미국 대입 필수 영단어

AMERICAN COLLEGE VOCABULARY 101

헤르몬하우스
HERMONHOUSE

미국 대학에 진학한다는 것은 무엇을 의미하는 걸까요?

Columbia University에서 발표된 2007년 논문에 따르면 미국의 최상위 14개의 대학에서 한국 유학생의 약 45%가 중도 탈락하는 것으로 알려졌습니다. 힘들게 아이비리그 대학에 합격했는데, 왜 그토록 많은 학생들이 중간에 포기해 버리는 걸까요? 어쩌면 이는 당연한 현상입니다. 미국 대학 시스템에 익숙하지 않은 학생들에게는 학교를 다니는 하루하루가 그야말로 배틀 그라운드일 테니까요.

미국 대학 생활이란 짧은 시간 안에 어마어마한 분량의 수준 높은 텍스트를 빠르고 정확하게 읽고, 그에 대해 논리적, 분석적으로 또는 문학적으로 글을 쓴 뒤, 쓴 글을 가지고 수업 시간에 진행되는 토론에서 전사 같은 미국 학생들에 맞서 버티고, 이겨내야 하는 것을 말합니다. 그런 상황이 매일매일 여러 과목의 수업에 계속해서 이어지는 것입니다.

외국인이라서 말을 잘 못하는 것은 어쩔 수 없다고 생각하신다면? 글을 잘 쓰면 됩니다. 모국어가 영어가 아니라고 알아서 학점을 잘 주는 일은 없습니다. 만약 대학원에 진학한다면 앞의 모든 상황은 기본으로 깔리고, 그 위에 교수 백업에 티칭, 자료 조사, 논문 읽고 쓰기의 무한 반복 루프가 당신을 기다리고 있습니다. 경영 대학원에 진학한다? 당신이 느끼는 은근한 무시와 자존심 상하는 순간순간은 인종 차별만은 아닐 겁니다. 당신의 지적 우수함은 인정받을지 몰라도, 그들의 입장에서 함께 토론하고 연구하고 편하게 논의할 수 있는 마음 맞는 팀원이 되기에는 걸리는 것이 많기 때문이죠. 그리고 이 모든 과정에서 걸리는 대부분은, 언어능력, 즉 어휘력 때문입니다.

따라서 어휘력이 갖춰지지 않은 상태로 유학 간다는 것은, 무기 하나 없이 격전지 한가운데로 떨어지는 것과 다름없습니다. 어휘는 무기입니다. 아주 좋은 아이템이죠. 그래서 늘 학생들을 보면서 간절히 바랍니다. '제발, 맨몸으로 맨땅에 헤딩하지 말기를...'

당신은 이제,
완전히 다른 레벨의 게임을
시작하게 된다는 뜻입니다.

이 책은 그런 마음에서 썼습니다. 여기 있는 단어 하나하나가 당신의 실탄이자, 헬멧이고, 낙하산이 되어 줄 것입니다. 처음부터 완벽하게 외우지 않아도 좋습니다. 다만 완전히 익힐 때까지 반복하는 일을 멈추지 말아 주십시오.

이 책은 정말 많은 고마운 분들의 큰 도움이 있었기에 세상에 나올 수 있었습니다. 언제나 나의 빛이자 영광이신 나의 하나님, 감사합니다. 늘 따뜻한 응원과 사랑을 아낌없이 보내주는 나의 사랑하는 가족들, 너무 고맙고 사랑합니다. 마음과 정성을 다해 애써 주셨던 우리 SSATKorea 팀원들, 헤르몬하우스 대표님과 직원들, 미국 학교 교사로 바쁜 와중에도 열심히 함께해 주신 감수자 Veronica L. Wilson, 그리고 디자이너님께 깊은 감사의 마음 전합니다.

하나님의 크신 축복이 큰 꿈에 도전하는 당신의 한 걸음 한 걸음에 함께 하시기를 기도합니다.

한세희 드림

왜 Vocabulary 101이 필요한가?

세상에 나와 있는 수많은 어휘집은 대부분 너무 어렵습니다.

모국어로 한글을 구사하는 고등학생이라면 학교에서 배우는 수준의 어휘로 책이나 신문을 보거나, 대학에 진학해 공부하는 것이 충분히 가능합니다. 일상생활에서 의사소통을 위한 영어를 원한다면 그 정도도 필요 없지요. 대학이나, 대학원, 나아가 경영 대학원 등 아카데믹한 곳에서 더 공부하길 바라는 사람들의 기본 어휘 대부분은 고등학교 수준으로 충분합니다.

어떤 단어 책은 단어가 너무 많아 시작도 하기 전에 엄두가 나질 않죠. 또 어떤 책은 터무니없이 어렵고, 또 어떤 책은 요령이나 순간적인 단순 암기를 돕기 위한 책들도 많습니다. 미안하지만 이 책에는 재미있는 그림도, 보자마자 쏙쏙 암기되는 특별한 비법도 없습니다. 하지만, 당신은 이 책이 반드시 필요합니다.

이 책은 BASIC 그 자체입니다. 고급 어휘의 기본서이자, 미국 대학 이상을 진학하려 할 때 반드시 알아야 할 기본이며 필수 어휘들입니다. 그래서 제목도 〈American College Vocabulary 101〉입니다.

이 책은 미국 고등학교 Grade 8th-11th 수준에 맞춰져 내용이 구성되어 있습니다. 적어도 미국 고등학교를 나온 아이들과 비교했을 때 어휘력에서 많이 차이가 나지 않도록, 대학에 진학할 때 문제가 없도록, 수년간의 연구 끝에 핵심 필수 어휘만 모은 도서입니다. 간혹 조금 쉬워 보이는 단어들도 있을 겁니다. 그런 것은 꼭 알아야 하는데 혹시라도 모르고 넘어갈까 봐 고심 끝에 넣은 것입니다.

당신이 SAT, ACT, GRE, GMAT 등 어떤 시험을 보든 미국 대학 이상의 시험을 준비한다면 바로 이 책이, 당신이 봐야 할 그 첫 번째 책입니다.

이 책은 기존 책들과는 확연히 다릅니다

■ 어휘의 선별이 다르다.

지성인들을 위해 대학과 대학원, 전문대학원, 학계 필드에서 현실 상황에 필요한 아카데믹 기본 어휘를 모았습니다. 어휘의 수준은 Grade 8th-11th 사이로 쉽지만, 필수인 단어와 적절한 고급 단어가 잘 섞여 있습니다.

■ 만든 사람이 다르다.

SSAT에 대해 들어보셨나요?

SSAT는 'Secondary School Admission Test'의 약자로 미국 사립학교 입학시험을 말합니다. 우리나라에도 영재고나 과학고, 특목고 등 시험을 봐서 들어가는 소수의 우월한 학습 집단을 위한 입학시험이 존재하듯, 미국에도 특별한 사립학교 입학을 위해 치러야 하는 시험이 SSAT이죠.

미국 학생들이 공부도 안 하고 대부분 놀면서 고등학교 시절을 편하게 보낸다고 생각하지만, 전 세계에서 내로라하는 톱클래스는 의외로 미국 학생인 경우가 많습니다. 전체적으로는 우리나라 학생이 수학과 과학에 뛰어난 편이지만, 세계적인 탑티어 인재들은 아직도 미국에 있는 경우가 많지요. 이들이 밤낮으로 치열하게 공부하며, 세계적인 네트워크를 이루고 지내는 우수한 고등학교의 대부분이, 미국에 있는 명문 사립학교들입니다.

이 책은 그러한 미국 특목고나 영재고 수준 시험에 해당하는 SSAT를 가르치고 연구한 저희 연구팀이 심혈을 기울여 만든 책입니다. 우리는 SSAT라는 미국 고등학교 수준의 어휘를 지난 20년간 연구해 왔습니다. 그리고 그 분야는 명실공히 우리가 대한민국 탑이라고 자부합니다.

■ Your Seed Vocabulary

투자를 할 때도 Seed Money 종잣돈이 있듯이, 영어의 어휘에도 Seed Vocabulary가 있습니다. 종잣돈이 일단 모여야 투자의 규모도 커지고 이익도 기하급수로 커지는 것처럼, 어휘도 일단 한번 탄탄하게 다져진 뒤에서야 빠르게 확장되며 단단해지게 되죠.

이는 마치 눈사람을 만드는 것과 비슷합니다. 눈사람을 만들 때 처음으로 눈을 단단하게 뭉치고 굴리는 과정은 힘이 듭니다. 하지만 이 과정을 통해 어느 정도 눈덩이의 크기가 커지면 나중엔 눈밭에 살짝 굴리기만 해도 엄청나게 불어나죠. 이처럼 처음 눈을 뭉치는 그 과정이 지금 이 책을 공부하는 것과 비슷합니다. 힘들고 어려워 보여도, 일단 한번 Seed Vocabulary가 갖춰지면 따로 외우지 않고, 원어민들처럼 독서만을 통해서도 어휘가 늘어나게 됩니다.

'유치원 때부터 영어를 배웠지만 실력이 늘지 않는다'는 생각이 든다면, 아마도 Seed Vocabulary가 제대로 형성되지 않은 때문일 것입니다. 그러니 이 책을 통해서 제대로 Seed Vocabulary를 만들어 보는 것은 어떨까요?

■ 인생에 한 번은 제대로 된 단어 정리

우리는 계속해서 생각해 왔습니다. 왜 초등 영어와 대학 영어 사이의 중요한 간극을 비워둔 채 한국 학생들은 대학생이 되는 걸까?

'초등학교 때 수능 영어까지 떼자'가 영어 선행의 기본 원칙이 된 지 오래여서 그런지, 아니면 고등학교 진학과 동시에 수학, 물리 같은 학교 수업만으로는 해결되지 않는 어려운 과목들이 대거 등장하기 때문인지는 모르겠지만, 한국인에게는 이 중간 수준의 교양이자 핵심, 그리고 필수인 영어 어휘들은 비어 있습니다.

그리고 그리 많지도 않은 기본 단어들을 몰라 '영포자'로 살아가기를 택한 학생들이 많다는 사실에 항상 안타까웠습니다. 영어 원서와 신문, 잡지, 인터넷, 학위 논문에 이르기까지, 미국 고등학교 수준의 어휘 정도면 충분히 가능한 것을 왜 이토록 어렵고 많은 단어들을 나열하여 사람들을 지치고 포기하게 만드는 것인지 이해할 수 없습니다.

그렇다고 이 책의 단어가 그리 적은 것도 아닙니다. 하지만 이를 실제로 '할만하게' 만드는 것은 당신의 몫입니다. 가능한 플랜을 세워 시간, 장소, 개수를 정해서 실행하는 방법에 대해서는 이어서 나오는 '이 책의 활용 방법'을 참고하면 됩니다.

이렇게 공부하면 됩니다

이 책은 하루에 36개씩 60일 분량의 단어들로 구성되어 있습니다. 익숙한 구성이죠?

■ 하루의 단어는 36개로 12개씩 3번에 나누어 외운다.

이 세상 불가능해 보이는 모든 미션도 쪼개고 쪼개어 한 스텝씩 나아가면 분명히 도달할 수 있습니다. 그리고 그런 식으로 계획을 짜서 실행하지 않으면, 아무리 시간을 길게 준다 해도 목표를 이룰 수 없지요. 나에게 주어진 시간이 얼마인지. 그 시간 안에 뭘 해야 하는지, 충분히 생각하고 계획해서 실행합니다.

■ 12개의 단어는 6개씩 두 번으로 나누어 외운다.

한 자리에서 12개를 외우는 것은 좋습니다. 그렇다면 1-6까지 처음 6개를 외우고 한번 체크, 나머지 7-12까지 6개 외우고 다시 체크, 1-12까지 다시 한번 체크하고 잘 외워지지 않는 것만 하이라이트나 별표 표시를 하세요. 이렇게 세 번으로 나눠 하는 것을 추천합니다.

■ 정해진 시간, 정해진 장소에서 외운다.

언제, 어디에 가면, 무엇을 한다. 이렇게 정해져 있는 형식이 루틴 routine입니다. 단어를 외우는 것이 루틴으로 만들어지면 훨씬 편안하게 할 수 있습니다. 단어가 잘 외워지는 자기만의 장소, 자기만의 시간을 찾아낸다면, 훨씬 수월해질 것입니다.

단어 잘 외우는 방법이 따로 있다고요?

어휘를 가르치다 보니 '단어 잘 외우는 방법'이 있냐는 질문을 많이 받습니다. 제가 묻겠습니다. 가장 좋은 다이어트 방법이 뭘까요? 최첨단 과학 기술을 이용한 획기적인 약물이나 수술과 단식 같은 방법보다는 모두가 다 아는 것처럼, 적게 먹고 많이 움직이는 것, 그리고 그것이 습관이 되는 것, 바로 이것이 아닐까요?

단어 역시 마찬가지입니다. 현란한 암기법이나 재미있는 그림은 몇몇 강한 인상을 줄 수 있습니다. 하지만 그 암기에 도움이 되는 스토리나 이미지를 매번 자기 스스로 만들어내지 않는 이상, 그것만으로는 그 많은 어휘들을 다 외울 수는 없죠. 그러니 가장 좋은 방법은, 자기에게 잘 맞는 좋은 습관을 만들어 '부담 없이 여러 번, 반복하는 것'입니다. 그것이 오래 갈 수 있는 정석이겠죠.

다음은 조금 더 구체적으로 단어 외우는 팁을 추천합니다.

■ 단어는 책상에 앉아 외우는 것이 아니라 돌아다니며 외운다.

책상에 앉아 쓰면서 외우는 것이 체질에 맞는 사람이 있습니다. 하지만 일단 저 스스로도 그 부류가 아닙니다. 저는 차라리 보드판 앞에 서서 쓰면 더 잘 외워집니다. 오히려 돌아다니면서, 걸으면서, 운동하면서 몸을 쓰면서 외우면 잘 외워집니다. 그래서 앉아서 공부할 때는 읽고, 쓰고, 집중해서 길게 해야 하는 일을 합니다.

■ 한번 외우고 잊어버릴 수 있다는 것을 당연하게 받아들여라.

어휘라는 것은 부담 없이 여러 번 봐서 익숙하게 만드는 것이 제일 좋습니다. 요즘은 단어 외우는 것을 도와주는 App도 많으니 반복하는 방식은 자기에게 맞는 것으로 고르면 됩니다. 저는 개인적으로 Quizlet App을 추천합니다. 플래시 카드와 Self-test를 의외로 유용하게 쓸 수 있습니다. 이때 외운 것도 자꾸 잊어버린다고 자책하는 학생들이 많은데요, 한번 외우고 잊어버릴 수 있는 것은 당연한 것이므로 이를 괴로워하지 않기 바랍니다. 괴로워할 시간에 그냥 한 번 더 보십시오. 나중에는 읽기만 해도 외워집니다.

■ 한 번에 많이 외우려 하지 마라.

'밀러의 Magic Number, 7±2'

1956년 프린스턴 대학의 교수인 조지 A. 밀러는 인간이 단기적으로 받아들일 수 있는 정보량이 어느 정도 정해져 있다는 연구 결과를 발표했습니다. 보통 인간의 단기 기억 용량은 7개이고, 잘 기억하는 사람은 7+2로 9개, 잘 못하는 사람은 7-2로 5개 정도를 기억한다는 것이지요. 이 연구 결과에 따르면 대부분의 사람들이 비슷한 수준의 기억 용량을 가지고 있다는 뜻이 됩니다. 때문에, 우리나라나 미국이나 전화번호는 7자리라는 이야기가 있지요.

아마도 처음 외우는 분들도 6개 정도면 한 번에 외울 수 있을 겁니다. 6개가 많다면 3개+3개로 나누어 외워도 좋습니다. 하지만 기본 세트는 6개로 보면 됩니다. 하루에 6개씩 x 6번 = 36개의 단어를 외우는 것이지요.

■ Memory Building!

근육질로 태어나는 아기는 없습니다. 조금씩 꾸준한 트레이닝으로 근력을 늘려나가는 것이 Body Building 보디빌딩이지요. 전문가들의 말에 따르면, 근육을 키우려면 약간의 고통이 느껴질 정도까지 운동을 해주어야 한다고 합니다. 그러면 상처 입은 근섬유가 몸이 쉬는 동안 회복되면서 그 위에 더 단단한 근육이 빌드 된다는 것이죠. 어휘력을 키우는 것도 이와 비슷합니다. 한 번에 기억되는 기억 용량을 Memory Chunk 덩어리라고 하는데, 이 기억 용량을 늘이는 것이 근육을 키우는 것과 매우 비슷합니다.

오늘부터 열심히 하겠다고 첫날 100개 외운다면, 한 번도 운동 안 하던 사람이 운동 첫날 윗몸 일으키기 100개를 한 것과 비슷한 역효과가 날 것입니다. 다음 날은 드러눕고, 그 다음 날까지 앓는 소리를 하다가 셋째 날부터는 어떻게든 피하고 싶어지는 것처럼 말이지요. 우리의 목표는 처음 반짝이 아니고 끝까지 여러 번 하는 것입니다. 그러니 무리하지 말고, 처음에 6개, 그리고 조금씩 조금씩 늘립니다.

■ 스스로에게 성공의 기회를 줘라

어떤 일을 할 때 스스로 '난 이건 잘 할 수 있어!'라고 생각하는 것을 자기 효능감 (self-efficacy)이라고 합니다. 그렇다면 이 자기 효능감, 즉 자신감은 어떻게 생기는 걸까요? 바로 작은 성공의 경험이 쌓이는 것, 그로 인한 긍정적인 피드백이 자신감의 원천이 됩니다.

아이가 처음 걸음마를 할 때, 온 가족이 그 몸짓 하나하나에 경탄하며 칭찬을 쏟아붓는 것을 본 적이 있지요? 이처럼 여러분이 단어를 외울 때마다 누군가 긍정적인 피드백을 해준다면 고맙겠지만, 그러기는 어렵기 때문에 스스로 성공 경험을 만들어줘야 합니다. 스스로에게 성공 경험을 많이 만들어주려면 어떻게 해야 할까요?

일단 이길만한 싸움을 하도록 해야겠죠. 이기는 것도 습관입니다. 많이 이겨본 사람이 이기는 데 익숙하고, 이기는 법을 잘 알게 되어 이길 수 있습니다. 그러니 해볼 만한 싸움으로 만들어 여러 번 이기게 하세요. 미리 포기하지 않도록, 못한다고 생각하지 않도록, 할만하다, 해낼 수 있겠다는 생각이 들도록 계획을 세우고 상황을 설정하는 것이 중요합니다. 즉, 해볼 만한 작은 일로 만드는 것이죠. 3200개나 외워야 한다는 것이 아니라, 지금은 10분동안 6개만 외우면 돼! 이렇게 생각할 수 있도록 말이죠. 그렇게 실행 가능한 학습 계획을 세우세요. 그리고 여러 번 반복해서 해내는 겁니다. 절대 무리한 계획을 잡아 그만두는 일이 없도록 공부 계획을 세우는 것이 중요합니다.

■ 정해진 시간, 정해진 장소에서 루틴을 만들라

돌아다니면서 단어를 외우더라도 하나의 루틴(routine)으로 만들어 놓으면 그보다 좋은 것이 없습니다. "몇 시에 어디에 가면 이렇게 한다." "학교에서 집으로 오는 지하철에서 외운다."는 식의 루틴을 정해서 해당 시간, 해당 장소에 도착하면 바로 시작하는 것이죠. 간단한 워킹이나 조깅을 하면서도 도움이 됩니다.

■ 자신의 목소리를 이용하라

책을 보고, 단어장을 들고 외울 수 없을 때는 자기 목소리로 녹음해서 들으면 됩니다. 여러분의 뇌는 여러분의 목소리를 가장 사랑합니다. 그런데 신기하게도 다른 사람이 단어를 읽어주면, 바로 잠들게 되죠. 단어를 처음 외울 때 핸드폰에 쭉 단어를 읽으며 녹음해보세요. 자기만의 힌트도 더하고, 스스로를 응원해주는 이야기도 한두 마디 넣어서 녹음해 놓는 겁니다. 그리고 돌아다닐 때, 움직이며, 머릿속으로 단어를 떠올리며 외워보세요. 음악을 좋아하는 당신, 당신의 목소리로 녹음한 단어 듣기도 의외로 많은 도움이 될 겁니다.

■ 간격을 두고 반복하고, 반복하라

한번에 완벽하게 할 필요는 없습니다. 단, 간격을 두고 반복하는 것이 포인트.

이것은 마치 풍선 띄우기와 비슷합니다. 풍선을 불어 손으로 여러 번 쳐서 위로 띄우는 놀이가 있다고 해봅시다. 가만히 몇 초 두면 스르르 내려와 땅에 닿을 것입니다. 땅에 닿기 직전에 다시 쳐서 올리려 하면 중간에 살짝 올리는 것보다 훨씬 힘듭니다. 조금 내려온 듯할 때 한 번 다시 쳐주고, 또 조금 내려온 듯할 때 한번 다시 올려 준다고 생각하면 됩니다. 단어를 외우는 것도 이와 비슷합니다. 한번 외운 단어가 계속, 영원히, 꾸준히 기억되어 한참 뒤 볼 시험에서 생각이 팍팍 날 것이라고, 절대 기대하지 마십시오. 그런 일은 거의 없습니다. 그래서 반복과 다지기가 필요합니다. 그렇지 않다면 시험에서 그 단어를 봤을 때 '이거 외웠던 건데 생각이 안나네…'라는 슬픈 기억만 남기게 될 테니까요.

■ 반복할 때는 다른 방식을 쓰면 더 효과적

보통 어떤 단어가 완전히 자신의 어휘가 되려면 6번 정도 반복해야 한다고 합니다. 그런데 같은 방식으로 6번 반복하는 것보다는 매번 다른 방식으로 반복하는 것이 훨씬 효과적입니다. 한번 작정해서 외우고 난 뒤, 우연히 신문보다 한 번, SNS 보다가 한 번, 해리포터 다시 읽다가 한 번, 미드 보다가 대사에서 한 번, 이런 식으로 다양한 곳에서 다른 방식으로 6번을 만난다면 그 단어는 이제 당신의 것, 당신의 친한 친구가 될 겁니다.

그 전까지는 그냥 얼굴만 아는 사람 정도의 관계랄까요? 한참 있다 다시 보면 기억 안 나도 이상하지 않은 사이, 딱 그 정도이죠. 그러니 한 번 외우고 끝났다고 생각 말고, 간격을 두고 다른 방식으로 반복, 또 반복하세요.

■ 한 번 외울 때 완벽하게 외우려 애쓰지 마라

단어를 외울 때 너무 세세하고 완벽하게 외우려 애쓰지 마세요. 첫 번째 목표는 그 단어를 알아보는 것입니다. 100번씩 쓰면서 정확한 스펠링과 예문까지 외우려 애쓰지 마세요. 36개도 완벽하게 마스터하지 못했다고 괴로워하지 마세요. 어차피 반복할 거니까요. 36개 중에 6개 정도는 틀려도 괜찮습니다. 결국은 반복하면서 틀리는 개수를 줄여주는 거죠.

처음은 인식할 수 있으면 되고, 그렇게 여러 번 반복하면 저절로 외워질 겁니다. 단, 처음에

한 번 볼 때는 "정확하게" 인식하고 외워 줘야 합니다. 잘못된 정보가 들어가면, 그다음 수정은 훨씬 더 어렵습니다. 한 번 정확하게 읽고, 인식하며 외우고 난 뒤부터는 부담 없이 여러 번 빠르게 보는 것이 좋습니다. 단어 외우는 것이 너무 느려서 걱정이시라고요? 속도는 걱정할 것 없습니다. 여러 번 반복하면 속도는 저절로 붙게 됩니다.

■ 플래시 카드 공부 비법

App을 쓰든, 전통 방식으로 종이에 만들든, 플래시 카드는 좋은 암기법입니다. 그런데 그 방법이 중요합니다. 모르는 단어를 다 카드로 만드는 것은 시간과 자원만 낭비됩니다. 제대로 잘 하려면 이렇게 하면 됩니다.

1. 먼저 자신이 잘 외워지는 방법으로 단어를 공부한다. 처음 한 번 '제대로' 읽고, 꼼꼼히 이해한 뒤, 외워본다.

2. 한 번에 6개씩 외운 단어를 빠르게 한 번 테스트해 본다. 이때 매일 외울 단어 첫 부분의 Words to Learn 표를 이용하면 편리하다.

3. 6개 중, 잘 기억 나지 않는 단어가 1~2개 정도라면, 넘어간다. 완벽하게 하려다 지치는 게 더 문제이다. 그러나 3~5개 이상을 모른다면 제대로 외운 것이 아니니 다시 한번 외우고 테스트해 본다.

4. 다음 6개씩도 그런 식으로 진행한다. 중요한 것은 앞으로 나아가는 것이다. 36개를 6x6으로 끝까지 마무리하는 것이 중요하다.

5. 잘 안 외워지는 단어만 모아본다. 이때 다시 외울 단어가 6개 이하라면, 그것으로 플래시 카드를 만든다. 만약 6개 이상이면 그 단어들만 모아 다시 한번 외우고 테스트해 모르는 단어를 6개 이내로 줄인다.

6. 만들어진 플래시 카드는 그날 더 외우려 하지 말고 일주일치를 모아둔다.

7. 이 책은 1세트가 7일로 구성되어 있다. 매일매일 외울 단어 Day1~6 + weekly test 포맷이다. 월, 화, 수, 목, 금, 토, 6일 동안 단어를 외우고, 따로 플래시카드로 '보관'된 단어들만 7번째에 모아서 외운다. 그런 뒤에 Weekly Test를 보도록 한다.

■ 중요하고 긴급한 것부터

'왜 못했는가'에 대한 가장 흔한 변명은 '시간이 없어서'일 것입니다. 시간이 없는 것이 아니라 시간을 어떻게 써야 할지 모른다는 것이 더 정확한 의미이겠죠. 20세기 최고의 경영학자인 피터 드러커 Peter Drucker도 '시간의 부족은 부족의 문제가 아니라 관리의 문제'라고 했습니다. 시간 관리를 잘하려면 우선순위를 잘 잡는 것이 중요합니다. 우선순위를 잘 잡으려면 어떻게 해야 할까요?

미국의 제34대 대통령이자 나토 최고 사령관이었던 아이젠하워 Dwight David Eisenhower는 일의 긴급성과 중요성에 따라 다음의 네 가지로 분류하여 우선순위를 정한 바 있습니다.

A. 긴급하고 중요한 일 (생존에 관계된 일, 바로 해야 할 공부, 치료해야 할 질병)
B. 급하지 않으나 중요한 일 (운동, 자기계발, 가족과 시간을 보내는 일)
C. 긴급하나 중요하지 않은 일 (거절하지 못해, 하게 되는 일)
D. 긴급하지도 중요하지도 않은 일 (SNS 하기, Youtube 보기, 게임하기)

당연히 처리 순서는 A → B → C → D일 것입니다. 그러나 오늘 하루 어떻게 보냈는지 생각해 보세요. 혹시 D → C → B → A인가요? 남들보다 더 나은 선택을 하고 싶다면, 중요하고 긴급한 것부터 처리하는 것으로 바꾸십시오.

함께 더 빨리, 더 강하게

■ 카테고리별 그룹 지어 외우기

쉽게 관련 있는 것끼리 함께 외우는 것입니다. 예를 들어 과일은 과일끼리, 동물은 동물끼리 함께 외우면 연관 관계가 생겨 더 잘 기억될 수 있으며, 여러 단어를 한꺼번에 외우기 쉽습니다.

■ 동의어 그룹 같이 외우기

"한 번에 하나 외우기도 힘든데 동의어까지 외우라니요?"라고 분노하실 분도 계실지 모르겠습니다만, 동의어를 하나씩만 같이 외워도 어휘 실력을 빠르게 늘릴 수 있습니다. 이 책의 미니 단어책에 실린 동의어 하나씩만 들고 다니면서 같이 외우세요. 한 발 더 나아가 동의어 그룹을 같이 외워준다면 기하급수적으로 어휘가 늘어나는 놀라운 효과를 볼 수 있습니다. 예를 들어 friendly를 뜻하는 단어인 amiable을 외운다고 할 때, amiable, amicable, agreeable, affable, genial, congenial 등 비슷한 뜻의 단어를 그룹으로 묶어 함께 외워주면 더 좋습니다. 동의어를 함께 외우는 것은 Writing을 쓸 때나 말을 할 때 "Redundancy: 같은 단어를 반복해서 사용하는 실수"를 피할 수 있게 됩니다. 당신의 Writing에서 Redundancy를 없애는 것, 이런 것이 의외로 학교 GPA를 올리는 기본적인 테크닉입니다.

■ Greek Roman Prefixes & Roots를 이용하여 외우기

예를 들어 배울 '학學'자가 쓰인 단어가 '배우다'라는 뜻을 가진 단어들을 알면 '학교, 학자, 학원, 학습, 학생, 학부모' 등등의 단어를 처음 보았을 경우라도 "혹시 배운다는 뜻이거나 학교나 이런 것에 관련되어 있는 것 아닐까?"라고 쉽게 추측하실 수 있지요? 영어 단어도 마찬가지로 친구를 뜻하는 라틴어인 'ami'가 들어있는 단어 amiable, amicable, amity 같은 경우가 '친구'라는 뜻과 관련이 있다고 추측할 수 있습니다. 이런 어휘들은 Written Text에서 많이 나오기 때문에 학교나 학습 상황에서 자주 나오므로 외워두면 유리합니다.

이렇듯 모르는 단어라도 그 안에 내가 아는 그리스어나 라틴어 Prefix, Root가 있으면 뜻을 유추하기가 쉽지요. Prefix는 접두어로 단어의 앞쪽에 붙어 뜻을 강조하거나 뒤집어 줄 때 주로 사용되며, Root는 뿌리라는 뜻 그대로 어근으로써 단어의 뿌리 부분, 즉 의미를 나타내주는 부분입니다. 예를 들어 'incredible'이란 단어에서 'in' 부분이 반대의 뜻을 나타내는 Prefix이고, 'cred'는 '믿다'라는 뜻의 Root이고, ible는 '~을 할 수 있는'이란 뜻의 어미 suffix로 품사가 형용사인 것을 알려주는 부분입니다.

자, 그런데 여기 주의할 점이 있습니다. 모든 한글 단어에 '학'자가 들어갔다고 '배울 學'에서 유래된 것은 아닌 것처럼, 모든 단어에 'ami'가 들어갔다고 해서 다 '친구'를 의미하지는 않는다는 것이죠. 그렇지만 Prefix와 Root는 추측의 가능성을 높일 근거 있는 힌트로 충분히 잘 사용되는 경우가 많으니, 알아두면 매우 효과적인 어휘력 부스터가 될 것입니다.

이 책에는 매일매일 하나씩 쉽고도 잘 쓰이는 Prefix와 Root를 소개해 놓고 있습니다. 한자를 많이 알아야 국어 어휘의 수준이 수월하게 올라간다는 것을 이미 알고 계실 테니, 이 부분도 꼭 빼놓지 말고 공부하기를 바랍니다.

■ 라틴어 기반 외국어와 함께 배우기

영어 어휘를 잘 배워 놓으면, 같은 라틴어를 근원으로 하는 프랑스어, 스페인어, 독일어 등등 다양한 유럽어를 훨씬 더 빠르게 배울 수 있습니다. 미국인이나 유럽인이 라틴어 기반의 언어를 배우는 것은 한국인이 한자 기반의 외국어를 빠르게 배울 수 있는 것과 같습니다. 한글에도 한자어에서 유래된 어휘가 많듯이 영어의 대부분은 그리스어와 라틴어에서 유래된 것이 많기 때문이죠. 게다가 영어는 외래어를 그대로 받아들여 사용하는 경우가 많기 때문에 영어와 다른 라틴어 기반의 외국어를 함께 배우는 것도 추천합니다. 양쪽 언어에서 서로 도움을 받을 수 있는 부분이 어휘 쪽에서는 확실히 많습니다. 저는 개인적으로 프랑스어를 함께 공부했는데, 영어 배울 때는 프랑스어 단어가 도움이 되고, 프랑스어 배울 때는 영어 어휘를 가지고 유추가 가능한 부분이 많아 더 좋았던 것 같습니다.

ACV 발음 기호 표시 안내

강세 표시 안내 : [파란색 색상체]가 강세를 뜻합니다.

예를 들어 newspaper는 [nooz-pey-per]로 information은 [in-fer-mey-sh*uh* n]으로 표기됩니다.

자음 CONSONANTS	
[b]	**b**oy, **b**a**b**y, ro**b**
[d]	**d**o, la**dd**er, be**d**
[f]	**f**ood, o**ff**er, sa**f**e
[g]	**g**et, bi**gg**er, do**g**
[h]	**h**appy, a**h**ead
[j]	**j**ump, bu**dg**et, a**g**e
[k]	**c**an, spea**k**er, sti**ck**
[l]	**l**et, fo**ll**ow, sti**ll**
[m]	**m**ake, su**mm**er, ti**m**e
[n]	**n**o, di**nn**er, thi**n**
[ng]	si**ng**er, thi**n**k, lo**ng**
[p]	**p**ut, a**pp**le, cu**p**
[r]	**r**un, ma**rr**y, fa**r**, sto**r**e
[s]	**s**it, **c**ity, pa**ss**ing, fa**c**e
[sh]	**sh**e, sta**ti**on, pu**sh**
[t]	**t**op, be**tt**er, ca**t**
[ch]	**ch**ur**ch**, wat**ch**ing, na**t**ure, wit**ch**
[th]	**th**irsty, no**th**ing, ma**th**
[*th*]	**th**is, mo**th**er, brea**th**e
[v]	**v**ery, se**v**en, lo**v**e
[w]	**w**ear, a**w**ay
[wh]	**wh**ere, some**wh**at
[y]	**y**es, on**i**on
[z]	**z**oo, ea**s**y, bu**zz**
[zh]	mea**s**ure, televi**s**ion, bei**ge**

모음 VOWELS	
[a]	**a**pple, c**a**n, h**a**t
[ey]	**ai**d, h**a**te, d**ay**
[ah]	**a**rm, f**a**ther, ah**a**
[air]	**air**, c**are**ful, w**ear**
[aw]	**a**ll, **o**r, t**a**lk, l**o**st, s**aw**
[e]	**e**ver, h**ea**d, g**e**t
[ee]	**ea**t, s**ee**, n**ee**d
[eer]	**ear**, h**e**ro, b**eer**
[er]	teach**er**, afterw**ar**d, murd**er**er
[i]	**i**t, b**i**g, f**i**nishes
[ai]	**I**, **i**ce, h**i**de, den**y**
[o]	**o**dd, h**o**t, w**a**ffle
[oh]	**o**we, r**oa**d, bel**ow**
[oo]	**oo**ze, f**oo**d, s**ou**p, s**ue**
[*oo*]	g**oo**d, b**oo**k, p**u**t
[oi]	**oi**l, ch**oi**ce, t**oy**
[ou]	**ou**t, l**ou**d, h**ow**
[uh]	**u**p, m**o**ther, m**u**d
[*uh*]	**a**bout, anim**a**l, probl**e**m, circ**u**s
[ur]	**ear**ly, b**ir**d, st**ir**ring

외국어 FOREIGN SOUNDS	
[a]	*Fr.***a**mi
[kh]	*Scot.* lo**ch**, *Ger.* a**ch** or i**ch**
[œ]	*Fr.* f**eu**, *Ger.* sch**ö**n
[r]	*Fr.* au **r**evoir, *Yiddish* **r**ebbe
[*uh*]	*Fr.* oeuv**r**e
[y]	*Fr.* t**u**, *Ger.* **ü**ber

비음화된 모음 NASALIZED VOWELS	
[an]	*Fr.* bi**en**
[ahn]	*Fr.* croiss**ant**
[awn]	*Fr.* b**on**
[œn]	*Fr.* parf**um**
[*in*]	*Fr.* Pr**in**cipe

CONTENTS

"Give up making wishes. Instead, set goals."

소원 비는 일은 포기하라 대신,
목표를 세워라.

Greek and Latin Roots & Prefixes 1

★ PED = foot

-al (n.)	pedal	페달, 페달을 밟다
stall (seat)	pedestal	받침대
er (person)	peddler	행상인
an (person)	pedestrian	보행자
cure (care)	pedicure	페디큐어, 발 관리
bi (two)	biped	두발 동물
quad (four)	quadruped	네발 동물
centi (100)	centipede	지네
tri (three)	tripod	삼각대
ex (out)	expedition	탐험, 원정

DAY

01

WORDS TO LEARN

☐ abandon   ☐ distinctive   ☐ infectious   ☐ reprehensible

☐ agile   ☐ embezzle   ☐ interrogation   ☐ rudimentary

☐ archive   ☐ eternal   ☐ keynote   ☐ skewed

☐ berate   ☐ facsimile   ☐ manipulate   ☐ spatter

☐ caliber   ☐ foil   ☐ misgiving   ☐ stringent

☐ collusion   ☐ genteel   ☐ nettle   ☐ temperament

☐ contrite   ☐ hallucination   ☐ oratory   ☐ temperence

☐ deferential   ☐ hurtle   ☐ pensive   ☐ velocity

☐ devoid   ☐ imprudent   ☐ predecessor   ☐ wrath

01

abandon
[*uh*-ban-d*uh*n]

v. to leave completely
버리다, 그만두다
The captain gave an order to **abandon** the ship.[1]

syn. forsake, desert, discard

02

agile
[aj-*uh*l]

adj. able to move or change direction quickly and easily
민첩한, 재빠른
He was sleek and **agile** as an acrobat.[2]

syn. nimble, supple, lithe, prompt

03

archive
[ahr-kaiv]

n. a collection or a place of historical records
공적 기록, 공문서 보관소
The library has an enormous amount of confidential papers in the **archive**.[3]

syn. records, annals

예문 해석

01 선장은 배를 버리라고 명령했다.   **02** 그는 곡예사처럼 유연하고 민첩했다.   **03** 도서관의 고문서 보관소에는 방대한 양의 기밀 문서가 있다.

04

berate
[bi-reyt]

v. to scold someone severely

몹시 꾸짖다

She **berated** her son for the noise he made.[4]

syn. criticize severely, reprove, reproach

05

caliber
[kal-*uh*-ber]

n. degree of capacity or competence

능력, 도량, (총의) 구경

She was a mathematician of high **caliber**.[5]

syn. capacity, ability, quality

06

collusion
[k*uh*-loo-zh*uh*n]

n. secret agreement

음모

Some of his employees were acting in **collusion** to rob him.[6]

syn. plot, ruse, conspiracy

07

contrite
[k*uh*n-trahyt]

adj. showing sincere remorse

회개하는, 뉘우치는

He looked **contrite** after he yelled at his friend.[7]

syn. regretful, rueful, repentant

08

deferential
[def-*uh*-ren-sh*uh*l]

adj. showing politeness

공손한, 예를 표하는

She is always **deferential** to all the guests.[8]

syn. respectful, deferent

09

devoid
[dih-void]

adj. lacking or empty

결여된, 전혀 없는

She is **devoid** of any sense of humor.[9]

syn. wanting, lacking, deficient

예문 해석

04 그녀는 소란을 피운 아들을 몹시 꾸짖었다.   **05** 그녀는 수준 높은 수학자였다.   **06** 몇몇 직원들이 그를 강탈하려는 음모를 꾸몄다.   **07** 그는 친구에게 소리를 지른 후 뉘우치는 표정을 지었다.   **08** 그녀는 모든 손님들에게 늘 공손하다.   **09** 그녀는 유머감각이라고는 전혀 없는 사람이다.

10 ·······

distinctive
[di-stingk-tiv]

adj. easily recognized and very individual
특이한, 차이를 나타내는, 구별되는
Her voice was **distinctive**.[10]

syn. distinguishing, characteristic

11 ·······

embezzle
[em-bez-*uhl*]

v. to take or use dishonestly (money or property with which one has been entrusted)
횡령하다
He **embezzled** public funds.[11]

syn. misappropriate, misuse, appropriate

12 ·······

eternal
[i-tur-nl]

adj. without beginning or end
영원한, 불후의
People all over the world are fascinated with the idea of **eternal** life.[12]

syn. timeless, unending, endless

13 ·······

facsimile
[fak-sim-*uh*-lee]

n. an exact copy
복사, 복사본, 복제
Johnson published a fine **facsimile** of the book.[13]

syn. duplicate, replica

14 ·······

foil
[foil]

v. to prevent the success of
좌절시키다, 뒤엎다
She has **foiled** his attempts to steal her secrets.[14]

syn. frustrate, balk, thwart

15 ·······

genteel
[jen-teel]

adj. polite and well-bred
품위 있는, 가문이 좋은
With a **genteel** curtsy, she approached the queen.[15]

syn. well-bred, refined, cultivated

📖 예문 해석

10 그녀의 목소리는 특이했다. **11** 그는 공금을 횡령했다. **12** 전 세계 사람들은 영원한 삶이라는 생각에 매료되었다. **13** 존슨은 그 책의 정교한 카피본을 출판했다. **14** 그녀는 비법을 뺏어가려는 그의 시도를 무산시켰다. **15** 예의를 갖춰, 그녀는 여왕에게 다가갔다.

16

hallucination
[h*uh*-loo-s*uh*-ney-sh*uh*n]

n. the observation of something which is not actually present
환각, 환영
The drug induces **hallucinations** at high doses.[16]

syn. delusion, illusion

17

hurtle
[hur-tl]

v. to move or throw very quickly or noisily
질주하다
The car **hurtled** down the highway.[17]

syn. dash, fling, race

18

imprudent
[im-prood-nt]

adj. unwise or thoughtless
건방진, 예의 없는, 분별없는
She gave an **imprudent** answer to the teacher's question.[18]

syn. rude, saucy, pert

19

infectious
[in-fek-sh*uh*s]

adj. disease or movement easily passed from one person to another
전염성의, 옮기 쉬운
The **infectious** disease affected my entire class.[19]

syn. contagious, communicable

20

interrogation
[in-ter-*uh*-gey-sh*uh*n]

n. the act of questioning
심문, 질문, 취조
They were driven to the police station for **interrogation**.[20]

syn. questioning, investigation, interview

21

keynote
[kee-noht]

n. the main idea or central principle of a speech, program, thought, action, etc.
기조, 중심생각, 요지
A **keynote** address is a speech, as at a political convention, that presents principles or policies.[21]

syn. theme, gist, point

 예문 해석

16 약물은 과다복용시 환각증세를 가져온다.　**17** 자동차가 고속도로로 질주했다.　**18** 그녀는 선생님 질문에 예의없는 대답을 했다.　**19** 그 전염병은 우리 반 전체에 영향을 미쳤다.　**20** 그들은 취조를 받으러 경찰서로 끌려갔다.　**21** 기조연설이란 정당회의 등에서 원칙, 정책 등에 대한 연설을 말한다.

22 ....

manipulate
[m*uh*-nip-y*uh*-leyt]

v. to handle, manage, or use secretly
교묘하게 조종하다, 조작하다
He is very good at **manipulating** public opinion.[22]

syn. juggle, falsify, control

23 ....

misgiving
[mis-giv-ing]

n. fear and apprehension
불안, 의심, 걱정, 염려
He read her letter without any **misgivings**.[23]

syn. uneasiness, solicitude, qualm

24 ....

nettle
[net-l]

v. to make somebody sightly angry
초초하게 만들다, 화나게 하다
My remarks clearly **nettled** her.[24]

syn. upset, provoke, annoy

25 ....

oratory
[awr-*uh*-tawr-ee]

n. the art of public speaking
웅변술
He displayed determination as well as powerful **oratory**.[25]

syn. rhetoric, public speaking, eloquence

26 ....

pensive
[pen-siv]

adj. preoccupied with one's thoughts
생각에 잠긴, 곰곰이 생각하는
He looked somber and **pensive**.[26]

syn. thoughtful, contemplative, meditative

27 ....

predecessor
[pred-*uh*-ses-er]

n. the person who formerly held a job or position now held by someone else
전임자, 선배
He learned everything he knew from his **predecessor**.[27]

syn. precursor, forerunner, ancestor

 예문 해석

22 그는 여론을 조작하는 일에 능숙하다. **23** 그는 그녀의 편지를 아무런 의심 없이 읽었다. **24** 내 말은 분명 그녀를 화나게 했다. **25** 그는 힘있는 웅변술 외에도 결단을 보여주었다. **26** 그는 우울하고 생각에 잠겨 보였다. **27** 그가 아는 모든 것은 그의 전임자로부터 배운 것이다.

28

reprehensible
[rep-ri-hen-*suh*-b*uh*l]

adj. deserving of reproof, rebuke, or censure
비난할 만한, 괘씸한
It is hard to stand such **reprehensible** things.[28]

> *syn.* blameworthy, culpable, blamable

29

rudimentary
[roo-d*uh*-men-t*uh*-ree]

adj. pertaining to basics or first principles
기본의, 초보의
He had only a **rudimentary** knowledge of French.[29]

> *syn.* fundamental, basic, elementary

30

skewed
[skyood]

adj. having an oblique or slanting direction or position
왜곡된, 편향된, 삐딱한
People accused the news reports of being **skewed** toward one political viewpoint.[30]

> *syn.* crooked, distorted, biased

31

spatter
[spat-er]

v. to scatter or dash in small particles or drops
(물이나 진탕 등을) 튀기다, 물장구치다, 흩뿌리다
The car **spattered** her new coat with mud.[31]

> *syn.* splash, splatter, sprinkle

32

stringent
[strin-j*uh*nt]

adj. very severe or strictly controlled
엄격한, 강력한
He announced that there would be more **stringent** controls on the possession of weapons.[32]

> *syn.* exacting, severe, strict

33

temperament
[tem-per-*uh*-m*uh*nt]

n. the combination of mental, physical, and emotional traits of a person
성격, 기질
Her **temperament** will not let her endure such a tedious job.[33]

> *syn.* personality, nature, disposition

예문 해석

28 그런 괘씸한 일을 참는 것은 어렵다.   **29** 그는 불어의 아주 기초적인 지식만을 가지고 있었다.   **30** 사람들은 그 뉴스 보도가 하나의 정치적 견해에 치우쳐 있다고 비난했다.   **31** 차가 그녀의 새 코트에 진흙탕을 튀겼다.   **32** 그는 무기 소지에 관한 더 강한 통제가 있을 것이라 발표했다.   **33** 그녀는 성질 때문에 그런 지루한 일을 견디지 못할 것이다.

temperance
[tem-per-*uh*ns]

n. total abstinence from alcoholic liquors

금주, 절제

Exercise and **temperance** can preserve something of our early strength even in old age.[34]

syn. self-restraint, abstinence, moderation

velocity
[v*uh*-los-i-tee]

n. the speed at which something moves in a particular direction

속도, 속력

There is nothing faster than the **velocity** of light.[35]

syn. speed, rate, celerity

wrath
[rath]

n. strong, stern, or fierce anger

분노, 화

To avoid his father's **wrath**, he ran away.[36]

syn. ire, rage, fury, indignation

 예문 해석

34 운동과 절제로 노년기에도 우리의 초기 체력을 보존할 수 있다.   **35** 빛의 속도보다 빠른 것은 없다.   **36** 그는 아버지의 노여움을 피하기 위해 도망쳤다.

Directions Each of the following questions consists of one word followed by five words or phrases. You are to select the one word or phrase whose meaning is closest to the word in capital letters.

1. ABANDON :
- (A) blend
- (B) eject
- (C) give
- (D) forsake
- (E) complain

2. AGILE :
- (A) gleeful
- (B) furrow
- (C) optimal
- (D) jolly
- (E) nimble

3. CALIBER :
- (A) admission
- (B) hint
- (C) goodness
- (D) protection
- (E) capacity

4. COLLUSION :
- (A) oration
- (B) plot
- (C) frankness
- (D) tirade
- (E) determination

5. CONTRITE :
- (A) vexed
- (B) asked
- (C) excited
- (D) regretful
- (E) barren

6. DEFERENTIAL :
- (A) respectful
- (B) drunk
- (C) asking
- (D) diverse
- (E) reduced

7. EMBEZZLE :
- (A) misappropriate
- (B) lubricate
- (C) entice
- (D) laud
- (E) violate

8. FACSIMILE :
- (A) staff
- (B) duplicate
- (C) expert
- (D) vine
- (E) thesis

9. HALLUCINATION :
- (A) tune
- (B) delusion
- (C) obstacle
- (D) infection
- (E) rustler

10. MISGIVING :
- (A) tendril
- (B) deliberation
- (C) escape
- (D) uneasiness
- (E) trait

Greek and Latin Roots & Prefixes 2

★ MANU = hand

-al (n.)	manual	설명서
cure (care)	manicure	매니큐어, 손 관리
er (person)	manager	관리자
scribere (write)	manuscript	원고, 필사본
factura(make)	manufacture	제조하다, 생산하다
dare(give)	mandate	명령하다, 지시하다
operari (work)	maneuver	책략, 술책, 작전 행동
plere (fill)	manipulate	조종하다, 조작하다
acle (fetter)	manacles	수갑
ex (out)	emancipate	풀어주다, 해방시키다

DAY

02

WORDS TO LEARN

☐ abbreviate	☐ distort	☐ infernal	☐ quaint
☐ aghast	☐ embrace	☐ intersect	☐ repress
☐ ardent	☐ etymology	☐ kidnap	☐ shabby
☐ beseech	☐ faculty[1]	☐ manual	☐ specific
☐ callow	☐ foliage	☐ mislead	☐ strive
☐ colossal	☐ gentry	☐ neutralize	☐ tarnish
☐ convene	☐ halt	☐ orchard	☐ trim
☐ deft	☐ hub	☐ perceive	☐ vend
☐ devour	☐ impudent	☐ phony	☐ winnow

01

abbreviate
[*uh*-bree-vee-eyt]

v. to shorten
줄이다, 줄여 쓰다
You can **abbreviate** the word, "volume" to "vol."[1]

syn. shorten, reduce, curtail

02

aghast
[*uh*-gast]

adj. shocked
경악한, 겁에 질린
She was **aghast** at the disaster.[2]

syn. shocked, horrified, petrified

03

ardent
[ahr-dnt]

adj. passionate and fervent
열정적인, 불타는 듯한, 열렬한
He was an **ardent** patriot who fought for his country.[3]

syn. fervid, eager, impassioned

예문 해석

01 "volume"이란 단어를 "vol."로 줄여 쓸 수 있다.　**02** 그녀는 재난에 경악하였다.　**03** 그는 나라를 위해 싸우는 열렬한 애국자였다.

04

beseech
[bi-seech]

v. to ask someone earnestly
애원하다, 진심으로 부탁하다
She **beseeched** him to stop smoking.[4]

syn. implore, beg, entreat, petition

05

callow
[kal-oh]

adj. immature or inexperienced
미숙한, 풋내기인
The **callow** baseball player missed an incredibly easy ball.[5]

syn. immature, inexperienced, unfledged

06

colossal
[kuh-los-uhl]

adj. extraordinarily great in size
거대한, 엄청난
The singer earned a **colossal** amount of money.[6]

syn. immense, huge, enormous

07

convene
[kuhn-veen]

v. to come together or assemble
모이다, 소집하다, 개최하다
The members **convened** for a conference.[7]

syn. congregate, meet, gather

08

deft
[deft]

adj. skillful in physical movements
재빠른, 솜씨 좋은, 능숙한
With her **deft** fingers, she untangled the wire.[8]

syn. agile, clever, adroit

09

devour
[di-vour]

v. to eat quickly and eagerly
게걸스레 먹다, 탐식하다
The tiger **devoured** its prey.[9]

syn. gobble, swallow, consume

예문 해석

04 그녀는 그에게 담배를 끊으라고 애원했다.　**05** 그 미숙한 야구 선수는 믿을 수 없을 정도로 쉬운 공을 놓쳤다.　**06** 그 가수는 엄청난 돈을 벌었다.　**07** 회원들은 회의를 위해 모였다.　**08** 재빠른 손놀림으로 그녀는 엉켜있는 줄들을 풀었다.　**09** 호랑이는 게걸스럽게 먹이를 먹었다.

10

distort
[di-stawrt]

v. to twist something out of shape
(형체나 모습을) 비틀다, 일그러뜨리다
The mass media **distorts** reality.[10]

syn. deform, falsify, disfigure

11

embrace
[em-breys]

v. to hold someone closely in one's arms
포옹하다, 껴안다
They **embraced** each other with joy.[11]

syn. hug, hold, cuddle

12

etymology
[et-*uh*-mol-*uh*-jee]

n. the study of the origin and history of words
어원학, 말의 어원을 공부하는 것
Finding out the **etymology** of a word can help clarify its meaning.[12]

syn. word history, word origin, derivation

13

faculty[1]
[fak-*uhl*-tee]

n. any of one's mental or physical abilities
능력, 재능
He has a **faculty** for making friends easily.[13]

syn. talent, flair, gift, caliber

14

foliage
[foh-lee-ij]

n. the green leaves on a tree or plant
나뭇잎, 낙엽
Pay special attention to those enemies who might be hiding in the **foliage**.[14]

syn. leaves, leafage, greenery

15

gentry
[jen-tree]

n. wellborn and well-bred people
상류 사회, 귀족
The **gentry** are not concerned by worrisome financial matters.[15]

syn. aristocracy, nobility, peerage

예문 해석

10 대중매체는 현실을 왜곡시킨다.　**11** 그들은 기쁨으로 서로 껴안았다.　**12** 말의 어원을 찾아보는 것이 뜻을 명확히 이해하는 데 도움을 줄 것이다.　**13** 그는 친구를 잘 사귀는 재능이 있다.　**14** 나뭇잎 뒤에 숨어 있을 수 있는 적들을 특히 조심하라.　**15** 상류층은 걱정스러운 재정 문제에 대해 염려하지 않는다.

16

halt
[hawlt]

v. to stop
멈추다
They **halted** at the red light.[16]

> *syn.* stop, cease, discontinue

17

hub
[h*uh*b]

n. the central part or focal point of a region
중심지, 중추
This city is the commercial **hub** of the nation.[17]

> *syn.* center, focal point, nerve center

18

impudent
[im-py*uh*-d*uh*nt]

adj. rude or disrespectful
뻔뻔스러운, 염치없는
Their responses were **impudent** and insulting.[18]

> *syn.* cheeky, impertinent, audacious

19

infernal
[in-fur-nl]

adj. very annoying or unpleasant
극도로 심하고 괴로운, 지옥같은
The garbage bin has an **infernal** smell.[19]

> *syn.* hellish, outrageous, diabolical

20

intersect
[in-ter-sekt]

v. to cut or divide by passing through or across
가로지르다, 교차하다
This road **intersects** with the highway.[20]

> *syn.* cross, converge, meet

21

kidnap
[kid-nap]

v. to abduct by force to ask for ransom
유괴하다, 납치하다
Terrorists attempted to **kidnap** soldiers.[21]

> *syn.* abduct, hijack, hold for ransom

예문 해석

16 그들은 빨간 불에서 멈춰 섰다.   **17** 이 도시는 그 나라의 상업 중심지이다.   **18** 그들의 반응은 모욕적이고 뻔뻔했다.   **19** 쓰레기통에서 지독한 냄새가 난다.   **20** 이 길은 고속도로와 교차한다.   **21** 테러리스트들은 병사들을 납치하려 했다.

22

manual
[man-yoo-*uhl*]

adj. using the hands or physical strength
손의, 수동의
They are skilled **manual** workers.[22]

> *syn.* hand-operated, done by hand, physical

23

mislead
[mis-leed]

v. to deceive
속이다, 나쁜 일에 꾀어 들이다
It was a device to **mislead** the voters.[23]

> *syn.* misinform, deceive, delude

24

neutralize
[noo-tr*uh*-laiz]

v. to make something ineffective
효력을 없애다, 중립을 선언하다
The intruder **neutralized** the alarm system.[24]

> *syn.* counteract, counterbalance, nullify

25

orchard
[awr-cherd]

n. a garden or piece of land where fruit trees are grown
과수원, 정원
I walked through a peach **orchard** with my friends.[25]

> *syn.* garden, grove

26

perceive
[per-seev]

v. to become aware of
인식하다, 이해하다
They could **perceive** what the problem was.[26]

> *syn.* recognize, discern, understand

27

phony
[foh-nee]

adj. not real or genuine
가짜의, 위조의
He was a **phony** scientist saying he knew everything about quantum physics.[27]

> *syn.* counterfeit, deceiving, fake

 예문 해석

22 그들은 손을 사용해서 일하는 숙련된 일꾼들이다.　**23** 그것은 투표자들을 속이기 위한 장치였다.　**24** 침입자는 경계시스템을 해제시켰다.　**25** 나는 친구들과 복숭아 과수원을 걸었다.　**26** 그들은 문제가 무엇인지 이해할 수 있었다.　**27** 그는 양자 물리학에 대해 모든 것을 안다고 말하는 가짜 과학자였다.

28

quaint
[kweynt]

adj. attractive in an unusual or old- fashioned way
기묘한, 특이한
I grew up in a small, **quaint** town.[28]

syn. odd, unusual, strange

29

repress
[ree-pres]

v. to keep under control, check, or suppress
억제하다, 진압하다
The regime **repressed** the minority race.[29]

syn. suppress, quell, subdue

30

shabby
[shab-ee]

adj. something that is in poor condition because it has been used a lot
초라한, 낡은
He was in **shabby** clothes.[30]

syn. run-down, worn, dilapidated

31

specific
[spi-sif-ik]

adj. stated explicitly or in detail
구체적인, 세세한
The witness told us a **specific** and detailed account of the accident.[31]

syn. precise, particular, definite

32

strive
[strahyv]

v. to try hard
노력하다, 애쓰다
She **strove** to make herself understood.[32]

syn. exert, attempt, endeavor

33

tarnish
[tahr-nish]

v. to spoil or damage something
녹슬게 하다, 변색되다, 더럽히다
The affair could **tarnish** the reputation of the principal.[33]

syn. blemish, taint, stain

🧘 **예문 해석**

28 나는 작고 특이한 마을에서 자랐다.   **29** 그 정권은 소수 민족을 탄압했다.   **30** 그는 낡은 옷을 입고 있었다.   **31** 목격자는 우리에게 그 사고에 대한 구체적이고 상세한 설명을 해주었다.   **32** 그녀는 자신을 이해시키려 애썼다.   **33** 그 사건은 교장의 명예를 더럽힐 수 있었다.

34

trim
[trim]

v. to make something neater, smaller, or better
다듬다, 장식하다
My mother **trimmed** my hair when I was a boy.[34]

syn. curtail, cut

35

vend
[vend]

v. to sell
팔다
I bought a soda from the **vending** machine.[35]

syn. peddle, sell

36

winnow
[win-oh]

v. to free grain from chaff by wind or driven air
(곡식에서 쭉정이 등을 가려내려고) 골라내다
At the farm, I saw a machine **winnow** the chaff off of the grain of rice.[36]

syn. sieve, sift, cull

 예문 해석

34 내가 어렸을 때 엄마가 내 머리를 다듬어주셨다.　**35** 나는 자판기에서 탄산음료를 샀다.　**36** 농장에서, 나는 기계가 쌀알의 껍질을 제거하는 것을 보았다.

Directions   Each of the following questions consists of one word followed by five words or phrases. You are to select the one word or phrase whose meaning is closest to the word in capital letters.

1. ABBREVIATE :
(A) walk
(B) cover
(C) captivate
(D) instigate
(E) shorten

2. ARDENT :
(A) fervid
(B) rash
(C) profitable
(D) shallow
(E) undesirable

3. BESEECH :
(A) implore
(B) detest
(C) swarm
(D) pour
(E) spellbind

4. COLOSSAL :
(A) moist
(B) cruel
(C) immense
(D) rude
(E) tolerant

5. DISTORT :
(A) reply
(B) innovate
(C) dive
(D) prevent
(E) deform

6. HALT :
(A) stop
(B) increase
(C) renew
(D) judge
(E) consider

7. HUB :
(A) festival
(B) ruin
(C) ornament
(D) center
(E) distraction

8. MISLEAD :
(A) exfoliate
(B) feign
(C) sparkle
(D) whiten
(E) misinform

9. PHONY :
(A) counterfeit
(B) figurative
(C) sincere
(D) deferential
(E) impudent

10. QUAINT :
(A) intentional
(B) military
(C) deceptive
(D) odd
(E) unrehearsed

"Live as if you were to die tomorrow. Learn as if you were to live forever."

— Mahatma Gandhi —
Indian political and spiritual leader

내일 죽을 것처럼 살고, 영원히 살 것처럼 배워라.

Greek and Latin Roots & Prefixes 3

★ SPEC = see, look

-acle (n.)	spectacle	구경거리, 장관
-acle (n.)	spectacles	안경
-or (person)	spectator	(스포츠 경기) 관중
-ion (n.)	speculation	추측, 짐작
-er (object)	specter	유령
in (in)	inspect	점검하다
into (into)	introspection	자기 성찰, 내성
re (back)	respect	존경, 경의
per (forward)	perspective	관점, 시각
retro (back)	retrospective	회고하는, 뒤돌아 보는

DAY

03

WORDS TO LEARN

☐ abdicate	☐ distracted	☐ infiltrate	☐ qualm
☐ agitate	☐ embroidery	☐ interval	☐ reprimand
☐ arduous	☐ eulogy	☐ limb	☐ rumple
☐ besiege	☐ faculty[2]	☐ manuscript	☐ sham
☐ callous	☐ foolhardy	☐ mitigate	☐ stroll
☐ comatose	☐ genuine	☐ nuisance	☐ tart
☐ dawdle	☐ hamlet	☐ ordeal	☐ trip
☐ defiance	☐ hustle	☐ perennial	☐ venerate
☐ dexterous	☐ impugn	☐ preface	☐ wriggle

01

abdicate
[ab-di-keyt]

v. to give up one's right to the throne
(왕위나 권리 등을) 버리다, 포기하다
The king **abdicated** the throne.[1]

syn. abandon, forsake, desert

02

agitate
[aj-i-teyt]

v. to move or force into violent, irregular action
자극하다, 동요시키다
People who worked in this factory began to **agitate** for better conditions.[2]

syn. instigate, stir, incite, perturb

03

arduous
[ahr-joo-*uhs*]

adj. difficult and tiring
힘든, 고된
The task was more **arduous** than he had calculated.[3]

syn. difficult, hard, grueling

예문 해석

01 그 왕은 왕위에서 물러났다.　**02** 공장에서 일하는 사람들은 더 좋은 조건을 위해 동요하기 시작했다.　**03** 그 일은 그가 계산했던 것보다도 훨씬 힘이 들었다.

04

besiege
[bih-seej]

v. to crowd around
에워싸다, 둘러싸다
Many students **besieged** her with requests to get into her class.[4]

syn. surround, encompass, encircle

05

callous
[kal-*uhs*]

adj. unconcerned for the feelings of others
무감각한, 냉담한
She was **callous** to their misery.[5]

syn. insensitive, apathetic, nonchalant

06

comatose
[kom-*uh*-tohs]

adj. in a coma
혼수 상태의, 의식이 없는
She arrived at the hospital in critical condition and was **comatose**.[6]

syn. unconscious, senseless

07

dawdle
[dawd-l]

v. to hang back or fall behind in movement, progress, development, etc.
꾸물거리다, 어정거리다
When Ted took a lot more time, his companion said, "Don't **dawdle**!"[7]

syn. delay, loiter, waste time

08

defiance
[di-fai-*uh*ns]

n. a bold resistance to authority
반항, 도전, 저항
His eyes flashed with **defiance**.[8]

syn. resistance, opposition, confrontation

🧘 **예문 해석**

04 많은 학생들이 그녀를 에워싸고는 수업에 들어가게 해달라고 요청했다. **05** 그녀는 그들의 불행에 무감각했다. **06** 그녀는 매우 위중한 상태로 의식 없이 병원에 도착했다. **07** 테드가 훨씬 더 많은 시간을 끌었을 때, 그의 동료가 "꾸물대지 마!"라고 말했다. **08** 그의 눈은 반항심으로 번뜩였다.

09

dexterous
[dek-str*uh*s]

adj. skillful or adroit in the use of the hands or body
(손이나 몸놀림이) 재빠른, 솜씨 좋은
He is very **dexterous** in sports.[9]

syn. proficient, ingenious, deft

10

distracted
[di-strak-tid]

adj. having one's attention diverted
산만해진, 심란한
She had seemed curiously **distracted**.[10]

syn. disturbed, troubled, panicked

11

embroidery
[em-broi-d*uh*-ree]

n. the art of needlework
(천에 놓는 무늬 등의) 자수
The seamstress learned sewing, knitting and **embroidery**.[11]

syn. fancy stitching, decoration, brocade

12

eulogy
[yoo-l*uh*-jee]

n. a speech or piece of writing in high praise
찬미, 칭송, 찬양
The song was a **eulogy** to the joys of life.[12]

syn. tribute, acclamation

13

faculty[2]
[fak-*uh*l-tee]

n. the professors and lecturers of an academy
강사진, 교수진
Here's a list of **faculty** members of Phillips Exeter Academy.[13]

syn. teaching staff

14

foolhardy
[fool-hahr-dee]

adj. extremely risky
무모한
When he tested an early vaccine on himself, many described the act as **foolhardy**.[14]

syn. reckless, rash, risky

예문 해석

09 그는 스포츠에 매우 능하다.   **10** 그녀는 호기심에 마음이 산만해진 듯 보였다.   **11** 그 재봉사는 바느질, 뜨개질, 자수를 배웠다.   **12** 그 노래는 인생의 즐거움을 찬양한 것이다.   **13** 여기, Phillips Exeter Academy의 선생님들 명단이야.   **14** 그가 초기 백신을 자신에게 테스트했을 때 많은 사람들은 무모하다고 했다.

15

genuine
[jen-yoo-in]

adj. real or actual
진짜의, 진품의
Her personality was described as **genuine**.[15]

> *syn.* authentic, original

16

hamlet
[ham-lit]

n. a small village
작은 마을
The president was a native of a farming **hamlet**.[16]

> *syn.* small village, small town, community

17

hustle
[h*uhs-uh*l]

v. to push or force one's way
난폭하게 밀치다
He **hustled** the villain into the car.[17]

> *syn.* jostle, push, shove

18

impugn
[im-pyoon]

v. to challenge as false
비난하다, 공격하다, 반박하다
I didn't mean to **impugn** your ideas.[18]

> *syn.* assail, challenge, criticize

19

infiltrate
[in-fil-treyt]

v. to filter into or through
침투 시키다, 스며들게 하다
His platoon **infiltrated** the enemy lines.[19]

> *syn.* penetrate, permeate

20

interval
[in-ter-v*uh*l]

n. the period of time between two events
(장소나 시간의) 간격, 중간 쉬는 시간
The athlete ran using **intervals** training, in order to increase his speed.[20]

> *syn.* gap, time, hiatus, period

예문 해석

15 그녀의 성격은 진실한 것으로 묘사되었다. **16** 그 대통령은 작은 농촌 출신이었다. **17** 그는 악당을 차에 세게 밀어 넣었다.
18 네 생각을 비난하려는 것은 아니었다. **19** 작전 부대는 적진을 뚫었다. **20** 그 선수는 속도를 높이기 위해 간격을 두고 달렸다.

limb
[lim]

n. an arm or a leg
팔과 다리, 사지
He usually sleeps with his **limbs** outstretched.[21]

> *syn.* extremity, branch

manuscript
[man-*yuh*-skript]

n. the original text of an author's work
필사본
His works are still in **manuscript** form.[22]

> *syn.* document, article, composition

mitigate
[mit-i-geyt]

v. to partially excuse something or make it less serious
완화하다, 누그러뜨리다, 덜어주다, 진정시키다
We tried hard to **mitigate** circumstances.[23]

> *syn.* alleviate, soothe, pacify, mollify

nuisance
[noo-*suh*ns]

n. an obnoxious or annoying person or thing
성가신 사람, 골칫거리
I don't want to be a **nuisance**, so please tell me if you want to be alone.[24]

> *syn.* annoyance, blister, bore

ordeal
[awr-deel]

n. any extremely severe test or experience
시련, 고난
The **ordeal** has affected both her mental and physical health.[25]

> *syn.* trouble, suffering, trial

perennial
[*puh*-ren-ee-*uh*l]

adj. lasting for an indefinitely long time
다년생의, 연중 계속되는
A **perennial** plant lives more than two years.[26]

> *syn.* enduring, perpetual, continuing

예문 해석

21 그는 보통 팔다리를 쭉 뻗고 잔다.　**22** 그의 작품들은 아직도 원고 상태로 있다.　**23** 우리는 상황을 진정시키느라 애썼다.
24 나는 귀찮은 존재가 되고 싶지 않으니 혼자 있고 싶으면 말해요.　**25** 그 시련은 그녀의 정신 건강과 신체 건강, 둘 다에 영향을 끼쳤다.　**26** 다년생 식물은 2년 이상 산다.

preface
[pref-is]

n. an explanatory statement at the beginning of a book
책의 서문, 머리말
I don't have time for **prefaces**.[27]

syn. foreword, preamble, introduction

qualm
[kwahm]

n. a scruple, misgiving, or pang of conscience
양심의 가책, 불안
She has no **qualms** of conscience.[28]

syn. misgiving, scruple, pang

reprimand
[rep-*ruh*-mand]

v. to scold severely
공개적으로 꾸짖다, 질책하다
The president does not have the legal right to **reprimand** the police chief.[29]

syn. blame, scold, admonish

rumple
[*ruh*m-p*uh*l]

v. to crumple or crush into wrinkles
구기다, 헝클어놓다
The wind **rumpled** her hair.[30]

syn. crumple, ruffle

sham
[sham]

n. not real or not really what it seems to be
거짓, 속임수, 허위
His promises were exposed as a hollow **sham**.[31]

syn. pretense, fake, fraud

stroll
[strohl]

n. a leisurely walk
이리저리 거닐기, 산책
After dinner, I took a **stroll** around the park.[32]

syn. walk, amble, saunter

예문 해석

27 본론만 말하시오.　**28** 그녀는 양심의 가책이 없다.　**29** 대통령은 경찰청장을 징계할 법적인 권리가 없다.　**30** 바람이 그녀의 머리를 헝클어 놓았다.　**31** 그의 약속들은 얕은 속임수로 밝혀졌다.　**32** 저녁을 먹고 나는 공원을 산책했다.

33

tart
[tahrt]

adj. brief and sarcastic, sour
맛이 시큼한, 신맛 나는, 신랄한
The words were more **tart** than I had intended.[33]

syn. sour, sarcastic, sharp

34

trip
[trip]

v. to miss a step and fall or nearly fall
발에 걸려 넘어지다, 헛디디다
He **tripped** over his child's toy.[34]

syn. fall, err, stumble

35

venerate
[ven-*uh*-reyt]

v. to regard someone or something with deep respect or awe
존경하다, 숭배하다
Many **venerate** Mother Teresa.[35]

syn. revere, hallow, esteem, defer

36

wriggle
[rig-*uhl*]

v. to twist to and fro
(지렁이 등이) 이리저리 꿈틀거리며 움직이다, 꿈틀거리다
A caterpillar **wriggles** along.[36]

syn. crawl, wiggle, drag

예문 해석

33 내가 의도했던 것보다 더 신랄한 말이 나왔었다.   **34** 그는 아이의 장난감에 발이 걸려 넘어졌다.   **35** 많은 사람들이 테레사 수녀를 존경한다.   **36** 애벌레가 꿈틀거린다.

Directions   Each of the following questions consists of one word followed by five words or phrases. You are to select the one word or phrase whose meaning is closest to the word in capital letters.

1. ABDICATE :
   (A) acclaim
   (B) soothe
   (C) enlarge
   (D) abandon
   (E) reduce

2. ARDUOUS :
   (A) alleviated
   (B) positive
   (C) agreeable
   (D) hospitable
   (E) difficult

3. CALLOUS :
   (A) insensitive
   (B) boundless
   (C) deceitful
   (D) wayward
   (E) charitable

4. DEFIANCE :
   (A) extremity
   (B) purification
   (C) resistance
   (D) accord
   (E) revenge

5. GENUINE :
   (A) authentic
   (B) clever
   (C) malleable
   (D) resolute
   (E) inflexible

6. HAMLET :
   (A) small village
   (B) head gear
   (C) young tree
   (D) huge construction
   (E) small waterfall

7. MITIGATE :
   (A) reprise
   (B) shake
   (C) confirm
   (D) alleviate
   (E) shorten

8. NUISANCE :
   (A) indifference
   (B) annoyance
   (C) scarcity
   (D) reconciliation
   (E) drop

9. REPRIMAND :
   (A) compel
   (B) blame
   (C) harmonize
   (D) remain
   (E) absorb

10. VENERATE :
    (A) separate
    (B) revere
    (C) compare
    (D) discourage
    (E) postpone

"People only see what they are prepared to see."

— Ralph Waldo Emerson —

American essayist, philosopher, poet, and leader of the Transcendentalist movement in the early 19th century

사람들은 자기가 볼 수 있는 것만 본다.

Greek and Latin Roots & Prefixes 4

★ DICT = to speak

-ion (n.)	diction	말투, 용어 선택
-um (status)	dictum	격언, 금언
-ion (n.)	dictation	받아쓰기, 구술
-or (person)	dictator	독재자
pre (before)	predict	예언하다
contra (against)	contradict	부정하다, 반박하다
ver (true)	verdict	평결, 판결
ex (out)	edict	명령, 포고령
in (in)	indictment	기소, 기소장

DAY

04

WORDS TO LEARN

☐ abash	☐ distress	☐ inflame	☐ reproach
☐ affront	☐ eminent	☐ intervene	☐ rustic
☐ arid	☐ euphemism	☐ limerick	☐ shard
☐ bestow	☐ fainthearted	☐ mar	☐ specter
☐ camouflage	☐ forage	☐ mnemonic	☐ superfluous
☐ comprehensive	☐ getaway	☐ nimble	☐ taut
☐ conventional	☐ hamper[1]	☐ perfunctory	☐ trite
☐ deficient	☐ hybrid	☐ prejudiced	☐ venomous
☐ despise	☐ impunity	☐ quandary	☐ writhe

01

abash
[*uh*-bash]

v. to make ashamed or embarrassed
무안하게 하다, 당황하게 하다
The boy was **abashed** by the laughter of his classmates.[1]

syn. embarrass, disconcert, baffle

02

affront
[*uh*-fru*h*nt]

n. a personally offensive act or word
모욕, 상처
Nonconformists saw slavery as an **affront** to their religion.[2]

syn. insult, indignity, provocation

03

arid
[ar-id]

adj. very dry
건조한, 메마른, 불모의
We traveled through an **arid** desert.[3]

syn. parched, dehydrated, waterless

예문 해석

01 그 소년은 반 친구들의 웃음소리에 당황했다.　**02** 비순응주의자들은 노예제도를 자신들의 종교에 대한 모욕으로 여겼다.　**03** 우리는 건조한 사막을 여행했다.

04 ···

bestow
[bi-stoh]

v. to give or to present
주다
He **bestowed** a gift on the child.[4]

> *syn.* give, confer, bequeath, grant

05 ···

camouflage
[kam-*uh*-flahzh]

v. to disguise or conceal
가장하다, 변장하다
They'd be very well **camouflaged**.[5]

> *syn.* conceal, disguise, cover

06 ···

comprehensive
[kom-pri-hen-siv]

adj. covering or involving much
포괄적인, 종합적인
He has a **comprehensive** grasp of this issue.[6]

> *syn.* inclusive, broad, extensive

07 ···

conventional
[k*uh*n-ven-sh*uh*-nl]

adj. adhering to accepted standards
관습적인, 전통적인, 틀에 박힌
Three times as many people are using the **conventional** system rather than a brand-new one.[7]

> *syn.* customary, traditional

08 ···

deficient
[di-fish-*uh*nt]

adj. lacking some element or characteristic
모자라는, 부족한
Since Sloane was **deficient** in her daily dose of iron, she had to take supplemental vitamins.[8]

> *syn.* insufficient, inadequate, defective

예문 해석

04 그는 그 아이에게 선물을 주었다. **05** 그들은 잘 변장했을 것이다. **06** 그는 이 문제를 포괄적으로 파악하고 있다. **07** 세 배나 많은 사람들이 완전 새로운 시스템보다는 전통적인 것을 사용하고 있다. **08** 슬론은 매일 철분 섭취가 부족했기 때문에 비타민 보충제를 먹어야 했다.

09

despise
[dih-spaiz]

v. to regard with contempt or disgust
경멸하다
They **despised** him for being greedy.[9]

syn. scorn, abhor, deride

10

distress
[di-stres]

n. extreme sorrow, suffering, or pain
고통
Jealousy causes painful **distress**.[10]

syn. suffering, pang, agony

11

eminent
[em-*uh*-nu*h*nt]

adj. famous and admired
저명한, 탁월한, 훌륭한
She has been an **eminent** scholar for many years.[11]

syn. prominent, noted, respected

12

euphemism
[yoo-f*uh*-miz-*uh*m]

n. a polite word or expression
완곡 어법
"To pass away" is a **euphemism** for "to die."[12]

syn. circumlocution, substitute

13

fainthearted
[feynt-hahr-tid]

adj. lacking boldness or courage
소심한, 용기 없는, 겁 많은
There is no time to be **fainthearted**.[13]

syn. cowardly, afraid, fearful

14

forage
[fawr-ij]

v. to search for food
마구 뒤지며 찾다, 약탈하다
The wild cat **forages** for food.[14]

syn. scavenge, rummage

 예문 해석

09 그들은 그가 욕심이 많다고 경멸했다. **10** 질투는 극심한 고통을 낳는다. **11** 그녀는 수 년간 저명한 학자였다. **12** "돌아가셨다"는 것은"죽다"의 완곡한 표현이다. **13** 겁 먹고 있을 시간이 없다. **14** 야생 고양이가 먹을 것을 뒤지며 찾고 있다.

15

getaway
[get-*uh*-wey]

n. a getting away or fleeing

도주, 휴가

My parents went on a two-week **getaway** in the Maldives.[15]

syn. escape, break

16

hamper[1]
[ham-per]

v. to hinder the progress or movement of someone or something

방해하다, 구속하다

The bad weather **hampered** rescue operations.[16]

syn. hinder, impede, deter

17

hybrid
[hai-brid]

n. offspring of two different breeds

잡종, 혼혈아, 혼성물

Environmentally conscious **hybrid** cars are gaining popularity.[17]

syn. mongrel, composite, mixture

18

impunity
[im-pyoo-ni-tee]

n. exemption from punishment

처벌 받지 않음, 면제

His honest answer provided him with some **impunity**.[18]

syn. exemption, freedom, immunity

19

inflame
[in-fleym]

v. to make something more heated or intense

화나게 하다, 자극시키다, 흥분시키다

They were **inflamed** with enthusiasm.[19]

syn. excite, anger, aggravate

20

intervene
[in-ter-veen]

v. to involve oneself in something which is happening in order to affect an outcome

사이에 끼어들다, 개입하다

The situation calmed down soon after the police **intervened**.[20]

syn. arbitrate, mediate, intercede

예문 해석

15 우리 부모님은 몰디브로 2주 동안 여행을 가셨어. **16** 나쁜 날씨가 구조 작업을 방해했다. **17** 환경을 의식한 하이브리드 자동차가 인기를 끌고 있다. **18** 그의 솔직한 답변이 처벌을 면하게 해주었다. **19** 그들은 열정으로 불타올랐다. **20** 경찰이 개입하자 곧 상황은 잠잠해졌다.

limerick
[lim-er-ik]

n. a humorous poem which has five lines
리머릭, 5행으로 된 유머러스한 시
The story was written in the **limerick** form of poetry.[21]

> *syn.* verse, poem, ballad

mar
[mahr]

v. to spoil or damage
망치다, 손상시키다
A number of problems **marred** this convention.[22]

> *syn.* injure, disgrace, spoil

mnemonic
[ni-mon-ik]

n. something intended to assist the memory
연상하여 기억을 돕게 만드는 말이나 방법, 기억술
You can remember the colors of the rainbow, use the **mnemonic** "Richard Of York Gave Battle In Vain".[23]

> *syn.* cue, hint, inkling

nimble
[nim-buhl]

adj. agile or acrobatic
민첩한, 솜씨 좋은
Nimble fingers are always an asset.[24]

> *syn.* adroit, agile, shrewd

perfunctory
[per-fuhngk-tuh-ree]

adj. done merely as a duty or routine
아무렇게나 하는, 형식적인
He asked me how I was, as a **perfunctory** courtesy.[25]

> *syn.* desultory, cursory

prejudiced
[prej-uh-dis]

adj. having an unreasonable dislike of or preference
편견을 가진, 선입견을 가진
Some employers are racially **prejudiced**.[26]

> *syn.* biased, intolerant, bigoted

예문 해석

21 그 이야기는 리머릭 형태로 쓰여졌다. **22** 많은 문제들이 이 회의를 망쳐놓았다. **23** 당신은 무지개의 색깔들을 "Richard Of York Gave Battle In Vain"이라는 기억을 돕는 말로 외울 수 있다. (Red, Orange, Yellow, Green, Blue, Indigo, Violet의 앞 글자를 따서 만든 말) **24** 솜씨 좋은 손놀림은 언제나 자산이다. **25** 그는 형식적인 예의로 나에게 안부를 물었다. **26** 어떤 고용주들은 인종에 대한 선입견이 있다.

27

quandary
[kwon-*duh*-ree]

n. the state of not being able to decide what to do in a difficult situation

당황, 곤경, 난처한 처지

They were in a hopeless **quandary**.[27]

syn. difficulty, puzzle, uncertainty

28

reproach
[ri-prohch]

v. to find fault with

비난하다, 꾸짖다, 책망하다

She is quick to **reproach** anyone who doesn't live up to her own standards.[28]

syn. censure, criticize, upbraid

29

rustic
[*ruhs*-tik]

adj. of living in the country

시골 풍의, 소박한

He loved his **rustic** life.[29]

syn. rural, arcadian, bucolic, pastoral

30

shard
[shahrd]

n. a fragment, especially of broken earthenware

(도자기, 유리 등의) 조각, 파편

When the vase hit the wall, the **shards** of glass flew in all directions.[30]

syn. fragment, piece, particle

31

specter
[spek-ter]

n. a ghost or a great fear

유령, 망령, 공포

The boy saw a **specter** in his nightmare.[31]

syn. ghost, apparition, phantom

🔖 예문 해석

27 그들은 어찌할 바를 몰랐다.　**28** 그녀는 자기 기준에 맞지 않은 행동을 하는 사람들은 바로 꾸짖었다.　**29** 그는 전원적인 자신의 삶을 사랑했다.　**30** 꽃병이 벽에 부딪혔을 때, 유리 조각들은 사방으로 날아갔다.　**31** 그 소년은 악몽 속에서 유령을 보았다.

32

superfluous
[soo-pur-floo-*uh*s]

adj. being more than is sufficient or required
불필요한
It works by eliminating information from the file that the program deems **superfluous**.[32]

> *syn.* unnecessary, redundant, excessive

33

taut
[tawt]

adj. tightly drawn
팽팽한, 팽팽하게 당겨진
Make sure the line is pulled **taut**, otherwise the ball won't move across the line.[33]

> *syn.* tight, tense

34

trite
[trahyt]

adj. dull and boring
흔한, 평범한, 진부한
This movie is teeming with **trite** scenes.[34]

> *syn.* clichéd, banal, hackneyed

35

venomous
[ven-*uh*-m*uh*s]

adj. full of or containing venom
독이 있는, 악의에 찬
This snake is a highly **venomous** one.[35]

> *syn.* malicious, spiteful, poisonous

36

writhe
[rahyth]

v. to twist the body as in pain
괴로워서 몸부림치다, 뒤틀다
The sentry **writhed** in pain when the door fell on his foot.[36]

> *syn.* twist, squirm, distort

 예문 해석

32 프로그램이 불필요한 정보를 파일에서 제거함으로써 작동합니다. **33** 줄을 팽팽하게 당겨라, 그렇지 않으면 공이 줄을 따라 움직이지 않는다. **34** 이 영화는 진부한 장면들로 가득 차 있다. **35** 이 뱀은 맹독을 가졌다. **36** 보초는 문이 발 위로 떨어지자 고통으로 몸부림쳤다.

Directions   Each of the following questions consists of one word followed by five words or phrases. You are to select the one word or phrase whose meaning is closest to the word in capital letters.

1. ARID :
   (A) waterfall
   (B) parched
   (C) pardon
   (D) power
   (E) breeze

2. BESTOW :
   (A) alter
   (B) aristocracy
   (C) give
   (D) shocked
   (E) rural

3. CAMOUFLAGE :
   (A) conceal
   (B) reprimand
   (C) unveil
   (D) berate
   (E) hurtle

4. DEFICIENT :
   (A) reckless
   (B) hellish
   (C) insufficient
   (D) quandary
   (E) kindle

5. EUPHEMISM :
   (A) circumlocution
   (B) stroll
   (C) meat-eating
   (D) force
   (E) ramble

6. IMPUNITY :
   (A) harmful
   (B) mean
   (C) stumble
   (D) exemption
   (E) garrulous

7. MNEMONIC :
   (A) captivate
   (B) cue
   (C) anticipate
   (D) suppress
   (E) fickle

8. NIMBLE :
   (A) adroit
   (B) pertinacious
   (C) opening
   (D) anticipate
   (E) swerve

9. PREJUDICED :
   (A) related
   (B) foolish
   (C) titular
   (D) forgo
   (E) biased

10. REPROACH :
   (A) intentional
   (B) bow
   (C) censure
   (D) blend
   (E) demand

"A woman is like a tea bag-you never know how strong she is
until she gets in hot water."

— Eleanor Roosevelt —
U.S. diplomat & reformer

여자는 마치 티백과 같다. 뜨거운 물에 들어가기 전까지는
얼마나 강한지 알 수 없다.

LESSON

Greek and Latin Roots & Prefixes 5

★ JECT = throw

on (overboard)	jettison	(항공기나 선박이 무게를 줄이기 위해) 버리다
pro (forward)	project	기획, 프로젝트
re (back)	reject	거부하다, 거절하다
ex (out)	eject	튀어나오게 하다, 탈출하다
in (in)	injection	주사, 투입
con (together)	conjecture	추측, 추측한 내용
de (down)	dejected	낙담한, 실망한
ob (against)	objection	반대
ob (towards)	objective	목적, 목표
trans(beyond)	trajectory	탄도, 궤적

DAY

05

WORDS TO LEARN

☐ abhor	☐ emit	☐ kindle	☐ reprove
☐ akin	☐ euphoria	☐ limp	☐ rustle
☐ armada	☐ force¹	☐ malignant	☐ sheath
☐ bewildered	☐ germane	☐ maraud	☐ stalwart
☐ candid	☐ hamper²	☐ nocturnal	☐ stronghold
☐ converge	☐ hyperbole	☐ ornamental	☐ tedious
☐ deflect	☐ imprint	☐ peril	☐ trivial
☐ didactic	☐ inflammable	☐ preliminary	☐ veracity
☐ diverge	☐ intimate¹	☐ quarry¹	☐ wry

01

abhor
[ab-hawr]

v. to hate or dislike
몹시 싫어하다, 혐오하다, 질색하다
I **abhor** violence.¹

syn. detest, hate, loathe, abominate

02

akin
[*uh*-kin]

adj. similar or being of the same kind
유사한, 비슷한
His life story is **akin** to a good adventure novel.²

syn. similar, parallel, analogous, alike

03

armada
[ahr-mah-d*uh*]

n. any fleet of warships
함대
His whole thoughts were directed to the preparation of an invincible **armada** for the conquest of England.³

syn. fleet, flotilla, squadron

예문 해석

01 나는 폭력을 혐오한다.　**02** 그의 인생 이야기는 흥미로운 모험소설과도 같다.　**03** 그의 모든 생각은 영국 정복을 위한 무적 함대를 준비하는 데 집중되어 있었다.

04

bewildered
[bi-wil-derd]

adj. confused
당황한
Some people looked **bewildered** by the news that he was back.[4]

syn. confounded, perplexed, puzzled

05

candid
[kan-did]

adj. open and sincere
솔직한, 숨김없는
She is famous for her **candid** criticism.[5]

syn. frank, open, outspoken

06

converge
[kuhn-vurj]

v. to come together from different directions
한 점으로 모이다
The lines **converge** at this point.[6]

syn. concentrate, gather, assemble

07

deflect
[dih-flekt]

v. to turn from a true course or straight line
(무엇엔가 부딪히고) 방향을 바꾸다
Prisms **deflect** rays of light towards their bases.[7]

syn. bounce off, turn aside, avert

08

didactic
[dai-dak-tik]

adj. intended for instruction
교훈적인
His novels for children are certainly **didactic**, and they are certainly moral.[8]

syn. instructive, educational, academic

📖 예문 해석

04 어떤 사람들은 그의 귀환 소식에 당황한 듯 보였다. **05** 그녀는 솔직한 비평으로 유명하다. **06** 선들은 이 점에서 한 곳으로 모인다. **07** 프리즘은 빛을 밑부분으로 향하게 합니다. **08** 아이들을 위한 그의 소설들은 확실히 교훈적이고 도덕적이다.

09 ....

diverge
[di-vurj]

v. to move in different directions from a common point
갈라지다, 분기하다
They **diverged** from the right way[9]

syn. branch off, separate, deviate

10 ....

emit
[i-mit]

v. to give off liquid, light, heat, sound, particles, etc.
발산하다, 내뿜다
The sun **emits** light and heat.[10]

syn. discharge, release, give off

11 ....

euphoria
[yoo-fawr-ee-*uh*]

n. a feeling of intense happiness and excitement
행복감
I was in a state of **euphoria** after I received the surprising news.[11]

syn. elation, exhilaration, glee

12 ....

force[1]
[fors]

n. a powerful effect or influence
힘, 체력
He was a **force** to be reckoned with.[12]

syn. power, strength

13 ....

germane
[jer-meyn]

adj. closely related
적절한, 관계있는
She asks **germane** questions that are central to the issue.[13]

syn. relevant, pertinent

14 ....

hamper[2]
[ham-per]

n. basket usually with a cover
바구니, 광주리
Put your dirty clothes in the **hamper**.[14]

syn. container, holder, box

예문 해석

09 그들은 바른 길에서 벗어났다. **10** 태양은 빛과 열을 방출한다. **11** 나는 놀라운 소식을 듣고 행복감에 빠졌다. **12** 그는 무시할 수 없는 힘이었다. **13** 그녀는 이슈의 핵심을 찌르는 적절한 질문을 했다. **14** 너의 더러운 옷은 바구니에 넣어라.

15 ....

hyperbole
[hai-pur-b*uh*-lee]

n. obvious and intentional exaggeration
과장법, 과장어구
Hyperbole is used to create emphasis.[15]

syn. exaggeration, overstatement

16 ....

imprint
[im-print]

n. any impression or impressed effect
(마음 속에 새겨진) 각인
The terrible scenes of wars were indelibly **imprinted** on this child's mind.[16]

syn. signature, impression, symbol

17 ....

inflammable
[in-flam-*uh*-b*uh*l]

adj. easily being set on fire
가연성의, 불이 잘 붙는
The building was built of wood and other **inflammable** materials.[17]

syn. flammable, combustible, volatile

18 ....

intimate[1]
[in-t*uh*-mit]

adj. close or very private
친한, 매우 사적인
She knew all of my secrets because she was an **intimate** friend.[18]

syn. close, near, dear, cherished

19 ....

kindle
[kin-dl]

v. to start a fire
불이 붙다, 불을 붙이다
A mischievous light **kindled** in his eyes.[19]

syn. ignite, inflame, start a fire

20 ....

limp
[limp]

adj. not stiff or firm
흐느적거리는, 부드러운, 축 늘어진
She went **limp**.[20]

syn. flabby, flaccid, soft

예문 해석

15 과장법은 강조를 하기 위해 사용된다.　**16** 전쟁의 참혹한 장면들이 이 아이의 마음에 지울 수 없이 각인되었다.　**17** 그 건물은 나무와 다른 가연성 물질들로 지어졌다.　**18** 그녀는 친한 친구였기 때문에 나의 비밀을 모두 알고 있었다.　**19** 그의 눈은 장난기로 번뜩였다.　**20** 그녀는 축 처졌다.

malignant
[m*uh*-lig-n*uh*nt]

adj. disposed to cause harm, suffering, or distress deliberately
악성의

A **malignant** tumor grew uncontrollably and spread to the patient's whole body.[21]

syn. diseased, cancerous, fatal

maraud
[m*uh*-rawd]

v. to wander in search of people to attack and property to steal
약탈하다, 습격하다

His town had been **marauded** by a band of soldiers.[22]

syn. plunder, pillage

nocturnal
[nok-tur-nl]

adj. belonging or relating to the night
밤의, 야행성의

A bat is an example of a **nocturnal** animal.[23]

syn. nightly, nighttime, happening at night

ornamental
[awr-n*uh*-men-tl]

adj. serving a decoration rather than a useful purpose
장식적인, 장식용의

It is a popular **ornamental** plant in gardens due to its bright and attractive color.[24]

syn. decorative, exquisite, ornate

peril
[per-*uhl*]

n. grave danger and a hazard
큰 위험

Liberty without learning is always in **peril**; learning without liberty is always in vain. -John F. Kennedy [25]

syn. danger, threat, risk

예문 해석

21 악성 종양이 걷잡을 수 없이 커져 환자의 온몸으로 퍼졌다. **22** 그의 마을은 한 무리의 군인들에게 약탈당했다. **23** 박쥐는 야행성 동물의 한 예이다. **24** 이것은 밝고 매력적인 색깔 때문에 인기 있는 장식용 식물이다. **25** 배움 없는 자유는 항상 위험하고, 자유 없는 배움은 항상 헛되다.

26

preliminary
[pri-lim-*uh*-ner-ee]

adj. happening before a more important action or event
준비의, 준비 단계의
The **preliminary** findings in the investigation led the detective to the potential suspects.[26]

syn. initial, first, opening

27

quarry[1]
[kwawr-ee]

n. a place with large amounts of stone
채석장, 돌 캐는 곳
Stone from the **quarry** was used in the Middle Ages for both ecclesiastical and military buildings.[27]

syn. pit, stone pit, excavation

28

reprove
[ri-proov]

v. to criticize gently
타이르다, 야단치다
The teacher **reproved** a pupil for talking loudly in the corridor.[28]

syn. admonish, scold gently, reprimand

29

rustle
[r*uhs-uhl*]

v. to make a succession of slight, soft sounds
살랑살랑 소리 내다, 옷 스치는 소리를 내다
There was a **rustle** of paper as people turned the pages.[29]

syn. swish, whisper, sigh

30

sheath
[sheeth]

n. a case or covering for the blade of a sword or knife
칼집, 덮개
He placed his sword in its **sheath**.[30]

syn. cover, case

 예문 해석

26 그 수사에서 나온 예비 소견은 그 형사를 잠재적인 용의자로 이끌었다.   **27** 중세시대 채석장의 돌은 교회와 군용 건물들에 사용되었다.   **28** 그 선생님은 복도에서 크게 떠드는 학생을 타일렀다.   **29** 사람들이 페이지를 넘길 때 바스락거리는 소리가 났다.
30 그는 그의 칼을 칼집에 넣었다.

31

stalwart
[stawl-wert]

adj. strongly and stoutly built
충실한, 튼튼한
When the **stalwart** bodyguards accompanied the movie stars, she felt much safer.[31]

syn. sturdy, strong, robust

32

stronghold
[strawng-hohld]

n. a well-fortified place
요새, 성채, 근거지
The region had long been a **stronghold** of the party.[32]

syn. bulwark, fort, fortress

33

tedious
[tee-dee-*uhs*]

adj. boring and rather frustrating
지루한, 지겨운
Such essays are long and **tedious** to read.[33]

syn. boring, dull, monotonous

34

trivial
[triv-ee-*uhl*]

adj. not important or serious
하찮은, 시시한
Don't sweat **trivial** matters.[34]

syn. unimportant, insignificant, trifling

35

veracity
[v*uh*-ras-i-tee]

n. the quality of being true or the habit of telling the truth
진실, 진실을 말함
We questioned the **veracity** of his account.[35]

syn. truthfulness, credibility, authority

36

wry
[rai]

adj. humorously sarcastic or mocking
비꼬는, 풍자적인
When my co-worker asked how my horrible morning was, I replied with a **wry** tone, "couldn't be better." [36]

syn. sarcastic, mocking, twisted

예문 해석

31 그 충실한 경호원들이 영화배우들과 동행했을 때, 그녀는 훨씬 더 안전함을 느꼈다. **32** 그 지역은 그 정당에게는 오랜 본거지이다. **33** 이런 에세이들은 너무 길고 읽기 지루하다. **34** 사소한 일로 힘 빼지 마라. **35** 우리는 그가 하는 이야기의 진실성에 의문이 들었다. **36** 직장 동료가 나의 끔찍한 아침이 어땠냐고 묻자 나는 "더 좋을 수가 없다"고 비꼬는 어조로 대답했다.

Directions Each of the following questions consists of one word followed by five words or phrases. You are to select the one word or phrase whose meaning is closest to the word in capital letters.

1. ABHOR :
(A) alter
(B) consent
(C) belittle
(D) detest
(E) mislead

2. AKIN :
(A) deficient
(B) perilous
(C) imprisoned
(D) peculiar
(E) similar

3. CANDID :
(A) frank
(B) unkempt
(C) obscure
(D) priceless
(E) nebulous

4. DEFLECT :
(A) wipe down
(B) bounce off
(C) throw away
(D) clean up
(E) put up

5. EMIT :
(A) creep
(B) discharge
(C) originate
(D) dilute
(E) propagate

6. EUPHORIA :
(A) elation
(B) vestige
(C) trek
(D) garment
(E) circumlocution

7. FORCE :
(A) power
(B) massacre
(C) dogma
(D) satire
(E) pedestal

8. KINDLE :
(A) revoke
(B) mitigate
(C) rescue
(D) ignite
(E) request

9. PERIL :
(A) flood
(B) danger
(C) scene
(D) gadget
(E) scabbard

10. TRIVIAL :
(A) quaint
(B) unimportant
(C) reasonable
(D) passive
(E) helpless

"People learn more on their own rather than being forced."

— Socrates —
Greek philosopher

사람들은 강압적인 때가 아닌 스스로가 원할 때 더 많은 것을 배운다.

Greek and Latin Roots & Prefixes 6

★ SECT = to cut

-ct (n.)	sect	종파, 같은 종교의 갈린 갈래
-ion (n.)	section	부분
-or (part)	sector	(특히 국가 경제 활동) 부문
-an (person)	sectarian	종교 분파의, 종파의
bi (two)	bisect	이등분 하다
dis (apart)	dissect	해부하다
in (into)	insect	곤충
inter (between)	intersection	교차로
viv (life)	vivisection	생체 해부

DAY

06

WORDS TO LEARN

- ☐ abominable
- ☐ alacrity
- ☐ aroma
- ☐ biased
- ☐ cantankerous
- ☐ commencement
- ☐ convert
- ☐ defunct
- ☐ degenerate

- ☐ diction
- ☐ empathy
- ☐ evade
- ☐ far-fetched
- ☐ hangar
- ☐ hypnotize
- ☐ inadvertent
- ☐ infringe
- ☐ intimate[2]

- ☐ kindred
- ☐ lineage
- ☐ marginal
- ☐ moderate
- ☐ nomad
- ☐ ornate
- ☐ paradigm
- ☐ prelude
- ☐ quarry[2]

- ☐ repudiate
- ☐ ruthless
- ☐ shed[1]
- ☐ speculate
- ☐ stunning
- ☐ teem
- ☐ trot
- ☐ verbalize
- ☐ xenophobia

01

abominable
[*uh*-bom-*uh*-nuh-b*uh*l]

adj. very bad, poor, or inferior
지긋지긋한, 혐오스러운, 무시무시한
The refugees were forced to live in **abominable** conditions.[1]

syn. hateful, detestable, loathsome

02

alacrity
[*uh*-lak-ri-tee]

n. cheerful readiness
활발, 민첩
He accepted her invitation with **alacrity**.[2]

syn. liveliness, briskness, willingness

03

aroma
[*uh*-roh-m*uh*]

n. an agreeable odor
향기, 좋은 냄새
A pleasant coffee **aroma** wafted in from the kitchen.[3]

syn. fragrance, odor

예문 해석

01 난민들은 어쩔 수 없이 끔찍한 환경에서 생활해야 했다.   **02** 그는 그녀의 초대를 얼른 받아들였다.   **03** 주방으로부터 기분 좋은 커피향이 풍겨왔다.

04

biased
[bai-*uh*st]

adj. having or showing bias
선입견이 있는, 편견을 가진
Many people are **biased** toward other religions.[4]

> *syn.* prejudiced, partial, slanted

05

cantankerous
[kan-tang-ker-*uh*s]

adj. disagreeable to deal with
심술궂은, 성질 나쁜
He was a **cantankerous**, argumentative man.[5]

> *syn.* contentious, peevish, crabby

06

commencement
[k*uh*-mens-m*uh*nt]

n. the act of starting something
시작, 개시(졸업식, 학위 수여식이란 의미로도 쓰임)
Please put out cigarettes before the **commencement** of the flight.[6]

> *syn.* start, beginning, initiation

07

convert
[k*uh*n-vurt]

v. to change the nature, purpose, or function of something
바꾸다, 전환하다
Convert yards into meters.[7]

> *syn.* switch, change, alter

08

defunct
[dih-f*uh*ngkt]

adj. no longer in effect or use
사용되지 않는, 사망한
A hurricane swept through the city, leaving many houses ruined and **defunct**. [8]

> *syn.* extinct, obsolete, vanished

예문 해석

04 많은 사람들이 다른 종교에 관해 편견을 가지고 있다.   **05** 그는 심술궂고 논쟁적인 사람이었다.   **06** 비행 시작 전에 담배는 꺼주십시오.   **07** 야드를 미터법으로 변환하라.   **08** 허리케인이 도시를 휩쓸면서 많은 집들이 파괴되고 버려졌다.

09

degenerate
[dih-jen-*uh*-reyt]

v. to pass from a higher to a lower condition
퇴보하다, 전락하다
As time went on, our relationship **degenerated**.[9]

syn. worsen, decline, backslide, retrogress

10

diction
[dik-sh*uh*n]

n. style of speaking or writing
어법, 말투
Even the harshest critics agree that Shakespeare's **diction** is perfect.[10]

syn. choice of words, phraseology, phrasing

11

empathy
[em-p*uh*-thee]

n. the ability to share another person's feelings
공감, 감정 이입
Having begun my life in a children's home, I have great **empathy** for the little ones.[11]

syn. understanding, fellow feeling, sympathy

12

evade
[i-veyd]

v. to avoid
피하다, 회피하다
They tried to **evade** military service.[12]

syn. avoid, dodge, escape, shun, eschew

13

far-fetched
[fahr-fecht]

adj. highly imaginative but unlikely
믿기지 않는, 설득력 없는
For her mother, becoming a pop star is a **far-fetched** idea.[13]

syn. unlikely, implausible, unfeasible

14

hangar
[hang-er]

n. a large building in which aircraft are kept
격납고 (비행기 보관소)
The airplane entered the **hangar**.[14]

syn. garage, shed, shelter

예문 해석

09 시간이 지날수록 우리의 관계는 악화되었다. **10** 가장 신랄한 비평가들조차 세익스피어의 어법은 완벽하다고 동의한다. **11** 고아원에서 자란 나는 아이들의 마음을 잘 알 수 있었다. **12** 그들은 병역을 기피하려 했다. **13** 그녀의 어머니에게 팝스타가 되는 것은 말이 안되는 생각이다. **14** 비행기가 격납고로 들어갔다.

15

hypnotize
[hip-n*uh*-taiz]

v. to control completely as by personal charm
최면을 걸다, 홀리다
The orator **hypnotized** the audience with his powerful speech.[15]

syn. spellbind, mesmerize, entrance

16

inadvertent
[in-*uh*d-vur-tnt]

adj. not done deliberately
고의가 아닌, 의도하지 않은
The **inadvertent** mistake caused her great shame.[16]

syn. unintentional, unintended

17

infringe
[in-frinj]

v. to break a law or rule
어기다, 위반하다, 침해하다
Don't **infringe** on my privacy.[17]

syn. violate, transgress, encroach

18

intimate[2]
[in-t*uh*-meyt]

v. to make known
암시하다, 힌트를 주다
Although she had **intimated** her retirement, the announcement was still a shock.[18]

syn. imply, hint, suggest

19

kindred
[kin-drid]

adj. related by blood or marriage
관련된, 비슷한
She sees him as a **kindred** spirit.[19]

syn. related, connected, similar

20

lineage
[lin-ee-ij]

n. the series of families
혈통, 계통
They could trace their **lineage** with their family record.[20]

syn. pedigree, bloodline, ancestry

예문 해석

15 그 연설가는 힘있는 연설로 관중들을 매혹시켰다.　**16** 그 무심코 저지른 실수는 그녀에게 큰 부끄러움을 주었다.　**17** 내 사생활을 침해하지 마시오.　**18** 그녀가 은퇴에 대해 암시했음에도 불구하고 그 발표는 여전히 충격적이었다.　**19** 그녀는 그를 동족으로 본다.　**20** 그들은 족보를 가지고 혈통을 따져볼 수 있었다.

21

marginal
[mahr-j*uh*-nl]

adj. minimal or barely enough
미미한, 근소한
There has been only a **marginal** improvement in the patient's health condition. [21]

> *syn.* slight, negligible, insignificant

22

moderate
[mod-er-it]

adj. of medium quantity or amount
절제 있는, 보통의, 온건한
Moderate exercise is good for your health.[22]

> *syn.* temperate, judicious, reasonable

23

nomad
[noh-mad]

n. a person who has no permanent home but moves about from place to place
유목민, 방랑자
They lived as **nomads**.[23]

> *syn.* wanderer, itinerant, vagabond

24

ornate
[awr-neyt]

adj. covered with a lot of decoration
화려하게 장식한, 잘 꾸민
They bought an **ornate** sofa.[24]

> *syn.* fancy, decorative, flowery

25

paradigm
[par-*uh*-daim]

n. an example serving as a model
전형적인 예
After the economic fiasco, the government created a new **paradigm** for financial stability.[25]

> *syn.* example, model, exemplar

26

prelude
[prel-yood]

n. a short piece of music as an introduction to a longer piece
서곡
This is just a **prelude** to the main act.[26]

> *syn.* introduction, overture, prologue

예문 해석

21 그 환자의 건강 상태는 극히 일부 좋아졌을 뿐이다.　**22** 적당한 운동은 건강에 좋다.　**23** 그들은 유목민으로 살았다.　**24** 그들은 화려하게 장식된 소파를 샀다.　**25** 경제 실패 이후, 정부는 금융 안정을 위한 새로운 패러다임을 만들었다.　**26** 이것은 우리가 기대한 것의 서곡에 불과하다.

27

quarry²
[kwawr-ee]

n. an animal hunted or caught for food
사냥감
The hunter was hunting his **quarry**.[27]

> *syn.* game, prey, aim

28

repudiate
[ri-pyoo-dee-eyt]

v. to reject as having no authority or binding force
거절하다, 부인하다
He **repudiated** the report.[28]

> *syn.* disclaim, reject, renounce

29

ruthless
[rooth-lis]

adj. without pity or compassion
무자비한, 잔인한
He was a **ruthless** tyrant.[29]

> *syn.* cruel, callous, brutal

30

shed¹
[shed]

n. a wooden or metal outbuilding, usually small, for storage or for shelter
오두막
My parents store their gardening equipment in a **shed**.[30]

> *syn.* hovel, hut, shack

31

speculate
[spek-yuh-leyt]

v. to indulge in conjectural thought
사색하다, 추정하다
The doctors **speculate** that he died of a cerebral hemorrhage caused by a blow to the head.[31]

> *syn.* conjecture, surmise, guess

32

stunning
[stuhn-ing]

adj. of striking beauty or excellence
굉장히 멋진
She was the most **stunning** woman he'd ever seen.[32]

> *syn.* marvelous, beautiful, fabulous

🔖 **예문 해석**

27 사냥꾼은 사냥감을 쫓고 있었다. **28** 그는 그 보고를 부인했다. **29** 그는 무자비한 독재자였다. **30** 우리 부모님은 원예용품을 헛간에 보관하신다. **31** 의사들은 그가 머리를 맞아 뇌출혈로 사망했을 것이라 추정했다. **32** 그녀는 그가 본 사람 중 가장 아름다운 여자였다.

33 ···

teem
[teem]

v. to abound or swarm
충만하다, 풍부하다, 가득하다
This region is always **teeming** with tourists.[33]

syn. swarm, abound, be full

34 ···

trot
[trot]

v. to move at a steady, fairly fast pace
빠른 걸음으로 가다, 바쁘게 걷다
The horses **trotted** around the track.[34]

syn. jog, run

35 ···

verbalize
[vur-b*uh*-laiz]

v. to express in words
말로 표현하다
She couldn't **verbalize** her feelings.[35]

syn. communicate, express

36 ···

xenophobia
[zen-*uh*-foh-bee-*uh*]

n. strong and unreasonable dislike or fear of people from other countries
이방인 공포증, 외국인 혐오증
A plague came to France, and the people's fear turned into **xenophobia**.[36]

syn. fear of strangers, prejudice, bias

 예문 해석

33 이 지역은 항상 관광객들로 가득하다. **34** 말들이 트랙 주위를 속보로 달렸다. **35** 그녀는 자신의 감정을 말로 표현할 수 없었다. **36** 프랑스에 전염병이 찾아왔고, 사람들의 공포는 외국인 혐오증으로 변했다.

Directions   Each of the following questions consists of one word followed by five words or phrases. You are to select the one word or phrase whose meaning is closest to the word in capital letters.

1. **ALACRITY :**
   (A) liveliness
   (B) poem
   (C) routine
   (D) carriage
   (E) dwelling

2. **BIASED :**
   (A) applicable
   (B) ecstatic
   (C) habitual
   (D) prejudiced
   (E) convincing

3. **CANTANKEROUS :**
   (A) shocked
   (B) contentious
   (C) secured
   (D) disguise
   (E) rascal

4. **CONVERT :**
   (A) slander
   (B) switch
   (C) stretch
   (D) reprieve
   (E) debate

5. **DEFUNCT :**
   (A) extinct
   (B) personable
   (C) attractive
   (D) insulting
   (E) vehement

6. **EMPATHY :**
   (A) aura
   (B) greeting
   (C) bitterness
   (D) delight
   (E) understanding

7. **HYPNOTIZE :**
   (A) befit
   (B) spellbind
   (C) comprehend
   (D) blend
   (E) rejuvenate

8. **INADVERTENT :**
   (A) unintentional
   (B) stilted
   (C) boring
   (D) secretive
   (E) fashionable

9. **LINEAGE :**
   (A) pedigree
   (B) amnesty
   (C) will
   (D) obedience
   (E) timidity

10. **MARGINAL :**
   (A) pertinent
   (B) acute
   (C) slight
   (D) outrageous
   (E) contented

Directions   Each of the following questions consists of one word followed by five words or phrases.
You are to select the one word or phrase whose meaning is closest to the word in capital letters.

1. PENSIVE :
(A) thoughtful
(B) inclined
(C) eroded
(D) conditional
(E) associated

2. REPREHENSIBLE :
(A) blameworthy
(B) quarrelsome
(C) implied
(D) mirrored
(E) victorious

3. TEMPERAMENT :
(A) moderation
(B) chronometer
(C) annoyance
(D) personality
(E) frowning

4. CONVENE :
(A) give
(B) resist
(C) congregate
(D) supervise
(E) minimize

5. DEFT :
(A) impractical
(B) pragmatic
(C) agile
(D) quaint
(E) obedient

6. EMBRACE :
(A) filch
(B) estimate
(C) divide
(D) grovel
(E) hug

7. AGITATE :
(A) banish
(B) gather
(C) instigate
(D) applaud
(E) confound

8. BESIEGE :
(A) blend
(B) surround
(C) commend
(D) swerve
(E) flatter

9. FOOLHARDY :
(A) reckless
(B) twisted
(C) tainted
(D) scanty
(E) indigent

10. INTERVAL :
(A) compliance
(B) mercy
(C) pastime
(D) vocation
(E) gap

11. ABASH :
  (A) indifferent
  (B) rural
  (C) absurd
  (D) shocked
  (E) embarrass

12. COMPREHENSIVE :
  (A) violate
  (B) tumult
  (C) sour
  (D) inclusive
  (E) initiate

13. DESPISE :
  (A) scorn
  (B) reckless
  (C) uncultivated
  (D) harmful
  (E) question

14. EMINENT :
  (A) hellish
  (B) absentee
  (C) prominent
  (D) contented
  (E) summary

15. ARMADA :
  (A) fleet
  (B) grove
  (C) archipelago
  (D) constellation
  (E) electorate

16. DIDACTIC :
  (A) stolid
  (B) sullen
  (C) instructive
  (D) narcissistic
  (E) collected

17. INFLAMMABLE :
  (A) uncultivated
  (B) anachronistic
  (C) flammable
  (D) clientele
  (E) deteriorated

18. GERMANE :
  (A) intermittent
  (B) catholic
  (C) ominous
  (D) relevant
  (E) subversive

19. AROMA :
  (A) article
  (B) fragrance
  (C) hesitation
  (D) procession
  (E) reverberation

20. COMMENCEMENT :
  (A) start
  (B) status
  (C) priority
  (D) abyss
  (E) impulsiveness

"What you do not wish for yourself, do not do to others."

– Confucius –
Chinese philosopher

네가 싫은 일은 다른 사람에게도 하지 말라

Greek and Latin Roots & Prefixes 7

★ CRED = to believe

-ible (capable of)	credible	믿을 수 있는
-ous (adj.)	credulous	잘 믿는, 잘 속는
-ed (n.)	creed	(종교적) 교리; 신념
-it (n.)	credit	신용 거래
-ial (n.)	credential	자격증을 수여하다
dis (not)	discredit	존경심을 떨어뜨리다
in (not)	incredible	믿을 수 없는
in (not)	incredulous	잘 안 믿는, 잘 안 속는

DAY

07

WORDS TO LEARN

- ☐ aboveboard
- ☐ affinity
- ☐ arouse
- ☐ bigoted
- ☐ candor
- ☐ commiserate
- ☐ convincing
- ☐ deity
- ☐ diffident

- ☐ diversion
- ☐ emphatic
- ☐ evanescent
- ☐ fallacy
- ☐ foreboding
- ☐ ghetto
- ☐ haphazard
- ☐ hypocrisy
- ☐ inalienable

- ☐ infirmity
- ☐ intimidate
- ☐ lenient
- ☐ mandatory
- ☐ modest
- ☐ nonchalant
- ☐ ostentatious
- ☐ penury
- ☐ premiere

- ☐ queasy
- ☐ repulse
- ☐ safeguard
- ☐ shed[2]
- ☐ shiver
- ☐ studious
- ☐ temperate
- ☐ truant
- ☐ verbose

01 ··

aboveboard
[*uh*-buhv-bawrd]

adj. legal and honest
정정당당한, 훤히 보이는
His action was open and **aboveboard**.[1]

syn. honest, open, candid

02 ··

affinity
[*uh*-fin-i-tee]

n. a natural liking
친밀감
They had much in common and felt a strong **affinity**.[2]

syn. liking, affection, fondness

03 ··

arouse
[*uh*-rouz]

v. to awaken
일깨우다, 각성시키다, 자극하다
His speech **aroused** the crowd.[3]

syn. awaken, stimulate, provoke

예문 해석

01 그의 행동은 정정당당했다. **02** 그들은 공통점이 많았고 강한 친화력을 느꼈다. **03** 그의 연설은 군중들을 일깨웠다.

04

bigoted
[big-*uh*-tid]

adj. obstinately attached to some opinion and intolerant toward others
고집 센, 편협한
Such a **bigoted** person is hard to deal with.[4]

syn. opinionated, unyielding

05

candor
[kan-der]

n. the state or quality of being frank or open
솔직함
While I appreciate your **candor**, I don't think we need to be friends anymore.[5]

syn. honesty, integrity, outspokenness

06

commiserate
[k*uh*-miz-*uh*-reyt]

v. to feel or express sorrow or sympathy for
위로하다, 동정하다
She **commiserated** with her brother over the sad loss of his puppy.[6]

syn. condole, comfort, console

07

convincing
[k*uh*n-vin-sing]

adj. causing one to believe the truth of something
설득력 있는, 납득 가게 하는
He provided **convincing** evidence.[7]

syn. assuring, persuasive, plausible

08

deity
[dee-i-tee]

n. god or goddess
신, 여신, 신성
Zeus and Aphrodite were ancient Greek **deities**.[8]

syn. god, immortal, idol

예문 해석

04 이런 고집 센 사람은 다루기가 힘들다. **05** 당신의 솔직함은 고맙지만, 우리는 더 이상 친구가 될 필요가 없다고 생각해요.
06 그녀는 강아지를 잃어버린 동생을 위로했다. **07** 그는 설득력 있는 증거를 제시했다. **08** 제우스와 아프로디테는 고대 그리스의 신들이다.

09

diffident
[dif-i-d*uh*nt]

adj. lacking confidence
수줍은, 자신이 없는
He was **diffident** about his own success.[9]

> *syn.* timid, bashful, sheepish

10

diversion
[dih-vur-zh*uh*n]

n. the activity that diverts the mind from more serious concerns
기분 전환, 주의를 다른 데로 돌리는 것
As a **diversion**, she plays the piano.[10]

> *syn.* recreation, distraction

11

emphatic
[em-fat-ik]

adj. expressed with emphasis
어조가 강한, 표현상 힘이 있는, 단호한
His response was immediate and **emphatic**.[11]

> *syn.* forceful, positive, definite

12

evanescent
[ev-*uh*-nes-*uh*nt]

adj. disappearing quickly
덧없는, 사라져가는
Popularity is **evanescent**.[12]

> *syn.* transitory, vanishing, fleeting

13

fallacy
[fal-*uh*-see]

n. mistaken notion
그릇된 생각, 오류
It's a **fallacy** that the affluent give relatively more to charity than the less prosperous.[13]

> *syn.* misconception, delusion

14

foreboding
[fawr-boh-ding]

n. a strong feeling of a future misfortune
예감, 전조, 불길한 징조
He had a **foreboding** of trouble when the door creaked open.[14]

> *syn.* omen, portent, prediction

 예문 해석

09 그는 자신의 성공에 대해 수줍어했다.　**10** 기분 전환을 위해 그녀는 피아노를 연주한다.　**11** 그의 대답은 즉각적이고 단호했다.　**12** 인기는 덧없는 것이다.　**13** 부유한 사람이 가난한 사람보다 자선을 더 베풀 것이라는 것은 잘못된 생각이다.　**14** 그는 문이 부서져 열려 있는 것을 보고 불길한 예감이 들었다.

15

ghetto
[get-oh]

n. a part of a city in which many poor people live
빈민가
Ghettos are avoided when traveling.[15]

syn. slum

16

haphazard
[hap-haz-erd]

adj. determined by or dependent on chance
아무렇게나, 준비 없이, 우연히
To enjoy a spontaneous road trip, we decided to take the
haphazard route.[16]

syn. random, casual, desultory

17

hypocrisy
[hi-pok-*ruh*-see]

n. the act of pretending to have feelings which one does
not actually have
위선, 위선 행위
The **hypocrisy** of the business officials make it nearly
impossible for trust to be built among the employers and
consumers.[17]

syn. insincerity, sanctimoniousness

18

inalienable
[in-eyl-y*uh*-nuh-b*uh*l]

adj. unable to be taken away from
떨어뜨릴 수 없는, 양도할 수 없는
It is important for each person to understand their **inalienable**
rights.[18]

syn. inviolable, absolute, unassailable

19

infirmity
[in-fur-mi-tee]

n. a physical weakness or sickness
병약, 질환
Her mental **infirmity** was caused by an early onset of
Alzheimer's disease.[19]

syn. frailty, malady, ailment

🧘 **예문 해석**

15 여행 중에는 게토(빈민가)를 피한다. **16** 즉흥적인 여행길을 즐기기 위해, 우리는 무계획적으로 길을 택하기로 했다. **17** 재계 관계자들의 위선은 고용주와 소비자 사이에 신뢰가 형성되는 것을 거의 불가능하게 만든다. **18** 각자가 양도할 수 없는 권리를 이 해하는 것은 중요하다. **19** 그녀의 정신 질환은 알츠하이머병의 조기 발병에 의한 것이었다.

20

intimidate
[in-tim-i-deyt]

v. to compel or deter by threats
협박하다, 위협하다
I didn't mean to **intimidate** you.[20]

> *syn.* browbeat, extort, blackmail

21

lenient
[lee-nee-*uh*nt]

adj. agreeably tolerant
관대한
This small school's teachers are more likely to be **lenient** and more understanding.[21]

> *syn.* tolerant, permissive, compassionate

22

mandatory
[man-d*uh*-tawr-ee]

adj. authoritatively ordered
법에 정해진, 의무적인
If you want to win this swimming race, weeknight practices are **mandatory**.[22]

> *syn.* obligatory, compulsory, required

23

modest
[mod-ist]

adj. showing a moderate or humble estimate of one's merits
겸손한, 신중한
She was **modest** about her success.[23]

> *syn.* humble, unassuming, self-effacing

24

nonchalant
[non-sh*uh*-lahnt]

adj. calmly or indifferently unconcerned
무관심한, 태연한, 냉담한
He has a **nonchalant** attitude to life.[24]

> *syn.* casual, unconcerned, indifferent

25

ostentatious
[os-ten-tey-sh*uh*s]

adj. intended to attract notice and impress others
자랑 삼아 드러내는, 과시하는
She was in an **ostentatious** dress at the garden party.[25]

> *syn.* showy, pretentious, affected

 예문 해석

20 당신을 위협할 생각은 아니었다.　**21** 이 작은 학교의 선생님들은 더 관대하고 이해심이 많을 것 같다.　**22** 당신이 이 수영 경기에서 우승하고 싶다면, 주중 야간 연습은 필수입니다.　**23** 그녀는 자신의 성공에 겸손했다.　**24** 그는 인생에 무관심한 태도를 가진다.　**25** 그녀는 가든파티 때 매우 화려하게 장식된 드레스를 입었다.

26

penury
[pen-*yuh*-ree]

n. extreme poverty
극빈, 빈곤
Economic downturns and job loss can lead to **penury**.[26]

syn. destitution, poverty, dearth

27

premiere
[pri-meer]

n. the first public performance
초연, 공개적인 첫 시연
Many famous actors were in attendance at the world **premiere**.[27]

syn. opening, first night, first performance

28

queasy
[kwee-zee]

adj. inclined to or feeling nausea
멀미하는 것 같은, 속이 불편한
He was very prone to seasickness and already felt **queasy**.[28]

syn. nauseous, sick, ill

29

repulse
[ri-p*uh*ls]

v. to drive back
격퇴하다, 물리치다
The troops available were not sufficient to **repulse** attack.[29]

syn. repel, rebuff, reject

30

safeguard
[seyf-gahrd]

n. something that serves as a protection or defense
안전 장치, 보호책, 예방책
The Defense Ministry says it has prepared enough **safeguards**.[30]

syn. protection, shield, security

31

shed[2]
[shed]

v. to emit and let fall, as tears
흘리다, 떨어지게 하다
She **shed** tears.[31]

syn. drop, spill

예문 해석

26 경기 침체와 일자리 감소는 빈곤으로 이어질 수 있다.　**27** 많은 유명한 배우들이 첫 시사회에 참석했다.　**28** 그는 배멀미를 잘해서 벌써부터 속이 불편한 것 같았다.　**29** 공격을 격퇴하기에 쓸 수 있는 군력이 충분하지 않다.　**30** 국방부는 충분한 안전장 치를 준비했다고 말하고 있다.　**31** 그녀는 눈물을 흘렸다.

32

shiver
[shiv-er]

v. to shake or tremble with cold, fear, or excitement
(몸을) 떨다
The involuntary **shiver** in chilly weather is a response meant to raise our body temperature to a safe level. [32]

syn. shake, shudder, tremble

33

studious
[stoo-dee-*uhs*]

adj. characterized by a serious hardworking approach, especially to study
열심인, 학구적인
I was a very quiet, **studious** little girl.[33]

syn. diligent, industrious, assiduous

34

temperate
[tem-per-it]

adj. not extreme or mild
절제하는, 삼가는, 온화한
The teacher admired the student's **temperate** attitude at school. [34]

syn. moderate, mild, clement

35

truant
[troo-*uhnt*]

n. someone who stays away from school or work without good reason or without permission
무단결석자, 게으름뱅이
She began to play **truant**.[35]

syn. absentee, malingerer, shirker

36

verbose
[ver-bohs]

adj. boringly or irritatingly long-winded
말이 많은, 장황한, 수다스러운
She detests having to read **verbose** reports.[36]

syn. garrulous, lengthy, wordy, loquacious

예문 해석

32 쌀쌀한 날씨에 무의식적으로 떨리는 것은 우리의 체온을 안전한 수준으로 올리기 위한 반응이다.　**33** 나는 굉장히 조용하고 열심히 노력하는 학생이었다.　**34** 선생님은 그 학생의 학교에서의 절제된 태도에 감탄했다.　**35** 그녀는 무단 결석을 하기 시작했다. **36** 그녀는 장황한 리포트를 읽는 것을 싫어했다.

Directions   Each of the following questions consists of one word followed by five words or phrases.
You are to select the one word or phrase whose meaning is closest to the word in capital letters.

1. ABOVEBOARD :
   (A) false
   (B) shrewd
   (C) honest
   (D) impolite
   (E) argumentative

2. AFFINITY :
   (A) elasticity
   (B) liking
   (C) bigot
   (D) formality
   (E) determination

3. CANDOR :
   (A) wealth
   (B) brevity
   (C) disguise
   (D) honesty
   (E) partnership

4. COMMISERATE :
   (A) emerge
   (B) condole
   (C) stray
   (D) charm
   (E) harmonize

5. DIVERSION :
   (A) recreation
   (B) cuisine
   (C) maze
   (D) formula
   (E) eviction

6. EMPHATIC :
   (A) forceful
   (B) irritating
   (C) redundant
   (D) humid
   (E) envious

7. FOREBODING :
   (A) approval
   (B) omen
   (C) eddy
   (D) inoculation
   (E) computation

8. INALIENABLE :
   (A) satirical
   (B) inviolable
   (C) captivating
   (D) obscene
   (E) irreprehensible

9. NONCHALANT :
   (A) charlatan
   (B) flammable
   (C) casual
   (D) short-sighted
   (E) deteriorated

10. OSTENTATIOUS :
   (A) corrupt
   (B) plain
   (C) competent
   (D) troublesome
   (E) showy

"Every artist was first an amateur."

— Ralph Waldo Emerson —

모든 예술가도 처음에는 아마추어였다.

Greek and Latin Roots & Prefixes 8

★ MIT, MISS = to send

-ion (n.)	mission	임무, 파견
-ile (n.)	missile	미사일
ad (toward)	admit	인정하다
ex (out)	emit	(빛이나 열등을) 배출하다
ob (intensive)	omit	빠뜨리다, 누락시키다
re (back)	remit	송금하다
trans (beyond)	transmit	전송하다
sub (under)	submit	제출하다

DAY

08

WORDS TO LEARN

☐ abridge	☐ divulge	☐ kinetic	☐ reputable
☐ allocate	☐ empirical	☐ linger	☐ sage
☐ arable	☐ evict	☐ masquerade	☐ sheen
☐ bilk	☐ fallow	☐ mortify	☐ splice
☐ capitulate	☐ foresee	☐ noncommittal	☐ stupendous
☐ commotion	☐ homage	☐ ostracize	☐ tempest
☐ convoluted	☐ idealistic	☐ plebeian	☐ trudge
☐ delegate	☐ inane	☐ premonition	☐ verdict
☐ diffuse	☐ ingenious	☐ quell	☐ zany

01 ····················

abridge
[*uh*-brij]

v. to shorten by omissions while retaining the basic contents
요약하다, 긴 이야기를 줄이다
This is an **abridged** version.[1]

syn. abbreviate, shorten, edit

02 ····················

allocate
[al-*uh*-keyt]

v. to distribute according to a plan or set apart for a purpose
(특정 목적을 위해) 할당하다, 배당하다
The leader of a camp **allocated** a loaf of bread to everyone daily.[2]

syn. assign, allot, apportion

03 ····················

arable
[ar-*uh*-buhl]

adj. capable of producing crops
경작이 가능한, 농사지을 수 있는
First, you need to find a patch of **arable** land to raise crops.[3]

syn. farmable, tillable, cultivable

📖 예문 해석

01 이것은 축약본이다. **02** 한 캠프의 지도자는 매일 모두에게 빵 한 덩어리를 나누어 주었다. **03** 먼저 당신은 농작물을 기를 수 있는 경작지를 찾아야 합니다.

04

bilk
[bilk]

v. to cheat
속이다, 빚을 떼어먹다
He **bilked** the government of almost a billion dollars.[4]

syn. deceive, swindle, hoax, gull

05

capitulate
[k*uh*-pich-*uh*-leyt]

v. to give in
항복하다
He finally **capitulated** and agreed to do the job my way.[5]

syn. surrender, yield

06

commotion
[k*uh*-moh-sh*uh*n]

n. a lot of noise, confusion, and excitement
동요, 소란
He heard a **commotion** outside.[6]

syn. agitation, tumult, uproar

07

convoluted
[kon-v*uh*-loo-tid]

adj. highly complex or intricate
꼬인, 뒤얽힌, 복잡한
He usually took a **convoluted** way to explain simple matters.[7]

syn. coiled, complicated, intricate

08

delegate
[del-i-geyt]

n. a person designated to act for or represent another or others
대표, 대리인
The United Nation **delegates** serve as the voice and face of their specific countries at various meetings.[8]

syn. deputy, representative, proxy

🧘 **예문 해석**

04 그는 정부를 상대로 거의 10억 원에 해당되는 금액을 사기쳤다.　**05** 그는 결국 항복하고 내 식대로 일하기로 동의했다.　**06** 밖에서 소란스러운 소리가 들려왔다.　**07** 그는 단순한 일들을 복잡하게 만들곤 했다.　**08** 유엔 대표단은 다양한 회의에서 특정 국가의 목소리와 얼굴 역할을 한다.

09

diffuse
[di-fyooz]

v. to spread
퍼지다, 퍼뜨리다
The perfume **diffused** throughout the room.[9]

syn. disseminate, disperse

10

divulge
[di-*vuh*lj]

v. to disclose or reveal
폭로하다, 누설하다
The secret must not be **divulged**.[10]

syn. reveal, debunk, disclose

11

empirical
[em-pir-i-k*uh*l]

adj. based on experiment, observation or experience, rather than on theory
경험적인, 실험에 근거한
There is no **empirical** evidence to support her thesis.[11]

syn. experiential, experimental, observed

12

evict
[i-vikt]

v. to force to leave
내쫓다
They were **evicted** from their apartment after they stopped paying their rent.[12]

syn. expel, exile, ostracize

13

fallow
[fal-oh]

adj. left unplanted
묵히고 있는, 휴경지의
The land was left **fallow** because the farmer had no seeds to plant.[13]

syn. uncultivated, unplanted, unsown

 예문 해석

09 향수의 향이 온 방으로 퍼졌다.   **10** 비밀은 누설되어서는 안된다.   **11** 그녀의 이론을 지지할 실험적 증거는 없다.   **12** 그들은 집세를 안 낸 뒤로는 아파트에서 쫓겨났다.   **13** 농부가 심을 씨앗이 없었기 때문에 그 땅은 휴경지로 남아 있었다.

14

foresee
[fawr-see]

v. realize beforehand
예견하다
In Greek mythology, Tiresias is known for **foreseeing** the future.[14]

syn. anticipate, foreknow, previse

15

homage
[hom-ij]

n. respect or reverence paid or rendered
경의, 존경의 표시
In her speech, she paid **homage** to great actors and actresses.[15]

syn. reverence, admiration, deference

16

idealistic
[ai-dee-*uh*-lis-tik]

adj. having a strong belief in perfect standards
이상주의적인, 완벽함을 추구하는
Don Quixote is an **idealistic** but impractical knight.[16]

syn. illusory, visionary, chimerical

17

inane
[i-neyn]

adj. silly or senseless
어리석은, 생각없는
The professor detested **inane** questions during class.[17]

syn. silly, senseless, void

18

ingenious
[in-jeen-y*uh*s]

adj. clever and original
독창적인, 창의력이 있는
The invention of the wheel was truly **ingenious**.[18]

syn. clever, resourceful, original

19

kinetic
[ki-net-ik]

adj. relating to or producing motion
운동의, 움직이는
Kinetic energy is the energy produced by something moving.[19]

syn. moving, energetic, peppy

예문 해석

14 그리스 신화에서, 테이레시아스는 미래를 예견하는 것으로 알려져 있습니다. **15** 그녀는 연설에서 위대한 배우들에게 경의를 표했다. **16** 돈키호테는 이상주의적이지만 비현실적인 기사이다. **17** 그 교수는 수업 중 엉뚱한 질문을 매우 싫어했다. **18** 바퀴의 발명은 정말 기발했다. **19** 운동 에너지란 움직여서 얻어지는 에너지를 말한다.

20

linger
[ling-ger]

v. to continue to exist for longer than expected
망설이다, 지체하다
We **lingered** for a while after the party.[20]

> *syn.* dawdle, procrastinate, delay

21

masquerade
[mas-kuh-reyd]

n. a party gathering of persons wearing masks
가면 무도회, 가장 무도회
A **masquerade** is a festive gathering of persons wearing masks and other disguises.[21]

> *syn.* disguise, camouflage

22

mortify
[mawr-tuh-fai]

v. to humiliate or shame
굴욕감을 주다, 모욕을 주다
He felt **mortified** because of his huge mistake.[22]

> *syn.* humiliate, embarrass, disgrace

23

noncommittal
[non-kuh-mit-l]

adj. avoiding expressing a definite opinion or decision
애매한, 이도 저도 아닌
He was **noncommittal** about the project he joined.[23]

> *syn.* evasive, vague, unrevealing

24

ostracize
[os-truh-saiz]

v. to exclude by general consent
추방하다, 배척하다
Her friends **ostracized** her after her father's arrest.[24]

> *syn.* banish, oust, exile

25

plebeian
[pli-bee-uhn]

adj. of a member of common people
(귀족이 아닌) 평민의
In Roman times, the lower class of people was the **plebeian** class; the upper class was the patrician class.[25]

> *syn.* base, lower-class, lowborn

예문 해석

20 우리는 파티가 끝난 뒤에도 조금 더 머물렀다. **21** 가면 무도회란 사람들이 가면을 쓰거나 변장을 하고 즐기는 축제이다. **22** 그는 자신의 큰 실수에 굴욕감을 느꼈다. **23** 그는 그가 참여한 프로젝트에 대해 애매한 태도를 취했다. **24** 그녀의 친구들은 그녀의 아버지가 체포된 이후 그녀를 멀리했다. **25** 로마 시대에 하층민들은 평민 계급이었고, 상류층은 귀족 계급이었다.

premonition
[pree-m*uh*-nish-*uh*n]

n. a feeling that something is about to happen before it actually does

전조, 예감

She had a **premonition** that an accident would happen.[26]

syn. foreboding, intuition, presentiment

quell
[kwel]

v. to suppress or crush completely

진압하다, 평정하다

The troops **quelled** the rebellion quickly.[27]

syn. vanquish, suppress, crush

reputable
[rep-*yuh*-t*uh*-b*uh*l]

adj. held in good repute

이름 높은, 평판이 좋은

Microsoft is one of the most **reputable** companies in the US.[28]

syn. respectable, honorable, commendable

sage
[seyj]

n. a person famed for wisdom

현명한 사람, 박식하고 경험이 풍부한 사람

He was a renowned **sage** of his age.[29]

syn. pundit, savant, scholar

sheen
[sheen]

n. shine, luster or radiance

광택, 윤

The carpet had a golden **sheen** to it.[30]

syn. shine, polish, luster, glossiness

splice
[splais]

v. to join two pieces of rope by weaving the strands of one into the other

밧줄을 꼬아 잇다, 연결하다

He taught me to edit and **splice** film.[31]

syn. conjoin, join, entwine

예문 해석

26 그녀는 사고가 일어날지도 모른다는 느낌이 들었다.　**27** 부대는 반란군을 재빨리 진압했다.　**28** 마이크로소프트사는 미국에서 가장 이름있는 회사들 중 하나다.　**29** 그는 그 시대의 유명한 현자였다.　**30** 카펫은 금빛 광택을 띄었다.　**31** 그는 나에게 필름을 편집하고 이어붙이는 법을 가르쳐주었다.

32

stupendous
[stoo-pen-*duhs*]

adj. surprisingly impressive or large

놀라운, 엄청난

He was a man of **stupendous** stamina and energy.[32]

syn. wonderful, amazing, impressive

33

tempest
[tem-pist]

n. a violent storm

폭풍

Because there was a **tempest** in the forecast, we went shopping for food and water to prepare.[33]

syn. storm, thunderstorm, gale

34

trudge
[tru*h*j]

v. to walk slowly and with heavy steps

터벅터벅 걷다, 무거운 발걸음으로 걷다

He **trudged** the desert for hours.[34]

syn. plod, lumber, tramp

35

verdict
[vur-dikt]

n. any decision, opinion or judgment

(배심원이 재판장에게 제출하는) 평결, 판정, 판단

The jury returned a unanimous "Not Guilty" **verdict**.[35]

syn. decision, judgment

36

zany
[zey-nee]

adj. ludicrous or foolish

우스꽝스러운, 어릿광대 같은

I saw many **zany** costumes at the annual masquerade.[36]

syn. funny, crazy, wacky

🧑‍🏫 **예문 해석**

32 그는 놀라운 스테미너와 에너지를 가진 사람이다.   **33** 일기예보에 폭풍우가 있어 우리는 대비를 위해 음식과 물을 사러 갔다.
34 그는 몇 시간 동안 사막을 무거운 발걸음으로 걸었다.   **35** 배심원 만장일치로 무죄 판결을 내렸다.   **36** 나는 매년 가장 무도
회에서 많은 우스꽝스러운 의상을 보았다.

Directions   Each of the following questions consists of one word followed by five words or phrases.
You are to select the one word or phrase whose meaning is closest to the word in capital letters.

1. **ABRIDGE :**
   (A) abbreviate
   (B) develop
   (C) help
   (D) arrest
   (E) detach

2. **ARABLE :**
   (A) brief
   (B) unselfish
   (C) farmable
   (D) knowledgeable
   (E) miserable

3. **DELEGATE :**
   (A) fervor
   (B) deputy
   (C) prudence
   (D) larceny
   (E) productivity

4. **DIFFUSE :**
   (A) access
   (B) grumble
   (C) incur
   (D) anticipate
   (E) disseminate

5. **FALLOW :**
   (A) timeless
   (B) agreeable
   (C) uncultivated
   (D) matchless
   (E) absorbed

6. **FORESEE :**
   (A) dilate
   (B) anticipate
   (C) retard
   (D) fade
   (E) conflict

7. **INGENIOUS :**
   (A) zealous
   (B) indistinct
   (C) clever
   (D) rambling
   (E) idiosyncratic

8. **KINETIC :**
   (A) early
   (B) precocious
   (C) senile
   (D) graphic
   (E) moving

9. **MORTIFY :**
   (A) tangle
   (B) startle
   (C) humiliate
   (D) litigate
   (E) trespass

10. **SPLICE :**
   (A) bore
   (B) invoke
   (C) conjoin
   (D) amuse
   (E) forgo

"Shallow men believe in luck. Strong men believe in cause and effect."

– Ralph Waldo Emerson –
U.S. essayist & poet

꾀가 얕은 자는 행운을 믿는다, 강한 자는 원인과 결과를 믿는다.

Greek and Latin Roots & Prefixes 9

★ BENE, BON = good, well

facere (to do)	benefit	혜택
	beneficial	유익한, 이로운
	benefactor	후원자
	beneficiary	수혜자
velle (to wish)	benevolent	자애로운
gignere (to bear)	benign	상냥한, 유순한
deu(to perform)	bonus	보너스, 상여금
fide(faith)	bona fide	진실된, 진짜의

DAY

09

WORDS TO LEARN

☐ absolve	☐ docile	☐ intoxicating	☐ retaliate
☐ affiliated	☐ emulate	☐ knack	☐ salute
☐ articulate	☐ evince	☐ massive	☐ sheepish
☐ bizarre	☐ falter	☐ molt	☐ splinter
☐ capricious	☐ forestall	☐ nondescript	☐ sturdy
☐ compelling	☐ giggle	☐ outburst	☐ thrust
☐ criterion	☐ idiosyncratic	☐ perish	☐ tumble
☐ deleterious	☐ inanimate	☐ preoccupied	☐ verify
☐ digress	☐ ingenuity	☐ quench	☐ zeal

---

01 ....

absolve
[ab-zolv]

v. to forgive someone formally
용서하다, 사면해주다
You could not **absolve** yourself of guilt by also showing someone else's guilt.[1]

syn. pardon, acquit, exonerate

---

02 ....

affiliated
[*uh*-fil-ee-ey-tid]

adj. connected or joined to a company, business, or school
연계된, 관련 있는
This prestigious school is deeply religious-**affiliated**.[2]

syn. associated, connected, related

---

03 ....

articulate
[ahr-tik-y*uh*-leyt]

v. to utter distinctly
똑똑히 발음하다
She had some trouble **articulating** her thoughts.[3]

syn. enunciate, utter clearly, express clearly

예문 해석

01 다른 사람도 잘못했다는 것을 보여줌으로써 자기 자신의 죄를 면할 수 있는 것은 아니다.   **02** 이 명문 학교는 종교와 밀접한 관련이 있다.   **03** 그녀는 자신의 생각을 또박또박 말하는 데 어려움이 있었다.

04

bizarre
[bi-zahr]

adj. weirdly odd or strange
이상한, 특이한
Many of the mental patients exhibit **bizarre** behavior.[4]

syn. strange, weird, peculiar

05

capricious
[kuh-prish-uhs]

adj. unpredictable or erratic
변덕스러운
The **capricious** bride left her groom standing at the wedding altar.[5]

syn. unpredictable, fickle, whimsical

06

compelling
[kuhm-pel-ing]

adj. having a powerful and irresistible effect
설득력 있는, 끌리지 않을 수 없는
There is no **compelling** evidence that she was guilty.[6]

syn. fascinating, enthralling, overpowering

07

criterion
[krahy-teer-ee-uhn]

n. a standard for judgment or criticism
판단 기준, 표준 (복수형 *criteria*)
Because Lisa has taught already for two years, she has met the **criterion** for teaching job experience.[7]

syn. standard, norm, yardstick

08

deleterious
[del-i-teer-ee-uhs]

adj. injurious to health
(건강에) 해로운, 유독한
The chemical is **deleterious** to the environment.[8]

syn. damaging, harmful, injurious

예문 해석

04 많은 정신질환자들이 이상한 행동을 보인다.　**05** 그 변덕스러운 신부는 신랑을 결혼식 제단에 세워두고 떠났다.　**06** 그녀에게 죄가 있다는 설득력 있는 증거는 없다.　**07** 리사는 이미 2년 동안 교편을 잡았기 때문에, 교직 경험의 기준을 충족시켰다.　**08** 그 화학물은 환경에 유해하다.

digress
[di-gres]

v. to wander away from the main topic
산만하게 굴다, 논지에서 벗어나다
I was tired of continuing the conversation, so I **digressed**.[9]

syn. stray, deviate, wander

docile
[dos-*uh*l]

adj. easy to manage or control
순종적인, 말 잘 듣는
The oldest daughter was the most **docile** out of the three children.[10]

syn. pliant, obedient, meek

emulate
[em-*yuh*-leyt]

v. to strive to equal or match by imitating
열심히 흉내 내다
She likes to **emulate** her favorite pop singers.[11]

syn. mimic, copy, imitate

evince
[i-vins]

v. to show or display something clearly
명시하다, 나타내다, 밝히다
She **evinced** her disappointment.[12]

syn. show, demonstrate

falter
[fawl-ter]

v. to speak or act in an unsteady way
비틀거리다, 말을 더듬다
The teacher's voice **faltered** as the giant mouse came into the classroom.[13]

syn. stumble, stutter, stammer

forestall
[fohr-stawl]

v. to prevent, delay, or hinder by acting in advance
미리 손쓰다, 선수를 치다
I'd like to **forestall** any possible crisis.[14]

syn. prevent, deter, hinder

예문 해석

09 나는 대화를 계속하는 것이 지겨워서 말을 돌렸다.　**10** 세 아이 중 첫째 딸이 가장 온순했다.　**11** 그녀는 자신이 좋아하는 팝 스타들을 따라하는 것을 좋아한다.　**12** 그녀는 그녀의 실망을 명백히 드러냈다.　**13** 거대한 쥐가 교실 안으로 들어오자 선생님은 말을 더듬었다.　**14** 나는 가능한 모든 위기를 미연에 방지하고 싶다.

15

giggle
[gig-*uh*l]

v. to laugh in a silly, high-pitched way
낄낄웃다
The young girls burst into **giggles** at the slightest provocation.[15]

> *syn.* snicker, chuckle, laugh

16

idiosyncratic
[id-ee-*uh*-sing-kr*uh*-tik]

adj. peculiar and odd
특유한, 기이한, 색다른
His singing style is highly original and **idiosyncratic**.[16]

> *syn.* eccentric, peculiar, quirky

17

inanimate
[in-an-*uh*-mit]

adj. not living
무생물의, 생기없는
Life is full of animate and **inanimate** objects.[17]

> *syn.* lifeless, dead, non-living

18

ingenuity
[in-*juh*-noo-i-tee]

n. the quality of being cleverly inventive
영리함, 발명의 재간
The **ingenuity** of her solution to the math problem astounded the teacher.[18]

> *syn.* inventiveness, cleverness, creativity

19

intoxicating
[in-tok-si-key-ting]

adj. causing or capable of causing intoxication
취하게 하는
As a college student, I was told to stay away from **intoxicating** beverages.[19]

> *syn.* exhilarating, stimulating, exciting

20

knack
[nak]

n. the ability to do something effectively and skillfully
기술, 요령, 교묘한 솜씨
Practice will give you the **knack** for it.[20]

> *syn.* ability, skill, talent

예문 해석

15 어린 소녀들은 작은 일에도 쉽게 깔깔거린다.　**16** 그의 창법은 매우 독창적이고 특이하다.　**17** 인생은 생물과 무생물로 가득 차 있다.　**18** 수학 문제를 푸는 그녀의 독창적인 해법에 선생님을 놀랐다.　**19** 대학생으로서, 나는 취하게 하는 음료를 멀리하라는 말을 들었다.　**20** 연습하면 요령을 알게 된다.

21

massive
[mas-iv]

adj. very big, bulky, solid and heavy
매우 큰, 거대한
A **massive** iceberg is floating.[21]

syn. bulky, ponderous, voluminous

22

molt
[mohlt]

v. to shed hair, feathers, shell, horns, or an outer layer periodically
털을 갈다, 탈피하다, 뿔을 갈다
Snakes **molt** as they grow, shedding the old skin and growing a larger new skin.[22]

syn. exfoliate, shed, cast off

23

nondescript
[non-di-skript]

adj. having no interesting or unusual features or qualities
정체를 알 수 없는, 특징 없는
Her house is one of hundreds of **nondescript** buildings along the road.[23]

syn. undistinguished, commonplace, unremarkable

24

outburst
[out-burst]

n. a sudden strong expression of an emotion
(갑작스러운) 감정의 폭발, 분출
The student's **outburst** disrupted the class.[24]

syn. burst, ebullition, effusion

25

perish
[per-ish]

v. to die as a result of very harsh conditions
멸망하다, 죽다
"We must learn to live together as brothers or **perish** together as fools." - Martin Luther King Jr.[25]

syn. die, expire, pass away

 예문 해석

21 커다란 빙산이 떠다니고 있다.　**22** 뱀들은 자라나면서 오래된 허물을 벗고 더 크고 새로운 피부로 탈피한다.　**23** 그녀의 집은 길을 따라 있는 수백 개의 정체불명 건물들 중 하나이다.　**24** 그 학생의 감정 폭발로 수업에 차질이 생겼다.　**25** "우리 모두 형제로서 더불어 사는 것을 배워야 한다. 아니면 모두가 바보로 멸망할 것이다." – 마틴 루터 킹 주니어

26

preoccupied
[pree-ok-yuh-paid]

adj. completely engrossed in thought
몰두한, 여념이 없는
He was totally **preoccupied** with his new project.[26]

syn. absorbed, engaged, engrossed

27

quench
[kwench]

v. to satisfy thirst by drinking
갈증을 해소하다, (불을) 끄다
Water is a thirst **quencher**.[27]

syn. extinguish, satisfy, sate

28

retaliate
[ri-tal-ee-yet]

v. to return like for like
받은 대로 되갚아 주다, 복수하다, 보복하다
He wants to **retaliate** for his injury.[28]

syn. revenge, get back, reciprocate

29

salute
[suh-loot]

n. a formal military gesture of respect
인사, 경례
The president was **saluted** with 21 guns.[29]

syn. greeting, address, salutation

30

sheepish
[shee-pish]

adj. embarrassed through having done something wrong or foolish
수줍어하는, 당황하는
He gave me a **sheepish** grin.[30]

syn. ashamed, shamefaced, embarrassed

31

splinter
[splin-ter]

n. a small, thin, sharp piece of wood
(나무나 돌의) 쪼개진 조각, 가시, 파편
The vase was broken into **splinters**.[31]

syn. piece, shard, fragment

예문 해석

26 그는 그의 새 프로젝트에 완전히 몰두해 있었다. **27** 물은 갈증을 해소해 준다. **28** 그는 그가 다친 대로 그대로 복수하길 원했다. **29** 대통령은 21발의 예포로 경례를 받았다. **30** 그는 내게 수줍은 미소를 보였다. **31** 그 꽃병은 산산조각 나버렸다.

32

sturdy
[stur-dee]

adj. thick and strong-looking
두껍고 억세 보이는, 건장한
He went to the gym every day to ensure he could maintain
his **sturdy** build.[32]

> *syn.* strong, powerful, stout

33

thrust
[thr*uh*st]

v. to push forward quickly and forcibly
(거칠게) 밀다, 밀치다, 찌르다
Jimmy **thrust** his hands deep into his pockets.[33]

> *syn.* push hard, shove, stab

34

tumble
[t*uh*m-b*uh*l]

v. to fall helplessly down by losing one's footing
헛디뎌 넘어지다, 구르다
He slipped and **tumbled** down the stairs.[34]

> *syn.* descend, fall, drop

35

verify
[ver-*uh*-fai]

v. to check that something is true
증명하다, 입증하다
Police could **verify** where the money had been deposited.[35]

> *syn.* validate, confirm, substantiate

36

zeal
[zeel]

n. great and sometimes excessive enthusiasm
열성, 열정
His teacher demonstrated great **zeal** and enthusiasm.[36]

> *syn.* passion, ardor, enthusiasm

예문 해석

32 그는 튼튼한 체격을 유지하기 위해 매일 체육관에 갔다.　**33** 지미는 두 손을 호주머니 깊숙이 찔러 넣었다.　**34** 그는 미끄러져서 계단에서 굴러 떨어졌다.　**35** 경찰은 어디에 돈이 예치되어 있는지 입증할 수 있었다.　**36** 그의 선생님은 굉장한 열성과 열정을 보여주었다.

Directions   Each of the following questions consists of one word followed by five words or phrases. You are to select the one word or phrase whose meaning is closest to the word in capital letters.

1. **ABSOLVE :**
   (A) prevent
   (B) scold
   (C) select
   (D) conceal
   (E) pardon

2. **AFFILIATED :**
   (A) formal
   (B) calm
   (C) associated
   (D) perilous
   (E) solemn

3. **BIZARRE :**
   (A) pertinacious
   (B) complicated
   (C) disabled
   (D) hearty
   (E) strange

4. **DIGRESS :**
   (A) taint
   (B) stray
   (C) encroach
   (D) swear
   (E) assuage

5. **DOCILE :**
   (A) pliant
   (B) intense
   (C) ruthless
   (D) intrepid
   (E) affected

6. **IDIOSYNCRATIC :**
   (A) eccentric
   (B) irritable
   (C) exacting
   (D) wily
   (E) talkative

7. **KNACK :**
   (A) method
   (B) excellence
   (C) incidence
   (D) ability
   (E) philanthropist

8. **PERISH :**
   (A) elaborate
   (B) claim
   (C) assert
   (D) mingle
   (E) die

9. **PREOCCUPIED :**
   (A) abominable
   (B) untamed
   (C) nautical
   (D) succinct
   (E) absorbed

10. **ZEAL :**
   (A) replica
   (B) plight
   (C) sentry
   (D) passion
   (E) rigidity

"Self-conceit may lead to self-destruction."

— Aesop —
Greek slave & fable author

자만은 자괴를 부른다.

Greek and Latin Roots & Prefixes 10

★ MAL, MALE = bad

habere (to have)	malady	심각한 문제, 병폐
aria (air)	malaria	말라리아
facere (to do)	mallefactor	악인, 악한
-ice (n.)	malice	악의, 적의
velle (to wish)	malevolent	악의 있는, 악의적인
gignere (to bear)	malignant	악성의
odor (smell)	malodorous	악취가 나는, 악취를 풍기는
practicare (to do)	malpractice	악습, 위법 행위

DAY

10

WORDS TO LEARN

☐ abstain	☐ doctrine	☐ intrusion	☐ requisite
☐ allay	☐ enchant	☐ knave	☐ salvation
☐ asperity	☐ evoke	☐ liquidate	☐ shimmer
☐ blackmail	☐ famine	☐ momentary	☐ spontaneous
☐ carnivorous	☐ forewarn	☐ nominal	☐ subdue
☐ compensate	☐ gimmick	☐ outdated	☐ tenable
☐ coordinate	☐ ignite	☐ perjury	☐ tumult
☐ deliberate	☐ inattentive	☐ plastic	☐ vernacular
☐ dilapidated	☐ ingenuous	☐ query	☐ zealot

01

abstain
[ab-stein]

v. to choose not to do something
자제하다, 삼가다
She usually **abstained** from eating meat.[1]

syn. forgo, desist, cease

02

allay
[*uh*-ley]

v. to lessen or relieve
고통을 줄여주다
An effective painkiller can **allay** pain.[2]

syn. mitigate, appease, calm, alleviate

03

asperity
[*uh*-sper-i-tee]

n. harshness or sharpness of tone
혹독함, 신랄함
When I disobeyed, my mother spoke to me with **asperity**.[3]

syn. severity, acrimony

🔖 예문 해석

01 그녀는 평소 고기를 먹는 것을 자제하고 있다.　**02** 효과적인 진통제는 고통을 줄여줄 수 있다.　**03** 내가 말을 안 듣자 어머니는 날카롭게 내게 말을 하셨다.

04

blackmail
[blak-meyl]

v. to extort money from a person by the use of threats
공갈하다, 갈취하다
The villain **blackmailed** them.[4]

> *syn.* threaten, extort, coerce

05

carnivorous
[kahr-niv-er-*uh*s]

adj. flesh-eating
육식의
A lion is a **carnivorous** animal.[5]

> *syn.* meat-eating

06

compensate
[kom-p*uh*n-seyt]

v. to make amends for
보상하다
You shall **compensate** for the loss.[6]

> *syn.* recompense, indemnify

07

coordinate
[koh-awr-dn-eyt]

v. to place or arrange in proper order or position
배열하다, 조정하다
The government **coordinated** the recovery effort of the earthquake zone.[7]

> *syn.* harmonize, arrange, align

08

deliberate
[di-lib-er-it]

adj. planned or intentional
고의적인, 심사숙고한, 신중한
I recognized his **deliberate** lie after I asked him for the truth.[8]

> *syn.* intentional, purposeful, planned

🧘 **예문 해석**

04 악당은 그들을 협박했다.　**05** 사자는 육식 동물이다.　**06** 네가 손해를 배상해야 한다.　**07** 정부에서 지진 지역의 복구를 통솔했다.　**08** 나는 그에게 진실을 묻고 나서 그의 고의적인 거짓말을 알아챘다.

dilapidated
[di-lap-i-dey-tid]

adj. reduced to ruin or decay

황폐한, 낡은

Many buildings in New York city are **dilapidated** and in a generally bad condition.[9]

syn. ramshackle, derelict, battered

doctrine
[dok-trin]

n. religious belief

종교 교리, 믿음

In Catholic school, I was taught Catholic **doctrines**.[10]

syn. principle, belief

enchant
[en-chant]

v. to attract somebody strongly

매혹하다, 황홀하게 만들다

Her gaiety and humor have **enchanted** me.[11]

syn. captivate, enthrall, fascinate

evoke
[i-vohk]

v. to summon or call forth

일깨우다

Pictures **evoke** memories.[12]

syn. arouse, elicit, provoke

famine
[fam-in]

n. extreme and general scarcity of food

기근, 굶주림

They suffered from severe **famine**.[13]

syn. starvation, shortage, dearth

forewarn
[fawr-wawrn]

v. to warn in advance

미리 경고하다

He had to **forewarn** me about the strictness of his parents.[14]

syn. caution, admonish

예문 해석

09 뉴욕시의 많은 빌딩들이 낡고 상태가 좋지 않다. **10** 가톨릭 학교에서 나는 가톨릭 교리를 배웠다. **11** 그녀의 명랑함과 유머가 나를 사로잡았다. **12** 사진은 기억을 일깨운다. **13** 그들은 극심한 기근으로 고통받았다. **14** 그는 자기 부모님의 엄격함에 대해 나에게 미리 주의를 주었어야만 했다.

15

gimmick
[gim-ik]

n. an novel device, scheme, or stratagem

비밀 장치, 속임수, 트릭

The discount was a clever **gimmick** to attract customers.[15]

> *syn.* scheme, ruse, trick

16

ignite
[ig-nait]

v. to set on fire

불을 붙이다, 점화하다

A fire sparked by a short circuit **ignited** the oil wagon.[16]

> *syn.* kindle, set on fire, inflame

17

inattentive
[in-*uh*-ten-tiv]

adj. lacking concentration

부주의한, 태만한

They may seem **inattentive**, but they avoid appearing aggressive.[17]

> *syn.* negligent, distracted, careless

18

ingenuous
[in-jen-yoo-*uhs*]

adj. innocent and frank

솔직 담백한, 꾸밈없는

He seemed too **ingenuous** to be a spokesperson.[18]

> *syn.* artless, honest, candid

19

intrusion
[in-troo-zh*uhn*]

n. an illegal act of entering

침해, 침입, 방해

People claim the noise from the plant is an **intrusion** on their lives.[19]

> *syn.* invasion, raid, encroachment

20

knave
[neyv]

n. an unprincipled or dishonest person

악당, 악한

"You rude **knave**!" the knight shouted at his opponent.[20]

> *syn.* rascal, rogue, scoundrel

🔖 **예문 해석**

15 할인은 손님을 끌기 위한 영리한 방법이다. **16** 회로에서 불꽃이 붙어 유조차로 옮겨 붙었다. **17** 그들은 부주의해 보일지는 몰라도 공격적으로 보이지 않으려 하고 있다. **18** 그는 대변인이기엔 너무 솔직하다. **19** 사람들은 공장에서 나는 소음이 생활에 방해가 된다고 주장했다. **20** "이 무례한 악당아!"라고 기사는 적에게 소리쳤다.

21

liquidate
[lik-wi-deyt]

v. to pay off a debt
(빚 등을) 청산하다, 갚다
The company **liquidates** a claim.[21]

syn. pay, pay off, repay

22

momentary
[moh-m*uhn*-ter-ee]

adj. lasting for a very short period of time
잠깐 동안의, 순간적인
This **momentary** life goes by in just a blink of an eye.[22]

syn. brief, fleeting, ephemeral

23

nominal
[nom-*uh*-nl]

adj. being such in name only
명목상의, 이름뿐인
The CEO is the **nominal** head of the company, but his assistant is really in charge of the day-to-day business.[23]

syn. titular, so-called, putative

24

outdated
[out-dey-tid]

adj. no longer useful because of being old-fashioned
구식의, 시대에 뒤진
Some of the plans are **outdated** and need to be eliminated.[24]

syn. obsolete, out-of-date, old-fashioned

25

perjury
[pur-*juh*-ree]

n. the willful giving of false testimony
위증, 위증죄
Commit **perjury** under trial, and you will get prosecuted.[25]

syn. lie, fib

26

plastic
[plas-tik]

adj. capable of being molded or modeled
형태를 만들기가 쉬운, 영향을 받기 쉬운
He has a **plastic** mind like a child.[26]

syn. malleable, susceptible, flexible

🧘 **예문 해석**

21 그 회사는 불만 사항을 처리했다.　**22** 이 순간적인 삶은 눈 깜짝할 사이에 지나간다.　**23** CEO는 명목상 회사의 수장이지만, 그의 비서가 일상 업무를 실제로 담당하고 있다.　**24** 몇몇 계획들은 시대에 뒤떨어져 폐지될 필요가 있다.　**25** 재판에서 거짓 증언을 하면 기소된다.　**26** 그는 아이처럼 영향을 받기 쉬운 마음을 가졌다.

27

query
[kweer-ee]

n. a question, especially one that raises a doubt or objection
질문, 의문, 의혹
The secretary replied to the **query**.[27]

syn. question, inquiry

28

requisite
[rek-*wuh*-zit]

adj. necessary for a particular purpose
필요한, 필수적인
She filled in the **requisite** paperwork.[28]

syn. necessary, needed, required

29

salvation
[sal-vey-sh*uh*n]

n. someone or something in the act of saving another from harm or destruction
구조, 구제, 구원
The ringing bells of the **Salvation** Army in front of the stores means Christmas is coming.[29]

syn. deliverance, rescue, recovery

30

shimmer
[shim-er]

v. to shine with a soft light
부드럽게 빛나다, 희미하게 반짝이다
The moonlight **shimmered** on the water.[30]

syn. gleam, glitter, glisten, glint

31

spontaneous
[spon-tey-nee-*uh*s]

adj. unplanned and voluntary
자발적인, 자진해서 하는, 임의의
There was a **spontaneous** movement of students to surround the car in which he was to be transported.[31]

syn. impulsive, intuitive, instinctive

 예문 해석

27 비서가 질문에 대한 답변을 했다. **28** 그는 필수적인 서류를 채워 넣었다. **29** 가게 앞 구세군의 벨소리는 크리스마스가 다가오는 것을 의미한다. **30** 달빛이 물에 은은하게 비쳤다. **31** 그가 이송되는 차를 에워싸는 학생들의 자발적인 움직임이 있었다.

32 ....

subdue
[*suhb*-doo]

v. to overpower and bring under control
정복하다, 진압하다
Sun Tzu said, "To **subdue** the enemy without fighting is the acme of skill." [32]

syn. quell, subjugate, conquer, vanquish

33 ....

tenable
[ten-*uh*-b*uhl*]

adj. capable of being held, maintained, or defended
공격에 견딜 수 있는
The grant was **tenable** as long as the requirements were met. [33]

syn. secured, protected, held

34 ....

tumult
[too-m*uh*lt]

n. a state of extreme confusion or agitation
소동, 소란
A **tumult** arose in the city center. [34]

syn. uproar, disturbance, commotion

35 ....

vernacular
[ver-nak-y*uh*-ler]

adj. spoken in a particular area
자국어의, 제 나라말의, 지방 사투리의
People identified him as a foreigner because of his **vernacular** language. [35]

syn. dialect, native

36 ....

zealot
[zel-*uht*]

n. a single-minded and determined supporter
열광자, 광신도, 광적인 팬
He was not a religious **zealot**. [36]

syn. partisan, advocate, proponent

🔖 예문 해석

32 손자는 "싸우지 않고 적을 제압하는 것이 기술의 최상이다."라고 말했다. **33** 그 보조금은 요구 조건을 충족하는 한 유지될 수 있었다. **34** 큰 소동이 도심에서 일어났다. **35** 사람들은 그의 사투리 때문에 그를 외국인이라고 여겼다. **36** 그는 종교적 광신자는 아니다.

Directions   Each of the following questions consists of one word followed by five words or phrases. You are to select the one word or phrase whose meaning is closest to the word in capital letters.

1. ALLAY :
(A) harden
(B) smoothen
(C) abbreviate
(D) mitigate
(E) intensify

2. BLACKMAIL :
(A) cling
(B) favor
(C) lessen
(D) inundate
(E) threaten

3. DILAPIDATED :
(A) ramshackle
(B) emotional
(C) accurate
(D) enigmatic
(E) terse

4. FOREWARN :
(A) caution
(B) absolve
(C) parole
(D) genuflect
(E) prognosticate

5. GIMMICK :
(A) scheme
(B) propriety
(C) generosity
(D) lubricant
(E) surrogate

6. NOMINAL :
(A) unwitting
(B) slack
(C) unwilling
(D) titular
(E) intermittent

7. OUTDATED :
(A) crucial
(B) obsolete
(C) refutable
(D) immediate
(E) unwarranted

8. PERJURY :
(A) lie
(B) steal
(C) walk
(D) mount
(E) swivel

9. PLASTIC :
(A) reversal
(B) masterful
(C) malleable
(D) petulant
(E) adorable

10. TENABLE :
(A) voracious
(B) inclusive
(C) vacant
(D) secured
(E) eternal

"Energy and persistence conquer all things."

— Benjamin Franklin —
U.S. author, diplomat, inventor, physicist, politician, & printer

힘과 인내가 모든 것을 이긴다.

Greek and Latin Roots & Prefixes 11

★ PHONO = sound

graph (draw)	phonograph	축음기 , 레코드 플레이어
-ics (study)	phonics	파닉스, 발음 중심 교수법
-ics (study)	phonetics	음성학
eu (good)	euphony	듣기 좋은 음조
caco (bad)	cacophony	불협화음
tele (far)	telephone	전화
micro (small)	microphone	마이크
xylo (wood)	xylophone	실로폰

DAY

11

WORDS TO LEARN

☐ abstract	☐ dodge	☐ intrepid	☐ resent
☐ allege	☐ encompass	☐ knead	☐ sanitary
☐ aspire	☐ evolve	☐ listless	☐ soundness
☐ blanch	☐ fanatic	☐ momentous	☐ sporadic
☐ carnage	☐ feud	☐ nonplussed	☐ submerge
☐ competent	☐ gird	☐ outlandish	☐ tenacious
☐ copious	☐ ignoble	☐ permanent	☐ turbulence
☐ delineate	☐ inaugurate	☐ prescription	☐ verse
☐ dilemma	☐ ingrained	☐ quest	☐ zenith

01

abstract
[ab-strakt]

n. a short document prepared from a longer one
개요, 요약, 초록
An **abstract** for a lab report includes a short summary of the main ideas found.[1]

syn. summary, synopsis, compendium

02

allege
[*uh*-lej]

v. to assert without proof
(충분한 증거도 없이) 강력히 주장하다, 우기다
He **alleged** his innocence.[2]

syn. claim, assert

03

aspire
[*uh*-spai*uh*r]

v. be eagerly desirous
간절히 원하다, 열망하다, 갈망하다
She **aspired** to become a famous actress.[3]

syn. yearn, pine, long for

📖 예문 해석

01 연구 보고서의 개요에는 발견된 주요 아이디어에 대한 간단한 요약이 포함되어 있다. **02** 그는 자신의 무죄를 주장했다. **03** 그녀는 유명한 여배우가 되기를 갈망했다.

04

blanch
[blanch]

v. to become pale

하얗게 만들다, 표백하다

He was **blanched** when his mother threatened to break his fishing rods.[4]

syn. whiten, bleach

05

carnage
[kahr-nij]

n. the slaughter of a great number of people

대학살

The correspondent saw a scene of **carnage** of a village after a bomb has been detonated.[5]

syn. massacre, slaughter, holocaust

06

competent
[kom-pi-t*uh*nt]

adj. able, efficient and effective

능력 있는

He was a very **competent** lawyer.[6]

syn. capable, knowledgeable

07

copious
[koh-pee-*uh*s]

adj. large in quantity or number

풍부한, 풍족한

I ate a **copious** amount of food for the holiday.[7]

syn. abundant, plentiful, ample

08

delineate
[di-lin-ee-eyt]

v. to trace the outline of

윤곽을 그리다, 묘사하다

He **delineated** Seoul on the map with a red pencil.[8]

syn. describe, portray, depict

예문 해석

04 어머니가 낚싯대를 부러뜨려 버리겠다고 협박했을 때 그는 하얗게 질렸다. **05** 그 특파원은 폭탄이 터진 후 한 마을에서 대학살이 벌어지는 장면을 목격했다. **06** 그는 매우 실력있는 변호사였다. **07** 나는 휴일에 음식을 많이 먹었다. **08** 그는 지도에서 서울의 윤곽을 빨간 연필로 표시했다.

dilemma
[dih-lem-*uh*]

n. a situation requiring a choice between equally undesirable alternatives

딜레마, 진퇴양난

Hamlet struggles with a **dilemma** in how to out the orders of his father's ghost to kill his stepfather.[9]

syn. perplexity, puzzle, difficulty

dodge
[doj]

v. to make a sudden movement in a new direction so as to avoid

재빨리 피하다, 날쌔게 비키다

They **dodged** a set of arrows.[10]

syn. evade, avoid, escape, shun, elude

encompass
[en-k*uh*m-p*uh*s]

v. to include comprehensively

둘러싸다, 포위하다, 포함하다

His job **encompassed** dealing with teachers, parents, and students.[11]

syn. include, encircle, surround

evolve
[i-volv]

v. to develop or produce gradually

서서히 발전시키다, 진화하다

Popular music **evolved** from folk songs.[12]

syn. develop, change, grow

fanatic
[f*uh*-nat-ik]

n. a person with an extreme and uncritical enthusiasm

광신자, 열광자

I am not a religious **fanatic**.[13]

syn. maniac, zealot

 예문 해석

09 햄릿은 의붓아버지를 죽이라는 아버지의 유령의 명령을 어떻게 물리쳐야 할지 딜레마와 씨름한다.   **10** 그들은 재빨리 화살들을 피했다.   **11** 그의 일에는 선생님, 학부모, 학생들을 상대하는 업무가 포함되어 있었다.   **12** 대중가요는 민중가요에서 발전했다.   **13** 나는 광신도는 아니다.

feud
[fyood]

n. a long-standing fight, often between two families
(오랜 동안의) 불화
In Romeo and Juliet, Shakespeare describes the lovers' long-**feuding** families, the Capulets and the Montagues.[14]

> *syn.* conflict, discord, altercation

15

gird
[gurd]

v. to encircle or bind with a belt or band
(칼 등을) 허리에 차다, 둘러매다, 에워싸다
The general **girded** on a sword.[15]

> *syn.* encircle, surround, strengthen

16

ignoble
[ig-noh-b*uh*l]

adj. of low character
저열한, 비열한, 불명예스러운
When begun, whether for noble or **ignoble** purpose, war is a reality.[16]

> *syn.* mean, base

17

inaugurate
[in-aw-gy*uh*-reyt]

v. to make a formal beginning of
정식으로 시작하다, 취임하다
Barack Obama was **inaugurated** as the first African-American President.[17]

> *syn.* initiate, launch, embark

18

ingrained
[in-greynd]

adj. firmly fixed
뿌리 깊이 박힌, 바뀌기 어려운
Nobody can change his **ingrained** bigotry.[18]

> *syn.* entrenched, embedded, inbuilt

예문 해석

14 '로미오와 줄리엣'에서 셰익스피어는 오랜 세월 동안 불화를 가진 연인들의 가족인 캐퓰릿가와 몬테규가를 묘사한다.　**15** 그 장군은 칼을 허리에 둘러 찼다.　**16** 고상한 이유든 비열한 이유든 어떤 목적이든 전쟁은 시작되면 현실이다.　**17** 버락 오바마는 첫 흑인 대통령으로 취임하였다.　**18** 그의 뿌리 깊이 박힌 고집은 아무도 바꿀 수 없다.

19

intrepid
[in-trep-id]

adj. invulnerable to fear or intimidation

겁 없는, 용감한

As he traveled through various uncertainties, people thought of him as an **intrepid** traveler.[19]

syn. fearless, bold, dauntless

20

knead
[need]

v. to work dough into a uniform mixture by pressing, folding, and stretching

반죽하다, 주무르다

Knead the dough for about five minutes until elastic.[20]

syn. blend, push, massage

21

listless
[list-lis]

adj. having no energy or enthusiasm

생기 없는, 맥 풀린, 나른한

He has looked **listless** over the past few weeks.[21]

syn. languid, lethargic, lackadaisical

22

momentous
[moh-men-t*uh*s]

adj. very important

매우 중요한

The birth of her first child was a **momentous** occasion.[22]

syn. important, significant, historic

23

nonplussed
[non-pl*uh*st]

adj. surprised and confused

어찌 할 바를 모르는, 당혹스런

I was **nonplussed** about what type of answer would be appropriate for the situation.[23]

syn. confused, confounded, baffled

24

outlandish
[out-lan-dish]

adj. strange or extremely unusual

이국적인, 특이한

This idea is not as **outlandish** as it sounds.[24]

syn. exotic, foreign

예문 해석

19 그가 여러 가지 생각지 못한 일들을 겪으면서, 사람들은 그를 용감한 여행자로 여겼다. **20** 반죽에 탄력이 생길 때까지 5분간 반죽하세요. **21** 지난 몇 주간 그는 맥없어 보였다. **22** 그녀의 첫 아이 탄생은 매우 중요한 사건이었다. **23** 나는 이 상황에 어떤 종류의 대답이 적당할지 당황스러웠다. **24** 이 아이디어는 들리는 것처럼 기이한 것은 아니다.

25

permanent
[pur-m*uh*-nuh*nt]

adj. lasting for a long time or forever
영원한
Kids should not play with **permanent** markers.[25]

syn. constant, perpetual, everlasting

26

prescription
[pri-skrip-sh*uh*n]

n. a set of written instructions from a doctor to a pharmacist
(의사가 써주는) 처방전
You should take your **prescription** to a pharmacist.[26]

syn. instruction, direction

27

quest
[kwest]

n. a long search for something
탐험, 탐구여행
They set off on a **quest** for the key.[27]

syn. mission, expedition, pursuit

28

resent
[ri-zent]

v. be angry about
분개하다, 화내다
She **resents** his arrogant attitude.[28]

syn. begrudge, dislike, grudge

29

sanitary
[san-i-ter-ee]

adj. of or pertaining to health
위생의, 건강상의
Sanitary workers are very important to our society.[29]

syn. hygienic, antiseptic

30

soundness
[soundnis]

n. a state or condition free from damage or decay
건전성, 안정성, 건실성
He paused and nodded as if testing and confirming the
soundness of his own words.[30]

syn. healthiness, solidity, durability

예문 해석

25 아이들은 지워지지 않는 마커를 가지고 놀지 말아야 한다.　**26** 당신은 처방전을 약사에게 전달해야 한다.　**27** 답을 찾으려는 그들의 탐험이 시작되었다.　**28** 그녀는 그의 무례한 태도에 분개했다.　**29** 환경미화원은 우리 사회에 매우 중요하다.　**30** 그는 잠시 멈춰 서서 자신의 말의 건전성을 시험하고 확인하는 것처럼 고개를 끄덕였다.

31

sporadic
[sp*uh*-rad-ik]

adj. occurring from time to time
때때로 일어나는, 우발적인, 단발성의
They staged **sporadic** rallies at various points in Seoul.[31]

syn. intermittent, irregular, periodic

32

submerge
[s*uh*b-murj]

v. to sink or plunge under water
물에 잠그다, 물속에 가라앉다
The flood **submerged** over 100 houses.[32]

syn. dive, sink, founder

33

tenacious
[t*uh*-ney-sh*uh*s]

adj. holding fast
고집하는, 끈기 있는, 꼭 쥐고 놓지 않는
The tyrant has kept its **tenacious** hold on power for more than ten years.[33]

syn. pertinacious, stubborn, obstinate

34

turbulence
[tur-by*uh*-l*uh*ns]

n. a disturbed, wild or unruly state
거칠게 몰아침, 휘몰아침, 난기류
His plane encountered severe **turbulence**.[34]

syn. tumult, uproar, commotion

35

verse
[vurs]

n. poetry, as opposed to prose
운문, 시(詩)
Her few lines of **verse** moved me.[35]

syn. poetry, rhyme

36

zenith
[zee-nith]

n. the highest point
정점, 극도, 절정
His career is now at its **zenith**.[36]

syn. peak, summit, pinnacle

 예문 해석

31 그들은 서울 곳곳에서 산발적인 시위를 벌였다. **32** 홍수는 100여 채가 넘는 집을 물에 잠기게 했다. **33** 그 독재자는 십 년 넘게 굳건한 권력을 쥐고 있었다. **34** 그의 비행기는 몇 번의 심한 난기류를 만났다. **35** 그녀의 시 몇 줄이 나를 감동시켰다. **36** 그의 커리어는 지금 정점에 달해있다.

Directions   Each of the following questions consists of one word followed by five words or phrases. You are to select the one word or phrase whose meaning is closest to the word in capital letters.

1. **ALLEGE :**
   - (A) claim
   - (B) reign
   - (C) stab
   - (D) consolidate
   - (E) plagiarize

2. **COMPETENT :**
   - (A) capable
   - (B) banal
   - (C) trifling
   - (D) neutral
   - (E) antagonistic

3. **COPIOUS :**
   - (A) abundant
   - (B) nuptial
   - (C) conclusive
   - (D) colloquial
   - (E) desultory

4. **FEUD :**
   - (A) filch
   - (B) conflict
   - (C) perjury
   - (D) faculty
   - (E) discrimination

5. **GIRD :**
   - (A) guess
   - (B) encircle
   - (C) obey
   - (D) distort
   - (E) acquit

6. **IGNOBLE :**
   - (A) coarse
   - (B) introspective
   - (C) jaunty
   - (D) mean
   - (E) disheartening

7. **LISTLESS :**
   - (A) complacent
   - (B) impractical
   - (C) patriotic
   - (D) wan
   - (E) languid

8. **OUTLANDISH :**
   - (A) aboveboard
   - (B) menacing
   - (C) chronic
   - (D) exotic
   - (E) fastidious

9. **SPORADIC :**
   - (A) tempting
   - (B) intermittent
   - (C) contrary
   - (D) tricky
   - (E) suspicious

10. **TENACIOUS :**
   - (A) clueless
   - (B) pertinacious
   - (C) hypothetical
   - (D) tardy
   - (E) unruly

"Facts don't cease to exist because they are ignored."

— Aldous Huxley —
English critic & novelist

무시한다고 해서 사실이 없어지는 것은 아니다.

Greek and Latin Roots & Prefixes 12

★ GRAPH = drawing

auto (self)	autograph	(유명인의) 싸인, 서명
para (beside)	paragraph	단락
photo (light)	photograph	사진
phono (sound)	phonograph	축음기 , 레코드 플레이어
seismos (shaking)	seismograph	지진계
bio (life)	biography	전기
carta (chart)	cartography	지도 제작(법)
kallos (beauty)	calligraphy	서예, 예쁜 글씨 쓰기
khoreia (dance)	choreography	안무, 춤 만들기
demos (people)	demography	인구통계학

DAY

12

WORDS TO LEARN

☐ abstruse	☐ dogged	☐ intricate	☐ reserved
☐ alleviate	☐ encounter	☐ knoll	☐ sanctimonious
☐ artifice	☐ exacerbate	☐ literacy	☐ shove
☐ bland	☐ fanciful	☐ maritime	☐ sprint
☐ cascade	☐ forgo	☐ momentum	☐ submissive
☐ complacent	☐ genuflect	☐ nostalgia	☐ tenant
☐ cordial	☐ hazardous	☐ outlook	☐ turmoil
☐ deliverance	☐ ignominy	☐ perfidy	☐ vertex
☐ dilatory	☐ inhabit	☐ quota	☐ zephyr

01

abstruse
[ab-stroos]

adj. hard to understand
난해한, 심오한
Some students have to stay after class in order to ask their professors about some **abstruse** theories learned.[1]

syn. unfathomable, esoteric, profound

02

alleviate
[*uh*-lee-vee-yet]

v. to relieve or lessen
고통을 줄여주다, 완화하다
To **alleviate** her pain, her daughter massaged warm oil on her painful joints.[2]

syn. abate, relieve, assuage

03

artifice
[ahr-*tuh*-fis]

n. a clever trick or stratagem
책략, 계략
The politician used a subtle and tricky **artifice** to get more votes.[3]

syn. wile, hoax, gimmick

예문 해석

01 일부 학생들은 교수들에게 난해한 이론들에 대해 물어보기 위해 수업이 끝난 후에도 남아 있어야 한다.　**02** 그녀의 고통을 덜어주기 위해 딸은 따뜻한 오일로 아픈 관절들을 마사지했다.　**03** 그 정치인은 표를 더 얻기 위해 미묘하고 교묘한 계략을 썼다.

04

bland
[bland]

adj. lacking taste or flavor
맛이 밍밍한, 특별한 맛이 안나는
The **bland** seasoning on the chicken was not one of my favorites.[4]

syn. flavorless, insipid, vapid

05

cascade
[kas-keyd]

n. a small waterfall
작은 폭포, 한꺼번에 쏟아지는 것
Her hair tumbled in a **cascade** down her back.[5]

syn. waterfall, avalanche, deluge

06

complacent
[kuhm-pley-suhnt]

adj. self-satisfied
현실에 안주하는, 자기만족적인
The fashion mogul had become **complacent** after years of success.[6]

syn. contented, pleased, smug

07

cordial
[kawr-juhl]

adj. sincere and gracious
마음에서 우러난, 진심의, 우호적인
Relations between the two countries are **cordial**.[7]

syn. heartfelt, friendly, warm

08

deliverance
[dih-liv-er-uhns]

n. an act or instance of rescue
구출, 구조, 석방
They planned the climactic **deliverance** of captives.[8]

syn. salvation, liberation, rescue

예문 해석

04 닭고기에 있는 밍밍한 양념은 내가 좋아하는 것이 아니었다. **05** 그녀의 머리는 등 뒤로 폭포처럼 풍성하게 출렁거렸다. **06** 그 패션계의 거물은 수년간 성공을 거둔 후 현실에 안주하게 되었다. **07** 그 두 나라 사이의 관계는 우호적이다. **08** 그들은 포로들의 극적 구출을 계획했다.

dilatory
[dil-*uh*-tawr-ee]

adj. tending to delay or procrastinate
지체하는, 시간 끄는
The staff was **dilatory** in acting on my complaint.[9]

syn. belated, procrastinating

dogged
[daw-gid]

adj. determined or resolute
완고한, 끈질긴, 고집 센
He showed us his **dogged** determination.[10]

syn. persistent, obstinate, tenacious

encounter
[en-koun-ter]

v. to meet someone or something unexpectedly
우연히 만나다, 마주치다
Every day of our lives we **encounter** stresses of one kind or another.[11]

syn. come across, bump into, meet by chance

exacerbate
[ig-zas-er-beyt]

v. to make worse
더욱 심하게 하다, 악화시키다
Severe heat **exacerbated** his pain.[12]

syn. aggravate, degrade, degenerate

fanciful
[fan-si-f*uh*l]

adj. (of a person or their thoughts) unpredictable, overimaginative, and unrealistic
변덕스러운, 공상적인
He is a **fanciful** person.[13]

syn. fickle, whimsical, capricious

forgo
[fawr-goh]

v. do without
없이 지내다, 삼가다, 그만두다
He was told he would have to **forgo** smoking.[14]

syn. abstain, refrain, give up

예문 해석

09 직원은 내 불만을 처리하는 데 꾸물거렸다.   **10** 그는 우리에게 끈질긴 결단을 보여주었다.   **11** 우리는 매일 이런저런 스트레스에 부딪치곤 한다.   **12** 심한 열기가 그의 고통을 더하게 했다.   **13** 그는 변덕스러운 사람이다.   **14** 그는 이제 담배를 끊어야 한다는 이야기를 들었다.

15

genuflect
[jen-yoo-flekt]

v. to bend one's knee and bow submissively
(무릎을 굽혀) 절하다
When the servant came to his monarch, he **genuflected** to show his respect.[15]

syn. bow, stoop

16

hazardous
[haz-er-d*uh*s]

adj. involving risk or danger
위험한, 해로운
These chemicals can be **hazardous** to your health.[16]

syn. risky, perilous, dangerous

17

ignominy
[ig-n*uh*-min-ee]

n. shame or public disgrace
치욕, 불명예
The **ignominy** of defeat was hard to bear.[17]

syn. disgrace, disrepute, discredit

18

inhabit
[in-hab-it]

v. to live or dwell in
살다, 거주하다
Many kinds of animals **inhabited** the woods.[18]

syn. occupy, dwell, reside

19

intricate
[in-tri-kit]

adj. full of complicated, interrelating or tangled details
복잡한, 뒤얽힌
The art consisted of **intricate** patterns.[19]

syn. complicated, tricky, convoluted

20

knoll
[nohl]

n. a small, rounded hill
둔덕, 작은 언덕
President John F. Kennedy was shot in Dallas just as his motorcade passed a grassy **knoll**.[20]

syn. mound, hillock, ridge

예문 해석

15 그 종이 군주를 찾아왔을 때, 그는 경의를 표하기 위해 몸을 내밀었다.　**16** 이런 화학물들은 당신의 건강에 해로울 수 있다.
17 패배의 수치심은 견디기 힘들었다.　**18** 많은 종류의 동물들이 그 숲에 살았다.　**19** 그 예술 작품은 복잡한 패턴으로 이루어져
있었다.　**20** 대통령 존 F. 케네디는 댈러스에서 자동차 행렬이 풀로 뒤덮인 둔덕을 지날 때 총에 맞았다.

21

literacy
[lit-er-acy]

n. the ability to read and write
글을 읽고 쓸 줄 아는 능력
Literacy is very important for success.[21]

syn. knowledge, proficiency, education

22

maritime
[mar-i-tahym]

adj. associated with the sea
바다의, 해양의
According to **maritime** law, ship captains have no authority to perform marriages.[22]

syn. nautical, seafaring, marine

23

momentum
[moh-men-tuhm]

n. continuous speed of progress
움직이게 하는 힘, 원동력
The car gained **momentum** going downhill.[23]

syn. impetus, drive, thrust

24

nostalgia
[no-stal-juh]

n. an affectionate feeling someone has for the past
향수, 과거나 고향을 그리워 함
He felt **nostalgia** for his happy youth.[24]

syn. reminiscence, longing, remembrances

25

outlook
[out-look]

n. prospect of the future
조망, 전망, 예측
He showed his employer a document demonstrating the business **outlook**.[25]

syn. viewpoint, prospect

26

perfidy
[pur-fi-dee]

n. deliberate breach of faith or trust
배신
He knew his close friend's **perfidy** and swore revenge.[26]

syn. treachery, betrayal, infidelity

예문 해석

21 글을 읽고 쓰는 능력은 성공을 위해 매우 중요하다.   **22** 해양법에 따르면 선장은 혼인을 주재할 권한이 없다.   **23** 차는 언덕을 내려가면서 움직일 힘을 얻었다.   **24** 그는 행복한 어린시절을 그리워했다.   **25** 그는 사업 전망을 증명하는 문서를 고용주에게 보여 주었다.   **26** 그는 친한 친구의 배신을 알고 복수를 맹세했다.

27 ···

quota
[kwoh-t*uh*]

n. the share or proportional part of a total
몫, 할당량
The company has imposed racial **quotas** on hiring.[27]

> *syn.* allocation, allotment, share

28 ···

reserved
[ri-zurvd]

adj. avoiding familiarity or intimacy with others
속 마음을 드러내지 않는, 내성적인
He was a **reserved** man.[28]

> *syn.* aloof, reticent, standoffish

29 ···

sanctimonious
[sangk-t*uh*-moh-nee-*uh*s]

adj. making a hypocritical show of religious devotion
독실한 체하는, 신성한 척 하는
They resented his **sanctimonious** comments.[29]

> *syn.* insincere, hypocritical

30 ···

shove
[sh*uh*v]

v. to push or thrust with force
떠밀다, 밀치다
He **shoved** her out of the way.[30]

> *syn.* push, thrust, heave

31 ···

sprint
[sprint]

v. to run at full speed
전속력으로 달리다, 전력 질주하다
He **sprinted** to the car.[31]

> *syn.* run, dash, race

32 ···

submissive
[s*uh*b-mis-iv]

adj. willing or tending to submit
복종하는, 순종하는
The **submissive** child continues to obey his parents with little pushback.[32]

> *syn.* obedient, meek, compliant

예문 해석

27 그 회사는 고용에 인종 할당제를 부과해 왔다.   **28** 그는 과묵한 남자였다.   **29** 그들은 그의 독실한 척하는 말에 격분했다.
30 그는 그녀를 길 밖으로 밀쳤다.   **31** 그는 차 쪽을 향해 전속력으로 뛰어갔다.   **32** 순종적인 아이는 부모에게 거의 물러서지
않고 계속 순종한다.

tenant
[ten-*uh*nt]

n. a person rents and occupies land or a house
(토지나 집 등의) 세입자, 소작인
The house owner sent his **tenant** a reminder.[33]

syn. occupant, resident, inhabitant

turmoil
[tur-moil]

n. a state of confusion, disorder, or great anxiety
소란, 소동, 혼란
They were in complete **turmoil**.[34]

syn. confusion, disorder, chaos

vertex
[vur-teks]

n. the highest point
최고점, 정상, 꼭지점
In geometry, we learn about **vertexes** in various shapes.[35]

syn. apex, summit, peak, zenith, acme

zephyr
[zef-er]

n. a gentle, mild breeze
서풍, 산들바람, 미풍
O gentle **zephyr**, tell me what they said as you pass'd by.[36]

syn. breeze, air, gust

 예문 해석

33 집 주인은 세입자에게 독촉장을 보냈다. **34** 그들은 극심한 혼란에 빠졌다. **35** 기하학에서, 우리는 다양한 모양의 꼭짓점에 대해 배운다. **36** 오, 부드러운 산들바람이여, 지나가며 그들이 무슨 이야기를 했는지 말하다오.

Directions   Each of the following questions consists of one word followed by five words or phrases. You are to select the one word or phrase whose meaning is closest to the word in capital letters.

1. ALLEVIATE :
   - (A) pardon
   - (B) grope
   - (C) fumble
   - (D) strut
   - (E) abate

2. ARTIFICE :
   - (A) refugee
   - (B) wile
   - (C) futility
   - (D) risk
   - (E) drivel

3. COMPLACENT :
   - (A) submissive
   - (B) unpredictable
   - (C) feeble
   - (D) contented
   - (E) pacific

4. CORDIAL :
   - (A) heartfelt
   - (B) unwilling
   - (C) alarming
   - (D) valiant
   - (E) logical

5. DILATORY :
   - (A) fiscal
   - (B) offensive
   - (C) belated
   - (D) unfounded
   - (E) versatile

6. EXACERBATE :
   - (A) vindicate
   - (B) assuage
   - (C) ebb
   - (D) aggravate
   - (E) wax

7. MARITIME :
   - (A) lively
   - (B) boastful
   - (C) nautical
   - (D) oriental
   - (E) generic

8. INHABIT :
   - (A) allay
   - (B) assign
   - (C) occupy
   - (D) perturb
   - (E) agitate

9. IGNOMINY :
   - (A) adaptability
   - (B) publicity
   - (C) device
   - (D) disgrace
   - (E) impunity

10. GENUFLECT :
   - (A) scathe
   - (B) resemble
   - (C) interrupt
   - (D) frown
   - (E) bow

Directions   Each of the following questions consists of one word followed by five words or phrases. You are to select the one word or phrase whose meaning is closest to the word in capital letters.

1. BIGOTED :
(A) exhausted
(B) opinionated
(C) peculiar
(D) slight
(E) exhilarated

2. EVANESCENT :
(A) aimless
(B) belated
(C) negligent
(D) transitory
(E) unrestricted

3. FALLACY :
(A) frightening
(B) style
(C) instruction
(D) misconception
(E) leisurely walk

4. LENIENT :
(A) heavy
(B) curative
(C) restful
(D) tolerant
(E) simulating

5. CAPITULATE :
(A) cater
(B) surrender
(C) converge
(D) provide
(E) collaborate

6. DIVULGE :
(A) shut
(B) reveal
(C) converge
(D) disprove
(E) pretend

7. HOMAGE :
(A) revision
(B) eccentricity
(C) deceit
(D) caprice
(E) reverence

8. NONCOMMITTAL :
(A) ailing
(B) mysterious
(C) evasive
(D) legitimate
(E) pertinacious

9. ARTICULATE :
(A) enunciate
(B) disgusting
(C) loyal
(D) disgraceful
(E) uneducated

10. COMPELLING :
(A) ornamental
(B) supreme
(C) quick-witted
(D) fascinating
(E) torrid

11. **SALUTE :**
   (A) deterrence
   (B) greeting
   (C) advocate
   (D) ignition
   (E) provocation

12. **ABSTAIN :**
   (A) aim
   (B) conspire
   (C) sedate
   (D) forgo
   (E) palpitate

13. **DELIBERATE :**
   (A) intentional
   (B) disreputable
   (C) bewildered
   (D) timid
   (E) callous

14. **MOMENTARY :**
   (A) brief
   (B) gloomy
   (C) ancient
   (D) important
   (E) unqualified

15. **QUERY :**
   (A) protocol
   (B) deference
   (C) obeisance
   (D) question
   (E) conduct

16. **ABSTRACT :**
   (A) derision
   (B) truth
   (C) captivity
   (D) summary
   (E) euphemism

17. **DELINEATE :**
   (A) sob
   (B) belittle
   (C) wail
   (D) describe
   (E) roll

18. **INAUGURATE :**
   (A) accuse
   (B) initiate
   (C) exploit
   (D) plot
   (E) tease

19. **RESENT :**
   (A) dive
   (B) pulverize
   (C) begrudge
   (D) raze
   (E) thrill

20. **RESERVED :**
   (A) facile
   (B) officious
   (C) aloof
   (D) contrite
   (E) mournful

Greek and Latin Roots & Prefixes 13

★ BIO = life

logy (science)	biology	생물학
logy (science)	biological	생물학적, 생물학의
de (down) + grade (to go)	biodegradable	생분해성의
ingeniare (to invent)	bioengineering	생명 공학
oma (result)	biome	생물군계
opsis (sight)	biopsy	생체 검사
sphaera (globe)	biosphere	생물권
graph (drawing)	biography	(인물의) 전기, 일대기
syn (together)	symbiosis	공생
anti (against)	antibiotic	항생제

DAY

13

WORDS TO LEARN

- ☐ absurd
- ☐ alliance
- ☐ assertive
- ☐ blasé
- ☐ celerity
- ☐ compatible
- ☐ devout
- ☐ dilute
- ☐ dogmatic

- ☐ encumber
- ☐ exalt
- ☐ fetch
- ☐ formidable
- ☐ glance
- ☐ hapless
- ☐ ignorance
- ☐ incendiary
- ☐ inhumane

- ☐ intuition
- ☐ knotty
- ☐ literal
- ☐ milieu
- ☐ notable
- ☐ outpost
- ☐ perpetrate
- ☐ prestigious
- ☐ quirk

- ☐ resigned
- ☐ sanction
- ☐ showy
- ☐ spur
- ☐ subordinate
- ☐ tenet
- ☐ turncoat
- ☐ veer
- ☐ zest

---

01 ....

absurd
[ab-surd]

adj. utterly or obviously senseless

터무니없는, 불합리한, 우스운

He gave the **absurd** excuse that the dog ate his homework.[1]

syn. ridiculous, silly, preposterous

02 ....

alliance
[uh-lai-uhns]

n. a formal agreement or treaty between two or more nations to cooperate for specific purposes

동맹

The two countries sought a military **alliance** for their overall safety.[2]

syn. union, league, association

03 ....

assertive
[uh-sur-tiv]

adj. inclined to expressing wishes and opinions in a firm and confident manner

자기 주장이 강한, 확신에 찬

Be more **assertive**![3]

syn. self-assured, insistent, pushy

예문 해석

01 그는 개가 숙제를 먹어 버렸다는 말도 안 되는 핑계를 둘러댔다.   **02** 두 나라는 전반적인 안전을 위해 군사 동맹을 모색했다.
03 자신의 주장을 강력히 피력하라!

04

blasé
[blah-zey]

adj. indifferent to or bored with life as if from an excess of worldly pleasures

(이미 여러 번 겪은 일이라) 심드렁한, 향락에 지친

He tried to act **blasé** as he unwrapped the present.[4]

syn. bored, indifferent, jaded

05

celerity
[suh-ler-i-tee]

n. speed or swiftness

민첩함, 속도

The demanding coach will punish a player if his **celerity** is not fast enough.[5]

syn. swiftness, velocity, speed

06

compatible
[kuhm-pat-uh-buhl]

adj. capable of existing or living together in harmony.

(다른 구성원과) 잘 어울릴 수 있는, 화합할 수 있는

The grumpy student will never find a **compatible** roommate.[6]

syn. harmonious, agreeable, congruous

07

devout
[dih-vout]

adj. devoted to divine worship or service

독실한, 신앙이 깊은, 종교적인

She is a **devout** Christian keeping Sunday worship services.[7]

syn. pious, religious, faithful

08

dilute
[di-loot]

v. to make thinner

묽게 하다, 희석하다

Dilute the juice well with water.[8]

syn. thin, weaken, reduce

🔖 예문 해석

04 그는 선물을 풀어보며 아무렇지 않은 척 하려 애썼다.   **05** 그 까다로운 감독은 속도가 충분히 빠르지 않으면 선수를 처벌할 것이다.   **06** 그 심술궂은 학생은 결코 어울리는 룸메이트를 찾지 못할 것이다.   **07** 그녀는 주일 예배를 지키는 독실한 기독교 신자이다.   **08** 주스를 물에 잘 섞으세요.

dogmatic
[dawg-mat-ik]

adj. of a doctrine or code of beliefs
독단적인, 교리에 관한
Many writers hold **dogmatic** views.[9]

syn. dictatorial, opinionated, stubborn

encumber
[en-kuhm-ber]

v. to prevent free and easy movement
방해하다, 거추장스럽게 하다
The tape **encumbers** all our attempts at action.[10]

syn. hamper, impede, hinder

exalt
[ig-zawlt]

v. to raise in rank, honor, power, quality, etc.
위로 떠받들다, 칭찬하다
He was **exalted** to the position of Prime Minister.[11]

syn. glorify, praise, acclaim

fetch
[fech]

v. to go and bring back
가지고 오다
The dog saw the boomerang and ran to **fetch** it.[12]

syn. return with, go get, carry

formidable
[fawr-mi-duh-buhl]

adj. causing fear, apprehension, or dread
무서운, 무시무시한, 엄청난
He was a **formidable** opponent.[13]

syn. horrible, overwhelming, appalling

glance
[glans]

v. to look quickly or briefly
힐끗 보다, 잠깐 보다
She **glanced** at her watch.[14]

syn. glimpse, peek, peep

 예문 해석

09 많은 작가들이 독단적인 시각을 가지고 있다. **10** 테이프 때문에 우리는 쉽게 움직일 수 없었다. **11** 그는 국무총리로 격상됐다. **12** 그 개는 부메랑을 보고 그것을 가지러 달려갔다. **13** 그는 무시무시한 적수였다. **14** 그녀는 시계를 흘끗 보았다.

hapless
[hap-lis]

adj. unfortunate and deserving pity
불운한, 운이 없는
Many children are **hapless** victims of this war.[15]

syn. unlucky, miserable, unfortunate

ignorance
[ig-ner-*uh*ns]

n. lack of knowledge
무지, 무식
"The **ignorance** of one voter in a democracy impairs the security of all." — John F. Kennedy[16]

syn. unawareness, inexperience, illiteracy

incendiary
[in-sen-dee-er-ee]

adj. of or pertaining to the criminal setting on fire of property
방화의, 불을 지르는
The major conflagration was caused by **incendiary** grenades.[17]

syn. inflammatory, combustible

inhumane
[in-hyoo-meyn]

adj. lacking humanity or compassion
비인간적인, 잔혹한
The nursing home treated patients in an **inhumane** way.[18]

syn. brutal, cruel, pitiless

intuition
[in-too-ish-*uh*n]

n. the ability to know things without conscious reasoning
직감, 본능
Her **intuition** was always right.[19]

syn. instinct, hunch, insight

knotty
[not-ee]

adj. highly complex or intricate and occasionally devious
복잡한, 어려운
A **knotty** legal issue involves complicated constitutional issues.[20]

syn. complex, difficult, troublesome

예문 해석

15 많은 어린이들이 이 전쟁의 불행한 희생자이다.   **16** "민주주의에서 한 유권자의 무지는 모두의 안전을 해친다." – 존 F. 케네디
17 대화재는 방화용 수류탄에 의하여 일어났다.   **18** 그 요양원은 환자들을 비인간적으로 대했다.   **19** 그녀의 직감은 항상 맞았다.   **20** 난해한 법적 문제에는 복잡한 헌법적 문제가 수반된다.

21

literal
[lit-er-*uh*l]

adj. the basic meaning of a word or phrase
글자대로의, 문자의
I had to buy the **literal** translation of Don Quixote.[21]

> *syn.* exact, denotative, explicit

22

milieu
[mil-yoo]

n. a surrounding culture
(사회적) 환경
There is very little hope for quality leadership in the current political **milieu** for years to come.[22]

> *syn.* surroundings, atmosphere, ambiance

23

notable
[noh-t*uh*-b*uh*l]

adj. important or famous
유명한, 저명한
This place is **notable** for fine foods.[23]

> *syn.* renowned, distinguished, prominent

24

outpost
[out-pohst]

n. a small military camp
전초지, 전초 부대
We keep only a small number of men at our desert **outposts**.[24]

> *syn.* frontier, boundary

25

perpetrate
[pur-pi-treyt]

v. to commit, or be guilty of a crime or misdeed
나쁜 짓을 범하다, 과오를 저지르다
A high proportion of crime is **perpetrated** by young males in their teens and twenties.[25]

> *syn.* commit, carry out, pull off

 예문 해석

21 나는 돈키호테의 직역본을 사야 했다. **22** 현재 정치 환경에서 양질의 리더십에 대한 희망은 앞으로 몇 년 동안 거의 없다.
23 이곳은 근사한 음식들로 유명하다. **24** 우리는 사막 전초 부대들에 적은 인원만을 유지한다. **25** 범죄의 많은 비율이 십대나 이십대 때의 젊은 남성들에 의해 저질러진다.

26 ··

prestigious
[pre-stij-*uhs*]

adj. having a great reputation
고급의, 일류의, 명문의
Most of the graduates were hoping to go on to a **prestigious** college.[26]

syn. honored, esteemed, prominent

27 ··

quirk
[kwurk]

n. an odd habit
기벽, 특이한 버릇이나 성격
He is full of strange **quirks**.[27]

syn. idiosyncrasy, peculiarity, quirkiness

28 ··

resigned
[ree-sahynd]

adj. accepting that something unpleasant cannot be changed or avoided
단념한, 체념한
He is **resigned** to the noise and mess.[28]

syn. reconciled, acquiescent, submissive

29 ··

sanction
[sangk-sh*uh*n]

v. to give permission for something
승인하다, 인가하다
The government has **sanctioned** the establishment of private boarding schools.[29]

syn. authorize, permit, approve

30 ··

showy
[shoh-ee]

adj. making an imposing display
화려한, 과시하는
Since he was color blind, he favored large, **showy** flower prints.[30]

syn. ostentatious, flashy, flamboyant

 예문 해석

26 대부분의 졸업생들은 명문대학으로 진학하길 희망했다.   27 그는 모든 면이 특이하다.   28 그는 소음과 난동에 대해 단념했다.   29 정부는 사립 기숙 학교들의 설립을 인가해 왔다.   30 그는 색맹이어서 크고 화려한 꽃무늬를 좋아했다.

spur
[spur]

v. to proceed hurriedly
박차를 가하다
The jockey **spurred** his horse.[31]

syn. goad, provoke, stimulate, impel

subordinate
[*suh*-bawr-dn-it]

n. someone lower in rank or status
부하, 아랫사람
The king did not want to seek guidance from **subordinates**.[32]

syn. assistant, junior, underling

tenet
[ten-it]

n. a belief, opinion or doctrine
집단이 신봉하는 주의(主義), 교의(敎義)
Non-violence and patience are their central **tenets**.[33]

syn. doctrine, principle, theory, belief

turncoat
[turn-koht]

n. someone who turns against or leaves his or her party or principles
변절자, 배반자
He was criticized for being a political **turncoat**.[34]

syn. betrayer, renegade, traitor

veer
[veer]

v. to change direction or turn about or aside
방향을 홱 틀다, 방향을 바꾸다
He **veered** away from an oncoming truck on the highway to avoid getting crushed.[35]

syn. swerve, deflect, shift

zest
[zest]

n. an enjoyably exciting quality
열성, 열정
He has a **zest** for life.[36]

syn. ardor, zeal, passion

예문 해석

31 기수는 말에 박차를 가했다.　**32** 왕은 부하들의 호위를 받지 않길 원했다.　**33** 비폭력과 인내가 그들 교리의 핵심이다.　**34** 그는 정치적인 변절자로 비난받았다.　**35** 그는 충돌하지 않기 위해 고속도로에서 마주 오던 트럭으로부터 방향을 틀었다.　**36** 그는 삶에 대한 열정이 있다.

Directions Each of the following questions consists of one word followed by five words or phrases. You are to select the one word or phrase whose meaning is closest to the word in capital letters.

1. **ABSURD :**
   (A) ajar
   (B) stormy
   (C) babbling
   (D) ridiculous
   (E) partial

2. **ASSERTIVE :**
   (A) biased
   (B) irregular
   (C) impulsive
   (D) unpredictable
   (E) self-assured

3. **CELERITY :**
   (A) swiftness
   (B) animals
   (C) hint
   (D) shackle
   (E) foreboding

4. **DEVOUT :**
   (A) pious
   (B) convinced
   (C) checked
   (D) blended
   (E) stretching

5. **EXALT :**
   (A) dangle
   (B) crinkle
   (C) forgo
   (D) stumble
   (E) glorify

6. **HAPLESS :**
   (A) slight
   (B) harmful
   (C) unlucky
   (D) misgiving
   (E) acute

7. **IGNORANCE :**
   (A) destiny
   (B) force
   (C) unawareness
   (D) elixir
   (E) ghost

8. **INCENDIARY :**
   (A) evasive
   (B) fascinated
   (C) interested
   (D) inflammatory
   (E) winced

9. **KNOTTY :**
   (A) unruly
   (B) complex
   (C) forbidden
   (D) excessive
   (E) modest

10. **SANCTION :**
   (A) sink
   (B) interfere
   (C) jostle
   (D) authorize
   (E) petrify

"For small creatures such as we,
the vastness is bearable only
through love."

— Carl Sagan —
American astronomer

우리 같은 작은 생물들에게 광활함은
오직 사랑을 통해서만 견딜 수 있다.

Greek and Latin Roots & Prefixes 14

★ VIV, VIT = life

amine (compound)	vitamin	비타민
-al (adj.)	vital	필수적인
-ity (n.)	vitality	활력
-id (adj.)	vivid	생생한
-ous (adj.)	vivacious	명랑한, 쾌활한
-ize (v.)	vitalize	활력을 북돋아 주다
-a (n.)	viva	만세! (격려하는 뜻으로)
re (again)	revitalize	새로운 활력을 주다
re (again)	revive	활기를 되찾다
super (beyond)	survive	살아남다

DAY

14

WORDS TO LEARN

- [ ] abundant
- [ ] allusion
- [ ] assess
- [ ] blast
- [ ] catastrophe
- [ ] compliant
- [ ] corpse
- [ ] deluge
- [ ] diminutive

- [ ] doldrums
- [ ] encyclopedia
- [ ] exasperated
- [ ] fastidious
- [ ] fortify
- [ ] glare
- [ ] hatchet
- [ ] illegitimate
- [ ] inception

- [ ] iniquity
- [ ] inundate
- [ ] label
- [ ] literary
- [ ] maternal
- [ ] mongrel
- [ ] notion
- [ ] outrage
- [ ] perpetual

- [ ] preposterous
- [ ] resilient
- [ ] sanctuary
- [ ] shred
- [ ] spurious
- [ ] subsequent
- [ ] table
- [ ] tentative
- [ ] vestige

01

abundant
[uh-buhn-duhnt]

adj. existing in large amounts
풍부한
Calcium is the most **abundant** mineral in the body.[1]

syn. plentiful, copious, rich, ample

02

allusion
[uh-loo-zhuhn]

n. something said or written that refers to another person in an indirect way
암시, 언급
The teacher made no **allusion** to her efforts.[2]

syn. implication, hint, inkling

03

assess
[uh-ses]

v. to estimate officially the value of something
가치를 평가하다, 감정하다
The value of this property was **assessed** at five million dollars.[3]

syn. appraise, estimate, evaluate

예문 해석

01 칼슘은 몸에서 가장 풍부한 미네랄이다.　**02** 선생님은 그녀의 노력에 대해서는 언급하지 않았다.　**03** 이 자산의 가치는 오백만 달러로 평가되었다.

04

blast
[blast]

n. a big explosion, especially one caused by a bomb
거센 폭발, 센 바람
Hundreds of people were killed in the **blast**.[4]

syn. gale, explosion

05

catastrophe
[k*uh*-tas-tr*uh*-fee]

n. a sudden and widespread disaster
대재앙, 대재난
The tornado caused **catastrophe**.[5]

syn. calamity, fiasco, debacle

06

compliant
[k*uh*m-plai-*uh*nt]

adj. obedient
유순한, 시키는 대로 하는, 고분고분한
The employer preferred to hire docile and **compliant** workers.[6]

syn. docile, submissive, amenable

07

corpse
[korps]

n. a dead body, usually of a human being
시체, 사체
A **corpse** resolves itself into dirt.[7]

syn. dead body, cadaver, carcass

08

deluge
[del-yooj]

n. huge flood
대홍수
Last week's **deluge** flooded every basement in the village.[8]

syn. downpour, flood, inundation

09

diminutive
[di-min-y*uh*-tiv]

adj. very small
아주 작은
They could not notice the **diminutive** figure standing at the gate.[9]

syn. tiny, microscopic, minute

예문 해석

04 폭발로 수백 명이 사망했다.　**05** 토네이도는 큰 재앙을 불러왔다.　**06** 고용주는 온순하고 순종적인 노동자를 고용하는 것을 선호했다.　**07** 사체는 먼지로 돌아간다.　**08** 지난 주 있었던 홍수로 마을 모든 집의 지하실에 물이 넘쳤다.　**09** 그들은 입구에 있던 작은 동상을 보지 못했다.

doldrums
[dohl-dr*uh*mz]

n. a state of inactivity

답답함, 우울

The economy is in the **doldrums**.[10]

syn. depression, gloom

encyclopedia
[en-sai-kl*uh*-pee-dee-*uh*]

n. a reference work containing information on every branch of knowledge

백과사전, 전문 사전

An **encyclopedia** is a good source of useful information.[11]

syn. reference book, book of facts, compilation

exasperated
[ig-zas-per-ate-id]

adj. angry and impatient

분노한, 화난

The passengers were **exasperated** by the senseless delays.[12]

syn. irritated, infuriated, enraged

fastidious
[fa-stid-ee-*uh*s]

adj. particular in matters of taste and detail

까다로운, 매우 꼼꼼한

She is a **fastidious** eater.[13]

syn. finicky, picky, meticulous

fortify
[fawr-t*uh*-fai]

v. to strengthen against attack

강화시키다, 요새화하다

The king ordered the guards to **fortify** the fort against an attack.[14]

syn. strengthen, reinforce, enhance

예문 해석

10 경제는 정체기에 있다.   **11** 백과사전은 유용한 정보의 좋은 보고이다.   **12** 승객들은 말도 안 되는 이유로 지연되는 것에 분통을 터뜨렸다.   **13** 그녀의 식성은 까다롭다.   **14** 왕은 공격에 대비해 요새를 강화할 것을 명령했다.

glare
[glair]

v. to stare angrily
노려보다, 눈을 부릅뜨다
The man **glared** and muttered something.[15]

> *syn.* stare, glower

hatchet
[hach-it]

n. a small axe that one can hold in one's hand
손도끼
"Bury the **hatchet**" is an American idiom, and it is said when you want someone to make amends and not look again at the past wrongdoing.[16]

> *syn.* ax, hack

illegitimate
[il-i-jit-*uh*-mit]

adj. not legitimate
위법의, 불법의
This **illegitimate** action guaranteed a lawsuit.[17]

> *syn.* unlawful, illegal, illicit

inception
[in-sep-sh*uh*n]

n. the start of an institution or activity
발단, 개시
She is the first woman to receive the award since its **inception** in 1982.[18]

> *syn.* beginning, outset, commencement

iniquity
[i-nik-wi-tee]

n. absence of moral or spiritual values
부정, 불법, 사악
If we do not study history, the **iniquities** of our past often become the downfall of our future.[19]

> *syn.* wickedness, evil, sinfulness

예문 해석

15 그 남자는 노려보며 무언가를 중얼거렸다.   **16** "손도끼를 묻는다"라는 표현은 미국의 관용어로, 과거의 잘못을 들추지 않고, 누군가 보상하기를 원할 때 하는 말이다.   **17** 이 불법적인 행동은 소송을 보장한다.   **18** 그녀는 1982년에 이상이 생긴 이후 처음으로 수상한 여성이다.   **19** 역사를 공부하지 않으면 과거의 죄악은 종종 미래의 몰락으로 이어진다.

20

inundate
[in-*uh*n-deyt]

v. to cover or overspread with water
범람시키다, 물에 잠기게 하다
The whole town was **inundated** with water.[20]

syn. flood, overwhelm, deluge, engulf

21

label
[ley-b*uh*l]

v. to designate or describe by, or on a label
라벨을 붙이다, 꼬리표를 붙여 분류하다
They **labeled** him a liar.[21]

syn. tag, brand, trademark

22

literary
[lit-*uh*-rer-ee]

adj. of relating to literature
문학의, 문학 작품의
After finishing our books, the class completed a **literary** analysis.[22]

syn. fictional, mythical, legendary

23

maternal
[m*uh*-tur-nl]

adj. related to the mother
어머니의, 모성의, 모계의
My **maternal** grandfather is a banker.[23]

syn. motherly, protective, nurturing

24

mongrel
[m*uh*ng-gr*uh*l]

n. an animal of mixed breeding
잡종, 잡종 동물
Every language is a **mongrel** language to some degree.[24]

syn. hybrid, cross, mutt

25

notion
[noh-sh*uh*n]

n. a general understanding
개념, 견해
He made me revise my **notion** of success.[25]

syn. belief, idea, apprehension

 예문 해석

20 마을 전체가 침수되었다.　**21** 그들은 그에게 거짓말쟁이라고 꼬리표를 붙였다.　**22** 우리 책을 다 읽고 나서, 그 반은 문학적 분석을 끝냈다.　**23** 내 외할아버지는 은행가이시다.　**24** 모든 언어는 어느 정도는 잡종이라고 할 수 있다.　**25** 그는 성공에 대한 나의 생각을 바꾸게 만들었다.

26

outrage
[out-reyj]

n. a wantonly cruel act

분노, 격분

The decision provoked **outrage** from women's rights groups.[26]

syn. rage, ire, wrath, indignation, resentment

27

perpetual
[per-pech-oo-*uhl*]

adj. continuing or enduring forever

영원한

I do not wish **perpetual** punishment on anyone.[27]

syn. everlasting, eternal, permanent

28

preposterous
[pri-pos-ter-*uhs*]

adj. completely contrary to nature, reason, or common sense

말도 안 되는, 터무니없는

As for the captain, leaving someone behind was a **preposterous** idea.[28]

syn. absurd, ridiculous, ludicrous

29

resilient
[ri-zil-y*uh*nt]

adj. able to return quickly to its original shape or position

원상태로 돌아가는, 탄력 있는

The company became more **resilient** to sudden changes.[29]

syn. elastic, flexible, pliant

30

sanctuary
[sangk-choo-er-ee]

n. a place of private refuge or retreat

보호구역, 피난처, 안식처

My family enjoyed visiting a wildlife **sanctuary**.[30]

syn. reserve, shelter, asylum

31

shred
[shred]

v. to cut or tear into small pieces

갈기갈기 찢다, 길고 가늘게 찢거나 썰다

We need to **shred** all the documents.[31]

syn. tear, cut

예문 해석

26 그 결정은 여성 인권 단체들을 격분시켰다. **27** 나는 그 누구에게든 영구적인 처벌을 바라지 않는다. **28** 선장 입장에서는 누군가를 두고 간다는 것은 말도 안 되는 생각이었다. **29** 회사는 갑작스러운 변화에 탄력적으로 대처할 수 있게 되었다. **30** 우리 가족은 야생 동물 보호 구역 방문을 즐겼다. **31** 우리는 모든 문서를 분쇄시켜야 한다.

spurious
[spyoor-ee-*uh*s]

adj. not genuine, authentic, or true
가짜의, 위조의
I'm not the only one here asking you to backup your **spurious** claim.[32]

syn. fake, false, bogus

subsequent
[s*uh*b-si-kw*uh*nt]

adj. occurring or coming later or after
다음의, 그 다음에 오는
A 20 percent cut will be carried out over the **subsequent** three years.[33]

syn. following, succeeding, ensuing

table
[tey-b*uh*l]

v. hold back to a later time
미루다, 유보하다
State senators can't compromise about new traffic laws; they might decide to **table** the issue.[34]

syn. postpone, delay, put off

tentative
[ten-t*uh*-tiv]

adj. not finalized or completed
시험적인, 시험 삼아 하는, 임시의
They all have a **tentative** agreement to hold a conference next week.[35]

syn. provisional, exploratory, speculative

vestige
[ves-tij]

n. a surviving trace of what has almost disappeared
자취, 흔적, 모습, 표적
I found a few columns which were the last **vestiges** of a Greek temple.[36]

syn. trace, sign, mark

🧑‍🏫 **예문 해석**

32 당신의 거짓 주장에 증거를 대라고 하는 사람이 나 하나는 아니다.　**33** 그 후 3년 동안은 20%가 감면된다.　**34** 주 상원 의원들은 새로운 교통법에 대해 타협할 수 없다. 그들은 그 문제를 보류하기로 결정할지도 모른다.　**35** 그들은 다음 주에 총회를 열기로 임시적으로 동의했다.　**36** 나는 그리스 신전의 마지막 흔적인 기둥 몇 개만을 발견했다.

Directions Each of the following questions consists of one word followed by five words or phrases. You are to select the one word or phrase whose meaning is closest to the word in capital letters.

1. **ASSESS :**
   (A) hurl
   (B) alter
   (C) qualify
   (D) ruffle
   (E) appraise

2. **CATASTROPHE :**
   (A) savior
   (B) rubbish
   (C) taint
   (D) succession
   (E) calamity

3. **COMPLIANT :**
   (A) docile
   (B) exotic
   (C) brazen
   (D) shuddered
   (E) grabbed

4. **FASTIDIOUS :**
   (A) slovenly
   (B) tardy
   (C) finicky
   (D) brutal
   (E) scowling

5. **ILLEGITIMATE :**
   (A) illegal
   (B) wilted
   (C) laden
   (D) impending
   (E) intuitive

6. **INUNDATE :**
   (A) flood
   (B) segregate
   (C) corrode
   (D) stride
   (E) enfeeble

7. **MONGREL :**
   (A) hybrid
   (B) agility
   (C) lament
   (D) muster
   (E) blend

8. **NOTION :**
   (A) cascade
   (B) posture
   (C) apothecary
   (D) divination
   (E) belief

9. **PREPOSTEROUS :**
   (A) detestable
   (B) absurd
   (C) raucous
   (D) sumptuous
   (E) congenital

10. **RESILIENT :**
    (A) elastic
    (B) deranged
    (C) ruined
    (D) pitted
    (E) haggard

"Courage is resistance to fear, mastery of fear—not absence of fear."

— Mark Twain —
U.S. humorist, novelist, short story author

용기는 공포에 저항하고, 공포를 극복하는 것이다 – 공포가 없는 것이 아니라.

Greek and Latin Roots & Prefixes 15

★ SCRIB, SCRIPT = to write

-ipt (n.)	script	대본
-e (person)	scribe	(인쇄술이 발명되기 전의) 필경사
-le (n.)	scribble	휘갈겨 쓴 글씨
de (down)	describe	묘사하다
manu (hand)	manuscript	(책이나 악보 등의) 원고, 필사본
in (in)	inscription	(금속이나 돌에) 적힌 글, 제문
pre (before)	prescription	처방전
post (after)	postscript	추신
sub (down)	subscription	구독
trans (across)	transcribe	(생각이나 말을 글로) 기록하다

DAY

15

WORDS TO LEARN

☐ afflict	☐ doleful	☐ initiate	☐ presumptuous
☐ aloof	☐ endeavor	☐ insofar	☐ quintessence
☐ assiduous	☐ excess	☐ laborious	☐ recluse
☐ blatant	☐ fathom	☐ majesty	☐ seasoned
☐ cater	☐ fortitude	☐ maternity	☐ shrewd
☐ compliment	☐ glean	☐ monitor	☐ spurn
☐ corpulent	☐ haughty	☐ novel	☐ subservient
☐ delusion	☐ iconoclast	☐ overbearing	☐ tenuous
☐ dingy	☐ incessant	☐ perplex	☐ vessel

---

01 ·······

afflict
[*uh*-flikt]

v. to cause suffering, pain, or misery
괴롭히다, 피해를 입히다
Carpal Tunnel Syndrome may **afflict** someone who spends many hours typing on computers every day.[1]

syn. bother, distress, torment

02 ·······

aloof
[*uh*-loof]

adj. reserved or reticent
냉담한, 무관심한
He stood **aloof** from their arguments.[2]

syn. indifferent, nonchalant, apathetic

03 ·······

assiduous
[*uh*-sij-oo-*uh*s]

adj. diligent
지치지 않는, 근면한
Teachers knew him as an **assiduous** student.[3]

syn. industrious, laborious, conscientious

예문 해석

01 손목 터널 증후군은 매일 많은 시간을 컴퓨터로 타이핑하는 사람을 괴롭히는 것이다. **02** 그는 논쟁에 가담하지 않고 있었다.
03 선생님들은 그를 성실한 학생으로 알고 있었다.

04

blatant
[bleyt-nt]

adj. very obvious and without shame
명백한, 뻔뻔한
Foreign workers suffer from **blatant** discrimination.[4]

syn. obvious, unconcealed

05

cater
[key-ter]

v. to provide food and service
음식과 연회서비스를 제공하다
Her company **caters** for the banquet.[5]

syn. provide, help, furnish

06

compliment
[kom-pluh-muhnt]

n. an expression of praise or admiration
찬사, 칭찬, 듣기 좋은 말
Her sincere **compliment** boosted his morale.[6]

syn. accolade, kudos, extolment

07

corpulent
[kawr-pyuh-luhnt]

adj. excessively fat
뚱뚱한
His **corpulent** body would not allow him to ride on a roller coaster.[7]

syn. obese, portly, stout, chubby

08

delusion
[di-loo-zhuhn]

n. the act of misleading
속임, 현혹, 착각
He has **delusions** of his competence.[8]

syn. deception, illusion, hallucination

🔖 예문 해석

04 외국인 근로자들은 명백한 차별에 고통을 겪는다. **05** 그녀의 회사는 연회 음식과 서비스를 제공한다. **06** 그녀의 진심 어린 찬사는 그의 사기를 북돋아 주었다. **07** 그의 뚱뚱한 몸 때문에 롤러코스터를 타는 것이 어려울 것이다. **08** 그는 자신의 역량에 대해 착각을 하고 있다.

09

dingy
[din-jee]

adj. dirty or discolored
우중충한, 거무스레한
His **dingy** jeans looked like they hadn't been washed in a year.[9]

syn. grimy, dirty, shabby

10

doleful
[dohl-*fuh*l]

adj. expressing or suggesting sadness
슬픈, 수심에 잠긴
She expressed a **doleful** look after hearing the sad news.[10]

syn. rueful, mournful, deplorable

11

endeavor
[en-dev-er]

v. to exert oneself to do or effect something
노력하다
He is **endeavoring** to get in shape.[11]

syn. attempt, try, strive

12

excess
[ik-ses]

n. the fact of exceeding something else in amount or degree
초과, 초과량
His wealth is in **excess** of one million dollars.[12]

syn. overabundance, surfeit, surplus

13

fathom
[fath-*uh*m]

v. to understand
이해하다
I couldn't **fathom** what he was talking about.[13]

syn. understand, work out, figure out

14

fortitude
[fawr-ti-tood]

n. mental and emotional strength in facing difficulty
용기, 불굴의 의지
Never once did her **fortitude** waver during that long illness.[14]

syn. determination, courage, bravery

예문 해석

09 그의 거무죽죽한 바지는 일년은 빨지않은 것처럼 보였다.　**10** 그녀는 그 슬픈 소식을 듣고 수심에 잠긴 표정을 지었다.　**11** 그는 몸매를 만들려 노력하고 있다.　**12** 그는 재산이 백 만 달러가 넘는다.　**13** 나는 그가 무슨 말을 하는지 이해할 수 없었다.　**14** 오랜 병중에도 그녀의 의지는 흔들리지 않았다.

15

glean
[gleen]

v. to collect something patiently
(사실이나 정보 등을) 조금씩 모으다
We're **gleaning** information from all sources.[15]

syn. collect, cull, gather

16

haughty
[haw-tee]

adj. very proud, or arrogant
오만한, 거만한
He spoke in a **haughty** tone.[16]

syn. arrogant, pompous, cocky

17

iconoclast
[ai-kon-*uh*-klast]

n. a person who attacks cherished beliefs or traditional institutions
우상 파괴자, 인습 타파주의자
The entrepreneur is an **iconoclast** who is not afraid to introduce something innovative to the market.[17]

syn. nonconformist, cynic, sceptic

18

incessant
[in-ses-*uh*nt]

adj. continuing without interruption
끊임없는, 계속 되는
Stop your **incessant** whining.[18]

syn. ceaseless, constant, continuous

19

initiate
[i-nish-ee-eyt]

v. to start
시작하다, 착수하다
They wanted to **initiate** a discussion about politics.[19]

syn. commence, begin, start

20

insofar
[in-*suh*-fahr]

adv. to the degree or extent that
～하는 한에 있어서는
I will do my best **insofar** as I am able.[20]

syn. to such an extent, inasmuch as

예문 해석

15 우리는 가능한 모든 정보를 모으고 있다.　**16** 그는 거만한 말투로 이야기했다.　**17** 그 기업가는 혁신적인 것을 시장에 내놓는 것을 두려워하지 않는 인습 타파주의자이다.　**18** 우는 소리 그만해.　**19** 그들은 정치에 대한 토론을 시작하고 싶어 했다.　**20** 나는 내가 할 수 있는 한 최선을 다할 것이다.

laborious
[luh-bawr-ee-uhs]

adj. requiring much work
힘든, 고된, 근면한
Checking all the details will be **laborious**.[21]

> syn. onerous, arduous

majesty
[maj-uh-stee]

n. impressiveness in scale or proportion
장엄함, 위풍당당함
A chain of mountains of Himalayan **majesty** runs from Paris to Calcutta.[22]

> syn. grandeur, greatness, loftiness

maternity
[muh-tur-ni-tee]

n. the state of being or becoming a mother
모성
The instinct of **maternity** was natural to her.[23]

> syn. motherhood

monitor
[mon-i-ter]

v. to check regularly
지켜보다, 감독하다
We **monitor** their routes and locate their domestic habitats.[24]

> syn. check, watch, observe

novel
[nov-uhl]

adj. fresh and new
새로운, 신기한
His idea was **novel** in 1970.[25]

> syn. new, original, unconventional

overbearing
[oh-ver-bair-ing]

adj. too powerful and proud
거만한, 고압적인
Sometimes his father is quite **overbearing** with his son.[26]

> syn. domineering, insolent, haughty

예문 해석

21 모든 세세한 부분까지 점검하는 것은 힘들 것이다. **22** 파리에서 캘커타까지 히말라야의 웅장한 산줄기가 이어져 있다. **23** 모성 본능은 그녀에게는 자연스러운 것이었다. **24** 우리는 그들의 이동경로를 감시하고 서식지를 찾는다. **25** 그의 생각은 1970년에는 참신했다. **26** 가끔 그의 아버지는 그에게 꽤 고압적인 자세로 대했다.

perplex
[per-pleks]

v. to puzzle, confuse or baffle someone
난처하게 하다, 당황케 하다
Her strange response **perplexed** him.[27]

syn. bewilder, confuse, confound

presumptuous
[pri-*zuh*mp-choo-*uhs*]

adj. impertinent or arrogant
주제넘은, 뻔뻔한, 건방진
It would be **presumptuous** to judge what the outcome will be.[28]

syn. audacious, brazen, impertinent

quintessence
[kwin-tes-*uh*ns]

n. the pure and concentrated essence of a substance.
핵심, 정수
She has always been the **quintessence** of honesty, so I was shocked by her apparent lies.[29]

syn. essence, core, kernel

recluse
[rek-loos]

n. a person who lives in seclusion or apart from society
은둔자
He had no intention of becoming a **recluse**.[30]

syn. hermit, anchorite, eremite

seasoned
[see-*zuh*nd]

adj. having a lot of experience doing something
경험 많은, 노련한
A **seasoned** politician knows what the public wants.[31]

syn. experienced, accomplished, qualified

shrewd
[shrood]

adj. sharp in practical matters
기민한, 영민한
He is a **shrewd** politician.[32]

syn. sharp, acute, astute

예문 해석

27 그녀의 이상한 반응이 그를 당황하게 만들었다. **28** 결과가 어떨지 예측하는 것은 주제넘은 일일지도 모른다. **29** 그녀는 항상 정직의 정수였기 때문에 나는 그녀의 명백한 거짓말에 충격을 받았다. **30** 그는 스스로 은둔자가 되려는 의도는 없었다. **31** 노련한 정치인은 국민이 무엇을 원하는지 안다. **32** 그는 영민한 정치인이다.

spurn
[spurn]

v. to reject with disdain
쫓아내다. 내쫓다
He **spurned** the beggar.[33]

syn. reject, snub, refuse

subservient
[*suhb*-sur-vee-*uhn*t]

adj. too willing to obey other people
비굴한, 아첨하는
Some people never escape that **subservient** position and are envious of others who have.[34]

syn. submissive, obedient, compliant

tenuous
[ten-yoo-*uhs*]

adj. weak or uncertain
희박한, 얇은, 가는
To him, this was a **tenuous** argument.[35]

syn. feeble, flimsy, slight, insubstantial

vessel
[ves-*uhl*]

n. a ship or boat
배, 보트
We came aboard the **vessel** to travel to the islands.[36]

syn. ship, boat

 예문 해석

33 그는 그 거지를 내쫓았다.　**34** 어떤 사람들은 굴종적인 위치에 머무르면서 계속해서 다른 사람이 가진 것을 부러워하기만 한다.　**35** 그에게 이것은 사소한 논쟁이었다.　**36** 우리는 섬으로 여행하기 위해 배를 탔다.

Directions   Each of the following questions consists of one word followed by five words or phrases. You are to select the one word or phrase whose meaning is closest to the word in capital letters.

1. ALOOF :
   (A) awakened
   (B) portly
   (C) indifferent
   (D) reminiscent
   (E) strict

2. CATER :
   (A) grin
   (B) overwhelm
   (C) provide
   (D) scowl
   (E) dismantle

3. DINGY :
   (A) regretful
   (B) grimy
   (C) tense
   (D) blankly
   (E) rambling

4. ENDEAVOR :
   (A) snort
   (B) drawl
   (C) convert
   (D) plunge
   (E) attempt

5. FATHOM :
   (A) avoid
   (B) hiss
   (C) understand
   (D) defend
   (E) soar

6. GLEAN :
   (A) collect
   (B) stride
   (C) dart
   (D) mean
   (E) ignite

7. HAUGHTY :
   (A) tiny
   (B) crackling
   (C) arrogant
   (D) protrude
   (E) decay

8. ICONOCLAST :
   (A) snicker
   (B) suppressor
   (C) predecessor
   (D) nonconformist
   (E) dabbler

9. NOVEL :
   (A) illegal
   (B) glinting
   (C) new
   (D) spiteful
   (E) unoriginal

10. SEASONED :
   (A) nonchalant
   (B) experienced
   (C) tangled
   (D) startled
   (E) apprehensive

"Whatever you do will be insignificant,
but it is very important that you do it."

– Mahatma Gandhi –
Indian political and spiritual leader

당신이 어떤 하찮은 일을 하든, 중요한 것은 그것을 당신이 했다는 것이다.

Greek and Latin Roots & Prefixes 16

★ JUD, JUR, JUS = to judge

-ly (adverb)	justly	바르게, 정당하게
-ice (n.)	justice	정의, 공정함
-fy (to make)	justify	정당화하다
dicere (to say)	judge	판결을 내리다, 판사
lus (law)	jury	(재판의) 배심원
-ist (person)	jurist	법학자, 법률문제 전문가
dictio (saying)	jurisdiction	관할권
prudentia (knowledge)	jurisprudence	법학
ab (away from)	abjure	(공식적으로) 포기하다
per (away)	perjury	위증하다, 위증죄

DAY

16

WORDS TO LEARN

☐ abyss	☐ domicile	☐ initiative	☐ pretentious
☐ alter	☐ endorse	☐ irritable	☐ quixotic
☐ assuage	☐ excruciating	☐ lackluster	☐ resonant
☐ bleak	☐ fatigue	☐ lithe	☐ sarcastic
☐ chamber	☐ fortnight	☐ mayhem	☐ snub
☐ complimentary	☐ grope	☐ mollify	☐ subside
☐ correspondence	☐ haul	☐ novice	☐ tepid
☐ demise	☐ illicit	☐ overdue	☐ twine
☐ diplomatic	☐ incense	☐ persecution	☐ veto

01

abyss
[*uh*-bis]

n. a bottomless gulf or pit
끝없는 심연, 나락
After finding out about my parents' death, I mentally fell into an **abyss** of despair.[1]

syn. gulf, pit, chasm

02

alter
[awl-ter]

v. to change
바꾸다, 변하다
She had **altered** her appearance so much I hardly recognized her.[2]

syn. convert, transmute, transform

03

assuage
[*uh*-sweyj]

v. to make milder or less severe
누그러뜨리다, 달래다
To **assuage** her doubts about his skill, the magician changed his hat into a rose.[3]

syn. relieve, ease, mitigate, appease

예문 해석

01 부모님의 죽음을 알게 된 후, 나는 정신적으로 절망의 나락으로 빠져들었다.   **02** 그녀는 너무 변해서 나는 그녀를 거의 알아보지 못했다.   **03** 실력에 대한 그녀의 의심을 잠재우기 위해 마법사는 모자를 장미로 바꾸었다.

04

bleak
[bleek]

adj. seems unlikely to improve
암담한, 우울한
Many predicted a **bleak** future.[4]

> syn. murky, gloomy, dim

05

chamber
[cheym-ber]

n. a large room
방, 실, 회의장
The prisoners were kept in a **chamber** in the basement.[5]

> syn. room, hall, assembly room

06

complimentary
[kom-pl*uh*-men-t*uh*-ree]

adj. given free
무료의, 선물로 주어진
I was given a **complimentary** ticket for admission to a well-known museum.[6]

> syn. free, gratis, gratuitous

07

correspondence
[kawr-*uh*-spon-d*uh*ns]

n. similarity by virtue of corresponding
일치, 조화
There is often **correspondence** between sounds and meanings.[7]

> syn. similarity, equivalence

08

demise
[dih-maiz]

n. death or decease
죽음, 사망
The antagonist met his inevitable **demise** at the end of the story.[8]

> syn. death, decease, termination

🧘 예문 해석

04 많은 사람들이 우울한 미래를 예측했다.　**05** 죄수들은 지하 방에 갇혀 있었다.　**06** 나는 유명한 박물관 입장권을 무료로 받았다.　**07** 소리와 의미는 종종 일치한다.　**08** 그 적수는 이야기의 마지막에 피할 수 없는 죽음을 맞이했다.

diplomatic
[dip-*luh*-mat-ik]

adj. skilled in dealing with sensitive matters or people
외교적 수완이 있는, 교섭에 능한
It was **diplomatic** to make such demands.[9]

syn. tactful, politic, strategic

domicile
[dom-*uh*-sail]

n. a legally recognized place of permanent residence
거주지, 주소
When applying to universities, one must include their **domicile** in the application.[10]

syn. abode, address

endorse
[en-dawrs]

v. to state one's approval of something
승인하다, 인정하다
I **endorse** their opinion wholeheartedly.[11]

syn. affirm, confirm, corroborate

excruciating
[ik-skroo-shee-ey-ting]

adj. causing great physical or mental pain
고문받는 것 같은, 몹시 괴로운
I was in **excruciating** pain.[12]

syn. torturous, painful, grueling

fatigue
[f*uh*-teeg]

n. temporary loss of strength and energy resulting from hard physical or mental work
피로, 피곤
I felt the **fatigue** of driving for many hours.[13]

syn. tiredness, lethargy, weariness

fortnight
[fawrt-nait]

n. two weeks
2주간, 14일간
We only had a **fortnight** to study for our entrance exams.[14]

syn. fourteen nights, two weeks

 예문 해석

09 그런 요구를 하다니 수완이 좋다.　**10** 대학에 지원할 때는 지원서에 주소를 포함해야 한다.　**11** 나는 그들의 의견을 진심으로 받아들인다.　**12** 나는 너무나 고통스럽게 아팠다.　**13** 나는 몇 시간 동안 운전의 피로를 느꼈다.　**14** 우리는 입학시험을 대비해 공부할 시간이 2주밖에 없었다.

15

grope
[grohp]

v. to feel about uncertainly or blindly
(손으로) 더듬다, 더듬어 찾다
He **groped** for his glasses in the darkness of the bedroom.[15]

syn. fumble, look for, search

16

haul
[hawl]

v. to pull or draw with force
세게 잡아 당기다, 끌다
The sailor **hauled** up an anchor.[16]

syn. drag, pull, tug

17

illicit
[i-lis-it]

adj. not allowed by law
불법의, 부정의
He paid for expensive things with an **illicit** income.[17]

syn. illegal, unlawful, illegitimate

18

incense
[in-sens]

v. to make someone very angry
몹시 화나게 하다
He **incensed** just about everyone in the room.[18]

syn. enrage, infuriate, exasperate

19

initiative
[i-nish-ee-*uh*-tiv]

n. the ability or skill to initiate things
솔선, 시작, 주도권, 진취적인 마음
She took the **initiative** to make new friends.[19]

syn. leadership, action, eagerness to do something

20

irritable
[ir-i-t*uh*-b*uh*l]

adj. easily irritated or annoyed
짜증을 잘 내는, 화를 잘 내는
His **irritable** sister loses her temper so quickly.[20]

syn. cranky, fractious, testy

예문 해석

15 그는 침실의 어둠 속에서 안경을 더듬어 찾았다. **16** 그 선원은 닻을 감아 올렸다. **17** 그는 부정한 수입으로 비싼 물건을 샀다. **18** 그는 그 방에 있던 거의 모든 사람을 몹시 화나게 했다. **19** 그녀는 친구를 만드는데 적극적이다. **20** 그의 짜증을 잘 내는 여동생은 쉽게 화를 낸다.

21

lackluster
[lak-*luhs*-ter]

adj. lacking brilliance or radiance
광택을 잃은, 흐리멍덩한
Her **lackluster** eyes did not intrigue me.[21]

syn. dull, flat, lusterless

22

lithe
[lahyth]

adj. moving easily, in a way that is graceful
나긋나긋한, 유연한
Her **lithe** movements enthralled thousands of spectators.[22]

syn. supple, flexible, pliable

23

mayhem
[mey-hem]

n. the crime of willfully inflicting a bodily injury on another
신체 상해, 상해죄
Antipathy between two parties boiled over, and **mayhem** finally ensued.[23]

syn. violence, damage, offence

24

mollify
[mol-*uh*-fai]

v. to soften in feeling or temper, as a person
달래다, 진정시키다
The editor tried to **mollify** readers with an apology.[24]

syn. pacify, assuage, allay

25

novice
[nov-is]

n. a person who is new and has little experience
초보자, 풋내기
I'm not good with a sword, but I'm not a complete **novice** either.[25]

syn. beginner, tyro, neophyte

26

overdue
[oh-ver-doo]

adj. not paid, done or returned by the required or expected time
기한이 넘은, 마감이 늦은
This debate is long **overdue**.[26]

syn. late, belated, tardy

예문 해석

21 그녀의 흐리멍덩한 눈은 내 흥미를 끌지 못했다.   **22** 그녀의 유연한 움직임은 수천 명의 관중을 매료시켰다.   **23** 두 정당 사이에는 반감이 끓어올라, 결국 난동이 발생하게 되었다.   **24** 편집자는 사과로 독자들을 달래려 했다.   **25** 저는 검을 잘 다루지는 못하지만, 완전히 초보자는 아닙니다.   **26** 이 논의는 한참 뒤늦었다.

27

persecution
[pur-si-kyoo-sh*uh*n]

n. cruel and unfair treatment

박해, 학대

The students were taught about the **persecutions** of Christians by the Romans.[27]

syn. harassment, maltreatment, bullying

28

pretentious
[pri-ten-sh*uh*s]

adj. making an exaggerated outward show

가식적인, 허세 부리는

His **pretentious** attitude makes others not like him.[28]

syn. affected, snobbish, conceited

29

quixotic
[kwik-sot-ik]

adj. having ideas that show imagination but are usually not practical

돈키호테 같은, 공상적인

He is **quixotic** like Don Quixote.[29]

syn. visionary, impractical, impracticable

30

resonant
[rez-*uh*-nu*h*nt]

adj. continuing to sound

소리가 울리는

The **resonant** thundering of cannons being fired was heard throughout the country.[30]

syn. echoing, resounding

31

sarcastic
[sahr-kas-tik]

adj. mocking in speech

빈정대는

She was hurt by his **sarcastic** laugh.[31]

syn. satirical, cynical, sardonic

예문 해석

27 학생들은 로마인들이 기독교인들을 박해한 것에 대해 배웠다.　**28** 그의 잘난 체하는 태도는 다른 사람들이 그를 좋아하지 않게 만든다.　**29** 그는 돈키호테처럼 공상적이고 비현실적이다.　**30** 대포가 발사되는 굉음이 온 나라에 들렸다.　**31** 그의 빈정대는 웃음에 그녀는 상처 받았다.

snub
[sn*uh*b]

v. to ignore or refuse to acknowledge someone
무시하다, 모욕하다
She **snubbed** him by pretending not to notice him.[32]

syn. ignore, disregard, rebuff

subside
[s*uh*b-said]

v. to sink to a lower level
아래로 가라앉다, 푹 꺼지다
Does that mean the whole house is **subsiding**?[33]

syn. collapse, sink, abate

tepid
[tep-id]

adj. moderately warm
미지근한, 열의가 없는
The critics have been **tepid** in their response.[34]

syn. lukewarm, warm, unenthusiastic

twine
[twain]

v. to twist together
꼬다, 꼬아 합치다, 감다
My sister **twined** flowers into a wreath.[35]

syn. coil, interweave, interlace

veto
[vee-toh]

n. the right to formally reject a proposal
거부권
The president holds the power to **veto**.[36]

syn. rejection, refusal

 예문 해석

32 그녀는 그를 못 본 척하며 무시했다.　**33** 그럼 집 전체가 가라앉고 있다는 뜻인가요?　**34** 평론가들은 미지근한 반응을 보였다.　**35** 내 여동생은 꽃을 꼬아 화관을 만들었다.　**36** 대통령은 거부권을 발휘할 힘을 가진다.

Directions   Each of the following questions consists of one word followed by five words or phrases. You are to select the one word or phrase whose meaning is closest to the word in capital letters.

1. **ALTER :**
   (A) convert
   (B) swagger
   (C) drench
   (D) suffice
   (E) billow

2. **COMPLIMENTARY :**
   (A) communicable
   (B) isolated
   (C) weary
   (D) free
   (E) candid

3. **DIPLOMATIC :**
   (A) forceful
   (B) indistinct
   (C) tactful
   (D) imperceptible
   (E) disenchanted

4. **ENDORSE :**
   (A) affirm
   (B) disregard
   (C) baffle
   (D) sort
   (E) mortify

5. **FATIGUE :**
   (A) peril
   (B) celerity
   (C) vanity
   (D) tiredness
   (E) sabotage

6. **GROPE :**
   (A) execute
   (B) allocate
   (C) utter
   (D) swoop
   (E) fumble

7. **HAUL :**
   (A) harmonize
   (B) subdue
   (C) avert
   (D) drag
   (E) quench

8. **INCENSE :**
   (A) alarm
   (B) pierce
   (C) tear
   (D) gloat
   (E) enrage

9. **LACKLUSTER :**
   (A) clever
   (B) dull
   (C) physical
   (D) resigned
   (E) tricky

10. **PRETENTIOUS :**
   (A) rural
   (B) stealthy
   (C) affected
   (D) malicious
   (E) conspicuous

"The time to repair the roof is when the sun is shining."

— John F. Kennedy —
35th president of the U.S.

지붕을 고쳐야 할 때는 햇빛이 비칠 때이다.

Greek and Latin Roots & Prefixes 17

★ FLEX, FLECT = to bend

ex (v.)	flex	(준비 운동으로) 몸을 풀다
-ible (adj.)	flexible	유연한
-ity (n.)	flexibility	유연성, 나긋나긋함
de (down)	deflect	(부딪쳐) 방향을 바꾸다
re (back)	reflect	비추다, 반영하다, 반사하다
	reflection	반사
	reflex	반사 작용, 반사적인 반응
	reflex nerve	반사 신경
in (not)	inflexible	융통성 없는

DAY

17

WORDS TO LEARN

- ☐ accelerate
- ☐ altercation
- ☐ assorted
- ☐ boycott
- ☐ champion
- ☐ concede
- ☐ corroborate
- ☐ demeanor
- ☐ dire
- ☐ drawback
- ☐ endowment
- ☐ excursion
- ☐ fatuous
- ☐ foster
- ☐ galactic
- ☐ haven
- ☐ illiterate
- ☐ incision
- ☐ inkling
- ☐ invaluable
- ☐ lad
- ☐ litigation
- ☐ matriculate
- ☐ monologue
- ☐ noxious
- ☐ overhaul
- ☐ perseverance
- ☐ piquant
- ☐ relentless
- ☐ resort
- ☐ shrine
- ☐ squander
- ☐ surge
- ☐ terminate
- ☐ truncate
- ☐ viable

01

accelerate
[ak-sel-*uh*-reyt]

v. to speed up
가속하다, 속력을 높이다
He **accelerated** his car.[1]

syn. speed up, hasten, quicken

02

altercation
[awl-ter-key-sh*uh*n]

n. a heated or angry dispute
언쟁, 논쟁
An **altercation** occurred between a plaintiff and a defendant.[2]

syn. argument, bickering, wrangle

03

assorted
[*uh*-sawr-tid]

adj. consisting of different or various kinds
여러 가지의, 갖은
The candy jar contained **assorted** treats.[3]

syn. various, diversified, miscellaneous

🧘 **예문 해석**

01 그는 차의 속력을 높였다. **02** 원고와 피고 사이에 언쟁이 일어났다. **03** 그 캔디 통에는 다양한 종류가 담겨 있었다.

04

boycott
[boi-kot]

v. to stop buying or using the goods or services of a certain company or country as a protest
구매나 사용을 거부하다, 보이콧하다
Boycotts are an effective way to use your spending money to effect change.[4]

syn. ban, avoid, snub

05

champion
[cham-pee-*uhn*]

v. to support or defend
옹호하다, 지지하다
Many financial experts **champion** this new investment approach.[5]

syn. advocate, support, defend

06

concede
[k*uhn*-seed]

v. to acknowledge as true
인정하다, 수긍하다
They **conceded** defeat in the war.[6]

syn. admit, acknowledge, surrender

07

corroborate
[k*uh*-rob-*uh*-reyt]

v. to make certain
확인하다, 확실하게 하다
Investigators were initially unable to **corroborate** Anderson's claims.[7]

syn. confirm, authenticate, substantiate

08

demeanor
[di-mee-ner]

n. manner of behaving
처신, 행실, 품행
There was a sharp change in his **demeanor**.[8]

syn. behavior, manner, attitude

📖 예문 해석

04 불매 운동은 변화를 일으키기 위해 당신의 돈을 사용하는 효과적인 방법이다. **05** 많은 재무 전문가들이 이 새로운 투자 방식을 지지한다. **06** 그들은 전쟁에서 패배를 인정했다. **07** 수사관들은 앤더슨의 주장이 맞는지 처음엔 확인할 수 없었다. **08** 그의 태도에 극명한 변화가 있었다.

dire
[dai-*uh*r]

adj. causing or involving great fear
무서운, 무시무시한
The lawyer was threatened with **dire** consequences.[9]

syn. dreadful, terrible, horrible

drawback
[draw-bak]

n. a disadvantage or slight problem
결점, 문제점
Jessie loved her job working at the library on weekends, despite the **drawback** of needing to get up early on Saturday mornings.[10]

syn. disadvantage, snag, problem

endowment
[en-dou-m*uh*nt]

n. the property with which an institution is given
기부금
The school is supported by a $1 billion **endowment**.[11]

syn. gift, grant, bequest

excursion
[ik-skur-zh*uh*n]

n. a short journey or trip
야유회, 소풍
The family's **excursion** to Italy was much better than last year's trip to France.[12]

syn. expedition, trip, jaunt

fatuous
[fach-oo-*uh*s]

adj. lacking intelligence
얼빠진, 어리석은
The renowned chef was left speechless by this **fatuous** remark.[13]

syn. foolish, stupid, silly

 예문 해석

09 그 변호사는 끔찍한 결과를 초래할 위협을 받았다. **10** 토요일 아침 일찍 일어나야 한다는 단점에도 불구하고, 제시는 주말에 도서관에서 일하는 그녀의 직업을 좋아했다. **11** 그 학교는 기부금 10억 원을 지원받았다. **12** 가족의 이번 이탈리아 여행은 작년 프랑스 여행보다 훨씬 좋았다. **13** 그 유명한 요리사는 말도 안 되는 발언에 할 말을 잃었다.

14

foster
[faw-ster]

v. to encourage development

양육하다, 기르다

The president thought that it was important to **foster** nationalism in the hearts of his nations' people.[14]

syn. nurture, cultivate, nurse

15

galactic
[guh-lak-tik]

adj. inconceivably large

(은하처럼) 거대한, 엄청 큰

Did you see her **galactic** house? It's huge![15]

syn. huge, immense, vast

16

haven
[hey-vuhn]

n. a place of safety or rest

피난처, 쉴 곳

She sought a **haven** from the arid desert.[16]

syn. shelter, asylum, refuge

17

illiterate
[i-lit-er-it]

adj. not knowing how to read or write

문맹의, 읽고 쓸 줄 모르는

A large percentage of the population was **illiterate** in his country.[17]

syn. uneducated, uninformed, ignorant

18

incision
[in-sizh-uhn]

n. a sharp cut

절개

Because the tumor was so large, the surgeon made an **incision** 5 inches long.[18]

syn. cut, slit

19

inkling
[ingk-ling]

n. a slight hint or indication

눈치챔, 느낌, 힌트

She had an **inkling** something was wrong when the blaring siren began to sound.[19]

syn. hint, intimation, hunch

예문 해석

14 대통령은 사람들 마음속에 애국심을 기르는 것이 중요하다고 여겼다.　**15** 그녀의 거대한 집을 봤나요? 엄청 커요.　**16** 그녀는 바짝 마른 사막에서 쉴 곳을 찾았다.　**17** 그의 나라에서는 대부분의 국민이 문맹이다.　**18** 종양이 너무 컸기 때문에 외과의사는 5인치 길이의 절개를 했다.　**19** 시끄러운 사이렌이 울리기 시작했을 때 그녀는 무언가 잘못되어 가고 있다는 느낌을 받았다.

20

invaluable
[in-val-yoo-*uh*-buhl]

adj. having a value that is too great to be measured

값을 헤아릴 수 없는, 평가 못할 만큼 매우 귀중한

I was able to gain **invaluable** experience over that year.[20]

syn. priceless, precious

21

lad
[lad]

n. a boy or youth

젊은이, 소년, (친근한 호칭으로) 녀석

He was a smart **lad**.[21]

syn. boy, youth, fellow

22

litigation
[lit-i-gey-sh*uh*n]

n. a lawsuit

소송, 기소

The case was in **litigation**.[22]

syn. lawsuit, case, trial

23

matriculate
[m*uh*-trik-y*uh*-leyt]

v. to enroll in a college or university as a candidate for a degree

대학에 입학하다, 대학 입학 허가를 받다

One hundred fifteen Phillips Academy Andover students were allowed to **matriculate** at Harvard from 2004 to 2010.[23]

syn. enroll, register

24

monologue
[mon-*uh*-lawg]

n. a long speech by one person during a conversation

독백, 1인극

She ignored the question and continued her **monologue**.[24]

syn. monodrama, soliloquy, speech by one person

25

noxious
[nok-sh*uh*s]

adj. poisonous or very harmful

유해한, 유독한

Many household products give off **noxious** fumes.[25]

syn. harmful, toxic, poisonous

예문 해석

20 그해 나는 매우 값진 경험을 할 수 있었다.　**21** 그는 영리한 젊은이였다.　**22** 그 사건은 소송 중이었다.　**23** 2004년부터 2010년까지 필립스 아카데미 앤 도버에서 115명의 학생이 하버드에 입학했다.　**24** 그녀는 질문을 무시하고 독백을 이어갔다.　**25** 많은 가정용품이 해로운 연기를 배출한다.

overhaul
[oh-ver-hawl]

v. to examine a machine or system
정밀 검사하다, 분해 수리하다
My car was **overhauled** by an expert mechanic.[26]

syn. mend, repair, fix up

perseverance
[pur-*suh*-veer-*uh*ns]

n. the quality of continuing to try to achieve a particular aim
인내, 끈기
They had enough **perseverance** to finish the job.[27]

syn. persistence, tenacity, doggedness

piquant
[pee-k*uh*nt]

adj. agreeably pungent or sharp in taste or flavor
(맛이 상큼하게) 톡 쏘는 듯한
This story is filled with **piquant** details with charm and wit.[28]

syn. pungent, biting, zesty

relentless
[ri-lent-lis]

adj. not easing or slackening
수그러들지 않는, 끈질긴
This **relentless** business mogul is not taking "no" for an answer.[29]

syn. merciless, harsh, unforgiving

resort
[ree-sawrt]

n. use of or appeal to some person or thing for aid, satisfaction, service
의지, 수단
I hope the conflict can be resolved without either party needing to **resort** to violence.[30]

syn. alternative, recourse, chance

 예문 해석

26 내 차는 전문 수리공에게 대대적인 검사를 받았다.　**27** 그들은 그 일을 끝까지 해낼 충분한 끈기를 가지고 있었다.　**28** 이 이야기는 매력과 재치가 넘치는 톡 쏘는 디테일로 가득 차 있다.　**29** 이 가차 없는 재계 거물은 "아니오"라는 대답을 받아들이지 않는다.　**30** 나는 양쪽이 폭력에 의존하지 않고 충돌을 해결하기를 희망한다.

31

shrine
[shrain]

n. any place or object hallowed by its history or associations
성소, 성역, 제단
He visits the **shrine** to pray for peace of mind.[31]

> *syn.* altar, chapel, sanctuary

32

squander
[skwon-der]

v. to use up money wastefully
돈을 펑펑 쓰다, 낭비하다
Do not **squander** money.[32]

> *syn.* waste, spend

33

surge
[surj]

n. a sudden strong swelling
급증, 급등
Whenever she watches a sad movie, she experiences a sudden **surge** of emotion.[33]

> *syn.* deluge, flood, rush

34

terminate
[tur-m*uh*-neyt]

v. to end completely
완전히 끝내다, 종결되다
Her contract **terminates** at the end of the season.[34]

> *syn.* end, finish, come to an end

35

truncate
[tr*uh*ng-keyt]

v. to shorten by cutting off a part
길이를 줄이다, 짧게 하다
Although the director loved all of the scenes with this actress, he had to **truncate** the movie so its runtime would be less than ninety minutes.[35]

> *syn.* cut short, prune, shorten

36

viable
[vai-*uh*-b*uh*l]

adj. capable of doing what it is intended to do
생존 가능한, 실행 가능한
Her inventions can become commercially **viable** products.[36]

> *syn.* feasible, plausible, practical

예문 해석

31 그는 마음의 평화를 기도하기 위해 성소를 찾는다.　**32** 돈을 펑펑 낭비하지 말아라.　**33** 그녀는 슬픈 영화를 볼 때마다 갑자기 감정이 솟구친다.　**34** 이번 시즌 후에 그녀의 계약이 끝난다.　**35** 감독은 이 여배우와 함께 하는 모든 장면이 마음에 들었지만, 상영시간이 90분도 채 되지 않도록 영화를 잘라내야 했다.　**36** 그녀의 발명은 상업적으로 가능성 있는 상품이 될 수 있다.

Directions   Each of the following questions consists of one word followed by five words or phrases. You are to select the one word or phrase whose meaning is closest to the word in capital letters.

1. ASSORTED :
(A) grave
(B) exotic
(C) various
(D) clairvoyant
(E) ashamed

2. BOYCOTT :
(A) illuminate
(B) diminish
(C) encircle
(D) ban
(E) dilapidate

3. CHAMPION :
(A) advocate
(B) murky
(C) biased
(D) gaze
(E) violate

4. DEMEANOR :
(A) fortitude
(B) behavior
(C) insurance
(D) emperor
(E) quagmire

5. ENDOWMENT :
(A) vengeance
(B) duty
(C) revenge
(D) lunacy
(E) gift

6. FOSTER :
(A) monitor
(B) nurture
(C) summon
(D) precursor
(E) arouse

7. HAVEN :
(A) outcast
(B) bedlam
(C) entertainment
(D) prospect
(E) shelter

8. LAD :
(A) pyramid
(B) rumor
(C) boy
(D) senior
(E) inmate

9. PIQUANT :
(A) pungent
(B) shrinking
(C) inconstant
(D) awkward
(E) deliberate

10. RELENTLESS :
(A) timeless
(B) eccentric
(C) waspy
(D) beneficial
(E) merciless

Greek and Latin Roots & Prefixes 18

★ FRAIL, FRACT, FRAG = to break

-ion (n.)	fraction	부분, 일부
-ure (n.)	fracture	골절
-ity (n.)	fragment	조각, 파편
-ile (adj.)	fragile	깨지기 쉬운
-il (adj.)	frail	노쇠한
in (not)	infraction	위반
re (back)	refract	굴절시키다
	refraction	굴절, 굴절 작용
	refractory	다루기 힘든, 불량한
sub (under)	suffrage	선거권, 참정권

DAY

18

WORDS TO LEARN

☐ accolade	☐ dismay	☐ innate	☐ rabble
☐ altruistic	☐ enervate	☐ invective	☐ redeem
☐ astounding	☐ execute	☐ laden	☐ satire
☐ blight	☐ fauna	☐ litter	☐ shun
☐ chaotic	☐ founder	☐ monopoly	☐ stipulate
☐ composed	☐ glut	☐ nuance	☐ substantiate
☐ corrosion	☐ havoc	☐ overhear	☐ terminology
☐ debacle	☐ illuminate	☐ prevalent	☐ tyro
☐ disapproving	☐ incisive	☐ proportion	☐ vibrant

01

accolade
[ak-*uh*-leyd]

n. any award, honor, or laudatory notice
칭찬, 영예
This award is the highest **accolade** in the fashion industry.[1]

syn. award, praise, distinction

02

altruistic
[al-troo-is-tik]

adj. unselfishly concerned for or devoted to the welfare of others
이타적인
Altruistic individuals often make many sacrifices.[2]

syn. philanthropic, unselfish, selfless

03

astounding
[*uh*-stoun-ding]

adj. shocking or amazing
몹시 놀라게 하는
The results are quite **astounding**.[3]

syn. astonishing, breathtaking, amazing

예문 해석

01 이 상은 패션 업계에서 최고의 영예입니다. **02** 이타적인 사람들은 종종 많은 희생을 감수한다. **03** 결과는 매우 놀라웠다.

04

blight
[blait]

v. to frustrate, spoil or destroy something
망치다, 말라 죽게 하다
His behavior yesterday has **blighted** his career.[4]

syn. mar, spoil

05

chaotic
[key-ot-ik]

adj. completely disordered
혼돈된, 무질서한
The traffic in New Delhi is **chaotic** at rush hour.[5]

syn. disorganized, disordered, uncontrolled

06

composed
[k*uh*m-pohzd]

adj. calm
평온한, 잠잠한
His **composed** face reassured the nervous passengers.[6]

syn. tranquil, serene, peaceful

07

corrosion
[k*uh*-roh-zh*uh*n]

n. the gradual wearing away
부식
Zinc protects other metals from **corrosion**.[7]

syn. disintegration, decomposition, deterioration

08

debacle
[dee-bah-k*uh*l]

n. a sudden and complete disaster
대실패, 큰 낭패
His army ended in a **debacle**, surrounded on all sides by the enemy.[8]

syn. catastrophe, disaster, fiasco

예문 해석

04 어제 행동은 그의 커리어를 망쳐 놓았다.   **05** 뉴델리의 러시아워 교통상황은 혼돈스럽다.   **06** 그는 침착한 얼굴로 불안한 승객들을 안심시켰다.   **07** 아연은 다른 금속이 부식되는 것을 막아준다.   **08** 그의 군대는 사방이 적에게 포위되어 대실패로 끝이 나게 되었다.

disapproving
[dis-*uh*-proo-ving]

adj. expressing disapproval
불만스런, 비난하는
She gave him a **disapproving** look.[9]

syn. complaining, grumbling, protesting

dismay
[dis-mey]

v. to dishearten thoroughly
크게 실망시키다, 경악하게 만들다
They watched in **dismay** as the house burned.[10]

syn. disappoint, daunt, horrify

enervate
[en-er-veyt]

v. to take energy from something
기력을 빼앗다
A hot climate **enervates** people.[11]

syn. weaken, exhaust, sap

execute
[ek-si-kyoot]

v. to perform or carry out something
직무나 계획을 실행하다
We are going to **execute** our campaign.[12]

syn. carry out, effect, implement

fauna
[faw-n*uh*]

n. the animals living in an area or in a particular period of history
동물군
Hawaii has a vast variety of flora and **fauna**.[13]

syn. animals

founder
[foun-der]

v. to fall or sink down
가라앉다, 허물어지다
The building has **foundered**.[14]

syn. sink, collapse

 예문 해석

09 그녀는 불만스러운 눈빛으로 그를 보았다.   **10** 그들은 그 집이 불타는 것을 낙담하여 지켜보았다.   **11** 더운 기후는 사람들의 기력을 빼앗는다.   **12** 우리는 우리의 캠페인을 곧 실행할 예정이다.   **13** 하와이에는 다양한 식물군과 동물군이 있다.   **14** 빌딩이 허물어졌다.

15

glut
[gl*uh*t]

n. an excessive supply or amount
과잉
The decline is blamed mainly on a global **glut** of sugar.[15]

syn. surfeit, excess, surplus

16

havoc
[hav-*uh*k]

n. ruinous damage
대규모의 황폐
The **havoc** wrought by the hurricane was devastating.[16]

syn. ruin, devastation

17

illuminate
[ih-loo-m*uh*-neyt]

v. to light up
(~에 불을) 비추다
She pushed the doors open enough for the room's light to
illuminate the contents.[17]

syn. brighten, flash, spotlight

18

incisive
[in-sai-siv]

adj. demonstrating ability to recognize or draw fine distinctions
예리한, 재빠른, 날카로운
It is difficult to produce a documentary that is both **incisive**
and probing.[18]

syn. intelligent, sharp, acute

19

innate
[ih-neyt]

adj. existing in an individual from birth
타고난, 천부적인, 선천적인
She has an **innate** musical talent.[19]

syn. inborn, inherent, congenital

20

invective
[in-vek-tiv]

n. harsh or abusive langauge
심한 독설이나 비난
They hurled **invective** at each other.[20]

syn. verbal abuse, denunciation, diatribe

예문 해석

15 이러한 감소는 전 세계적인 설탕 과잉 탓으로 주로 지목된다.　**16** 허리케인으로 인한 대재앙은 참혹했다.　**17** 그녀는 방의 불빛이 내용물을 비추도록 문을 밀어서 열었다.　**18** 예리하면서도 제대로 진상을 규명하는 다큐멘터리를 만드는 것은 쉽지 않다. **19** 그녀는 천부적인 음악적 재능이있다.　**20** 그들은 서로 간에 심한 독설을 주고 받았다.

laden
[leyd-n]

adj. loaded down

(짐을) 잔뜩 실은, 가득한

The **laden** suitcase was full of clothes for the month long trip.[21]

syn. loaded, burdened

---

litter
[lit-er]

v. to scatter objects in disorder

어질러 놓다

The streets were **littered** with newspapers.[22]

syn. strew, disseminate, straw

---

monopoly
[m*uh*-nop-*uh*-lee]

n. the only one providing a particular product

독점, 독점기업

Sales of tobacco in Korea are controlled by a state-owned **monopoly**.[23]

syn. exclusive ownership, control, domination

---

nuance
[noo-ahns]

n. a slight difference

뉘앙스, 미묘한 차이

The **nuances** of various famous artworks are evident to the keen eye.[24]

syn. subtlety, hint, shade

---

overhear
[oh-ver-heer]

v. to hear without the speaker's knowledge

우연히 듣게 되다

She **overheard** us discussing our plans.[25]

syn. monitor, eavesdrop, tap

 예문 해석

21 짐을 실은 여행 가방은 한 달 동안의 여행용 옷들로 가득 차 있었다. **22** 거리는 신문지로 어지럽혀 있었다. **23** 한국에서 담배 판매는 국영 독점 기업에 의해 통제된다. **24** 다양한 유명 예술 작품의 미묘한 차이는 예리한 눈에는 분명히 드러난다. **25** 그녀가 우리가 계획을 이야기하는 것을 우연히 들었다.

26

prevalent
[prev-*uh*-lu*h*nt]

adj. common and widespread
일반적으로 행해지는, 유행하는, 널리 퍼진
The epidemic is **prevalent** in the area.[26]

syn. common, rife, widespread

27

proportion
[pr*uh*-pawr-sh*uh*n]

n. comparative relation between things or magnitudes
(전체에서 차지하는) 부분, 비율
A large **proportion** of older adults live alone.[27]

syn. ratio, fraction, magnitude

28

rabble
[rab-*uh*l]

n. a noisy disorderly crowd or mob
오합지졸, 무질서한 군중
A **rabble** of noisy teenagers outside of his building woke him up.[28]

syn. mob, throng, crowd, multitude

29

redeem
[ri-deem]

v. to make up for
만회하다, 보완하다
After being irritable and snappy with her mother, he **redeemed** himself by bringing her flowers and apologizing.[29]

syn. compensate, offset, rehabilitate

30

satire
[sat-ai*uh*r]

n. the use of irony or sarcasm in exposing vice or folly
풍자
This story should be read as a **satire**, not as "obscene" content.[30]

syn. sarcasm, mockery

31

shun
[sh*uh*n]

v. to keep away from
피하다, 회피하다
From that time forward, everybody **shunned** them.[31]

syn. eschew, avoid, evade

예문 해석

26 이 지역에는 그 전염병이 널리 퍼졌다.   **27** 노인들 중 많은 비율이 혼자 산다.   **28** 건물 밖에서 나는 시끄러운 청소년 무리 때문에 그는 잠이 깼다.   **29** 어머니에게 짜증을 내고 화를 낸 후, 그는 어머니에게 꽃을 가져다 드리고 사과함으로써 자신을 속죄했다.   **30** 이 이야기는 불건전한 것이 아니라 풍자로 해석되어야 한다.   **31** 그 때부터 모든 사람이 그들을 피했다.

stipulate
[stip-y*uh*-leyt]

v. to make an express demand or arrangement as a condition of agreement

규정하다, 명시하다

The contracts of the players **stipulate** they must attend all practices and games.[32]

syn. designate, impose, specify

substantiate
[s*uh*b-stan-shee-eyt]

v. to prove or support something

증거를 들어 입증하다, 구현시키다

There is little scientific evidence to **substantiate** the claims.[33]

syn. prove, confirm, verify, validate

terminology
[tur-m*uh*-nol-*uh*-jee]

n. the words and phrases used in a particular subject or field

용어

In order to do well on a math test, it is necessary to understand math **terminology**.[34]

syn. terms, jargon, expressions

tyro
[tai-roh]

n. a beginner in learning anything

초보자

Sammy was still a **tyro** in ballet, but her enthusiasm to learn was fervent.[35]

syn. amateur, novice, beginner

vibrant
[vai-br*uh*nt]

adj. extremely lively or exciting

활기 넘치는, 활발한, 선명한

He likes the **vibrant** atmosphere in class.[36]

syn. lively, animated, cheerful, vivacious

예문 해석

32 선수들의 계약서에는 그들이 모든 연습과 경기에 참석해야 한다고 명시되어 있다. **33** 주장을 입증할 과학적인 증거는 거의 없다. **34** 수학 시험을 잘 보기 위해서는 수학 용어를 이해하는 것이 필요하다. **35** 새미는 여전히 발레 초보였지만 배우려는 열정은 뜨거웠다. **36** 그는 클래스의 활기 넘치는 분위기가 좋았다.

Directions   Each of the following questions consists of one word followed by five words or phrases.
You are to select the one word or phrase whose meaning is closest to the word in capital letters.

1. ACCOLADE :
   (A) talent
   (B) award
   (C) uneasiness
   (D) priority
   (E) achievement

2. COMPOSED :
   (A) tranquil
   (B) ardor
   (C) rascal
   (D) chipped
   (E) ordinary

3. ENERVATE :
   (A) weaken
   (B) prolong
   (C) enunciate
   (D) coalesce
   (E) uproar

4. FOUNDER :
   (A) grab
   (B) dissolve
   (C) stare
   (D) sink
   (E) mourn

5. GLUT :
   (A) dearth
   (B) surfeit
   (C) restriction
   (D) maniac
   (E) expulsion

6. ILLUMINATE :
   (A) lean
   (B) nod
   (C) brighten
   (D) dab
   (E) stammer

7. LADEN :
   (A) loaded
   (B) derisive
   (C) miserable
   (D) obligatory
   (E) mortal

8. NUANCE :
   (A) swish
   (B) starvation
   (C) topple
   (D) subtlety
   (E) debatable

9. RABBLE :
   (A) trepidation
   (B) shoot
   (C) purpose
   (D) mob
   (E) timidity

10. VIBRANT :
   (A) soggy
   (B) rumbling
   (C) lively
   (D) mild
   (E) fishy

Directions   Each of the following questions consists of one word followed by five words or phrases.
You are to select the one word or phrase whose meaning is closest to the word in capital letters.

1. **COMPATIBLE :**
   (A) brawny
   (B) harmonious
   (C) introductory
   (D) final
   (E) battered

2. **ENCUMBER :**
   (A) cower
   (B) shorten
   (C) hamper
   (D) cringe
   (E) wrinkle

3. **FORMIDABLE :**
   (A) lifeless
   (B) horrible
   (C) exhausted
   (D) assorted
   (E) submissive

4. **INTUITION :**
   (A) discipline
   (B) instinct
   (C) enrollment
   (D) advantage
   (E) scheme

5. **PRESTIGIOUS :**
   (A) grasping
   (B) fortunate
   (C) irritated
   (D) gloomy
   (E) honored

6. **DIMINUTIVE :**
   (A) enraged
   (B) tiny
   (C) firm
   (D) stern
   (E) archaic

7. **FORTIFY :**
   (A) founder
   (B) waft
   (C) restart
   (D) strengthen
   (E) whack

8. **SANCTUARY :**
   (A) reserve
   (B) exemplar
   (C) gap
   (D) avalanche
   (E) bedlam

9. **TENTATIVE :**
   (A) threatening
   (B) sullen
   (C) provisional
   (D) wasteful
   (E) dawdling

10. **TABLE :**
   (A) rummage
   (B) postpone
   (C) admire
   (D) loosen
   (E) abide

11. **LABORIOUS :**
    (A) onerous
    (B) slight
    (C) lumpy
    (D) pithy
    (E) apathetic

12. **PRESUMPTUOUS :**
    (A) meticulous
    (B) jumbled
    (C) timid
    (D) audacious
    (E) simmering

13. **DOMICILE :**
    (A) loom
    (B) scoundrel
    (C) rascal
    (D) abode
    (E) bewilderment

14. **LITHE :**
    (A) mirthful
    (B) derelict
    (C) furtive
    (D) insolent
    (E) supple

15. **MAYHEM :**
    (A) fiend
    (B) analogy
    (C) violence
    (D) foreboding
    (E) suffering

16. **MOLLIFY :**
    (A) stumble
    (B) pacify
    (C) ruin
    (D) lurk
    (E) ponder

17. **VETO :**
    (A) theme
    (B) fawning
    (C) rejection
    (D) decipher
    (E) queue

18. **ACCELERATE :**
    (A) cast off
    (B) get rid of
    (C) speed up
    (D) deprive of
    (E) relevant to

19. **ALTERCATION :**
    (A) argument
    (B) trifle
    (C) margin
    (D) disrespect
    (E) marauder

20. **DISMAY :**
    (A) beautify
    (B) chant
    (C) jostle
    (D) commemorate
    (E) disappoint

"Bad gains are true losses."

— Benjamin Franklin —
one of the Founding Fathers of the United States of America

나쁜 이익은 진정한 손실이다.

Greek and Latin Roots & Prefixes 19

★ PORT = to carry

-able (adj.)	portable	휴대 할 수 있는, 휴대용 제품
-ure (n.)	porter	(공항이나 호텔의) 짐꾼
-ity (n.)	portfolio	작품 모음집, 포트폴리오
im (in)	import	수입하다
ex (out)	export	수출하다
sub (under)	deport	(국외로) 강제 추방하다
trans (beyond)	transport	운송하다
sub (under)	support	지지하다

DAY

19

AMERICAN COLLEGE VOCABULARY 101

WORDS TO LEARN

☐ acclaim	☐ engraving	☐ inventory	☐ radiant
☐ amass	☐ exemplary	☐ lag	☐ respiration
☐ astute	☐ feint	☐ longevity	☐ saturate
☐ blinding	☐ fraction	☐ meager	☐ sift
☐ compulsory	☐ glum	☐ monotonous	☐ stagnant
☐ cosmopolitan	☐ headlong	☐ nudge	☐ surrogate
☐ demur	☐ impale	☐ overlook	☐ terrestrial
☐ disarming	☐ incite	☐ perspective	☐ ubiquitous
☐ drab	☐ innocuous	☐ proprietor	☐ vicinity

01

acclaim
[*uh*-kleym]

n. an enthusiastic approval, expression of enthusiasm, etc.
갈채, 환호, 찬사
The actor won critical **acclaim** for his performance.[1]

syn. applause, priase, kudos

02

amass
[*uh*-mas]

v. to collect into a mass
쌓다, 모으다
Both husband and wife worked together to **amass** property.[2]

syn. gather, assemble, collect

03

astute
[*uh*-stoot]

adj. of keen penetration or discernment
예리한, 날카로운
Astute managers can see how well employees get along
with their co-workers.[3]

syn. perceptive, shrewd, keen

🔖 **예문 해석**

01 그 배우의 연기는 비평가들의 찬사를 받았다.　**02** 남편과 부인 모두 재산을 모으기 위하여 함께 일했다.　**03** 예리한 관리자는
종업원이 다른 직원들과 잘 지내는지 알 수 있다.

04

blinding
[blain-ding]

adj. extremely bright
눈을 멀게 할 만큼 강한 빛의, 너무 눈부신
The doctor worked beneath the **blinding** lights of the operation room.[4]

syn. dazzling, glaring, radiant

05

compulsory
[k*uh*m-p*uh*l-s*uh*-ree]

adj. required
필수적인, 강요되는
Compulsory education has positive societal outcomes.[5]

syn. required, obligatory, necessary

06

cosmopolitan
[koz-m*uh*-pol-i-tn]

adj. belonging to or representative of all parts of the world
전 세계적인, 국제적인
Music is one of the most **cosmopolitan** arts.[6]

syn. ecumenical, universal, ubiquitous

07

demur
[di-mur]

v. to raise objections
이의를 제기하다
The doctor **demurred**, but she was adamant.[7]

syn. protest, object

08

disarming
[dis-ahr-ming]

adj. removing hostility or suspicion
상대방을 무장 해제시키는, 마음을 누그러뜨리는
Because the actress had a **disarming** smile, she could easily get what she wants.[8]

syn. charming, persuasive, seductive

예문 해석

04 그 의사는 수술실의 강한 불빛 아래 일했다. **05** 의무 교육은 긍정적인 사회적 결과를 낳는다. **06** 음악은 전 세계적인 예술 중 하나이다. **07** 의사는 난색을 표명했지만 그녀는 확고했다. **08** 그 여배우는 매력적인 미소를 가져 원하는 것을 쉽게 얻을 수 있었다.

drab
[drab]

adj. lacking in spirit or brightness
칙칙한, 단조로운
This **drab** advertisement is dull and unattractive.[9]

> *syn.* colorless, dull, flat

epicure
[ep-i-kyoor]

n. a person devoted to refined sensuous enjoyment
미식가, 식도락가
The food critic is an **epicure** who loves the highest levels of food.[10]

> *syn.* gourmet, connoisseur

exemplary
[ig-zem-pl*uh*-ree]

adj. worth following as an example
모범적인, 훌륭한
Exemplary conduct in school will lead to great success.[11]

> *syn.* outstanding, commendable

feint
[feynt]

n. a movement made in order to deceive an adversary
상대방을 속이는 동작
Ali **feinted** with a jab, and Frazier threw one of his own, missing.[12]

> *syn.* mock attack, pretense, ruse

fraction
[frak-sh*uh*n]

n. a very small part or segment of anything
파편, 단편, 단수
Only a **fraction** of the work was completed.[13]

> *syn.* part, portion, piece

glum
[gl*uh*m]

adj. moody or sorrowful
침울한
The **glum** folks are usually sullen, brooding, or moody - seldom smile, giggle, or laugh.[14]

> *syn.* sullen, depressed, melancholy

예문 해석

09 이 칙칙한 광고는 따분하고 매력적이지 않아요. **10** 그 음식 평론가는 최고 수준의 음식을 사랑하는 미식가이다. **11** 학교에서의 모범적인 행동은 큰 성공을 가져올 것이다. **12** 알리는 잽을 날리는 척했고, 프레이저는 잽을 날려 빗나갔다. **13** 작업의 아주 일부만이 완료되었다. **14** 우울한 사람들은 보통 시무룩하거나 침울하거나 기분이 나쁘다 – 거의 미소 짓거나, 낄낄거리거나, 소리 내어 웃지 않는다.

headlong
[hed-lawng, -long]

adj. undertaken quickly and suddenly
무모한, 앞뒤를 가리지 않는
The **headlong** boxing fight lasted 30 seconds.[15]

syn. impetuous, rash, reckless

impale
[im-peyl]

v. to fasten or stick
찌르다, 꽂다
When he donated blood, the nurse seemed to **impale** the needle in his arm with great force.[16]

syn. pierce, stab, spike

incite
[in-sait]

v. to stir up or provoke to action
자극하다, 격려하다, 선동하다
He **incited** his colleagues to take their revenge.[17]

syn. provoke, instigate, rouse

innocuous
[i-nok-yoo-*uhs*]

adj. not harmful or offensive
해가 없는, 무독성의
These mushrooms look **innocuous** but are deadly and harmful.[18]

syn. harmless, inoffensive

inventory
[in-v*uhn*-tawr-ee]

n. a written list of all the objects in a particular place
재고 목록
He made an **inventory** of everything that was to be kept.[19]

syn. stock, list, account

lag
[lag]

v. to fall or stay behind
뒤에 처지다, 뒤떨어지다
He **lagged** behind the rest of the class.[20]

syn. retard, delay

예문 해석

15 그 치열한 권투 시합은 30초 동안 계속되었다. **16** 그가 헌혈했을 때, 간호사는 센 힘으로 그의 팔에 있는 바늘을 찌르는 것처럼 보였다. **17** 그는 복수를 하자고 동료들을 선동했다. **18** 이 버섯들은 독이 없을 것처럼 보이나 매우 위험하다. **19** 그는 갖춰야 할 모든 것의 재고 목록을 만들었다. **20** 그는 반에서 뒤처졌다.

longevity
[lon-jev-i-tee]

n. a long individual life
장수, 오래 지속됨
Better medical treatment has led to greater **longevity**.[21]

syn. durability, endurance, lastingness

meager
[mee-ger]

adj. very small or not enough
빈약한, 얼마 안 되는
He could not support his family earning a **meager** salary.[22]

syn. scanty, inadequate, puny

monotonous
[muh-not-n-uhs]

adj. boring
단조로운, 변화 없는
The **monotonous** voice of the principal could put anyone to sleep.[23]

syn. tedious, humdrum, droning

nudge
[nuhj]

v. to poke someone to get their attention
(팔꿈치로 쿡) 찌르다
He **nudged** me and whispered, 'Look who's just come in.'[24]

syn. poke, bump, push

overlook
[oh-ver-look]

v. to fail to notice, or perceive
보고도 못 본 체하다, 못보고 지나치다
She **overlooked** a misspelled word.[25]

syn. condone, neglect

perspective
[per-spek-tiv]

n. an individual way of regarding a situation
견해, 관점, 사고방식
The accident has given him a new **perspective** on life.[26]

syn. outlook, view, prospect

예문 해석

21 더 나은 의학적 치료는 더 많은 장수로 이어졌다.　**22** 그는 박봉으로 가족을 부양할 수 없었다.　**23** 교장 선생님의 단조로운 말투는 누구나 잠들게 할 수 있었다.　**24** 그가 나를 쿡 찌르며 말했다. "누가 왔는지 좀 봐봐".　**25** 그녀는 오자를 못보고 지나쳤다.　**26** 그 사고가 그에게 인생에 대한 새로운 시각을 가져다 주었다.

proprietor
[pr*uh*-prai-i-ter]

n. someone who owns a business
(사업체의) 소유주
A **proprietor** of a local donuts shop might make and sell his donuts, while the proprietor of a chain of donut shops might work from an office managing the stores.[27]

syn. owner, holder, possessor

radiant
[rey-dee-*uh*nt]

adj. emitting electromagnetic radiation
환한, 빛을 내는
On her wedding day, the bride looked truly **radiant**.[28]

syn. beaming, bright, luminous

respiration
[res-p*uh*-rey-sh*uh*n]

n. the act of respiring or breathing
호흡
Artificial **respiration** is much more effective without water in the lungs.[29]

syn. breathing, exhalation, inhalation

saturate
[sach-*uh*-reyt]

v. to soak thoroughly
푹 적시다, 흠뻑 적시다
She **saturated** a sponge with water.[30]

syn. impregnate, drench, soak

sift
[sift]

v. to put some fine substance through a sieve
체로 치다, 체로 거르다, 엄밀히 조사하다
Don't forget to **sift** the the flour, or use a fork to check for lumps.[31]

syn. sort, scrutinize, inspect

예문 해석

27 지역 도넛 가게의 주인은 도넛을 만들어 팔 수 있고, 도넛 가게 체인의 주인은 가게들을 관리하는 사무실에서 일할 것이다. **28** 결혼식 날 그녀는 정말 눈부시게 빛났다. **29** 인공호흡은 폐에 물이 없을 때 훨씬 효과적이다. **30** 그녀는 스폰지를 물에 푹 적셨다. **31** 체로 밀가루를 거르거나 포크를 사용하여 덩어리들이 있는지 확인하는 것을 잊지 마세요.

stagnant
[stag-n*uh*nt]

adj. not flowing
흐르지 않는, 정체된
Having a picnic by the **stagnant** water was peaceful.[32]

syn. stationary, static, motionless

surrogate
[sur-*uh*-geyt]

n. someone who takes the place of another person
대리인
When the movie star left her seat in the middle of the awards ceremony, a **surrogate** took her place until she returned.[33]

syn. proxy, deputy, delegate

terrestrial
[t*uh*-res-tree-*uh*l]

adj. relating to the planet Earth or its inhabitants
육지의, 지구의, 땅의
A variety of **terrestrial** life thrived in environments where preservation was possible.[34]

syn. earthly, earthbound

ubiquitous
[yoo-bik-wi-t*uh*s]

adj. existing, found or seeming to be found everywhere at the same time
동시에 도처에 있는, 어디에나 존재하는
Salt is **ubiquitous** in the ocean.[35]

syn. omnipresent, universal

vicinity
[vi-sin-i-tee]

n. the area or region near or about a place
근처, 부근
The Embassy has warned of potential threats in the **vicinity** of a college area.[36]

syn. proximity, propinquity, hood

예문 해석

32 그 고인 물가에서 피크닉을 하는 것은 평화로웠다. **33** 그 영화배우가 시상식 중간에 자리를 비웠을 때, 그녀가 돌아올 때까지 대리인이 그녀의 자리를 대신했다. **34** 보존이 가능한 환경에서 다양한 육상 생물이 번성했다. **35** 소금은 대양 어디에나 있다. **36** 대사관은 대학가 주변에 있을 수 있는 잠재적 위협에 대해 경고했다.

Directions   Each of the following questions consists of one word followed by five words or phrases. You are to select the one word or phrase whose meaning is closest to the word in capital letters.

1. **AMASS :**
   (A) frown
   (B) devise
   (C) ruffle
   (D) curtail
   (E) gather

2. **BLINDING :**
   (A) scuffling
   (B) dazzling
   (C) panting
   (D) despondent
   (E) grandiloquent

3. **COSMOPOLITAN :**
   (A) pointed
   (B) identical
   (C) disgraceful
   (D) meandering
   (E) ecumenical

4. **DISARMING :**
   (A) sulky
   (B) repugnant
   (C) charming
   (D) unraveling
   (E) meddlesome

5. **EPICURE :**
   (A) advocate
   (B) baler
   (C) gawker
   (D) gourmet
   (E) sentry

6. **EXEMPLARY :**
   (A) nasty
   (B) absurd
   (C) devout
   (D) outstanding
   (E) shrunken

7. **INNOCUOUS :**
   (A) lousy
   (B) conclusive
   (C) harmless
   (D) industrious
   (E) glistening

8. **MONOTONOUS :**
   (A) tedious
   (B) evasive
   (C) puzzled
   (D) brisk
   (E) bad-tempered

9. **OVERLOOK :**
   (A) condone
   (B) waft
   (C) collect
   (D) ramble
   (E) stroll

10. **PROPRIETOR :**
    (A) owner
    (B) supervisor
    (C) interviewee
    (D) retiree
    (E) professional

Greek and Latin Roots & Prefixes 20

★ JUNCT, JOIN, JUG = to meet

-in (v.)	join	합류하다
-int (adj.)	joint	공동의
-ity (n.)	junction	교차로, 나들목
-ure (n.)	juncture	특정 시점
con (together)	conjoin	결합하다
con (together)	conjunction	접속사
dis (not)	disjointed	일관성이 없는

DAY

20

WORDS TO LEARN

☐ accommodating	☐ dreadful	☐ invert	☐ rage
☐ ambiguous	☐ engulf	☐ lament	☐ respite
☐ asylum	☐ exemplify	☐ livid	☐ scald
☐ bliss	☐ fawn	☐ meander[1]	☐ singe
☐ catholic	☐ fractious	☐ moor	☐ stain
☐ charlatan	☐ gnarled	☐ nullify	☐ subtle
☐ conceal	☐ ill-timed	☐ overpower	☐ terse
☐ demure	☐ impair	☐ perspicacious	☐ ultimatum
☐ disband	☐ intrinsic	☐ plethora	☐ vicious

01

accommodating
[*uh*-kom-*uh*-dey-ting]

adj. willing to do what another person wants
호의적인, 친절한, 잘 돌봐주는, 싹싹한
The manager was **accommodating** to foreign workers.[1]

> *syn.* obliging, helpful, cooperative

02

ambiguous
[am-big-yoo-*uh*s]

adj. having more than one possible meaning
모호한
The politician insisted on giving **ambiguous** answers to reporters.[2]

> *syn.* vague, equivocal, nebulous

03

asylum
[*uh*-sai-*luh*m]

n. an institution for the care of the mentally ill
정신병원, 요양소, 은신처
The local **asylum** was overcrowded with people who thought they were aliens.[3]

> *syn.* haven, shelter, refuge

예문 해석

01 그 관리자는 외국인 근로자들에게 호의적이었다.   **02** 그 정치인은 기자들에게 애매한 대답을 해야 한다고 주장했다.   **03** 지역 정신병원은 자신이 외계인이라 믿는 사람들로 넘쳐났다.

04

bliss
[blis]

n. a state of complete happiness
완전한 행복, 큰 기쁨
Ignorance is **bliss**.[4]

syn. joy, happiness, euphoria

05

catholic
[kath-*uh*-lik]

adj. comprehensive or broad-minded in tastes or interests
폭 넓은, 일반적인
It's a **catholic** taste that everybody has in a way.[5]

syn. broad-minded, comprehensive, general

06

charlatan
[shahr-*luh*-tn]

n. a person who pretends or claims to have more knowledge or skill than he or she possesses
사기꾼, 돌팔이
The **charlatan** pretended to be a doctor to accumulate enormous wealth.[6]

syn. quack, impostor, swindler

07

conceal
[*kuhn*-seel]

v. to hide
감추다
He **concealed** the dagger under his coat.[7]

syn. hide, cover

08

demure
[di-myoor]

adj. quite and serious
얌전 피우는, 점잖은 척 하는
She enjoys a modest or **demure** outfit - high neckline and low hem.[8]

syn. modest, shy, meek

🔖 예문 해석

04 모르는 게 약이다. **05** 어떻게 보면 그것은 누구나 가진 일반적인 취향이다. **06** 그 사기꾼은 엄청난 부를 축적하기 위해 의사 행세를 했다. **07** 그는 단검을 코트 아래 감췄다. **08** 그녀는 단정하고 얌전한 복장을 즐긴다 – 목까지 올라오는 긴 네크라인에 긴 옷자락.

09

disband
[dis-band]

v. to break up
조직을 해산하다
The rebel army was **disbanded**.[9]

syn. break up, split up, scatter

10

dreadful
[dred-f*uh*l]

adj. causing great fear or terror
무서운, 무시무시한
Polio was a **dreadful** disease.[10]

syn. frightful, dire, terrible

11

engulf
[en-g*uh*lf]

v. to overwhelm or swallow up
집어삼키다
A landslide **engulfed** his town.[11]

syn. overwhelm, overcome, surround

12

exemplify
[ig-zem-pl*uh*-fai]

v. to be an example of something
예시하다
He **exemplified** the finest traditions of his family.[12]

syn. demonstrate, illustrate, represent

13

fawn
[fawn]

v. to flatter someome
아첨하다
People will **fawn** over you when you become famous.[13]

syn. grovel, blandish, ingratiate

14

fractious
[frak-shuhs]

adv. unruly or readily angered
성미가 까다로운, 다루기 어려운
The **fractious** child was sent off to boarding school.[14]

syn. unruly, irritable, petulant

 예문 해석

09 반란군은 해체되었다.　**10** 소아마비는 무시무시한 질병이었다.　**11** 산사태가 그의 마을을 집어삼켰다.　**12** 그는 집안에서 훌륭한 전통을 보여주었다.　**13** 네가 유명해지면 사람들은 아첨할 것이다.　**14** 그 말썽을 잘 부리는 아이는 기숙학교에 보내졌다.

15 ....

gnarled
[nahrld]

adj. (of trees) full of or covered with gnarls; bent; twisted
울퉁불퉁하고 비틀린
He tried to move but the **gnarled** branches of a dead bush blocked his path.[15]

syn. twisted, bent, contorted

16 ....

ill-timed
[il-taimd]

adj. badly timed
시기가 좋지 않은
The introduction of the new market now looks **ill-timed** as well.[16]

syn. inopportune, bad timed

17 ....

impair
[im-pair]

v. to make or cause to become worse
손상시키다, 악화시키다
Too much drinking can **impair** your health.[17]

syn. harm, mar, damage

18 ....

intrinsic
[in-trin-sik]

adj. belonging to a thing by its very nature
고유한, 본질적인
A man with a generous heart can see the **intrinsic** value in others.[18]

syn. basic, inborn, inherent

19 ....

invert
[in-vurt]

v. to turn upside down
거꾸로 뒤집다
He **inverted** an hourglass.[19]

syn. overturn, capsize, reverse

20 ....

lament
[luh-ment]

v. to express sadness, regret, or disappointment
슬퍼하다, 애도하다
He began to **lament** the death of the victims.[20]

syn. mourn, grieve, wail

예문 해석

15 그는 움직이려고 했지만 죽은 덤불의 구불구불한 나뭇가지가 그의 길을 가로막았다. **16** 새로운 시장을 개척하는 것도 지금은 시기가 좋지 않아 보인다. **17** 술을 너무 많이 마시면 건강을 악화시킬 수 있다. **18** 마음이 넓은 사람은 타인의 내적 가치를 알 수 있다. **19** 그는 모래시계를 뒤집어 놓았다. **20** 그는 희생양들의 죽음을 슬퍼했다.

livid
[liv-id]

adj. extremely angry
노발대발한, 격노한
She was **livid** that I lied to her.[21]

syn. furious, enraged, infuriated

meander[1]
[mee-an-der]

v. to wander randomly
정처 없이 걷다, 배회하다
We **meandered** through a landscape of mountains, rivers, and vineyards.[22]

syn. drift, wander, roam

moor
[moor]

v. to stop and tie a boat to the land
배를 정박시키다, 잡아매다
I decided to **moor** my boat at the nearest pier.[23]

syn. fasten, anchor, berth

nullify
[n*uhl*-*uh*-fai]

v. to cause or declare something to be legally invalid
취소하다, 무효로 하다, 파기하다
They insisted on **nullifying** the contract.[24]

syn. invalidate, revoke, cancel

overpower
[oh-ver-pou-er]

v. to defeat or gain control
이기다, 제압하다
Our players **overpowered** the team throughout the match.[25]

syn. conquer, defeat, vanquish

perspicacious
[pur-spi-key-shuhs]

adj. having keen mental perception
선견지명이 있는, 통찰력이 있는
He was a **perspicacious** young boy.[26]

syn. discerning, insightful, penetrating

예문 해석

21 내가 그녀에게 거짓말을 한 것에 그녀는 격분했다. **22** 우리는 산, 강, 포도원을 따라 정처없이 걸었다. **23** 나는 가장 가까운 부두에 배를 대기로 했다. **24** 그들은 계약을 취소해야 한다고 주장했다. **25** 우리 선수들은 경기 내내 그 팀을 제압했다. **26** 그는 통찰력 있는 어린 소년이었다.

27 ··········

plethora
[pleth-er-uh]

n. overabundance

과다, 과잉

Libraries have a **plethora** of books and movies to choose from.[27]

syn. glut, excess, surfeit

28 ··········

rage
[reyj]

n. violent anger

분노, 격노

He went into a wild **rage**.[28]

syn. wrath, ire, anger

29 ··········

respite
[res-pit]

n. a short period of rest from something unpleasant or difficult

일시적 중지, 휴식

We finally got a brief **respite**.[29]

syn. intermission, recess, rest

30 ··········

scald
[skawld]

v. to burn or affect painfully with or as if with hot liquid or steam

(끓는 물이나 증기로) 데게 하다, 데이다

He **scalded** himself with boiling water.[30]

syn. burn, scorch, sear

31 ··········

singe
[sinj]

v. to burn superficially or lightly

그을리다, 살짝 태우다

The boy was too close to his backyard fire pit; he **singed** his shirt sleeve.[31]

syn. scorch, char, cauterize

 예문 해석

27 도서관에는 선택할 수 있는 책과 영화가 너무 많다. **28** 그는 격노했다. **29** 우리는 마침내 잠깐 숨을 돌릴 수 있었다. **30** 그는 끓는 물에 데였다. **31** 그 소년은 그의 뒷마당 불구덩이에 너무 가까이 있었다; 그는 그의 셔츠 소매를 그을렸다.

stain
[steyn]

v. to discolor with spots or streaks
(얼룩으로) 더럽히다, (명예를) 훼손시키다
When your clothes become stained with blood, take soap and wash out the **stain** with cold water.[32]

syn. soil, smear, taint

subtle
[suht-l]

adj. not very noticeable or obvious
미묘한, 포착하기 어려운, 미세한
Nuance means a very **subtle** difference in meaning, sound, or color.[33]

syn. faint, slight, delicate

terse
[turs]

adj. brief and concise
간결한, 짧고 힘찬
She gave a **terse** reply to me.[34]

syn. succinct, concise, brief

ultimatum
[uhl-tuh-mey-tuhm]

n. a final warning
최후 통첩, 마지막 경고
The police issued an **ultimatum** to the hijacker.[35]

syn. final offer, warning, final proposal

vicious
[vish-uhs]

adj. having the nature of evildoing
나쁜, 부도덕한, 타락한, 사악한
Rabies caused the once docile dog to become **vicious**.[36]

syn. spiteful, malicious, mean

📖 예문 해석

32 옷에 피가 묻었을 때는 차가운 물과 비누로 얼룩을 씻어내라. **33** 뉘앙스란 뜻이나 소리, 색에 있어 매우 미묘한 차이를 뜻한다. **34** 그녀는 내게 간결한 대답을 했다. **35** 경찰은 비행기 납치범들에게 최후 통첩을 했다. **36** 광견병은 한때 유순했던 개를 사납게 만들었다.

Directions   Each of the following questions consists of one word followed by five words or phrases. You are to select the one word or phrase whose meaning is closest to the word in capital letters.

1. ACCOMMODATING :
(A) perilous
(B) exact
(C) imprecise
(D) obliging
(E) customary

2. BLISS :
(A) joy
(B) torrent
(C) pit
(D) precursor
(E) apprentice

3. CATHOLIC :
(A) unnecessary
(B) docile
(C) buoyant
(D) exceptional
(E) broad-minded

4. DISBAND :
(A) push back
(B) call off
(C) spur on
(D) break up
(E) miss out

5. FAWN :
(A) lasso
(B) fickle
(C) straggle
(D) falter
(E) grovel

6. GNARLED :
(A) bespectacled
(B) tripped
(C) abandoned
(D) twisted
(E) walloping

7. LIVID :
(A) furious
(B) gaunt
(C) lank
(D) morose
(E) grisly

8. MOOR :
(A) idiosyncrasy
(B) satirize
(C) fasten
(D) persistence
(E) pierce

9. NULLIFY :
(A) proxy
(B) expediency
(C) invalidate
(D) extravagant
(E) revenge

10. TERSE :
(A) raucous
(B) irksome
(C) flabbergasted
(D) mutinous
(E) succinct

"A friend is a second self."

— Aristotle —
Greek critic, philosopher, physicist, & zoologist

친구란 또 다른 자기 자신이다.

Greek and Latin Roots & Prefixes 21

★ CEDE = to go

pre (before)	precede	앞서다
pro (forward)	proceed	진행하다
re (back)	recede	물러나다
con (together)	concede	인정하다
ad (toward)	access	접근
re (back)	recess	쉬는 시간, 움푹 들어간 곳
sub (under)	succeed	성공하다

DAY

21

WORDS TO LEARN

☐ accomplice	☐ enhance	☐ invigorate	☐ rally
☐ ambivalent	☐ exert	☐ lampoon	☐ restive
☐ ameliorate	☐ feasible	☐ lucid	☐ scathing
☐ chastise	☐ fervent	☐ meander[2]	☐ skittish
☐ conceited	☐ glutton	☐ moot	☐ stammer
☐ conflagration	☐ headstrong	☐ numerous	☐ succinct
☐ deplete	☐ illumination	☐ overt	☐ testy
☐ disclaim	☐ incoherent	☐ pertinent	☐ upbraid
☐ dreary	☐ innuendo	☐ pretext	☐ winsome

01

accomplice
[*uh*-kom-plis]

n. a person who helps in a crime
공범
He and his **accomplice** Billy spread wax across the floor.[1]

syn. associate, accessory

02

ambivalent
[am-biv-*uh*-luht]

adj. having both good and bad feelings
좋으면서 싫은, 반대되는 감정을 동시에 가지는
As she grows older, she develops **ambivalent** feelings toward her mom.[2]

syn. conflicting, mixed, wavering

03

ameliorate
[*uh*-meel-yuh-reyt]

v. to make or become better
개선하다
Doctors wanted to **ameliorate** the patients' suffering.[3]

syn. improve, alleviate, lighten

예문 해석

01 그와 공범인 빌리는 바닥에 왁스를 발라 놓았다. **02** 커가면서 그녀는 엄마에게 좋으면서도 싫은 감정을 가지게 되었다. **03** 의사들은 그 환자들의 고통을 개선하기를 원했다.

04 ·······

chastise
[chas-taiz]

v. to punish someone severely
벌하다, 혼내주다
She **chastised** him for his arrogant remarks.[4]

syn. punish, scold, upbraid

05 ·······

conceited
[kuhn-see-tid]

adj. having too good an opinion of oneself
자부심이 강한, 우쭐한, 뽐내는
Don't be too **conceited**![5]

syn. pompous, insolent, haughty

06 ·······

conflagration
[kon-fluh-grey-shuhn]

n. an especially large and destructive fire that causes devastation
대화재, 큰 불
That tiny campfire somehow turned into a raging forest **conflagration**.[6]

syn. large fire, inferno, blaze

07 ·······

deplete
[di-pleet]

v. to decrease seriously
고갈시키다, 비우다
Extravagant spending soon **depleted** his funds.[7]

syn. exhaust, reduce

08 ·······

disclaim
[dis-kleym]

v. to deny or repudiate interest in or connection with
부인하다, 책임이 없다고 말하다
Although the suspect **disclaimed** responsibility for the murder, the police were sure that he was the culprit.[8]

syn. deny, disavow, disown

예문 해석

04 그녀는 그의 무례한 언행을 야단쳤다.　**05** 너무 자만하지 마라!　**06** 그 작은 캠프파이어가 어쩌다 보니 맹렬한 대형 산불로 번졌다.　**07** 사치가 그의 자산을 곧 탕진하게 했다.　**08** 용의자는 살인 혐의를 부인했지만 경찰은 그가 범인이라고 확신했다.

dreary
[dreer-ee]

adj. dull and depressing
단조로운, 우울한
November is generally **dreary** and wet.[9]

syn. depressing, dull, bleak

enhance
[en-hahns]

v. to improve value, quality, or attractiveness
개선시키다, 더 좋게 하다
She is keen to **enhance** her reputation.[10]

syn. reinforce, improve, augment

exert
[ig-zurt]

v. to bring something into use or action forcefully
힘을 쓰다, 애쓰다
She **exerted** every effort.[11]

syn. apply, strive, utilize

feasible
[fee-*zuh*-bu*h*l]

adj. capable of being done
실행할 수 있는, 가능한
It seemed **feasible** at the time, but the circumstances were more difficult than expected.[12]

syn. possible, plausible, likely

fervent
[fur-v*uh*nt]

adj. having great warmth or intensity of enthusiasm
열정적인, 열렬한
He was a **fervent** environmental activist of Greenpeace.[13]

syn. enthusiastic, ardent, vehement

glutton
[gl*uh*t-n]

n. a person who eats and drinks excessively or voraciously
대식가, 폭식가
After living his whole life as a **glutton**, he decided to go on a diet.[14]

syn. gourmand, gastronome

예문 해석

09 보통 11월은 음울하고 비가 많이 온다.　**10** 그녀는 그녀의 평판을 좋게 만드는 데 예리한 재능이 있다.　**11** 그녀는 모든 노력을 다했다.　**12** 그 당시에는 실현 가능한 것처럼 보였지만, 상황은 생각보다 어려웠다.　**13** 그는 그린피스의 열렬한 환경 운동가였다.　**14** 대식가로서 평생을 살아온 이후, 그는 다이어트에 돌입하기로 했다.

15

headstrong
[hed-strawng]

adj. determined to have one's own way
완고한, 고집센
He is very **headstrong** and independent.[15]

> *syn.* willful, stubborn, obstinate

16

illumination
[i-loo-m*uh*-ney-sh*uh*n]

n. the lighting that a place has
조명
The only **illumination** came from a small window high in the wall.[16]

> *syn.* light, lighting

17

incoherent
[in-koh-her-*uh*nt]

adj. without logical or meaningful connection
조리가 안 맞는, 논리적이지 못한
Submitting an **incoherent** paragraph resulted in a poor grade.[17]

> *syn.* rambling, irrational, disjointed

18

innuendo
[in-yoo-en-doh]

n. indirect reference to something rude or unpleasant
풍자, 빈정대는 말
She used subtle **innunedo** rather than obvious insults.[18]

> *syn.* insinuation, allusion, suggestion

19

invigorate
[in-vig-*uh*-reyt]

v. to fill with life and energy
기운 나게 하다, 활기차게 하다
To **invigorate** the economy, the president sent out stimulus checks.[19]

> *syn.* stimulate, revitalize, energize

 예문 해석

15 그는 매우 고집이 세고 독립적이다.   **16** 높은 벽에 붙은 작은 창에서 들어오는 것이 유일한 불빛이었다.   **17** 앞뒤가 맞지 않는 문단을 제출하여 나쁜 점수를 받았다.   **18** 그녀는 명백한 모욕보다는 은근한 풍자를 사용하고는 했다.   **19** 대통령은 경기를 활성시키기 위해 경기 부양책을 보냈다.

20

lampoon
[lam-poon]

v. to attack usually in the form of satirical prose or verse
풍자문으로 비방하다
He was often **lampooned** for his short stature and unique political views.[20]

syn. satirize, mock

21

lucid
[loo-sid]

adj. easily understood
명쾌한, 명료한
When you write your lab report, you must write clearly and **lucidly**.[21]

syn. evident, obvious, comprehensible

22

meander[2]
[mee-an-der]

v. to bend and curve
(강물 등이) 굽이쳐 흐르다
We crossed a wooden bridge over a **meandering** stream.[22]

syn. wind, zigzag, twist, turn

23

moot
[moot]

adj. open to argument
논란의 여지가 있는, 미결정의
How long he'll survive is a **moot** point.[23]

syn. debatable, doubtful, controversial

24

numerous
[noo-mer-uhs]

adj. presenting in large numbers
수많은
They had **numerous** difficulties, but they made it.[24]

syn. myriad, innumerable, countless

25

overt
[oh-vurt]

adj. shown in an open and obvious way
명백한, 공공연한
Although there is no **overt** hostility, older and younger students do not mix much.[25]

syn. clear, conspicuous, obvious

예문 해석

20 그의 작은 키와 독특한 정치적 신념은 자주 풍자되곤 했다.　**21** 실험실 보고서를 쓸 때는 명료하고 명쾌하게 써야 한다.　**22** 우리는 굽이쳐 흐르는 시내 위로 놓인 나무다리를 건넜다.　**23** 얼마나 그가 살아남을 수 있는지는 논란의 여지가 있다.　**24** 그들은 많은 어려움을 이겨내고 성공했다.　**25** 명백한 적대감은 없지만 나이 든 학생들과 어린 학생들은 잘 섞이지 않는다.

26

pertinent
[pur-tn-uhnt]

adj. relating directly to the matter
(특정한 상황에) 적절한, 관련 있는
When you relate the story, include all the **pertinent** details.[26]

syn. suitable, relevant, appropriate

27

pretext
[pree-tekst]

n. something that is put forward to conceal a true purpose or object
구실, 핑계
Her company fired her under the **pretext** of poor work ethics after she filed sexual harassment charges against her boss.[27]

syn. quibble, excuse, alibi

28

rally
[ral-ee]

v. gather and organize or inspire anew
다시 불러 모으다, 다시 모이다
The great general **rallied** his scattered army.[28]

syn. muster, assemble

29

restive
[res-tiv]

adj. impatient of control, restraint, or delay
침착성이 없는, 들떠 있는, 참을성이 없는
The crowd grew **restive**.[29]

syn. fidgety, jittery, nervous, unquiet

30

scathing
[skey-thing]

adj. marked by harshly abusive criticism
냉혹한, 상처를 입히는
His first novel suffered form **scathing** reviews.[30]

syn. biting, nasty, harsh

31

skittish
[skit-ish]

adj. apt to start or shy
겁이 많은, 잘 놀라는
The loud noises and crowds of people make **skittish** horses very nervous and jumpy.[31]

syn. edgy, jumpy, restive

예문 해석

26 이야기를 할 때는 관련 있는 세부 사항을 포함시키도록 하라. **27** 그녀가 상사를 성희롱 혐의로 고발한 후, 그녀의 회사는 잘못된 직업 윤리를 핑계로 그녀를 해고했다. **28** 위대한 장군은 그의 흩어진 군대를 다시 규합했다. **29** 군중들은 점점 동요되었다. **30** 그의 첫 소설은 가혹한 비평에 시달렸다. **31** 시끄러운 소리와 군중들은 잘 놀라는 말들을 매우 긴장시키고 뛰게 만든다.

stammer
[stam-er]

v. to speak or say something in a faltering or hesitant way
말을 더듬다
Five per cent of children **stammer**.[32]

syn. stutter, sputter, wobble

succinct
[suhk-singkt]

adj. brief, precise and to the point
간결한, 명료한
Keep your answers as **succinct** as possible.[33]

syn. pithy, brief, concise

testy
[tes-tee]

adj. irritably impatient
짜증 잘 내는
Contrary to his **testy** brother, she usually remains calm.[34]

syn. touchy, cantankerous, exasperated

upbraid
[uhp-breyd]

v. to find fault with or reproach severely
질책하다, 호되게 나무라다
His parents are going to **upbraid** him for not passing any of his classes this semester.[35]

syn. scold, censure, castigate

winsome
[win-suhm]

adj. sweetly or innocently charming
마음을 끄는, 매력적인
Even though the model is in her late fifties, she still uses her **winsome** looks to rule the stage.[36]

syn. appealing, charming, engaging

 예문 해석

32 5퍼센트 정도의 어린이들이 말을 더듬는다.   **33** 되도록 간결하게 대답하라.   **34** 그의 성질 사나운 오빠와는 달리, 그녀는 보통 침착하다.   **35** 그의 부모님은 이번 학기에 그가 수업을 하나도 통과하지 못한 것에 대해 그를 꾸짖을 것이다.   **36** 50대 후반의 모델임에도 불구하고 그녀는 여전히 그녀의 매력적인 외모를 이용해 무대를 지배한다.

Directions   Each of the following questions consists of one word followed by five words or phrases. You are to select the one word or phrase whose meaning is closest to the word in capital letters.

1. **AMBIVALENT :**
   (A) hairy
   (B) airborne
   (C) grisly
   (D) conflicting
   (E) putrid

2. **AMELIORATE :**
   (A) squelch
   (B) improve
   (C) blanch
   (D) humidify
   (E) purge

3. **CONFLAGRATION :**
   (A) small income
   (B) huge amount
   (C) short leash
   (D) large fire
   (E) tall tale

4. **DEPLETE :**
   (A) meanwhile
   (B) exhaust
   (C) torturous
   (D) lurid
   (E) arrogant

5. **FEASIBLE :**
   (A) vehement
   (B) soluble
   (C) injurious
   (D) frantic
   (E) possible

6. **ILLUMINATION :**
   (A) light
   (B) maze
   (C) plague
   (D) arcade
   (E) motto

7. **INNUENDO :**
   (A) insinuation
   (B) extrovert
   (C) hypochondriac
   (D) eloquence
   (E) relevancy

8. **MOOT :**
   (A) resourceful
   (B) unerring
   (C) rife
   (D) lavish
   (E) debatable

9. **PRETEXT :**
   (A) quibble
   (B) order
   (C) starvation
   (D) quantity
   (E) null

10. **SCATHING :**
    (A) intense
    (B) biting
    (C) forceful
    (D) wanton
    (E) nautical

"One glance at a book and you hear the voice of another person,
perhaps someone dead for 1,000 years.
To read is to voyage through time."

– Carl Sagan –
American astronomer

책을 한 번만 봐도 당신은 아마 죽은 지 1000년 된 사람의 목소리를 들을 수 있다.
독서는 시간을 거슬러 여행하는 것이다.

Greek and Latin Roots & Prefixes 22

★ RUPT = to break

-ure (n.)	rupture	(인체 내부 장기의) 파열
ab (away from)	abrupt	돌연한, 갑작스러운
bank (shelf)	bankrupt	파산시키다
co (together)	corrupt	부패하게 만들다, 타락시키다
dis (apart)	disrupt	방해하다, 지장을 주다
ex (out)	erupt	(화산이) 분출하다
inter (between)	interrupt	방해하다
dis (apart)	disruption	분열, 중단, 붕괴

DAY

22

WORDS TO LEARN

- ☐ accomplished
- ☐ amble
- ☐ atone
- ☐ blueprint
- ☐ comprise
- ☐ concerned
- ☐ counteract
- ☐ deplore
- ☐ disburse

- ☐ drench
- ☐ enigma
- ☐ exhaustive
- ☐ feeble
- ☐ filibuster
- ☐ gobble
- ☐ hymn
- ☐ impasse
- ☐ incompatible

- ☐ inordinate
- ☐ invincible
- ☐ leeway
- ☐ malinger
- ☐ morale
- ☐ obese
- ☐ overture
- ☐ peruse
- ☐ prodigal

- ☐ ramble
- ☐ resume
- ☐ shiftless
- ☐ simultaneous
- ☐ stance
- ☐ suffice
- ☐ theology
- ☐ unanswerable
- ☐ vigilant

---

01 ···

accomplished
[uh-kom-plisht]

adj. skillful at doing something
뛰어난, 능란한, 조예가 깊은
She is an **accomplished** painter.[1]

syn. skilled, skillful, proficient

02 ···

amble
[am-buhl]

v. to walk slowly
느긋하게 걷다
She **ambled** along the street.[2]

syn. stroll, saunter, ramble

03 ···

atone
[uh-tohn]

v. to make amends for a wrongdoing
속죄하다, 보상하다
Japan has yet to fully **atone** for its militaristic past.[3]

syn. repent, compensate

예문 해석

01 그녀는 숙련된 화가이다. **02** 그녀는 거리를 따라 느긋하게 걸었다. **03** 일본은 군국주의 과거에 대해 아직도 완전히 보상하지 않았다.

04 ·······

blueprint
[bloo-print]

n. a detailed original plan
청사진, 설계도
One of the famous architects made a **blueprint** for my house.[4]

syn. design, plan, guide

05 ·······

comprise
[kuhm-praiz]

v. to include or contain
~로 구성되다, ~로 이루어지다.
If X comprises A, B, and C, then A, B, and C compose X.[5]

syn. contain, make up, consist of

06 ·······

concerned
[kuhn-surnd]

adj. worried
걱정스러운, 염려하는, 근심하는
I was **concerned** about his security.[6]

syn. troubled, anxious

07 ·······

counteract
[koun-ter-akt]

v. to reduce or prevent the effect of something
거스르다, 방해하다
He has to take several pills to **counteract** high blood pressure.[7]

syn. counter, obstruct, prevent

08 ·······

deplore
[dih-plawr]

v. to regret deeply or strongly
비탄하다, 개탄하다, 몹시 한탄하다
Environmentalists **deplore** the fact that restoration has not been made.[8]

syn. lament, regret, bemoan, bewail

예문 해석

04 유명한 건축가 중 한 명이 우리 집의 설계도를 만들었다. **05** 만약 X가 A, B, C로 구성되어 있다면, A, B, C는 X를 구성한다.
06 나는 그의 안위가 걱정되었다. **07** 그는 고혈압을 막기 위해 몇 개의 약을 먹어야 한다. **08** 환경 운동가들은 아직도 복구가
이루어지지 않았다는 사실에 개탄하고 있다.

disburse
[dis-burs]

v. to pay out
지급하다
The bank has **disbursed** over a million dollars for the project.[9]

syn. expend, lay out, spend

drench
[drench]

v. to wet thoroughly
물에 흠뻑 적시다, 액체에 담그다
Trees were **drenched** with rain.[10]

syn. soak, wet, saturate, bathe

enigma
[*uh*-nig-m*uh*]

n. a person or thing that is mysterious
수수께끼, 수수께끼 같은 인물
Refrigerators are an **enigma** to my son.[11]

syn. mystery, riddle, conundrum

exhaustive
[ig-zaws-tiv]

adj. complete
철저한, 남김 없는
This is an **exhaustive** list.[12]

syn. thorough, comprehensive, complete

feeble
[fee-b*uh*l]

adj. weak
약한
Suffering from famine, the children became **feeble** in health.[13]

syn. frail, fragile, flimsy

filibuster
[fil-*uh*-b*uh*s-ter]

n. to obstruct legislation by talking at great length
의사 진행 방해 (의회에서 긴 연설로 투표를 지연시키는 것)
In the United States, a senator may **filibuster** on a bill by speaking on any topic.[14]

syn. obstruction, procrastination, delaying tactic

예문 해석

09 은행은 그 프로젝트를 위해 백만 달러 이상을 지급해왔다.　**10** 나무들이 비에 흠뻑 젖었다.　**11** 내 아들에게 냉장고는 미스터리다.　**12** 이것은 완벽한 리스트이다.　**13** 기아로 인해 아이들의 건강이 쇠약해졌다.　**14** 미국에서는 상원 의원이 어떤 주제에 대해서든 발언함으로써 법안을 필리버스터 할 수 있다.

15 ....

gobble
[gob-*uhl*]

v. to eat hurriedly and noisily
게걸스럽게 먹다
The beast might **gobble** you up.[15]

> *syn.* devour, gulp, guzzle

16 ....

hymn
[him]

n. a song or ode in praise or honor of God
찬송가
The worship service began with a **hymn**.[16]

> *syn.* chant, oratorio, psalm

17 ....

impasse
[im-pas]

n. a situation in which no progress can be made
교착 상태, 딜레마, 곤경
I was at an **impasse**. I couldn't move forward — I could only reverse.[17]

> *syn.* deadlock, stalemate, gridlock

18 ....

incompatible
[in-k*uhm*-pat-*uh*-b*uh*l]

adj. unable to exist together in harmony
서로 맞지 않는, 조화되지 않는
They were utterly **incompatible**.[18]

> *syn.* unsuited, mismatched

19 ....

inordinate
[in-awr-dn-it]

adj. immoderate and excessive
과도한, 지나친
It took an **inordinate** amount of time to do this task.[19]

> *syn.* excessive, exorbitant, extreme

20 ....

invincible
[in-vin-s*uh*-b*uh*l]

adj. unable to be defeated
무적의
He is virtually **invincible**.[20]

> *syn.* indestructible, unconquerable, impregnable

예문 해석

15 그 괴수가 너를 먹어버릴지도 모른다.　**16** 예배는 찬송가로 시작되었다.　**17** 나는 막다른 골목에 있었다. 앞으로 나아갈 수 없고 뒤로 물러설 수만 있었다.　**18** 그들은 서로 맞지 않는다.　**19** 이 작업에는 말도 안 될 만큼 엄청난 시간이 소요된다.　**20** 그는 사실상 무적이었다.

21

leeway
[lee-wey]

n. the amount of freedom available
재량, (자신이 원하는 대로 선택하거나 변경할 수 있는) 자유
She thinks everyone has a ten-minute **leeway** when meeting friends.[21]

syn. latitude, room to move, margin

22

malinger
[muh-ling-ger]

v. avoid responsibilities and duties by pretending to be ill
꾀병을 부리다, 아픈 척 해서 의무를 피하다
Lying about a stomachache, holding the thermometer near a light bulb, refusing to get out of bed, moaning — these are classic tactics of those who **malinger**.[22]

syn. dodge, shun, shirk

23

morale
[muh-ral]

n. the emotional condition of a person or group
사기, 의욕
The **morale** of his team had plummeted.[23]

syn. spirit, vigor, assurance

24

obese
[oh-bees]

adj. extremely fat
비만한
Obese people tend to have higher blood pressure than lean people.[24]

syn. corpulent, stout, overweight

25

overture
[oh-ver-cher]

n. an orchestral introduction to an opera, oratorio or ballet
(오페라나 발레 등의) 서곡
The program opened with the **overture**.[25]

syn. prelude, preliminary

 예문 해석

21 그녀는 모든 사람이 친구를 만날 때 10분 정도는 여유가 있다고 생각한다. **22** 배가 아파서 누워있고, 전구 근처에 온도계를 들고 있고, 침대에서 일어나기를 거부하고, 신음하는 것, 이것이 바로 꾀병을 부리는 사람들의 전형적인 전술이다. **23** 팀의 사기는 뚝 떨어졌다. **24** 비만한 사람들은 날씬한 사람들보다 고혈압일 경향이 많다. **25** 연주 프로그램은 서곡으로 시작되었다.

peruse
[puh-rooz]

v. to read through with thoroughness or care
꼼꼼하게 읽다, 정독하다, 탐독하다
The editor **perused** his manuscript, checking for grammatical errors.[26]

syn. read, pore over, examine

prodigal
[prod-i-guhl]

adj. heedlessly extravagant or wasteful
낭비하는, 방탕한
The **prodigal** expenditures were incurred for construction.[27]

syn. extravagant, lavish, profligate

ramble
[ram-buhl]

v. to walk for pleasure
어슬렁거리다, 산책하다, 거닐다
They **rambled** about in the countryside.[28]

syn. wander, amble, roam

resume
[ri-zoom]

v. to start again
다시 시작하다
The search will **resume** early tomorrow.[29]

syn. restart, recommence

shiftless
[shift-lis]

adj. lacking ambition or initiative
아무 의욕이 없는, 꿈도 야망도 없는
He was so **shiftless** that he tried to avoid hard work at any cost.[30]

syn. slothful, lazy, indolent

simultaneous
[sai-muhl-tey-nee-uhs]

adj. existing, occurring, or operating at the same time
동시에 일어난
Around the country, there was a **simultaneous** moment of silence in respect for the fallen heroes.[31]

syn. synchronous, coincident, concurrent

예문 해석

26 그 편집자는 원고에 문법적 오류가 있는지 체크하며 꼼꼼히 읽었다. **27** 건설에 낭비되는 비용이 발생했다. **28** 그들은 시골 길을 산책했다. **29** 수색은 내일 아침 일찍 다시 시작될 것이다. **30** 그는 아무 의욕이 없어서 무슨 수를 써서라도 힘든 일을 피하려고 했다. **31** 전국 곳곳에서는 희생된 영웅들을 추모하는 침묵이 동시에 흘렀다.

32

stance
[stans]

n. a position or manner of standing

발의 위치, 선 자세, 태도, 입장

Take a comfortably wide **stance** and flex your knees a little.[32]

syn. posture, carriage, deportment

33

suffice
[suh-fais]

v. to be enough

만족시키다. 충분하다

A shorter answer will **suffice**.[33]

syn. satisfy, be adequate, get by

34

theology
[thee-ol-uh-jee]

n. the study of the nature of God and of divine things

신학

He attended a college of **theology**.[34]

syn. religious theory, belief, creed

35

unanswerable
[uhn-an-ser-uh-buhl]

adj. not capable of being answered or not open to dispute or rebuttal

반박할 수 없는, 결정적인

The **unanswerable** proof convicted the suspect for murder.[35]

syn. conclusive, absolute, definite

36

vigilant
[vij-uh-luhnt]

adj. ready for possible trouble or danger

조심하는, 경계하는

The government warned the public to be **vigilant**, and report anything suspicious.[36]

syn. wary, watchful, cautious

 예문 해석

32 발을 편안하게 벌려 서고, 무릎을 약간 굽히세요.　**33** 짧은 대답이어도 충분하다.　**34** 그는 신학 대학을 다녔다.　**35** 그 반박할 수 없는 증거는 용의자에게 살인죄를 선고하게 했다.　**36** 정부는 대중들에게 경계하며 무엇이든 의심스러운 것은 신고하라고 경고했다.

Directions   Each of the following questions consists of one word followed by five words or phrases. You are to select the one word or phrase whose meaning is closest to the word in capital letters.

1. **ATONE :**
   (A) incite
   (B) lubricate
   (C) awaken
   (D) oblige
   (E) repent

2. **COMPRISE :**
   (A) contain
   (B) detain
   (C) enunciate
   (D) gallop
   (E) imbibe

3. **ENIGMA :**
   (A) inquisition
   (B) mystery
   (C) inventiveness
   (D) jaunt
   (E) discourse

4. **EXHAUSTIVE :**
   (A) savory
   (B) thorough
   (C) comely
   (D) offensive
   (E) casual

5. **FILIBUSTER :**
   (A) obstruction
   (B) figurine
   (C) epilogue
   (D) proscenium
   (E) epiphany

6. **IMPASSE :**
   (A) inequity
   (B) candor
   (C) deadlock
   (D) inkling
   (E) reluctance

7. **LEEWAY :**
   (A) lampoon
   (B) expert
   (C) unfathomable
   (D) latitude
   (E) sluggishness

8. **MORALE :**
   (A) spirit
   (B) anthology
   (C) placebo
   (D) lesson
   (E) confluence

9. **SHIFTLESS :**
   (A) genuine
   (B) slothful
   (C) wily
   (D) chary
   (E) prophetic

10. **STANCE :**
    (A) posture
    (B) remedy
    (C) gratis
    (D) vehemence
    (E) shortcomings

"Change is the law of life. And those who look only to the past
or present are certain to miss the future."

— John F. Kennedy —
35th president of the U.S.

변화는 삶의 법칙이다. 과거와 현재만 보는 사람은 미래를 분명 놓치게 될 것이다.

Greek and Latin Roots & Prefixes 23

★ PLI = to fold

ad (toward)	apply	신청하다, 지원하다, 적용하다
com (together)	comply	따르다, 순응하다
	compliant	순응하는, 말을 잘 듣는
	complicate	복잡하게 만들다
duo (two)	duplicate	복제하다
im/in (into)	imply	암시하다
	implicate	(범죄에) 연루되었음을 보여주다
	implication	함축, 암시
ex (out)	explicate	설명하다, 해석하다
in (not) + ex (out)	inexplicable	설명할 수 없는, 불가해한

DAY

23

WORDS TO LEARN

☐ accord	☐ divert	☐ inquire	☐ rampant
☐ amenable	☐ elevate	☐ invoke	☐ resurrect
☐ atrocity	☐ exhibit	☐ languid	☐ scoff
☐ bluff	☐ feign	☐ locomotive	☐ sink
☐ chide	☐ fraternal	☐ morbid	☐ stare
☐ concord	☐ gossamer	☐ obituary	☐ suffocate
☐ courteous	☐ heave	☐ parameter	☐ therapeutic
☐ demoralize	☐ illusory	☐ pervade	☐ unaffected
☐ discard	☐ incongruous	☐ pristine	☐ vigor

01

accord
[uh-kawrd]

n. an agreement between groups or even nations
일치, 화합
The two parties were in **accord**.[1]

syn. agreement, harmony, unanimity

02

amenable
[uh-mee-nuh-buhl]

adj. ready or willing to answer or agree, or yield
말을 잘 듣는, ~을 잘 받아들이는
She was **amenable** to change.[2]

syn. willing, obedient, cooperative

03

atrocity
[uh-tros-i-tee]

n. an act of extreme cruelty
잔혹 행위, 악행
The **atrocity** in Congo shocked us all.[3]

syn. cruelness, offensiveness, barbarity

📖 예문 해석

01 두 정당은 합의에 이르렀다.　**02** 그녀는 변화에 순응했다.　**03** 콩고에서 행해진 잔혹 행위는 우리 모두에게 충격을 주었다.

04

bluff
[bluhf]

v. to frighten someone by pretending to be stronger than one really is

허세 부려 속이다, 얻다

With his fake resume, he **bluffed** his way into a new job.[4]

syn. trick, deceive, pretend

05

chide
[chaid]

v. to criticize or blame

꾸짖다

She knew when to praise and when to **chide**.[5]

syn. criticize, blame, scold

06

concord
[kon-kawrd]

n. unity or harmony

일치, 조화, 화합

There was complete **concord** among the team members.[6]

syn. harmony, unity, agreement

07

courteous
[kur-tee-uhs]

adj. polite

예의 바른, 정중한, 친절한

Her answer was **courteous** but firm.[7]

syn. polite, decorous, civil

08

demoralize
[dih-mawr-*uh*-laiz]

v. to deprive a person of courage or spirit

사기를 꺾다, 의기소침하게 만들다

Those health problems **demoralized** him.[8]

syn. discourage, dishearten, unnerve

09

discard
[di-skahrd]

v. to cast aside or get rid of

버리다

Each player can **discard** some of his seven cards.[9]

syn. desert, abandon, forsake

예문 해석

04 가짜 이력서로 그는 새로운 일자리를 얻어냈다.   **05** 그녀는 칭찬할 때와 야단칠 때를 알고 있었다.   **06** 팀 멤버들 간 완벽한 조화가 있었다.   **07** 그녀의 대답은 정중했지만 확고했다.   **08** 그 건강 문제들은 그의 사기를 꺾었다.   **09** 그녀는 불신에 차서 그를 쳐다 보았다.

10

divert
[dih-vurt]

v. to shift or turn from one thing to another
기분 전환하다, (생각이나 분위기를) 바꾸다
Because her friend couldn't stop worrying about her grades, she **diverted** her with the latest school gossip.[10]

> syn. amuse, entertain, recreate

11

elevate
[el-*uh*-veyt]

v. to raise from a lower to a higher position
올리다, 높이다
One way to **elevate** your mood is to exercise or dance.[11]

> syn. lift up, heighten, raise

12

exhibit
[ig-zib-it]

v. to present
보여주다, 전시하다
The motor show **exhibits** the latest models of cars.[12]

> syn. manifest, display

13

feign
[feyn]

v. to pretend
가장하다, 척하다
She **feigned** sickness.[13]

> syn. pretend, affect, fake

14

fraternal
[fru*uh*-tur-nl]

adj. of a brother or brothers
형제의
My oldest friend and I have a **fraternal** relationship like real brothers.[14]

> syn. brotherly, congenial

15

gossamer
[gos-*uh*-mer]

adj. something extremely light, flimsy, or delicate
섬세한 거미줄 같은, 얇고 가벼운
The **gossamer** gold necklace was handled with care.[15]

> syn. delicate, flimsy

예문 해석

10 친구가 성적에 대한 걱정을 계속했기 때문에, 그녀는 최근 학교 소문으로 화제를 돌렸다.　**11** 기분을 좋게 하는 한 가지 방법은 운동이나 춤을 추는 것이다.　**12** 모터쇼는 최신 차 모델들을 전시한다.　**13** 그녀는 아픈 척 했다.　**14** 나의 가장 오래된 친구와 나는 친형제처럼 친하게 지낸다.　**15** 그 섬세한 금 목걸이는 조심스럽게 다뤄졌다.

16 ··

heave
[heev]

v. to raise or lift with effort or force
힘주어 들어올리다
He **heaved** the last stone into place.[16]

syn. hoist, lift

17 ··

illusory
[i-loo-*suh*-ree]

adj. based on illusion
(실제가 아니라) 환상에 불과한, 현혹시키는
The security of his mansion was **illusory**.[17]

syn. deceptive, misleading

18 ··

incongruous
[in-kong-groo-*uhs*]

adj. not harmonious
어울리지 않는, 부적절한
Her tutu looked **incongruous** with her army coat.[18]

syn. inharmonious, disharmonious, discordant

19 ··

inquire
[in-kwai*uhr*]

v. to ask for information
질문을 하다, 묻다
'Is something wrong?' she **inquired**.[19]

syn. ask, inspect, interrogate

20 ··

invoke
[in-vohk]

v. ask for aid or protection
빌다, 기원하다, 기도하다
She **invoked** God's blessing.[20]

syn. appeal, call for, pray

21 ··

languid
[lang-gwid]

adj. lacking in energy or vitality
나른한, 노곤한, 활발하지 못한, 축 늘어진
He was a tall and **languid** figure.[21]

syn. listless, flagging, lackadaisical

예문 해석

16 그는 마지막 돌을 들여다 놓았다. **17** 그의 대저택의 안전성은 환상에 불과했다. **18** 그녀의 발레 스커트는 군복 코트와는 안 어울리는 듯 했다. **19** '무슨 문제 있나요?' 그녀가 물었다. **20** 그녀는 신의 축복을 빌었다. **21** 그는 키가 크고 지친 모습이었다.

22

locomotive
[loh-kuh-moh-tiv]

n. a large vehicle that pulls a railway train

기관차

Thomas the Tank engine is a steam **locomotive**.[22]

syn. train, engine

23

morbid
[mawr-bid]

adj. unwholesomely gloomy, sensitive, extreme

병적인, 불건전한, 무시무시한

The scene of the accident was a **morbid** sight.[23]

syn. ghastly, nasty, sickly

24

obituary
[oh-bich-oo-er-ee]

n. a notice of the death of a person

부고 기사, 사망 기사

The **obituary** appeared in the local paper.[24]

syn. death notice, eulogy, obit

25

parameter
[puh-ram-i-ter]

n. any factor that defines a system and limits its performance

한도, 한계

The natural world sets specific **parameters**, like gravity and time.[25]

syn. boundary, rule, limit

26

pervade
[per-veyd]

v. to spread or extend throughout something

널리 퍼지다, 고루 미치다

The smell of happiness **pervaded** the whole house.[26]

syn. permeate, imbue, diffuse

27

pristine
[pris-teen]

adj. having its original purity

완전히 새것 같은, 아주 깨끗한

At dawn, the beaches were **pristine** and beautiful.[27]

syn. intact, unsullied, immaculate

예문 해석

22 토마스는 증기기관차이다.　**23** 사고 장면은 참혹했다.　**24** 그 부고 기사는 지역신문에 실렸다.　**25** 자연계는 중력과 시간과 같은 특정한 한도를 설정합니다.　**26** 행복의 향기가 온 집안에 퍼졌다.　**27** 새벽에 해변은 자연 그대로였으며 아름다웠다.

28

rampant
[ramp-ant]

adj. spreading everywhere in a way that cannot be controlled
(병이나 소문 등이) 마구 퍼지는, 무성한
Racism was illegal but **rampant**.[28]

syn. uncontrolled, wild, wanton

29

resurrect
[rez-uh-rekt]

v. to bring someone back to life
부활시키다, 소생시키다
The phoenix's ability to **resurrect** from its own ashes is its
defining characteristic.[29]

syn. revive, resuscitate, revitalize

30

scoff
[skawf]

v. to express scorn or contempt
비웃다, 조롱하다
You may **scoff**, but I honestly feel scared.[30]

syn. mock, ridicule, jeer, sneer scoundrel

31

sink
[singk]

v. to fall, drop, or descend gradually to a lower level
가라앉다, 침몰하다
The battleship **sank** within an hour.[31]

syn. founder, descend, fall

32

stare
[stair]

v. to look with a fixed gaze
응시하다, 노려보다
She **stared** at him in disbelief, shaking her head.[32]

syn. gaze, gape

33

suffocate
[suhf-uh-keyt]

v. to die because there is no air to breathe
질식하다, 질식시키다
They were **suffocated** as they slept.[33]

syn. smother, choke, stifle

예문 해석

28 인종차별은 불법이지만 만연하게 퍼져 있다. **29** 자신이 불탄 재에서 다시 부활하는 능력은 불사조만의 특징이다. **30** 당신은 비웃을지 모르지만 나는 두렵다. **31** 군함은 한 시간도 안돼 가라앉았다. **32** 그녀는 의심의 눈초리로 그를 노려보며 머리를 저었다. **33** 그들은 자면서 질식하였다.

34 ....

therapeutic
[ther-*uh*-pyoo-tik]

adj. tending to cure or restore to health
치료의, 치료법의
She considered shopping for shoes to be a **therapeutic** activity for her depression.[34]

syn. curative, remedial, healing

35 ....

unaffected
[uhn-uh-fek-tid]

adj. free from insincerity
진실된, 꾸미지 않은
She showed an **unaffected** smile at him.[35]

syn. sincere, genuine, unpretentious

36 ....

vigor
[vig-er]

n. great strength and energy of body or mind
정력, 힘, 활력
She still has **vigor**.[36]

syn. energy, power, strength

 예문 해석

34 그녀는 신발 쇼핑이 우울증에 대한 치료법이라고 생각했다. **35** 그녀는 그에게 꾸미지 않은 미소를 보여주었다. **36** 그녀는 아직 정정하다.

Directions Each of the following questions consists of one word followed by five words or phrases. You are to select the one word or phrase whose meaning is closest to the word in capital letters.

1. ACCORD :
(A) agreement
(B) defamation
(C) gorge
(D) conspiracy
(E) affiliation

2. ATROCITY :
(A) specter
(B) comprehension
(C) ignorance
(D) analogy
(E) cruelness

3. DEMORALIZE :
(A) allay
(B) vex
(C) discourage
(D) implore
(E) commence

4. DIVERT :
(A) bungle
(B) amuse
(C) smolder
(D) polish
(E) deceive

5. FEIGN :
(A) fabricate
(B) indict
(C) pretend
(D) jabber
(E) ruminate

6. INQUIRE :
(A) surpass
(B) give
(C) trick
(D) ask
(E) overrule

7. MORBID :
(A) collected
(B) ghastly
(C) efficient
(D) optimistic
(E) titular

8. PRISTINE :
(A) discriminating
(B) intact
(C) insolvent
(D) prolific
(E) fortuitous

9. RESURRECT :
(A) acquiesce
(B) improvise
(C) revive
(D) verify
(E) bewilder

10. VIGOR :
(A) patrician
(B) casualty
(C) power
(D) dispute
(E) forte

"We aim above the mark to hit the mark."

— Ralph Waldo Emerson —

American essayist, philosopher, poet, and leader of the Transcendentalist movement in the early 19th century

성공하고 싶다면 목표를 높게 잡아라.

Greek and Latin Roots & Prefixes 24

★ STRUCT = to build

-ure (n.)	structure	구조
con (together)	constructive	건설적인
de (down)	destructive	파괴적인
in (in)	instruct	지시하다
mis (badly)	misconstrue	오해하다
ob (in the way of)	obstruct	막다
re (again)	reconstruct	재건하다
sub (down)	substructure	하부구조

DAY

24

WORDS TO LEARN

☐ acme	☐ droop	☐ inquisitive	☐ proficient
☐ anomaly	☐ enlighten	☐ involuntary	☐ ranch
☐ attire	☐ exhilarate	☐ languish	☐ resuscitate
☐ bluster	☐ felony	☐ lofty	☐ scornful
☐ choleric	☐ frail	☐ meddlesome	☐ skeptical
☐ concoct	☐ gourmet	☐ moribund	☐ stark
☐ covet	☐ hectic	☐ objective	☐ suite
☐ depot	☐ illustrate	☐ palpable	☐ threshold
☐ discerning	☐ inconsolable	☐ petition	☐ vilify

01

acme
[ak-mee]

n. the highest point
절정, 정점
The team reached its **acme** when it won the Olympic gold medal.[1]

syn. summit, peak, apex

02

anomaly
[uh-nom-uh-lee]

n. a deviation from the common rule or type
변칙, 이례
He had to reproduce the experiment over a hundred times to find the **anomaly**.[2]

syn. irregularity, aberration, inconsistency

03

attire
[*uh*-tai*uh*r]

n. clothing of a distinctive style or for a particular occasion
의류
More schools are getting stricter about student **attire**.[3]

syn. apparel, garment, clothes

예문 해석

01 그 팀은 올림픽 금메달을 땄을 때 절정에 달했다. **02** 그는 변칙을 찾기 위해 백 번 이상 실험을 재현해야 했다. **03** 많은 학교가 학생들의 옷차림에 점점 더 엄격해지고 있다.

04

bluster
[bluhs-ter]

v. to make loud empty threats or protests
엄포를 놓다, 위협하다
"If you do such a thing again," **blustered** his coach, "You will never have a chance to run a race."[4]

syn. intimidate, bully, browbeat

05

choleric
[kol-er-ik]

adj. extremely irritable or easily angered
화를 잘 내는, 걸핏하면 화를 내는
Since she could not sleep well, she was **choleric** when someone called her again and again.[5]

syn. irascible, peevish, petulant

06

concoct
[kon-kokt]

v. to prepare or make by combining ingredients
섞어서 만들다, 이야기를 지어내다
She **concocted** a meal from leftovers.[6]

syn. devise, make up, contrive

07

covet
[kuhv-it]

v. to desire wrongfully
탐내다
She **covets** her friend's luck.[7]

syn. envy, crave, hanker

08

depot
[dee-poh]

n. a storehouse or warehouse
창고, 보관소
I went to a **depot** to get an assortment of building materials.[8]

syn. warehouse, silo, storehouse

📖 예문 해석

04 "한 번만 더 그런 행동을 하면 다시는 레이스에 참여하지 못할 거야"라고 코치는 엄포를 놓았다. **05** 그녀는 잠을 잘 자지 못했기 때문에, 누군가가 계속해서 그녀에게 전화를 걸었을 때, 그녀는 쉽게 화를 냈다. **06** 그녀는 남은 것들로 식사를 만들었다. **07** 그녀는 친구의 행운을 탐낸다. **08** 나는 건축 자재를 구하러 창고로 갔다.

discerning
[di-sur-ning]

adj. showing good or outstanding judgment
통찰력이 있는, 총명한
He was a **discerning** critic of English poetry. [9]

syn. discriminating, sharp, insightful

droop
[droop]

v, to hang down as from weakness, exhaustion, or lack of support
숙이다, 축 늘어지다
He **drooped** his head in shame.[10]

syn. stoop, bend, bow

enlighten
[en-lait-n]

v. to make the facts clear someone
계몽하다, 교육하다, 교화하다
He **enlightened** his sister about philosophy.[11]

syn. edify, teach, inform

exhilarate
[ig-zil-uh-reyt]

v. to make cheerful or merry
기분을 들뜨게 하다
The nice weather **exhilarated** us.[12]

syn. elate, thrill, excite

felony
[fel-uh-nee]

n. a serious crime
중죄 (살인, 방화, 강도 등)
Felonies are more serious crimes than misdemeanors.[13]

syn. offense, crime, assault

frail
[freil]

adj. weak, not robust
깨지기 쉬운, 약한, 건강하지 못한
The **frail** grandmother had gray hair, and she walked with a cane.[14]

syn. fragile, feeble, flimsy

예문 해석

09 그는 통찰력 있는 영시 비평가였다.　**10** 그는 부끄러움에 고개를 떨궜다.　**11** 그는 여동생에게 철학을 깨우치게 했다.　**12** 좋은 날씨가 우리를 들뜨게 만들었다.　**13** 중죄는 경범죄보다 심각한 범죄이다.　**14** 허약한 할머니는 머리가 희끗희끗해서 지팡이를 짚고 걸었다.

15

gourmet
[goor-mey]

n. a connoisseur of fine food and drink
식도락가, 미식가
He is a **gourmet** who is addicted to the pleasures of the table.[15]

syn. epicure, gastronome, bon vivant

16

hectic
[hek-tik]

adj. characterized by intense agitation or excitement
열광적인
It can be **hectic** when the whole family gets together.[16]

syn. frantic, frenzied, excited

17

illustrate
[il-uh-streyt]

v. to make clear
설명하다, 예시로 보여주다
To prevent misunderstandings, let me **illustrate**.[17]

syn. exemplify, demonstrate, present

18

inconsolable
[in-kuhn-soh-luh-buhl]

adj. very sad and cannot be comforted
매우 슬퍼하는, 너무 슬퍼 위로할 길이 없는
When my grandmother died, I was **inconsolable**.[18]

syn. brokenhearted, disconsolate, dejected

19

inquisitive
[in-kwiz-i-tiv]

adj. have a great interest in learning new things
알고 싶어하는, 호기심이 많은
She has an **inquisitive** mind.[19]

syn. curious, inquiring, investigative

20

involuntary
[in-vol-uhn-ter-ee]

adj. not voluntary
자기도 모르게 하는, 무심결의
She gave an **involuntary** shudder.[20]

syn. automatic, unintentional, unconscious

예문 해석

15 그는 맛있는 음식에 집착하는 미식가이다.　**16** 가족들이 다 모이면 정신이 하나도 없다.　**17** 오해를 미리 방지하기 위하여 제가 설명해 드리겠습니다.　**18** 할머니가 돌아가셨을 때 나는 너무 슬펐다.　**19** 그녀는 호기심이 많다.　**20** 그녀는 자기도 모르게 몸서리를 쳤다.

21 ···

languish
[lang-gwish]

v. to become dispirited
기운이 없어지다, 나른해지다
People were **languishing** during the prolonged heat wave.[21]

syn. droop, deteriorate, dwindle

22 ···

lofty
[lawf-tee]

adj. haughty or proud
높으신, 고상한, 거만한
She was considered **lofty** among her friends.[22]

syn. haughty, supercilious, superior

23 ···

meddlesome
[med-l-suhm]

adj. interfering
간섭하기 좋아하는, 참견하는
She is the most **meddlesome** person I know.[23]

syn. nosy, officious, intrusive

24 ···

moribund
[mawr-uh-buhnd]

adj. being on the point of death
다 죽어가는, 빈사 상태의, 소멸해가는
We need to provide financial support to revive the **moribund** venture companies.[24]

syn. dying, doomed, fated

25 ···

objective
[uhb-jek-tiv]

n. aim or purpose
목적, 목표
The **object** of this donation party is to raise funds for the children's charities.[25]

syn. purpose, aim, point, goal

 예문 해석

21 사람들은 오랫동안 온열이 지속되자 나른해졌다.   **22** 그녀는 친구들 사이에서 고귀한 사람으로 여겨졌다.   **23** 그녀는 내가 아는 사람 중 가장 참견하기 좋아하는 사람이다.   **24** 다 망해가는 벤처 회사들을 살리기 위해서는 재정적 지원을 제공하는 것이 필요하다.   **25** 이 자선 파티의 목적은 아동 자선 단체를 위한 모금이다.

palpable
[pal-puh-buhl]

adj. readily or plainly seen or heard
감지할 수 있는, 뚜렷한, 손에 만져질 듯한
There was a **palpable** excitement in the air as the city prepared for the New Year Countdown.[26]

syn. perceptible, obvious, apparent

---

petition
[puh-tish-uhn]

n. a request made for something desired
청원, 탄원
The pastor made a **petition** to God for courage and strength.[27]

syn. request, beg, entreaty

---

proficient
[pruh-fish-uhnt]

adj. skillful or skilled
솜씨 있는, 숙련된
You should be **proficient** in one or two foreign languages.[28]

syn. adept, talented, skillful

---

ranch
[ran-ch]

n. a large farm
농장, 목장
He breeds horses on his **ranch**.[29]

syn. farm, cattle farm, corral

---

resuscitate
[ri-suhs-i-teyt]

v. to make someone breathe again
(인공 호흡 등으로) 죽어가는 사람을 살리다
Once I realized she could not breath, I performed CPR to help **resuscitate** her.[30]

syn. resurrect, revive, revitalize

---

scornful
[skawrn-fuhl]

adj. full of scorn
조롱하는, 비웃는
He smiled in a **scornful** way.[31]

syn. derisive, contemptuous, disdainful

예문 해석

26 도시가 새해 카운트다운을 준비하자 흥분의 기운이 역력했다. **27** 목사는 용기와 힘을 달라고 하나님께 간청했다. **28** 외국어 한두 개 정도는 능통하게 해야 한다. **29** 그는 농장에서 말을 키운다. **30** 그녀가 숨을 쉴 수 없다는 것을 알았을 때, 나는 그녀를 소생시키는 것을 돕기 위해 심폐소생술을 시행했다. **31** 그는 비웃는 듯 웃었다.

32 ··

skeptical
[skep-ti-kuhl]

adj. showing doubt

의심 많은, 회의적인, 믿지 않는

Other archaeologists are **skeptical** about his findings.[32]

syn. doubtful, suspicious, dubious

33 ··

stark
[stahrk]

adj. extremely simple or severe

적나라한, 황량한

List at least five **stark** differences between A and B.[33]

syn. bleak, desolate, grim

34 ··

suite
[sweet]

n. a set of matching furniture or rooms

세트, 모음곡, (몇 개의 방으로 이루어진) 스위트룸

The traveling band has to sleep in hotel **suites** while on tour.[34]

syn. set, group, matching set

35 ··

threshold
[thresh-ohld]

n. the sill of a doorway

문지방, 입구, 발단, 시초

The home was so old, the **threshold** needed to be replaced.[35]

syn. sill, doorsill, opening

36 ··

vilify
[vil-*uh*-fai]

v. to speak ill of

비난하다, 비방하다

The politician wrote a column on the paper to **vilify** his opponent.[36]

syn. defame, slander, malign

 예문 해석

32 다른 고고학자들은 그의 발견에 대해 회의적이었다.　**33** A와 B 사이의 극명한 대조를 보이는 것을 적어도 5개 이상 열거하시오　**34** 여행 밴드는 투어 중에 호텔 스위트룸에서 자야 한다.　**35** 그 집은 너무 낡아서 문턱을 교체해야 했다.　**36** 그 정치인은 상대방을 비방하기 위해 그 신문에 칼럼을 썼다.

Directions   Each of the following questions consists of one word followed by five words or phrases. You are to select the one word or phrase whose meaning is closest to the word in capital letters.

1. **ACME :**
   (A) arbiter
   (B) confidant
   (C) apiary
   (D) summit
   (E) anticipation

2. **CHOLERIC :**
   (A) irascible
   (B) elusive
   (C) forceful
   (D) emphatic
   (E) notorious

3. **COVET :**
   (A) supersede
   (B) plunder
   (C) bewitch
   (D) enthrall
   (E) envy

4. **ENLIGHTEN :**
   (A) incur
   (B) censure
   (C) abut
   (D) genuflect
   (E) edify

5. **EXHILARATE :**
   (A) stratify
   (B) allocate
   (C) elate
   (D) betray
   (E) crucify

6. **FELONY :**
   (A) axiom
   (B) offense
   (C) gaffe
   (D) fission
   (E) aversion

7. **PALPABLE :**
   (A) perceptible
   (B) copious
   (C) impulsive
   (D) illegal
   (E) cowering

8. **RESUSCITATE :**
   (A) acquit
   (B) incriminate
   (C) resurrect
   (D) embellish
   (E) concur

9. **SUITE :**
   (A) set
   (B) embodiment
   (C) will
   (D) confrontation
   (E) incarnation

10. **VILIFY :**
   (A) align
   (B) condense
   (C) assault
   (D) repudiate
   (E) defame

Directions   Each of the following questions consists of one word followed by five words or phrases. You are to select the one word or phrase whose meaning is closest to the word in capital letters.

1. DISCLAIM :
- (A) vindicate
- (B) cheat
- (C) bestow
- (D) deny
- (E) compound

2. FERVENT :
- (A) bold
- (B) haughty
- (C) enthusiastic
- (D) extravagant
- (E) maritime

3. INVIGORATE :
- (A) commend
- (B) pray
- (C) broach
- (D) stimulate
- (E) condense

4. LUCID :
- (A) evident
- (B) academic
- (C) general
- (D) well-known
- (E) adaptable

5. BLUEPRINT :
- (A) husk
- (B) viewpoint
- (C) design
- (D) inventory
- (E) turncoat

6. DEPLORE :
- (A) lament
- (B) extol
- (C) facilitate
- (D) swerve
- (E) entreat

7. INVINCIBLE :
- (A) faux
- (B) indestructible
- (C) parched
- (D) jaded
- (E) auspicious

8. OBESE :
- (A) corpulent
- (B) immutable
- (C) sensible
- (D) manifest
- (E) humid

9. VIGILANT :
- (A) enduring
- (B) wary
- (C) harmful
- (D) lethargic
- (E) solicitous

10. SKEPTICAL :
- (A) mere
- (B) subjective
- (C) contrary
- (D) vague
- (E) doubtful

11. **CHIDE :**
    (A) criticize
    (B) adjust
    (C) proclaim
    (D) concur
    (E) nettle

12. **COURTEOUS :**
    (A) chic
    (B) listless
    (C) shrewd
    (D) tranquil
    (E) polite

13. **INVOKE :**
    (A) blow
    (B) cater
    (C) decant
    (D) comprehend
    (E) appeal

14. **SCOFF :**
    (A) compress
    (B) vanquish
    (C) mock
    (D) amass
    (E) forbid

15. **UNAFFECTED :**
    (A) drowsy
    (B) flabby
    (C) sincere
    (D) odd
    (E) inflexible

16. **CONCOCT :**
    (A) expunge
    (B) germinate
    (C) abolish
    (D) cloy
    (E) devise

17. **OBJECTIVE :**
    (A) thesis
    (B) purpose
    (C) gift
    (D) trivia
    (E) catalyst

18. **PETITION :**
    (A) accusation
    (B) indictment
    (C) annex
    (D) illegitimacy
    (E) request

19. **SCORNFUL :**
    (A) mild
    (B) assuring
    (C) grovel
    (D) derisive
    (E) broad-minded

20. **STARK :**
    (A) frank
    (B) bleak
    (C) singed
    (D) obedient
    (E) charred

"Repeat," "Repeat," that is the best medicine for memory.

— Talmud —
a record of rabbinic discussions pertaining to Jewish law, ethics, customs, and history

반복하고, 또 반복하라, 그것이 기억에 가장 좋은 약이다.

Greek and Latin Roots & Prefixes 25

★ TRACT = to pull

-able (adj.)	tractable	다루기 쉬운
ad (toward)	attractive	관심을 끄는
ab (away from)	abstract	추상적인
con (together)	contract	계약
de (down)	detract	나쁘게 말하다, 헐뜯다
dis (away)	distract	집중이 안 되게 하다, 주의를 딴 데로 돌리다
ex (out)	extract	추출하다, 뽑아내다
pro (in the way of)	protract	오래 끌다, 연장하다
re (again)	retract	(전에 한 말을) 철회하다
sub (down)	subtract	(계산식에서) 빼다

DAY

25

WORDS TO LEARN

☐ accrue	☐ dub	☐ insanity	☐ rancor
☐ amiable	☐ enmity	☐ iota	☐ reconciliation
☐ attribute	☐ exhort	☐ labyrinth	☐ scoundrel
☐ blunt	☐ ferment	☐ log	☐ skinflint
☐ complexion	☐ frantic	☐ mediate	☐ stupefy
☐ congenial	☐ groundless	☐ morose	☐ sullen
☐ crafty	☐ heed	☐ parole	☐ thrifty
☐ depravity	☐ illustrious	☐ petrify	☐ uncommitted
☐ discreet	☐ incorporate	☐ profound	☐ vindicate

01 ···

accrue
[*uh*-kroo]

v. to increase over a period of time
생기다, 붙다
The interest **accrued** at a rate of 8%.[1]

syn. accumulate, grow, increase

02 ···

amiable
[ey-mee-*uh*-b*uh*l]

adj. having or showing pleasant, goodnatured personal qualities
호감을 주는, 상냥한, 붙임성 있는
The student was presented with an award that amplified her **amiable** character.[2]

syn. agreeable, affable, friendly

03 ···

attribute
[a-trib-yoot]

n. a quality or feature
성격, 특징
Sympathy is a normal **attribute** of human beings.[3]

syn. disposition, characteristic, trait

예문 해석

01 그 이자는 8%씩 붙는다.　**02** 그 학생은 상냥한 성격을 더 강조해주는 상을 받았다.　**03** 동정은 인간의 일반적인 특성이다.

04

blunt
[bl*uh*nt]

adj. not sharp
둔한, 무딘
You can make thick marks with a **blunt** pencil.[4]

syn. callous, dull, worn

05

complexion
[k*uh*m-plek-sh*uh*n]

n. the natural color, texture, and appearance of the skin, especially of the face
안색, 피부색
His **complexion** was pale as if he seldom spent a lot of time outside.[5]

syn. appearance, hue, texture

06

congenial
[k*uh*n-jeen-y*uh*l]

adj. easy to get along with
마음이 맞는, 성격에 맞는
She loved the **congenial** atmosphere of her boarding school library.[6]

syn. compatible, affable, agreeable

07

crafty
[kraf-tee]

adj. skillful and underhanded
교활한
Their plot to evade taxes was very **crafty**.[7]

syn. sly, cunning, artful, deceitful, wily

08

depravity
[di-prav-i-tee]

n. very dishonest or immoral behavior
타락, 부패
Even he was surprised by his own **depravity**.[8]

syn. corruption, wickedness, vice

예문 해석

04 뭉툭한 연필로 두꺼운 선을 그릴 수 있다.   **05** 그의 안색은 거의 밖에서 시간을 보내지 않은 것처럼 창백했다.   **06** 그녀는 기숙학교 도서관의 화기애애한 분위기를 사랑했다.   **07** 그들의 탈세 음모는 매우 교활했다.   **08** 그조차도 스스로의 타락에 놀랐다.

discreet
[dih-skreet]

adj. judicious in one's conduct or speech
신중한, 조심스러운
His trusted **discreet** secretary is always quiet, prudent, and restrained.[9]

syn. prudent, attentive, considerate

dub
[duhb]

v. to give a name, especially a nickname, to someone
별명이나 호칭을 붙이다
He was **dubbed** a hero.[10]

syn. name, call, nickname

enmity
[en-mi-tee]

n. the state or quality of being an enemy
적개심, 악의, 원한
They have no **enmity** against us.[11]

syn. ill will, spite, hostility

exhort
[ig-zawrt]

v. to urge or advise someone strongly
열심히 타이르다, 권고하다
He **exhorted** her to deliver herself to the police.[12]

syn. urge, warn, advise

ferment
[fer-ment]

v. go sour or spoil
발효되다, 발효시키다
The **fermentation** turns juice or grain into alcohol due to the agitated development of bacteria.[13]

syn. ripen, fester, simmer

frantic
[fran-tik]

adj. desperate with fear or anxiety
광란의, 공포나 불안으로 제정신이 아닌
His silence drove her **frantic**.[14]

syn. frenzied, furious, distraught

예문 해석

09 그가 신뢰하는 신중한 비서는 항상 조용하고 신중하며 절제력이 있다. **10** 그는 영웅 칭호를 얻었다. **11** 그들은 우리에게 적개심은 없다. **12** 그는 그녀에게 경찰에 자백하라고 권고했다. **13** 발효는 박테리아의 움직임으로 인해 주스나 곡물을 알코올로 바꾼다. **14** 그의 침묵이 그녀를 미치게 만들었다.

15

groundless
[ground-lis]

adj. without a basis in reason or fact
근거없는
He made her cry with a **groundless** accusation that she stole the dog.[15]

syn. unfounded, baseless, idle

16

heed
[heed]

v. pay attention to
주의하다, 신경쓰다
They did not **heed** the warning.[16]

syn. care, listen, hear

17

illustrious
[ih-*luhs*-tree-*uhs*]

adj. extremely famous
유명한, 저명한
"The man who has nothing to boast of but his **illustrious** ancestry is like the potato - the best part under ground."
- Thomas Overbury[17]

syn. well-known, renowned

18

incorporate
[in-kawr-per-ey-t]

v. to contain something as part of a whole
통합시키다
This brand new model also **incorporates** a telephone.[18]

syn. absorb, include, integrate

19

insanity
[in-san-i-tee]

n. the state of being insane
광기, 정신 이상
The criminal pleaded **insanity**, so his consequences would be less dire.[19]

syn. madness, craziness, lunacy

20

iota
[ai-oh-t*uh*]

n. a very small amount
극소량, 아주 적은 양
He's never shown one **iota** of interest in any kind of work.[20]

syn. jot, bit, scrap

 예문 해석

15 그는 그녀가 개를 훔쳤다고 근거 없는 비난으로 그녀를 울렸다.　**16** 그들은 경고를 듣지 않았다.　**17** 유명한 조상 말고는 자랑할 것이 없는 사람은 가장 좋은 부분이 뿌리인 감자와 같다.　**18** 이 새로운 모델은 전화까지 된다.　**19** 그 범죄자는 정신 이상을 주장했기 때문에 결과가 덜 끔직하게 나올 것이다.　**20** 그는 어떤 일에도 조금도 관심을 보이지 않는다.

labyrinth
[lab-*uh*-rinth]

n. an intricate combination of paths or passages
미로
Each year, my family goes to an autumn cornstalk maze where we walk through the **labyrinth** together.[21]

syn. maze, tangle, riddle

log
[log]

n. record of a voyage or flight
항해 일지, 항공 일지
They found the **log** of the ship's voyage.[22]

syn. diary, journal, record

mediate
[mee-dee-ey-t]

v. to act as the agent seeking to reconcile the two sides
조정하다, 화해시키다
The teacher **mediated** between both sides.[23]

syn. negotiate, arbitrate, intercede

morose
[m*uh*-rohs]

adj. silently gloomy or bad-tempered
언짢은, 시무룩한, 침울한
He was **morose** and reticent.[24]

syn. miserable, sullen, glum

parole
[p*uh*-rohl]

n. the conditional release of a person from imprisonment
가석방
After serving five years, the criminal was released on **parole**, a promise to be good and check in regularly.[25]

syn. conditional release, discharge, pardon

petrify
[pe-tr*uh*-fai]

v. to benumb or paralyze with astonish
공포로 돌처럼 굳게 하다, 무섭게 하다
I was **petrified**.[26]

syn. horrify, appall, stupefy

 예문 해석

21 매년, 우리 가족은 미로를 함께 걷는 가을 옥수수 줄기 미로에 간다. 22 그들은 그 배의 항해일지를 발견했다. 23 선생님이 양측을 중재했다. 24 그는 시무룩하고 말이 없었다. 25 5년을 복역한 후, 범인은 선하게 행동하고 정기적으로 점검받겠다는 약속으로 가석방되었다. 26 나는 너무나 무서웠다.

27 ....

profound
[pr*uh*-found]

adj. having deep insight or understanding
깊은, 심오한
In my time of need, I expressed **profound** gratitude when others supported me with meals and clothing.[27]

syn. deep, abstruse, esoteric

28 ....

rancor
[ran-cur]

n. feelings of hatred
깊은 원한, 악의, 증오
She was told never to speak about others with **rancor**.[28]

syn. resentment, animosity, malice

29 ....

reconciliation
[rek-*uh*n-sil-ee-ey-sh*uh*n]

n. the reestablishment of cordial relations
화해, 조화
He had a **reconciliation** with his old enemy.[29]

syn. conciliation, accord, harmony

30 ....

scoundrel
[skoun-dr*uh*l]

n. an unprincipled or villainous rogue
건달, 불한당, 악당
He will be remembered as nothing more than a **scoundrel**.[30]

syn. rogue, rascal, villain

31 ....

skinflint
[skin-flint]

n. a person who would save, gain, or extort money by any means
구두쇠
The owner is a penny-pinching **skinflint**.[31]

syn. miser, tightwad

 예문 해석

27 내가 어려운 시기에 다른 사람들이 식사와 옷으로 나를 지지해 줄 때 나는 깊은 감사를 표했다.　**28** 그녀는 원한을 가지고 다른 사람에 대해 절대 말하지 말라는 말을 들었다.　**29** 그는 오랜 숙적과 화해했다.　**30** 그는 악당 이상으로 기억될 것이다.　**31** 주인은 인색한 구두쇠다.

32

stupefy
[stoo-p*uh*-fai]

v. to make stunned or senseless
깜짝 놀라게 하다, 멍하게 만들다
When she visited Seoul for the first time, she was **stupefied** by its unexpected dynamic energies.[32]

syn. stun, daze, amazed

33

sullen
[s*uh*l-*uh*n]

adj. showing irritation or ill humor by a gloomy silence or reserve
뿌루퉁한, 무뚝뚝한
He lapsed into a **sullen** silence.[33]

syn. surly, morose, dour, moody

34

thrifty
[thrif-tee]

adj. careful about spending money
절약하는, 검소한
You have some very good habits for **thrifty** living.[34]

syn. frugal, economical

35

uncommitted
[*uh*n-k*uh*-mit-id]

adj. not bound or pledged to support any particular party, policy, action, etc.
어느 편도 아닌, 미결의, 미수의
Convincing the **uncommitted** voter to vote for our candidate will be crucial.[35]

syn. neutral, unaffiliated, uninvolved

36

vindicate
[vin-di-keyt]

v. to prove that something is true
정당함을 입증하다
The experts' report **vindicated** his innocence.[36]

syn. justify, exonerate, exculpate

 예문 해석

32 그녀가 처음 서울을 방문했을 때, 그녀는 뜻밖의 역동적인 에너지에 정신을 잃었다. **33** 그는 뿌루퉁한 침묵에 빠졌다. **34** 당신은 절약하는 삶을 위한 좋은 습관들을 가지고 있다. **35** 아직 결정하지 못한 유권자들을 우리 후보에게 투표하도록 확신시키는 것은 매우 중요하다. **36** 전문가의 보고서가 그의 무고함을 증명했다.

Directions   Each of the following questions consists of one word followed by five words or phrases. You are to select the one word or phrase whose meaning is closest to the word in capital letters.

1. **AMIABLE :**
   (A) puzzling
   (B) free
   (C) gruff
   (D) tender
   (E) agreeable

2. **ATTRIBUTE :**
   (A) frontier
   (B) foreboding
   (C) crevice
   (D) disposition
   (E) record

3. **CONGENIAL :**
   (A) diligent
   (B) natal
   (C) compatible
   (D) grouchy
   (E) adorable

4. **CRAFTY :**
   (A) representative
   (B) indifferent
   (C) sly
   (D) artless
   (E) biased

5. **EXHORT :**
   (A) urge
   (B) frustrate
   (C) recede
   (D) provoke
   (E) deny

6. **FRANTIC :**
   (A) random
   (B) titular
   (C) frenzied
   (D) mammoth
   (E) tiny

7. **HEED :**
   (A) mend
   (B) describe
   (C) wander
   (D) depict
   (E) care

8. **LABYRINTH :**
   (A) fragment
   (B) gulf
   (C) maze
   (D) exemption
   (E) anecdote

9. **PAROLE :**
   (A) conditional release
   (B) innovative technology
   (C) wealthy suburb
   (D) rental car
   (E) modest price

10. **PROFOUND :**
   (A) deep
   (B) shallow
   (C) tardy
   (D) appeasing
   (E) roaming

"Excellency is not one act but a habit."

— Aristotle —
Greek critic, philosopher, physicist, & zoologist

우수함이란 한 번의 행동이 아니라 습관적인 행동을 말한다.

LESSON

Greek and Latin Roots & Prefixes 26

★ NAUT, NAUS, NAV = relating to the sea or ships

-y (n.)	navy	해군
-ate (v.)	navigate	(지도 등을 보며) 길을 찾다
-or (person)	navigator	(배나 항공기 등의) 조종사, 항해사
cal (adj.)	nautical	선박의, 해상의, 항해의
ous (adj.)	nauseous	토할 것 같은, 배 멀미 하는 것 같은
astra (star)	astronaut	우주 비행사
circum (circle)	circumnavigate	(세계) 일주를 하다

DAY

26

WORDS TO LEARN

- accumulate
- amicable
- audacious
- blithe
- catalyst
- concur
- covert
- deprecate
- dubious

- ennui
- exile
- ferret
- fraud
- gracious
- hegemony
- imbibe
- incorrigible
- insatiable

- irascible
- lapse
- loom
- mediocre
- motif
- oblique
- pacify
- plunder
- progeny

- relocate
- retentive
- sabotage
- skirmish
- stately
- summit
- thrive
- undaunted
- vindictive

01

accumulate
[*uh*-kyoo-my*uh*-leyt]

v. to build up
모으다, 축적하다
Assignments are **accumulating** on my desk.[1]

syn. amass, gather, stockpile

02

amicable
[am-i-k*uh*-b*uh*l]

adj. friendly
우호적인, 사이좋은, 원만한
We can solve all problems in **amicable** ways.[2]

syn. friendly, good-natured, cordial

03

audacious
[aw-dey-sh*uh*s]

adj. extremely bold or daring
대담한, 건방진
He made an **audacious** remark.[3]

syn. daring, venturesome, dauntless

예문 해석

01 숙제가 내 책상 위에 쌓여가고 있다. **02** 우리는 모든 문제를 우호적인 방법으로 해결할 수 있다. **03** 그는 대담한 발언을 했다.

04

blithe
[blaith]

adj. happy and carefree
쾌활한, 행복한, 태평한
She loved her daughter's happy and **blithe** spirit.[4]

syn. carefree, jaunty, jovial

05

catalyst
[kat-l-ist]

n. a substance that causes or accelerates a chemical reaction without itself being affected
촉매, 기폭제
Getting kicked out of his parents' house was a **catalyst** for becoming more independent.[5]

syn. motivation, impetus, incentive

06

concur
[kuhn-kur]

v. to agree or approve of something
동의하다
Do you **concur** with his statement?[6]

syn. agree, concord, hold

07

covert
[koh-vert]

adj. secret or hidden
비밀의, 은밀한
The platoon took part in a **covert** mission to infiltrate an enemy camp.[7]

syn. concealed, clandestine, underhanded

08

deprecate
[dep-ri-keyt]

v. to express disapproval of something
비난하다, 반대하다
He **deprecated** the low quality of school facilities.[8]

syn. denounce, disapprove, criticize

예문 해석

04 그녀는 딸의 행복하고 유쾌한 정신을 사랑했다.   **05** 부모의 집에서 쫓겨난 것이 그의 독립심을 키우는 촉매제였다.   **06** 그의 말씀에 동의하십니까?   **07** 그 소대는 적진에 침투하는 비밀 작전에 참가했다.   **08** 그는 학교 시설이 낙후한 것을 비난했다.

dubious
[doo-bee-*uhs*]

adj. of doubtful quality
의심스러운, 수상한
The teacher was **dubious** the students had studied adequately for the exam.[9]

syn. suspicious, questionable, skeptical

ennui
[ahn-wee]

n. boredom or discontent caused by a lack of activity or excitement
권태, 따분함, 무료함
She was just full of **ennui**.[10]

syn. boredom, tedium

exile
[eg-zail]

v. to expel someone from one's home country
추방하다, 망명하다
He was **exiled** for seven years.[11]

syn. deport, expel, banish

ferret
[fer-it]

v. to search out
샅샅이 찾아내다, 색출하다
She persistently continued to **ferret** about for possible jobs.[12]

syn. search, rummage, ransack, fumble

fraud
[frawd]

n. the crime of deceiving somebody
속임수, 사기
Their theory is a **fraud**.[13]

syn. deceit, trickery

gracious
[grey-sh*uhs*]

adj. characterized by good taste, comfort, ease, or luxury
상냥한, 우아한, 품위 있는
Her **gracious** manners and kind personality make her popular.[14]

syn. benevolent, accommodating, kind

 예문 해석

09 선생님은 학생들이 시험에 적합하게 공부했는지 의심했다.   **10** 그녀는 매우 지겨워했다.   **11** 그는 7년 동안 망명생활을 했다.
12 그녀는 끈질기게 할 수 있는 일을 샅샅이 찾았다.   **13** 그들의 이론은 사기다.   **14** 우아한 매너와 상냥한 성격 덕에 그녀는 유명해졌다.

15

hegemony
[hi-jem-*uh*-nee]

n. authority or control
헤게모니, 연맹 제국에 대한 지배권, 패권
They competed with each other for regional **hegemony**.[15]

> *syn.* domination, leadership, prominence

16

imbibe
[im-baib]

v. to drink, especially alcoholic drinks
(술을) 마시다
They were used to **imbibing** enormous quantities of alcohol when they got together.[16]

> *syn.* drink, swallow

17

incorrigible
[in-kawr-i-j*uh*-b*uh*l]

adj. bad beyond correction or reform
구제 불능의, 고쳐지지 못할
He is an **incorrigible** liar.[17]

> *syn.* incurable, hopeless, hardened

18

insatiable
[in-sey-sh*uh*-b*uh*l]

adj. not able to be satisfied
만족할 줄 모르는, 탐욕스러운
The media has an **insatiable** appetite for stories about celebrities.[18]

> *syn.* voracious, greedy

19

irascible
[i-ras-*uh*-b*uh*l]

adj. easily made angry
화를 잘 내는, 성급한
He had an **irascible** temper.[19]

> *syn.* irritable, bad-tempered, cantankerous

20

lapse
[laps]

n. a slight mistake or failure
실수, 깜빡함
I had a **lapse** of memory.[20]

> *syn.* error, failure, blunder

예문 해석

15 그들은 지역 패권 장악을 위해 경쟁했다.   **16** 그들은 함께 모이면 많은 양의 술을 마셔대곤 했다.   **17** 그는 구제불능 거짓말쟁이다.   **18** 미디어들은 유명인들의 이야기라면 만족할 줄 모른다.   **19** 그는 화를 잘 내는 성격을 가졌다.   **20** 나는 기억을 깜빡 깜빡 잃었다.

loom
[loom]

v. to come into view in indistinct and enlarged form
(어렴풋이) 보이기 시작하다, 나타나다
As he lay groggy on the soccer field, his coach suddenly **loomed** over him.[21]

syn. appear, emerge, brew

mediocre
[mee-dee-oh-ker]

adj. neither good nor bad
보통의, 평범한, 좋지도 나쁘지도 않은
He did well in math, although his grades were generally **mediocre**.[22]

syn. ordinary, moderate, common

motif
[moh-teef]

n. an idea or a phrase that is repeated and developed in a work
예술 작품에 표현된 작가의 중심 사상
This is a **motif** throughout the story.[23]

syn. main idea, theme, concept

oblique
[*uh*-bleek]

adj. not expressed in a direct way
비스듬한, 기울어진
She gave him an **oblique** glance.[24]

syn. sloping, slanting, slanted

pacify
[pas-*uh*-fai]

v. to calm, or soothe someone
진정시키다, 달래다
The speech was designed to **pacify** the irate crowd.[25]

syn. calm, allay, mitigate, soothe, placate

plunder
[pl*uh*n-der]

v. to rob of goods or valuables by open force
약탈하다, 강탈하다
They **plundered** the colony of many national treasures.[26]

syn. rob, pillage, despoil

 예문 해석

21 그가 축구장에 지쳐 누워 있을 때, 그 위로 갑자기 코치가 나타났다. **22** 비록 그의 성적은 대부분 보통 정도였지만 수학은 잘 했다. **23** 이것이 작품 전반에 나와 있는 모티브이다. **24** 그녀는 그를 비스듬히 쳐다보았다. **25** 그 연설은 성난 군중들을 달래기 위한 것이었다. **26** 그들은 식민지의 많은 국보들을 약탈했다.

27

progeny
[proj-*uh*-nee]

n. a descendant or offspring, as a child, plant, or animal
자손
Because the billionaire bachelor did not have a **progeny**, his entire estate went to charity when he died.[27]

syn. children, offspring, descendant

28

relocate
[ree-loh-keyt]

v. to move (a building, company, etc.) to a different location
이전하다, 이동시키다
The company **relocated** its product line to another country to reduce costs.[28]

syn. move, carry, change

29

retentive
[ri-ten-tiv]

adj. of the ability to remember experiences and things learned
기력이 좋은, 유지하는
She had an amazingly **retentive** memory.[29]

syn. holding, keeping

30

sabotage
[sab-*uh*-tahzh]

n. a deliberate act of destruction or disruption in which equipment is damaged
(항의의 표시인) 방해 행위, 파괴 행위
Furious workers were responsible for the **sabotage** of the plant machines.[30]

syn. destruction, damage, disruption

31

skirmish
[skur-mish]

n. a brief battle during a war
작은 접전, 크지 않은 전투
Border **skirmishes** between India and Pakistan were common.[31]

syn. fight, brawl, melee

 예문 해석

27 그 억만장자 독신남은 자손이 없었기 때문에, 그가 죽었을 때 그의 전 재산은 자선단체에 기부되었다.　**28** 그 회사는 비용 절감을 위해 제품군을 다른 나라로 이전했다.　**29** 그녀는 놀라울 만큼 기억력이 좋다.　**30** 격분한 노동자들은 공장 기계의 파괴에 책임이 있었다.　**31** 인도와 파키스탄 국경에서의 작은 접전은 흔한 일이다.

stately
[steyt-lee]

adj. impressive and graceful or dignified
위엄 있고 웅장한, 당당하고 멋진
Instead of moving at his usual **stately** pace, he was almost running.[32]

> *syn.* grand, splendid, dignified

33 ·········

summit
[suhm-it]

n. the highest point of a mountain or hill
정상, 꼭대기
They reached the **summit** of a mountain.[33]

> *syn.* top, apex, pinnacle, climax

34 ·········

thrive
[thraiv]

v. to prosper or be successful
번영하다, 번성하다
We want our business to **thrive**.[34]

> *syn.* flourish, prosper, succeed

35 ·········

undaunted
[uhn-dawn-tid]

adj. not discouraged
겁내지 않는, 두려워하지 않는
She remained **undaunted** by failure.[35]

> *syn.* indomitable, brave, fearless

36 ·········

vindictive
[vin-dik-tiv]

adj. trying to harm or upset someone
악의 있는 복수심을 가진, 보복성의
She angrily responded with a **vindictive** action.[36]

> *syn.* revengeful, hateful, malicious

예문 해석

32 평소 그의 위엄있는 걸음걸이와 다르게 그는 거의 뛰고 있었다.   33 그들은 산 정상에 도달했다.   34 우리는 우리 사업이 번창하기를 원한다.   35 그녀는 실패에도 꿈쩍하지 않았다.   36 그녀는 앙심을 품은 행동으로 화를 내며 응수했다.

Directions   Each of the following questions consists of one word followed by five words or phrases. You are to select the one word or phrase whose meaning is closest to the word in capital letters.

1. **ACCUMULATE :**
   (A) copy
   (B) justify
   (C) keep
   (D) abate
   (E) amass

2. **AMICABLE :**
   (A) friendly
   (B) resounding
   (C) awkward
   (D) ridiculous
   (E) bleak

3. **AUDACIOUS :**
   (A) elusive
   (B) profitable
   (C) daring
   (D) curious
   (E) infinite

4. **CONCUR :**
   (A) accumulate
   (B) indulge
   (C) escape
   (D) strive
   (E) agree

5. **DUBIOUS :**
   (A) murky
   (B) nautical
   (C) inopportune
   (D) suspicious
   (E) benevolent

6. **IRASCIBLE :**
   (A) inborn
   (B) secured
   (C) official
   (D) theatrical
   (E) irritable

7. **LAPSE :**
   (A) error
   (B) opening
   (C) realtor
   (D) declaration
   (E) knowledge

8. **LOOM :**
   (A) retain
   (B) displace
   (C) stamp
   (D) appear
   (E) misappropriate

9. **MEDIOCRE :**
   (A) ordinary
   (B) assuring
   (C) sharp
   (D) hateful
   (E) insignificant

10. **PROGENY :**
   (A) parchment
   (B) innuendo
   (C) respiration
   (D) implication
   (E) children

"Men are not prisoners of fate, but only prisoners of their own minds."

— Franklin Roosevelt —
32nd president of the U.S.

인간은 운명의 포로가 아니라 자기 마음의 포로일 뿐이다.

Greek and Latin Roots & Prefixes 27

★ VERS, VERT = to turn

-ile (adj.)	versatile	부분, 일부
ab (away from)	avert	(시선을) 피하다, (얼굴을) 돌리다
con (together)	convert	전환시키다, 개종 시키다
dis (aside)	divert	방향을 바꾸게 하다, 우회 시키다
intro (into)	diversion	기분 전환
ex (out)	introvert	내성적인 사람
in (in)	extrovert	외향적인 사람
re (back)	invert	도치 시키다, 뒤집다
ir (not)	reversible	뒤집어 입을 수 있는, 양면을 다 이용할 수 있는
sub (down)	revert	되돌아가는 것, 복귀하는 사람

DAY

27

WORDS TO LEARN

☐ acclimate	☐ established	☐ irate	☐ ransack
☐ assimilate	☐ exodus	☐ lash	☐ reticent
☐ augment	☐ felicity	☐ loquacious	☐ scroll
☐ blurb	☐ folly	☐ meditate	☐ slack
☐ chronic	☐ grandiose	☐ motley	☐ static
☐ conciliatory	☐ heinous	☐ obliterate	☐ summon
☐ depreciate	☐ incarnate	☐ pact	☐ tranquility
☐ discursive	☐ increment	☐ placid	☐ underhanded
☐ dulcet	☐ inscrutable	☐ proliferate	☐ virtue

01

acclimate
[ak-*luh*-meyt]

v. to get used to certian situations or surroundings
적응하다
She perfectly **acclimated** herself to her new school.[1]

syn. adapt, accustom, conform

02

assimilate
[*uh*-sim-*uh*-leyt]

v. to make similar
동화시키다, 흡수하다
This country **assimilates** immigrants very quickly.[2]

syn. accommodate, absorb, adapt

03

augment
[awg-ment]

v. to make larger or increase
늘리다, 증가시키다
He needs to **augment** his weapons to make them bigger, better, and stronger.[3]

syn. increase, reinforce, enhance

예문 해석

01 그녀는 새 학교에 완벽하게 적응했다. **02** 이 나라는 이민자들을 매우 빨리 동화시킨다. **03** 더 크고, 더 좋고, 더 강하게 만들기 위해 그는 무기를 증가시켰다.

04

blurb
[blurb]

n. a promotional statement
짧고 과장된 광고, 선전문
The **blurb** on the back of the book was full of the usual hyperbole.[4]

syn. advertisement, ad, announcement

05

chronic
[kron-ik]

adj. lasting for a very long time
고질적인, 만성적인
He suffered from severe **chronic** back pain.[5]

syn. incessant, never-ending, constant

06

conciliatory
[k*uh*n-sil-ee-*uh*-tawr-ee]

adj. tending to conciliate
달래는, 회유하기 위한
She invited him to her party to make a **conciliatory** gesture.[6]

syn. appeasing, placid, yielding

07

depreciate
[di-pree-shee-eyt]

v. to decrease in value
가치를 떨어뜨리다
The dollar is **depreciating** due to rapid inflation.[7]

syn. devalue, underestimate, undervalue

08

discursive
[dih-skur-siv]

adj. passing aimlessly from one subject to another
두서없는, 산만한
He has a **discursive** style rambling from topic to topic in his writing.[8]

syn. digressive, excursive, rambling

예문 해석

04 그 책 뒤의 광고는 과장법으로 가득차 있다. **05** 그는 심한 만성 요통을 앓았다. **06** 그녀는 유화적인 제스처를 취하기 위해 그를 파티에 초대했다. **07** 빠른 인플레이션 때문에 달러 가치가 떨어지고 있다. **08** 그는 글을 쓸 때 주제마다 횡설수설하는 문체를 가지고 있다.

dulcet
[d*uh*l-sit]

adj. pleasant or agreeable
상쾌한, 아름다운
She loves the **dulcet** tones of the cello.[9]

syn. pleasant, sweet, delightful

---

established
[ih-stab-lisht]

adj. brought about or set up or accepted
인정받는, 확실히 자리잡은
Becoming **established** doesn't happen overnight. You've got to put in the time and effort to prove yourself and build a good reputation.[10]

syn. accepted, settled, well-known

---

exodus
[ek-*suh*-d*uh*s]

n. a departure or emigration
(많은 사람들의) 대이동, 대탈출
The summer **exodus** to the shore was tiring but necessary.[11]

syn. evacuation, departure, leaving

---

felicity
[fi-lis-i-tee]

n. a state of happiness or the quality of joy
(더할 나위 없는) 행복
Sitting on her balcony with an iced coffee on a clear, starry night is her perfect **felicity**.[12]

syn. bliss, happiness, euphoria

---

folly
[fol-ee]

n. lack of understanding or sense
어리석음
Spending all night playing computer games when you have an exam the next day is total **folly**.[13]

syn. foolishness, nonsense, absurdity

 예문 해석

09 그녀는 첼로의 아름다운 소리를 좋아한다. **10** 자리를 잡는 것은 하루아침에 이루어지지 않습니다. 자신을 증명하고 좋은 평판을 쌓기 위해 시간과 노력을 기울여야 합니다. **11** 여름의 해안으로의 탈출은 피곤했지만 필요했다. **12** 맑고 별이 총총한 여름밤에 아이스커피를 들고 발코니에 앉아 있는 것은 그녀의 완벽한 행복이다. **13** 다음날 시험이 있는데 밤새도록 컴퓨터 게임을 하는 것은 어리석은 짓이다.

14 ···

grandiose
[gran-dee-ohs]

adj. affectedly grand or important
뽐내는, 과장된, 웅장한
He had **grandiose** ambitions of world conquest.[14]

syn. theatrical, bombastic, impressive

15 ···

heinous
[hey-n*uh*s]

adj. very evil or wicked
혐오스러운, 가증스러운
He committed a **heinous** crime, and he is now paying the consequences.[15]

syn. horrifying, abominable, monstrous

16 ···

incarnate
[in-kahr-ney-sh*uh*n]

v. to represent in bodily form
(생각이나 특징 등이 보통 인간의) 형태로 구현되다, 화신이 되게 하다
This new religion was embodied and made **incarnate** in the person of its leader.[16]

syn. embody, personify, be in bodily form

17 ···

increment
[in-kr*uh*-m*uh*nt]

n. the amount by which something is increased
증가, 증대
Profits increased in **increments** of one million dollars per year.[17]

syn. addition, increase, raise

18 ···

inscrutable
[in-skroo-t*uh*-b*uh*l]

adj. not easily understood
(사람이나 표정을) 이해하기 어려운
Henry's actions seemed **inscrutable**, but his mother knew why he was doing so.[18]

syn. mysterious, blank, enigmatic

 예문 해석

14 그는 세계 정복이라는 웅대한 야망을 가졌다. **15** 그는 극악무도한 범죄를 저질렀고, 그 대가를 치르고 있다. **16** 이 새로운 종교는 그 지도자의 인격으로 구체화되었고 화신화 되었다. **17** 연 백만 달러로 이익이 증가되었다. **18** 헨리의 행동은 이해하기 어려운 것처럼 보였으나, 그의 어머니는 그가 왜 그런지 알고 있었다.

irate
[ai-reyt]

adj. very angry

분노한, 격분한

The owner was so **irate** that he almost threw us out of the store.[19]

syn. enraged, ireful, incensed, furious

lash
[lash]

n. a sharp slap or strike with a rope or whip

매질, 채찍질

The bondman received ten **lashes** as a punishment. [20]

syn. whip, blow, stroke

loquacious
[loh-kwey-sh*uh*s]

adj. very talkative

수다스러운, 말이 많은

She was very **loquacious** about her experiences.[21]

syn. wordy, garrulous, talkative

meditate
[med-i-teyt]

v. to think deeply

명상하다, 계획하다

I **meditated** on my high school years.[22]

syn. contemplate, deliberate, ponder

motley
[mot-lee]

adj. exhibiting great diversity of elements

잡다하게 마구 섞인, 뒤죽박죽 섞인

This **motley** crew was a diverse and poorly organized group.[23]

syn. mixed, varied, disparate

obliterate
[*uh*-blit-*uh*-reyt]

v. to destroy something completely

지우다, 없애다

He tried to **obliterate** his sad memories.[24]

syn. efface, blot out, destroy

📖 **예문 해석**

19 주인은 너무 화가 나서 우리를 거의 내던지듯 쫓아내려 했다. **20** 그 노예는 벌로 10대의 채찍질을 당했다. **21** 그녀는 자신의 경험에 대해서는 매우 말이 많다. **22** 나는 고등학교 때를 곰곰이 생각해 보았다. **23** 이 잡다하게 섞인 조직은 다양한 사람들로 만들어진 조직력이 떨어지는 집단이었다. **24** 그는 슬픈 기억을 지우려 노력했다.

pact
[pakt]

n. an agreement between two or more parties
약속, 협정
The two governments signed a **pact**.[25]

syn. deal, promise, agreement

placid
[plas-id]

adj. pleasantly calm or peaceful
고요한, 평화로운
This **placid** lake has a smooth surface and no waves.[26]

syn. serene, tranquil, unruffled

proliferate
[pr*uh*-lif-*uh*-reyt]

v. to increase in numbers
급격히 증가하다
Computerized data bases are **proliferating** quickly.[27]

syn. multiply, flourish, thrive, prosper

ransack
[ran-sack]

v. to search thoroughly for plunder
샅샅이 뒤지다, 찾다
The enemy **ransacked** the entire town.[28]

syn. forage, rummage

reticent
[ret-*uh*-suhnt]

adj. not saying very much
과묵한, 말을 삼가는
She is **reticent** about her achievements.[29]

syn. reserved, taciturn

scroll
[skrohl]

n. a roll of paper or parchment usually containing an inscription
두루마리, 족자
Ancient **scrolls** were found in this cave.[30]

syn. roll, tube, spool

예문 해석

25 두 나라 정부는 조약에 서명했다. **26** 이 잔잔한 호수는 표면이 매끄럽고 물결이 없다. **27** 컴퓨터화된 데이터베이스들은 급격히 빠른 속도로 증가하고 있다. **28** 적들은 마을 전체를 샅샅이 뒤졌다. **29** 그녀는 자신의 성과에 대해서는 말을 아낀다. **30** 이 동굴에서 고대 족자가 발견되었다.

slack
[slak]

adj. loose
늘어진, 느슨한
The problem was a **slack** rope.[31]

> *syn.* loose, insecure, unfastened

static
[stat-ik]

adj. showing little or no change
정적인, 고정된, 움직이지 않는
The **static** relationship had no goals or signs of promise.[32]

> *syn.* still, stationary, motionless, immobile

summon
[*suhm-uhn*]

v. to order someone to appear in court
소환하다, 호출하다, 부르다
Suddenly, we were **summoned** to the interview room.[33]

> *syn.* call, send for, call for

tranquility
[trang-kwil-i-tee]

n. a state of peace and quiet
평온함, 고요함
Yoga or meditation can help bring **tranquility** by clearing your mind of constant worries.[34]

> *syn.* calmness, serenity, placidity

underhanded
[*uhn*-der-han-did]

adj. secret and crafty or dishonorable
공정하지 않은, 속이는, 부정한
Losing because my team is **underhanded** is unacceptable.[35]

> *syn.* dishonest, crooked, devious

virtue
[vur-choo]

n. the quality of being morally good
미덕, 덕목
Virtue is its own reward.[36]

> *syn.* goodness, moral excellence, righteousness

예문 해석

31 문제는 늘어진 로프였다. **32** 정적인 관계는 아무런 목표도 약속의 징후도 없다. **33** 갑자기 우리는 면접실로 불려 들어갔다. **34** 요가나 명상은 끊임없는 걱정으로부터 마음을 맑게 함으로써 평온을 가져오는데 도움을 줄 수 있다. **35** 내 팀이 공정치 못해서 졌다는 것은 받아들일 수 없다. **36** 선행은 그 자체가 보답이다.(다른 사람에게 칭찬이나 보답을 기대해서는 안된다.)

Directions   Each of the following questions consists of one word followed by five words or phrases. You are to select the one word or phrase whose meaning is closest to the word in capital letters.

1. ASSIMILATE :
(A) admonish
(B) blend
(C) inculpate
(D) swish
(E) accommodate

2. AUGMENT :
(A) contain
(B) abstain
(C) increase
(D) dawdle
(E) come across

3. CHRONIC :
(A) ferocious
(B) unclear
(C) banal
(D) skillful
(E) incessant

4. CONCILIATORY :
(A) questionable
(B) desultory
(C) appeasing
(D) timorous
(E) unintentional

5. ESTABLISHED :
(A) accepted
(B) immaterial
(C) irrelevant
(D) ostentatious
(E) timid

6. FOLLY :
(A) foolishness
(B) ecstasy
(C) deception
(D) arbiter
(E) souvenir

7. IRATE :
(A) unintentional
(B) illustrative
(C) deceptive
(D) enraged
(E) gloomy

8. OBLITERATE :
(A) amass
(B) misinform
(C) increase
(D) efface
(E) resound

9. RETICENT :
(A) conscientious
(B) visionary
(C) reserved
(D) decorative
(E) indifferent

10. SUMMON :
(A) decrease
(B) restrict
(C) associate
(D) call
(E) cringe

"Difficulties mastered are opportunities won."

— Winston Churchill —
British politician

극복해 낸 어려움은 새롭게 얻은 기회이다.

Greek and Latin Roots & Prefixes 28

★ SOCIO = friend, companion or ally

-al (adj.)	social	사회의
-able (adj.)	sociable	사교적인
-ity (n.)	society	사회, 모임
path (suffering)	sociopath	반사회적 인격 장애자
anti (against)	antisocial	반사회적인
ad (toward)	associate	연관 짓다
ad (toward)	association	협회
dis (aside)	disassociate	관계를 끊다

DAY

28

WORDS TO LEARN

☐ abscond	☐ dune	☐ ironic	☐ rectify
☐ amorphous	☐ enthrall	☐ lass	☐ redress
☐ auspicious	☐ exonerate	☐ lore	☐ scribe
☐ boisterous	☐ fete	☐ mettle	☐ slaughter
☐ chronicle	☐ frayed	☐ mien	☐ sneaky
☐ condemnation	☐ graphic	☐ oblivion	☐ sumptuous
☐ crave	☐ immaculate	☐ pageant	☐ syntax
☐ deputy	☐ incriminate	☐ poignant	☐ undermine
☐ disconcert	☐ iridescent	☐ prolific	☐ vent

01

abscond
[ab-skond]

v. to escape, often taking something along
도주하다, 종적을 감추다, 무단이탈하다
The Ponzi schemer **absconded** to Switzerland with his client's money.[1]

syn. leave secretly, flee, escape

02

amorphous
[*uh*-mawr-f*uh*s]

adj. having no specific form
형태가 없는, 무정형의
There must be an **amorphous** segment of society.[2]

syn. shapeless, formless

03

auspicious
[aw-spish-*uh*s]

adj. promising success
길조의, 좋은 징조의
Their house was built in the most **auspicious** of places.[3]

syn. propitious, opportune, favorable

예문 해석

01 그 폰지 사기꾼은 그의 고객의 돈을 가지고 스위스로 도망쳤다.   **02** 사회에는 보이지 않는 분열이 분명히 있다.   **03** 그들의 집은 가장 좋은 자리에 지어졌다.

04

boisterous
[boi-ster-*uhs*]

adj. noisy, lively, and full of energy
매우 시끄러운, 난리 법석의
Most of the children were active and **boisterous**.[4]

syn. uproarious, rambunctious

05

chronicle
[kron-i-k*uhl*]

n. the arrangement of events in order of occurrence
연대기, 역사책, 기록
The **Chronicles** of Narnia are a series of well known books.[5]

syn. annals, narrative

06

condemnation
[kon-dem-ney-sh*uh*n]

n. an expression of strong disapproval
비난, 규탄
Once the war ensued, international **condemnation** followed.[6]

syn. criticism, blaming, accusation

07

crave
[kreyv]

v. to desire eagerly
열렬히 원하다, 갈망하다
She **craves** water due to deadly thirst.[7]

syn. yearn for, hunger for, hanker

08

deputy
[dep-y*uh*-tee]

n. a person appointed to act as a substitute
대리인, 대리역
The **deputy** prime minister knew his role thoroughly.[8]

syn. representative, delegate, surrogate

09

disconcert
[dis-k*uh*n-surt]

v. to unsettle someone or make someone feel confused
당황하게 하다, 혼란시키다
She was **disconcerted** to find all of her classmates already seated.[9]

syn. confound, befuddle, confuse

🧘 예문 해석

04 대부분의 아이들이 활달하고 시끄럽다. **05** 나니아 연대기는 잘 알려진 책 시리즈이다. **06** 전쟁이 이어지자 국제적 비난이 뒤따랐다. **07** 그녀는 극도로 심한 갈증으로 물을 열렬히 원했다. **08** 부총리는 자신의 역할을 잘 알고 있었다. **09** 그녀는 반 친구들 모두가 이미 와서 앉아 있는 것을 보고 당황했다.

dune
[doon]

n. a natural hill made of sand, either on a beach or in a desert
모래 언덕, 사구
Namibia has some of the tallest **dunes** in the world.[10]

syn. sand dune, ridge

enthrall
[en-thrawl]

v. to captivate or charm
매혹시키다
The tourists were **enthralled** by the scenery.[11]

syn. enchant, bewitch, mesmerize

exonerate
[ig-zon-*uh*-reyt]

v. to free someone from blame
비난에서 해방시키다, 무죄임을 입증하다
He was **exonerated** from the accusation of cheating.[12]

syn. absolve, acquit, exculpate

fete
[fet]

n. a festive celebration
축제
The town seemed happy and festive because of the greatest **fete** of the season.[13]

syn. gala, fiesta, festival

frayed
[freyd]

adj. worn away or tattered along the edges
(천이나 옷감이) 닳은, 해어진
His hand-knit mittens became **frayed** around the cuffs after many winters.[14]

syn. worn, threadbare, tattered

graphic
[graf-ik]

adj. clear and detailed
생생한
The report described a **graphic** account of the earthquake.[15]

syn. vivid, lifelike, realistic

📖 **예문 해석**

10 나미비아에는 세계에서 제일 높은 모래 언덕이 있다.　**11** 관광객들은 광경에 매혹되었다.　**12** 그는 컨닝을 했다는 비난에서 벗어나게 되었다.　**13** 그 마을은 그 계절의 가장 큰 축제 때문에 행복한 축제 분위기처럼 보였다.　**14** 그의 손뜨개 벙어리장갑은 여러 해의 겨울 후에 주위가 닳았다.　**15** 그 보고서는 그 지진에 대한 생생한 이야기를 묘사했다.

16

immaculate
[i-mak-*yuh*-lit]

adj. extremely clean, tidy or neat
깨끗한, 순결한, 티 없는
Her desk was kept **immaculate** all the time.[16]

syn. fastidious, spotless

17

incriminate
[in-krim-*uh*-neyt]

v. to charge someone with a crime or fault
남에게 죄를 뒤집어 씌우다, 유죄로 하다
He was afraid of **incriminating** himself, so he said no more than was necessary.[17]

syn. inculpate, accuse, implicate

18

iridescent
[ir-i-des-*uh*nt]

adj. displaying a play of lustrous colors like those of the rainbow
보는 각도에 따라 색깔이 변하는, 무지갯빛의
Kingfisher is a bird with **iridescent** blue feathers.[18]

syn. lustrous, rainbow-colored, pearly

19

ironic
[ai-ron-ik]

adj. odd or amusing
말하고 있는 것과는 반대 내용을 의미하는, 빈정대는
She looked at him with an **ironic** expression at the dinner table.[19]

syn. cynic, sardonic, paradoxical, poignant

20

lass
[las]

n. a girl or young woman
소녀, 아가씨
Brad met an attractive **lass** named Scarlet.[20]

syn. girl, maiden, young woman

21

lore
[lawr]

n. traditional stories and history
민간 전승, 학문, 지식
Vampire **lore** goes way back.[21]

syn. information, wisdom

예문 해석

16 그녀의 책상은 항상 깨끗했다. **17** 그는 죄를 뒤집어 쓸 것이 두려워 필요 없는 것까지 다 말했다. **18** 킹피셔는 무지개빛 푸른 깃털을 가진 새이다. **19** 그녀는 저녁 식탁에서 아이러니한 표정으로 그를 바라보았다. **20** 브래드는 매력적인 아가씨인 스칼렛을 만났다. **21** 그 뱀파이어 이야기는 오래된 것들이다.

22 ···

mettle
[met-l]

n. the courage to carry on
패기, 용기
The king wanted to test his **mettle** to see if he had the heart to follow through when the going got tough.[22]

syn. boldness, caliber, fortitude

23 ···

mien
[meen]

n. a person's appearance, manner, or demeanor
표정, 태도, (풍기는) 분위기
Her cheerful **mien** radiates happiness and energy.[23]

syn. countenance, bearing, comportment

24 ···

oblivion
[uh-bliv-ee-uhn]

n. the state of being forgotten
망각, 잊혀진 상태
She is a former movie star who now lives in **oblivion**.[24]

syn. forgetfulness, obliteration

25 ···

pageant
[paj-uhnt]

n. an elaborate public spectacle
행렬, 구경거리, 쇼
She competed in many beauty **pageants** growing up.[25]

syn. spectacle, show, exhibition

26 ···

poignant
[poin-yuhnt]

adj. deeply moving
마음 아픈, 가슴에 사무치는
The movie was so **poignant** that the entire audience cried.[26]

syn. affecting, touching, moving

27 ···

prolific
[pruh-lif-ik]

adj. producing a large number of works
많은 작품을 만드는, 다작의
She is a **prolific** writer.[27]

syn. productive, creative, fertile

예문 해석

22 왕은 힘든 일이 닥쳤을 때 끝까지 갈 용기가 있는지 확인하기 위해 그의 기개를 시험하고 싶었다. **23** 그녀의 유쾌한 표정은 행복과 에너지를 발산한다. **24** 그녀는 지금은 잊혀진 예전 영화배우이다. **25** 그녀는 자라면서 많은 미인대회에 출전했다. **26** 영화가 너무 슬퍼서 관객 모두가 울었다. **27** 그녀는 다작하는 작가이다.

rectify
[rek-*tuh*-fai]

v. to make, put, or set right
바로잡다, 수정하다
His English teacher gave him a chance to **rectify** any mistakes he's made in an essay.[28]

syn. amend, fix, remedy

29

redress
[ree-dres]

n. compensation or satisfaction for a wrong or injury
보상, 배상
She demanded **redress** from the builder when her ceiling collapsed.[29]

syn. compensation, indemnity, atonement

30

scribe
[skraib]

n. someone employed to make written copies of documents
필경사, 서기
Before printing was invented, the **scribes** wrote copies of all the legal documents.[30]

syn. copyist, scrivener, secretary

31

slaughter
[slaw-ter]

n. the killing of animals for their meat
학살, 도살
During the primal years, every man knew how to **slaughter** animals.[31]

syn. killing, murder, massacre

32

sneaky
[snee-kee]

adj. marked by quiet and caution and secrecy
교활한, 엉큼한
Her **sneaky** sister slipped quietly into her room to borrow her favorite coat without asking first.[32]

syn. underhanded, furtive, sly

 예문 해석

28 그의 영어 선생님은 그가 에세이에서 한 실수를 바로잡을 기회를 주었다.　**29** 그녀는 천장이 무너지자 건축업자에게 배상을 요구했다.　**30** 인쇄술이 발명되기 전에, 필경사들은 모든 법적 문서의 사본을 썼다.　**31** 원시 시대에는 모든 사람들이 동물을 죽이는 방법을 알고 있었다.　**32** 그녀의 교활한 여동생은 먼저 묻지도 않고 그녀가 가장 좋아하는 코트를 빌리기 위해 조용히 그녀의 방으로 들어갔다.

33 ···

sumptuous
[s*uh*mp-choo-*uh*s]

adj. grand and obviously very expensive
사치스러운, 화려한, 호화로운, 값진
She produces elegant wedding gowns in a variety of
sumptuous fabrics.[33]

syn. costly, lavish, elaborate, expensive

34 ···

syntax
[sin-taks]

n. the study of the rules for forming admissible sentences
구문론 (언어에서 문장을 만드는 법칙)
The basic rules for arranging words and phrases in a
sentence are called **syntax**.[34]

syn. arrangement, structure, pattern

35 ···

undermine
[*uh*n-der-main]

v. to weaken or destroy something
명성 등을 훼손하다, 손상시키다
The repetitive failures **undermined** his confidence.[35]

syn. impair, weaken, damage

36 ···

vent
[vent]

n. a hole for the escape of gas or air
통풍구, 환기구
Fridge **vents** were placed along the surface between the
freezer and fridge.[36]

syn. outlet, venthole

 예문 해석

33 그녀는 다양하고 화려한 천으로 우아한 웨딩 드레스들을 만든다. **34** 문장에서 단어와 구를 배열하는 기본적인 규칙들은 구문론이라고 불린다. **35** 반복되는 실패는 그의 자신감을 훼손시켰다. **36** 냉장고와 냉장고 사이의 표면을 따라 냉장고 통풍구가 배치되어 있다.

Directions   Each of the following questions consists of one word followed by five words or phrases. You are to select the one word or phrase whose meaning is closest to the word in capital letters.

1. **ABSCOND :**
   (A) leave secretly
   (B) watch secretly
   (C) listen secretly
   (D) store secretly
   (E) eat secretly

2. **AMORPHOUS :**
   (A) amorous
   (B) digressive
   (C) unconquerable
   (D) impudent
   (E) shapeless

3. **AUSPICIOUS :**
   (A) propitious
   (B) customary
   (C) unique
   (D) anxious
   (E) sensible

4. **BOISTEROUS :**
   (A) visionary
   (B) uproarious
   (C) pungent
   (D) routine
   (E) nimble

5. **DEPUTY :**
   (A) representative
   (B) miserable
   (C) timid
   (D) priceless
   (E) latent

6. **PROLIFIC :**
   (A) secretive
   (B) productive
   (C) onerous
   (D) hypocritical
   (E) repulsive

7. **RECTIFY :**
   (A) amend
   (B) separate
   (C) tug
   (D) abate
   (E) plunge

8. **SNEAKY :**
   (A) enthusiastic
   (B) underhanded
   (C) taut
   (D) exact
   (E) mute

9. **SUMPTUOUS :**
   (A) tentative
   (B) civic
   (C) outrageous
   (D) rambling
   (E) costly

10. **UNDERMINE :**
   (A) collapse
   (B) subvert
   (C) petrify
   (D) skim
   (E) impair

"I've failed over and over and over again in my life.
And that is why I succeed. "

— Michael Jordan —
American Basketball Player

나는 인생에서 실패하고, 실패하고, 또 실패했다.
그것이 내가 성공한 이유이다.

Greek and Latin Roots & Prefixes 29

★ STRAIN, STRICT = to draw tight

-ain (n.)	strain	부담
-ed (adj.)	strained	긴장한, 부담되는
-ict (adj.)	strict	엄격한
-ent (adj.)	stringent	엄중한
con (together)	constrict	수축되다, 조이다
dis (aside)	district	지역, (특정) 지구
re (back)	restrain	저지하다
	restriction	제한, 규제

DAY

29

WORDS TO LEARN

☐ abate	☐ duplicate	☐ insight	☐ rapport
☐ amplify	☐ earnest	☐ irrelevant	☐ retort
☐ austere	☐ exorbitant	☐ lubricate	☐ scrupulous
☐ bearing	☐ felicitous	☐ meek	☐ slay
☐ chivalry	☐ freight	☐ motto	☐ stature
☐ circumspect	☐ gratitude	☐ obnoxious	☐ superimpose
☐ craven	☐ heterogeneous	☐ prerogative	☐ tribulation
☐ deranged	☐ immense	☐ poise	☐ unravel
☐ discontented	☐ incumbent	☐ promenade	☐ virulent

---

01 ....

abate
[*uh*-beyt]

v. to reduce in amount, degree or intensity

약해지다, 약화시키다

After falling off a ski lift, his enthusiasm for skiing surely **abated**.[1]

syn. lessen, diminish, dwindle

02 ....

amplify
[am-pl*uh*-fai]

v. to make larger, greater, or stronger

증폭시키다, 확대하다

Speakers **amplify** the volume of the noise coming through a microphone.[2]

syn. enlarge, extend, augment

03 ....

austere
[aw-steer]

adj. severe in manner

엄격한

The chapel is as simple and **austere** as the winter landscape.[3]

syn. stern, strict, severe

예문 해석

01 스키 리프트에서 떨어진 후, 스키에 대한 그의 열정은 확실히 사그라졌다. **02** 스피커는 마이크를 통해 나오는 소리의 크기를 증폭시킨다. **03** 교회당은 겨울 풍경처럼 단순하고 절제되어 있다.

04

bearing
[bair-ing]

n. a person's manner or conduct

태도, 자세

She has a noble **bearing** walking with her shoulders straight and her head up always.[4]

syn. conduct, manners, demeanor

05

chivalry
[shiv-*uhl*-ree]

n. the rules and customs of medieval knighthood

기사도

Picture a knight kneeling before a maiden and kissing her hand; It's a classic image of **chivalry** from the storybooks.[5]

syn. courtesy, knightliness, courtliness

06

circumspect
[sur-*kuhm*-spekt]

adj. careful of potential consequences

신중한, 조심스러운

He is now more **circumspect**, considering all circumstances and consequences.[6]

syn. cautious, discreet, prudent

07

craven
[krey-ven]

adj. lacking even the rudiments of courage

겁 많은, 비겁한

If you do not tell the truth, you will remain a **craven** coward.[7]

syn. weak, timid, cowardly

08

deranged
[di-reynjd]

adj. driven insane

미친, 제정신이 아닌

A **deranged** man shot and killed many people.[8]

syn. insane, mad, frantic

예문 해석

04 그녀는 항상 고개를 들고 어깨를 펴고 걷는 고상한 태도를 가지고 있다. **05** 한 기사가 여자 앞에 무릎을 꿇고 그녀의 손에 키스하는 모습을 상상해보라. 동화책에 나오는 전형적인 기사도의 이미지이다. **06** 그는 이제 모든 상황과 결과를 고려하여 더욱 신중해졌다. **07** 진실을 말하지 않으면, 너는 비겁한 겁쟁이로 남을 것이다. **08** 어떤 미친 남자가 총을 쏴 여러 사람이 죽었다.

09 ....

discontented
[dis-*kuhn*-ten-tid]

adj. not content or satisfied
불만스러운, 불편스러운
The government tried to appease the **discontented** workers.[9]

> *syn.* dissatisfied, displeased, unhappy

10 ....

duplicate
[doo-pli-keyt]

v. to make an exact copy of
복제하다, 되풀이 하다
He **duplicated** his house key.[10]

> *syn.* reproduce, copy, clone

11 ....

earnest
[ur-nist]

adj. serious and zealous in intention, purpose, or effort
진지한, 성실한, 진심인
Her parents were firmly against her dream as an actress,
but she was **earnest** about wanting a career.[11]

> *syn.* ardent, enthusiastic, passionate

12 ....

exorbitant
[ig-zawr-bi-t*uh*nt]

adj. highly excessive
말도 안 되는, 과도한
Due to her desire of having an **exorbitant**, luxurious
lifestyle, she needed to pursue a higher paying job.[12]

> *syn.* outrageous, extreme, unreasonable

13 ....

felicitous
[fi-lis-i-t*uh*s]

adj. well-suited for the occasion
아주 적절한, 절묘하게 어울리는
The weather was **felicitous** when she had a trip to the
amusement park.[13]

> *syn.* appropriate, opportune, apt

14 ....

freight
[freyt]

n. goods or cargo in transport
화물 운송
The packages were carried by air **freight**.[14]

> *syn.* carriage, shipment, cargo

예문 해석

09 정부는 불만에 가득 찬 직원들을 달래려 노력했다. **10** 그는 그의 집 열쇠를 복제했다. **11** 그녀의 부모님은 그녀의 배우로서 의 꿈을 단호히 반대했지만, 그녀는 직업을 원하는 것에 대해 진지했다. **12** 터무니없이 비싸고 사치스러운 생활을 하고 싶은 욕망 때문에, 그녀는 더 높은 보수의 직업을 추구할 필요가 있었다. **13** 그녀가 놀이공원에 여행을 갔을 때 날씨가 딱 맞게 좋았다. **14** 그 소포들은 항공 화물로 운송되었다.

gratitude
[grat-i-tyood]

n. feeling of being grateful or thankful
감사, 감사하는 마음
She expressed her **gratitude** to everyone.[15]

syn. thankfulness, appreciation, gratefulness

16

heterogeneous
[het-er-*uh*-jee-nee-*uh*s]

adj. composed of parts of different kinds
여러 다른 종류들로 이뤄진
This **heterogeneous** mixture contains two substances that do not combine, oil and water.[16]

syn. diversified, mingled, varied

17

immense
[i-mens]

adj. extremely large or great
엄청난, 굉장히 큰
The Pacific Ocean is **immense** and boundless.[17]

syn. gigantic, colossal, mammoth

18

incumbent
[in-k*uhm*-b*uh*nt]

adj. holding an indicated position currently
재직 중인, 재임 중인
The **incumbent** president was recently inaugurated.[18]

syn. official, occupant

19

insight
[in-sait]

n. penetrating mental vision or discernment
통찰력
The writer has great **insight**.[19]

syn. discernment, intuitiveness, awareness

20

irrelevant
[i-rel-*uh*-v*uh*nt]

adj. not applicable or pertinent
관련 없는, 적절하지 않은
His lectures often digress into **irrelevant** subjects.[20]

syn. immaterial, extraneous, unrelated

예문 해석

15 그녀는 모두에게 감사를 표했다. **16** 이 여러 다른 종류로 이루어진 혼합물은 결합하지 않는 기름과 물이라는 두 가지 물질을 포함하고 있다. **17** 태평양은 광활하고 한없이 넓다. **18** 현직 대통령이 최근에 취임했다. **19** 그 작가는 대단한 통찰력을 가졌다. **20** 그의 강의는 종종 관련없는 주제로 벗어날 때가 있다.

21

lubricate
[loo-bri-keyt]

v. to coat with oil or grease

기름칠을 하다

You can use mineral oils to **lubricate** machinery.[21]

syn. grease, anoint

22

meek
[meek]

adj. ready to do what other people want

온순한, 말 잘듣는

She was **meek** and mild.[22]

syn. compliant, shy, docile

23

motto
[mot-oh]

n. a maxim adopted as an expression of the guiding principle of a person or organization

모토, 좌우명

A **motto** I often think of was attributed to Aristotle, "We are what we repeatedly do. Excellence, then, is not an act, but a habit."[23]

syn. proverb, slogan, catchphrase

24

obnoxious
[*uh*b-nok-sh*uh*s]

adj. extremely unpleasant

몹시 불쾌한, 비위에 심하게 거슬리는

The boy was acting so **obnoxious**, his father asked him to leave the dinner table.[24]

syn. abhorrent, abominable, hateful

25

prerogative
[pri-rog-*uh*-tiv]

n. special right or privilege

특권

Legislative immunity is a **prerogative** of being partially exempted from prosecution.[25]

syn. privilege, immunity, right

 예문 해석

21 기계에 기름칠을 할 때 미네랄 오일을 사용해도 된다. **22** 그녀는 온순하고 착한 아이였다. **23** 내가 자주 생각하는 좌우명은 아리스토텔레스에게 기인했다. "우리는 우리가 반복적으로 하는 것이다. 그렇다면 탁월함은 행동이 아니라 습관이다." **24** 그 소년은 너무 불쾌하게 굴어서 그의 아버지는 그에게 저녁 식사 자리에서 나가라고 했다. **25** 입법 면책 특권은 기소가 일부 면제되는 특권이다.

26

poise
[poiz]

n. self-assurance
마음의 평정, 자신감에서 오는 평온함
It took a moment for her to recover her **poise**.[26]

syn. composure, aplomb, calmness

27

promenade
[prom-*uh*-neyd]

n. a stroll or walk
산책, 소요, 거닐기
We went on a **promenade** through the park.[27]

syn. leisurely walk, saunter, stroll

28

rapport
[ra-pawr]

n. a close emotional bond
우호적인 관계, 친밀감
Success depends on good **rapport** between coach and players.[28]

syn. relationship, fellowship, camaraderie

29

retort
[ri-tawrt]

v. to make a quick and clever or angry reply
반박하다, 말대꾸하다
She gave a quick and sharp **retort**.[29]

syn. rejoin, reply

30

scrupulous
[skroo-py*uh*-lu*h*s]

adj. thorough, exact, and careful about details
양심적으로 열심히 하는, 세세한 것까지 신경 쓰는
He was **scrupulous** in his negotiations.[30]

syn. conscientious, meticulous, thorough

31

slay
[sley]

v. to kill in a violent way
학살하다, 잔인하게 살해하다
In the fairy tale, the hero **slays** the monster dragon to save the princess.[31]

syn. kill, murder, assassinate

예문 해석

26 그녀가 평정을 찾는 데는 조금 시간이 걸렸다. **27** 우리는 공원을 거닐었다. **28** 성공은 코치와 선수들 사이의 우호적인 관계에 달려 있다. **29** 그녀는 바로 날카롭게 말대꾸했다. **30** 그는 협상시에 세세한 것까지 신경 썼다. **31** 동화에서 주인공은 공주를 구하기 위해 괴물 용을 죽인다.

32 ···

stature
[stach-er]

n. the height of a person, animal, or tree
키, 신장, 높이
His physical **stature** makes him remarkable.[32]

> *syn.* height, physique, build

33 ···

superimpose
[soo-per-im-pohz]

v. to lay or set one thing on top of another
위에 얹다, 포개어 놓다
He tried to **superimpose** his own story onto this ancient one.[33]

> *syn.* lay on a top, superpose, overlay

34 ···

tribulation
[trib-yuh-ley-shuhn]

n. severe trial or suffering.
고난, 시련
The **tribulations** of construction workers include a dangerous work environment and lung disease from dust and pollutants.[34]

> *syn.* adversity, grief, misery

35 ···

unravel
[uhn-rav-uhl]

v. to separate or disentangle the threads of (a knitted fabric or rope, etc.)
(실로 짠 직물이나 밧줄 등을) 풀다
When she pulled that straggly thread hanging from her sleeve, she found out she had **unraveled** her hand-knitted sweater.[35]

> *syn.* solve, resolve, untangle

36 ···

virulent
[vir-yuh-luhnt]

adj. having a rapidly harmful effect
맹독의, 치명적인, 매우 유해한
You should prepare to face **virulent** attacks from the mass media.[36]

> *syn.* baneful, malignant, pernicious

예문 해석

32 큰 키 덕에 그는 눈에 띈다. **33** 그는 고대의 이야기에 자신의 이야기를 포개어 덧붙이려 했다. **34** 건설 노동자들이 겪는 고충에는 위험한 작업 환경과 먼지와 오염 물질로 인한 폐 질환이 포함된다. **35** 그녀가 소매에 매달린 끈적끈적한 실을 잡아당겼을 때, 그녀는 자신이 손으로 짠 스웨터를 풀었다는 것을 알았다. **36** 당신은 대중 매체의 치명적인 공격을 대비해야 한다.

DAILY QUIZ 29

Directions   Each of the following questions consists of one word followed by five words or phrases.
You are to select the one word or phrase whose meaning is closest to the word in capital letters.

1. AMPLIFY :
   (A) chide
   (B) enlarge
   (C) abandon
   (D) drop
   (E) cover

2. AUSTERE :
   (A) tedious
   (B) relevant
   (C) stern
   (D) wary
   (E) secret

3. BEARING :
   (A) conduct
   (B) monodrama
   (C) relationship
   (D) adherence
   (E) rhetoric

4. DISCONTENTED :
   (A) timorous
   (B) dissatisfied
   (C) unfounded
   (D) shapeless
   (E) astonishing

5. DUPLICATE :
   (A) reproduce
   (B) avoid
   (C) conquer
   (D) demand
   (E) mistreat

6. EXORBITANT :
   (A) patronizing
   (B) traumatic
   (C) prominent
   (D) contented
   (E) outrageous

7. INSIGHT :
   (A) fury
   (B) motive
   (C) discernment
   (D) precursor
   (E) facsimile

8. IRRELEVANT :
   (A) immaterial
   (B) exotic
   (C) thorough
   (D) opinionated
   (E) clamorous

9. LUBRICATE :
   (A) deceive
   (B) grease
   (C) enrage
   (D) worsen
   (E) associate

10. OBNOXIOUS :
   (A) abhorrent
   (B) adroit
   (C) tedious
   (D) exotic
   (E) finicky

"The future belongs to those who believe in the beauty of their dreams."

— Eleanor Roosevelt —
First Lady of the United States from 1933 to 1945

미래는 자기 꿈의 아름다움을 믿는 사람들의 것이다.

LESSON

Greek and Latin Roots & Prefixes 30

★ TERR, TERRA, GEO = earth

-ory (adj.)	territory	지역, 영토
-ce (n.)	terrace	(집이나 식당의) 테라스
-ain (n.)	terrain	지형, 지역
-al (adj.)	terrestrial	육생의, 땅에서 생활하는
-ta (n.)	terra cotta	테라코타 (적갈색 점토를 유약을 바르지 않고 구운 것)
med (middle)	Mediterranean	지중해의
extra (outside)	extraterrestrial	외계인, 우주인
sub (under)	subterranean	지하의

DAY

30

WORDS TO LEARN

☐ acquiesce	☐ entice	☐ irrigate	☐ reparation
☐ analogy	☐ exotic	☐ latent	☐ revolt
☐ authentic	☐ feat	☐ lucrative	☐ scrutinize
☐ bore	☐ frenetic	☐ melancholy	☐ sleek
☐ churn	☐ gratuitous	☐ mourn	☐ statute
☐ condole	☐ herculean	☐ obscene	☐ supersede
☐ credulous	☐ immerse	☐ palatable	☐ timid
☐ discord	☐ incur	☐ polish	☐ unflagging
☐ duplicity	☐ insincere	☐ prominent	☐ visage

01

acquiesce
[ak-wee-es]

v. to accept, comply, or submit tacitly or passively
동의하다, 잠자코 따르다
They threatened him, and he **acquiesced**.[1]

syn. accede, agree, assent

02

analogy
[*uh*-nal-*uh*-jee]

n. resemblance in some particulars between things otherwise unlike
유사, 유추, 비슷한 관계
There is a close **analogy** between these two phenomena.[2]

syn. resemblance, similarity, correspondence

03

authentic
[aw-then-tik]

adj. not counterfeit or copied
진짜의, 진품의
CIA officials also believe that the tape is **authentic**.[3]

syn. genuine, real, valid

예문 해석

01 그들이 협박하자 그는 순순히 따랐다. **02** 두 현상 사이에는 매우 비슷한 점이 있다. **03** CIA 관계자들 역시 테이프가 진짜일 것이라고 믿고 있다.

04

bore
[bohr]

v. to make a hole
뚫다, 구멍을 내다, 파내다
They **bored** an oil well 2000 feet deep.[4]

> *syn.* drill, pierce, perforate

05

churn
[churn]

v. to move or swirl about violently
마구 휘젓다, 크림을 휘저어 버터로 만들다
His insides **churned** as the names were read out.[5]

> *syn.* stir, agitate, whip

06

condole
[kuhn-dohl]

v. to express sympathy
애도하다, 위로하다
He **condoled** with a friend whose grandmother has died.[6]

> *syn.* comfort, console

07

credulous
[krej-uh-luhs]

adj. willing to believe or trust too readily
너무 쉽게 믿어버리는, 잘 속는
This **credulous** man was constantly deceived by others.[7]

> *syn.* gullible, naive, easily fooled

08

discord
[dis-kawrd]

n. lack of concord or harmony
불일치, 불화
There was **discord** among the family.[8]

> *syn.* disagreement, conflict

예문 해석

04 그들은 오일 시추를 위한 구멍을 2천 피트 깊이로 팠다.　**05** 이름이 호명되자 그의 속이 뒤틀렸다.　**06** 그는 할머니가 돌아가신 친구를 위로했다.　**07** 이 잘 속는 남자는 끊임없이 다른 사람들에게 속았다.　**08** 가족 사이에 불화가 있었다.

duplicity
[doo-plis-i-tee]

n. deceitfulness in speech or conduct
사기, 이중성
I suspect her of **duplicity**.[9]

syn. artifice, deceit, chicanery

entice
[en-tais]

v. to lead on by exciting hope or desire
매혹하다, 유혹하다
They were **enticed** westward by dreams of diamonds.[10]

syn. allure, cajole, seduce

exotic
[ig-zot-ik]

adj. unusual and interesting
이국적인
During our time in South America, we went to an **exotic** resort.[11]

syn. foreign, outlandish, alien

feat
[feet]

n. a noteworthy or extraordinary act or achievement
위업, 솜씨
The man was honored when the king learned of his **feat**.[12]

syn. achievement, exploit, triumph

frenetic
[fruh-net-ik]

adj. wildly energetic
열광적인, 미친 듯이 흥분한
He featured a less **frenetic**, calmer style.[13]

syn. maniacal, frantic, frenzied

gratuitous
[gruh-too-i-tuhs]

adj. given without receiving any return value
무료의, 공짜의
The hotel guests enjoyed the **gratuitous** service.[14]

syn. free of charge, gratis, complimentary

📖 예문 해석

09 나는 그녀가 다른 마음이 있는지 의심된다.　**10** 그들은 다이아몬드의 꿈을 쫓아 서쪽으로 매혹되어 갔다.　**11** 남미에서 지내는 동안 우리는 이국적인 휴양지에 갔다.　**12** 그는 여왕이 그의 위업을 알았을 때 영예를 안았다.　**13** 그는 약간 덜 열광적인, 차분한 스타일이었다.　**14** 호텔 투숙객들은 그 무료 서비스를 즐겼다.

15

herculean
[hur-ky*uh*-lee-*uh*n]

adj. requiring great strength
큰 힘이 드는, 대단히 힘든
Digging the tunnel was a **herculean** task.[15]

syn. prodigious, arduous, onerous

16

immerse
[ih-murs]

v. to involve deeply
푹 빠지다, 깊이 연루되다
She was **immersed** in a book on the ancient secrets.[16]

syn. submerge, drench, saturate

17

incur
[in-kur]

v. to come into or acquire
초래하다
The terrible damage **incurred** during the past decade was devastating.[17]

syn. get, receive, obtain

18

insincere
[in-sin-seer]

adj. not honest in the expression of actual feeling
진심이 아닌, 꾸민
Crocodile tears are an **insincere** display of sadness.[18]

syn. hypocritical, pretended, dishonest

19

irrigate
[ir-i-geyt]

v. to supply land with water by artificial means
(토지에) 물을 대다, 관개하다
The farmer collected water to **irrigate** his crops.[19]

syn. water, moisten, wet

20

latent
[leyt-nt]

adj. existing as potential
잠재적인, 숨어 있는, 보이지 않는
She has a **latent** talent for acting.[20]

syn. dormant, inactive, hidden, unrevealed

예문 해석

15 터널을 뚫는 일은 엄청나게 힘이 든다.   **16** 그녀는 고대 마법에 대한 책에 푹 빠져 있었다.   **17** 지난 10년 동안 발생한 끔찍한 피해는 참혹했다.   **18** '악어의 눈물'이란 거짓으로 슬픈 척 하는 것을 말한다.   **19** 그 농부는 자신의 농작물에 물을 대주기 위해 물을 모았다.   **20** 그녀는 연기에 대한 잠재력이 있다.

lucrative
[loo-kr*uh*-tiv]

adj. making a large profit

수익이 되는, 이익이 있는

It is not easy to find **lucrative** jobs.[21]

syn. profitable, well-paid, gainful

melancholy
[mel-*uh*n-kol-ee]

adj. causing or expressing sadness

우울한, 슬픈

Listening to sad music all day long made me **melancholy**.[22]

syn. sad, depressed, downhearted

mourn
[mohrn]

v. to feel and show sadness for loss

슬퍼하다, 애통해하다

He **mourned** over the death of the former president.[23]

syn. bewail, bemoan, grieve

obscene
[*uh*b-seen]

adj. offensive to the mind

외설적인, 터무니없는

Refrain from using **obscene** language.[24]

syn. indecent, offensive, immoral

palatable
[pal-*uh*-t*uh*-b*uh*l]

adj. having a pleasant taste

맛 좋은, 입에 맞는

Artificial flavorings and preservatives make the food look more **palatable**.[25]

syn. delicious, agreeable, pleasant

polish
[pol-ish]

v. to make or become smooth and glossy by rubbing

닦다, 윤 내다

The marble floor was **polished** in a complicated process.[26]

syn. burnish, shine

예문 해석

21 수익이 되는 일을 찾기가 쉽지 않다. **22** 하루 종일 슬픈 노래를 들었더니 우울해졌다. **23** 그는 전직 대통령의 죽음을 애도했다. **24** 외설적인 말을 삼가세요. **25** 인공감미료와 보존제가 음식을 더 맛있어 보이게 한다. **26** 대리석 바닥은 복잡한 단계를 거쳐 윤이 난다.

27

prominent
[prom-*uh*-nu*h*nt]

adj. important and famous
저명한, 중요한
Several **prominent** political leaders were meeting to discuss the prospect of the treaty.[27]

syn. distinguished, eminent, famous

28

reparation
[rep-*uh*-rey-sh*uh*n]

n. the making of amends for wrong or injury done
보상, 보상금
A defeated nation was forced to pay **reparations** to its victorious enemies.[28]

syn. remuneration, compensation, amends

29

revolt
[ri-vohlt]

v. to rise up against an authority in an act of rebellion
반란을 일으키다, 저항하다, 봉기하다
She **revolted** against her oppressive 9:00 curfew.[29]

syn. rebel, mutiny, defy

30

scrutinize
[skroot-n-aiz]

v. to examine closely
세밀히 조사하다, 철저히 검사하다
The old lady **scrutinized** him through her spectacles.[30]

syn. ransack, investigate, search

31

sleek
[sleek]

adj. smooth and shiny and looking healthy
매끈한, 윤이 나는
The horse's **sleek** body gleamed.[31]

syn. smooth, shiny, glossy

32

statute
[stach-oot]

n. an act passed by a legislative body
법령, 법규
According to village **statute**, it was unlawful to drop anything from higher than ten feet.[32]

syn. act, law, decree

예문 해석

27 몇몇 저명한 정치 지도자들이 그 조약의 전망을 논의하기 위해 만나고 있었다.   **28** 패배한 국가는 승리한 적들에게 배상금을 지불해야만 했다.   **29** 그녀는 9시 통금 시간에 저항했다.   **30** 할머니는 안경 너머로 그를 찬찬히 훑어보았다.   **31** 말의 매끈한 몸은 윤이 났다.   **32** 마을법에 따르면 10피트 이상 상공에서 무엇이든 떨어뜨리는 것은 불법이었다.

33 ....

supersede
[soo-per-seed]

v. to take the place of something
대신하다, 대체하다
The TV has been **superseded** by the Internet.[33]

syn. displace, substitute

34 ....

timid
[tim-id]

adj. easily frightened or alarmed
겁 많은, 소심한
A **timid** child learned obedience at an early age.[34]

syn. timorous, shy, sheepish

35 ....

unflagging
[*uh*n-flag-ing]

adj. without ever becoming tired
지치지 않는, 지칠 줄 모르는
She was encouraged by the **unflagging** support of her
family and friends.[35]

syn. untiring, indefatigable, tireless

35 ....

visage
[viz-ij]

n. a person's face
얼굴, 용모, 외관
Think positive thoughts, and it will show on your **visage**.[36]

syn. face, countenance, feature

예문 해석

33 텔레비전은 인터넷으로 대체되었다.　**34** 겁 많은 아이는 일찍부터 순종을 배운다.　**35** 그녀는 그녀의 가족과 친구들의 끊임 없는 지지로 힘을 낼 수 있었다.　**36** 긍정적인 생각을 하세요, 그러면 당신의 얼굴에 드러날 것입니다.

Directions Each of the following questions consists of one word followed by five words or phrases. You are to select the one word or phrase whose meaning is closest to the word in capital letters.

1. ACQUIESCE :
(A) accede
(B) satirize
(C) revive
(D) apply
(E) stumble

2. ANALOGY :
(A) information
(B) expedition
(C) caliber
(D) disinformation
(E) resemblance

3. AUTHENTIC :
(A) genuine
(B) panicked
(C) impudent
(D) blameworthy
(E) obese

4. CONDOLE :
(A) comfort
(B) consult
(C) coordinate
(D) collaborate
(E) comprehend

5. CREDULOUS :
(A) moving
(B) flabby
(C) lethargic
(D) callow
(E) gullible

6. PALATABLE :
(A) delicious
(B) respectable
(C) biased
(D) dormant
(E) identical

7. FEAT :
(A) fragment
(B) canine
(C) achievement
(D) mandate
(E) conjecture

8. LUCRATIVE :
(A) foul
(B) ceaseless
(C) appealing
(D) slimy
(E) profitable

9. MOURN :
(A) bewail
(B) tread
(C) refuge
(D) revere
(E) stride

10. POLISH :
(A) abandon
(B) burnish
(C) sort
(D) comfort
(E) insinuate

Directions   Each of the following questions consists of one word followed by five words or phrases.
You are to select the one word or phrase whose meaning is closest to the word in capital letters.

1. RANCOR :
   (A) resentment
   (B) hypothesis
   (C) wile
   (D) authority
   (E) prompt

2. RECONCILIATION :
   (A) conciliation
   (B) premise
   (C) shortage
   (D) reasoning
   (E) implication

3. THRIFTY :
   (A) frugal
   (B) adverse
   (C) prodigal
   (D) miserable
   (E) philanthropic

4. VINDICATE :
   (A) justify
   (B) describe
   (C) abate
   (D) plunder
   (E) restart

5. COVERT :
   (A) obvious
   (B) concealed
   (C) disloyalty
   (D) complimentary
   (E) sumptuous

6. PACIFY :
   (A) squint
   (B) calm
   (C) retract
   (D) goad
   (E) split

7. PLUNDER :
   (A) filch
   (B) urge
   (C) abate
   (D) soothe
   (E) rob

8. SKIRMISH :
   (A) trajectory
   (B) summit
   (C) fight
   (D) distress
   (E) invigorated

9. HEINOUS :
   (A) prickly
   (B) decorative
   (C) horrifying
   (D) archaic
   (E) cautious

10. EXODUS :
   (A) gale
   (B) apex
   (C) doctrine
   (D) evacuation
   (E) mission

11. PACT :
  (A) melee
  (B) duel
  (C) deal
  (D) milestone
  (E) patron

12. PLACID :
  (A) repulsive
  (B) serene
  (C) dreadful
  (D) blameworthy
  (E) cumbersome

13. DISCONCERT :
  (A) confound
  (B) exert
  (C) resume
  (D) bleach
  (E) restrict

14. ENTHRALL :
  (A) enchant
  (B) vend
  (C) stir
  (D) reimburse
  (E) peddle

15. REDRESS :
  (A) domicile
  (B) surfeit
  (C) intuitiveness
  (D) transformation
  (E) compensation

16. FRAYED :
  (A) worn
  (B) cluttered
  (C) arid
  (D) languid
  (E) insane

17. PREROGATIVE :
  (A) privilege
  (B) lawsuit
  (C) etiquette
  (D) motherhood
  (E) wrath

18. POISE :
  (A) pagan
  (B) mecca
  (C) theme
  (D) composure
  (E) gap

19. PROMINENT :
  (A) still
  (B) prejudiced
  (C) fidgety
  (D) snappy
  (E) distinguished

20. REVOLT :
  (A) annul
  (B) amend
  (C) rebel
  (D) evade
  (E) insert

"The only limit to our realization of tomorrow will be our doubts of today."

— Franklin Roosevelt —
the 32nd president of the U.S.

내일 실현될 것에 대한 유일한 한계는 오늘 우리가 갖는 의심이다.

Greek and Latin Roots & Prefixes 31

★ AMBI = both

agere (to lead)	**ambi**guous	모호한, 확실하지 않은
valere (strong)	**ambi**valent	반대 감정을 동시에 가지는
bios (life)	**amphi**bian	양서류
dexter (right-handed)	**ambi**dextrous	양손잡이의, 양손을 다 잘 쓰는

★ AMBI = to surrond

ire (to go)	**ambi**tious	야심 있는
	ambience (**ambi**ance)	분위기
extra (outside)	**amphi**theater	(고대 로마의) 원형 극장

DAY

31

WORDS TO LEARN

☐ acquit	☐ dread	☐ insinuation	☐ premise
☐ anarchy	☐ entourage	☐ irrevocable	☐ ratify
☐ authority	☐ expansion	☐ latitude	☐ retreat
☐ bottomless	☐ fiasco	☐ ludicrous	☐ scurry
☐ circuitous	☐ frenzy	☐ mellow	☐ slender
☐ condescending	☐ grave	☐ muffle	☐ staunch
☐ coy	☐ hereditary	☐ obscure	☐ supreme
☐ deride	☐ imminent	☐ paltry	☐ unflappable
☐ discourse	☐ indomitable	☐ plausible	☐ unwarranted

01

acquit
[*uh*-kwit]

v. to declare not guilty
무죄를 선고하다
The jury **acquitted** her of murder.[1]

syn. exculpate, absolve

02

anarchy
[an-er-kee]

n. confusion and lack of order of any kind
무정부상태, 혼란
War and famine sent the nation plunging into **anarchy**.[2]

syn. disorder, chaos, lawlessness

03

authority
[*uh*-thawr-i-tee]

n. the power or right to give orders or make decisions
힘, 권한
The judge had the **authority** to send the man to prison.[3]

syn. right, power, ability

예문 해석

01 배심원단은 그녀의 살인에 무죄를 선고했다.　**02** 전쟁과 기근이 나라를 무정부 상태에 빠지게 만들었다.　**03** 판사는 남자를 감옥에 보낼 수 있는 권한을 가졌다.

04

bottomless
[bot-*uhm*-lis]

adj. extremely deep or plentiful
밑바닥 없는, 매우 깊은
We don't have a **bottomless** pit of resources.[4]

syn. extremely deep, boundless, abysmal

05

circuitous
[ser-kyoo-i-t*uhs*]

adj. not direct
간접적인, 돌려 하는
For the scenic route, he took a **circuitous** path.[5]

syn. roundabout, indirect, meandering

06

condescending
[kon-d*uh*-sen-ding]

adj. showing a patronizing descent from dignity or superiority
거들먹거리는, 잘난 체하는
His **condescending** attitude annoyed her.[6]

syn. patronizing, supercilious, arrogant

07

coy
[koi]

adj. artfully or affectedly shy or reserved
수줍어하는, 내숭을 떠는
The **coy** cheerleader pretends to be shy in front of the boy, but she really isn't.[7]

syn. bashful, evasive, timid

08

deride
[di-raid]

v. to laugh at in scorn or contempt
조롱하다, 비웃다
The professor **derided** his student's attempt to solve the problem.[8]

syn. jeer, sneer, mock, ridicule, scoff

🔖 예문 해석

04 자원이 무한정인 것은 아니다.   **05** 경치 좋은 길을 위해 그는 우회했다.   **06** 그의 거들먹거리는 태도에 그녀는 짜증을 냈다.
07 그 수줍은 치어리더는 그 소년 앞에서는 수줍은 척 하지만 실제로는 그렇지 않다.   **08** 교수는 문제를 풀려는 학생의 시도를 비웃었다.

discourse
[dis-kohrs]

n. formal and orderly and usually extended expression of thought on a subject
강연, 담화, 토론
He enjoyed intelligent **discourse** with his friends.[9]

syn. dialogue, conversation, discussion

dread
[dred]

n. the fear of something bad happening
(안 좋은 일이 생길까 봐 갖는) 두려움
People feel **dread** at the very thought of speaking in front of a large audience.[10]

syn. fear, apprehension, horror

entourage
[ahn-too-rahzh]

n. a group of people who travel with an important person
측근, 수행원, 주위 사람들
Movie star Lyla and her **entourage** - her manager, hair designer, trainer, bodyguard, massage therapist, doctor, and coordinator arrived at the theater.[11]

syn. attendants, retinue, escort

expansion
[ik-span-sh*uh*n]

n. the act or state of expanding
확장, 팽창
The **expansion** of territory was a great accomplishment for the country.[12]

syn. enlargement, growth, extension

fiasco
[fee-as-koh]

n. a complete and ignominious failure
큰 실수, 대실패
Their effort ended in **fiasco**.[13]

syn. debacle, catastrophe, failure

 예문 해석

09 그는 친구들과 나누는 지적인 담소를 즐겼다. **10** 사람들은 많은 청중 앞에서 연설한다는 생각만으로도 두려움을 느낀다. **11** 인기 영화배우인 라일라와 그의 측근들 – 매니저, 헤어 디자이너, 트레이너, 보디가드, 마사지사, 의사, 코디네이터 모두가 극장에 도착했다. **12** 영토의 확장은 그 나라에 큰 성과였다. **13** 그들의 노력은 대실패로 끝났다.

frenzy
[fren-zee]

n. wild agitation or excitement
격분, 열광
Once war broke out, a **frenzy** of fear was also felt among the people.[14]

syn. fury, anger, rage

grave
[greyv]

adj. serious or solemn
중대한, 심각한, 근엄한
The Korean government expresses **grave** concern over some of the Japanese textbooks that claim Dokdo's sovereignty.[15]

syn. serious, solemn, important

hereditary
[huh-red-i-ter-ee]

adj. naturally from parent to offspring through the genes
유전의, 물려받은
Blonde is **hereditary** in our family.[16]

syn. inherited, heritable, traditional

imminent
[im-uh-nuhnt]

adj. likely to happen in the near future
곧 닥쳐올 것 같은, 일촉즉발의
They are in **imminent** danger.[17]

syn. impending, forthcoming, immediate

indomitable
[in-dom-i-tuh-buhl]

adj. that cannot be subdued or overcome, as persons, will, or courage
불굴의, 정복되지 않는
The warrior has an **indomitable** spirit that comes from within.[18]

syn. unconquerable, invincible, obstinate

insinuation
[in-sin-yoo-ey-shuhn]

n. an indirect suggestion or hint
암시, 풍자
His methods of **insinuation** are ingenious.[19]

syn. innuendo, cue, hint

예문 해석

14 전쟁이 일어나자 국민들 사이에서도 공포의 광풍이 느껴졌다.　**15** 대한민국 정부는 독도의 영유권을 주장하는 일본의 몇몇 교과서에 대해 심각한 우려를 표명했다.　**16** 금발은 우리 가족의 유전이다.　**17** 그들은 즉각적인 위험에 처해 있다.　**18** 정말로 숙제 끝낸 것 맞아?　**19** 그의 풍자법은 천재적이다.

20 ·····

irrevocable
[i-rev-*uh*-kuh-bu*h*l]

adj. unable to be changed
취소할 수 없는, 되돌릴 수 없는
He said the decision was **irrevocable**.[20]

> *syn.* irreversible, final

21 ·····

latitude
[lat-i-tood]

n. freedom to choose
허용 범위, 위도
Parents must allow their children a fair amount of **latitude**.[21]

> *syn.* leeway, freedom, elbowroom

22 ·····

ludicrous
[loo-di-kr*uh*s]

adj. completely ridiculous
웃기는, 우스꽝스러운
It was **ludicrous** to believe that their meeting could be kept secret.[22]

> *syn.* preposterous, ridiculous, absurd

23 ·····

mellow
[mel-oh]

adj. pleasant and smooth
부드럽고 원숙한
Her voice was **mellow**, and I felt assured.[23]

> *syn.* soft, smooth, rich

24 ·····

muffle
[m*uhf-uh*l]

v. to make a sound quieter
소리를 줄이다, 소음하다
She tried to **muffle** the alarm clock by putting it under the pillow.[24]

> *syn.* mute, suppress, tone down

25 ·····

obscure
[*uh*b-skyoor]

adj. vague or hard to see
분명하지 않은
The **obscure** issue was seemingly unresolved.[25]

> *syn.* unclear, vague, murky

예문 해석

20 그는 결정을 되돌릴 수 없다고 말했다. **21** 부모는 아이들에게 어느 정도의 선택의 자유를 주어야 한다. **22** 그들의 만남이 비밀로 지켜질 것이라 믿는 것은 바보 같은 일이다. **23** 그녀의 목소리는 부드러웠고 나는 안도감을 느꼈다. **24** 그녀는 알람시계를 베개 밑으로 넣어 소리를 줄이려고 했다. **25** 그 애매한 문제는 겉으로 보기에는 해결되지 않았다.

26

paltry
[pawl-tree]

adj. utterly worthless
하찮은, 가치 없는
Only a **paltry** sum was set aside to support cultural programs.[26]

syn. insignificant, trivial, trifling

27

plausible
[plaw-*zuh-buhl*]

adj. having an appearance of truth or reason
이치에 맞는, 그럴듯한
When he forgot to do his homework, he tried to create a **plausible** excuse his teacher would believe.[27]

syn. probable, believable, feasible

28

premise
[prem-is]

n. a statement that is assumed to be true and from which a conclusion can be drawn
전제
You can criticize others' theories by demonstrating their false **premises**.[28]

syn. hypothesis, basis, argument

29

ratify
[rat-*uh*-fai]

v. to give formal consent to
승인하다, 인가하다
They had to **ratify** the constitution.[29]

syn. approve, confirm, sanction

30

retreat
[ree-treet]

n. the act of withdrawing or going backward
후퇴, 철수, 퇴각
In the military sense, **retreat** means the withdrawal of troops.[30]

syn. withdrawal, evacuation, departure

 예문 해석

26 극히 적은 예산만이 문화 프로그램에 할당되었다. **27** 그가 숙제하는 것을 잊었을 때, 그는 선생님이 믿을 만한 그럴듯한 변명을 지어내려 했다. **28** 다른 사람의 이론을 그릇된 전제를 들어 비판할 수 있다. **29** 그들은 헌법을 비준해야 했다. **30** 군사적 의미에서 후퇴는 군대의 철수를 의미한다.

31 ··

scurry
[skur-ee]

v. to go or move quickly or in haste
허둥지둥 달리다
The doctors were **scurrying** about the ward.[31]

> *syn.* scamper, sprint, scuttle

32 ··

slender
[slen-der]

adj. attractively slim
호리호리한, 가느다란
She is **slender**.[32]

> *syn.* slim, slight, lean

33 ··

staunch
[stawnch]

adj. firm or steadfast in principle, adherence or loyalty
견고한, 튼튼한, 믿음직한
A group of his **staunch** supporters discussed strategies to help him win the election.[33]

> *syn.* steadfast, resolute, firm

34 ··

supreme
[*suh*-preem]

adj. highest in rank, power, or importance
최고의, 최상의
To be a judge in the **Supreme** Court of the United States is quite an accomplishment.[34]

> *syn.* highest, best, ultimate

35 ··

unflappable
[*uhn*-flap-*uh*-buhl]

adj. remaining calm under pressure
침착한, 쉽게 흥분하지 않는
He always overcame difficulties in his usual **unflappable** manner.[35]

> *syn.* composed, calm, unflustered

36 ··

unwarranted
[*uhn*-wawr-*uhn*-tid]

adj. incapable of being justified or explained
부당한, 불필요한, 부적절한
To go into someone's home without a warrant would be **unwarranted**.[36]

> *syn.* unjustified, groundless, inexcusable

예문 해석

31 의사들이 황급하게 병동을 달렸다. **32** 그녀는 날씬하다. **33** 그의 충실한 지지자들은 선거에서 이길 수 있는 전략들을 논의했다. **34** 미국 대법원에서 판사가 되는 것은 대단한 업적이다. **35** 그는 늘 그래왔듯 어려움을 침착한 방식으로 극복했다. **36** 영장 없이 누군가의 집에 들어가는 것은 부당하다.

Directions   Each of the following questions consists of one word followed by five words or phrases. You are to select the one word or phrase whose meaning is closest to the word in capital letters.

1. ACQUIT :
(A) dissolve
(B) exculpate
(C) impregnate
(D) captivate
(E) reveal

2. AUTHORITY :
(A) game
(B) right
(C) attack
(D) shelter
(E) opponent

3. CONDESCENDING :
(A) aloof
(B) tricky
(C) complicated
(D) unconquerable
(E) patronizing

4. DREAD :
(A) youth
(B) fear
(C) euphoria
(D) locomotion
(E) vista

5. ENTOURAGE :
(A) proverb
(B) ecstasy
(C) cascade
(D) debacle
(E) attendants

6. FIASCO :
(A) tumult
(B) rundown
(C) mentor
(D) debacle
(E) revenge

7. INSINUATION :
(A) tapestry
(B) companion
(C) innuendo
(D) remuneration
(E) exemption

8. IRREVOCABLE :
(A) irreversible
(B) terse
(C) shaggy
(D) awful
(E) theatrical

9. LUDICROUS :
(A) wispy
(B) preposterous
(C) uproarious
(D) rambling
(E) ceaseless

10. OBSCURE :
(A) unclear
(B) tart
(C) weird
(D) unruffled
(E) probable

"Take time for all things; great haste makes great waste."

— Benjamin Franklin —
US author, diplomat, inventor, physicist, politician, & printer

모든 일을 여유를 가지고 처리하라. 더 크게 서두를수록 더 큰 낭비가 생긴다.

Greek and Latin Roots & Prefixes 32

★ GREG = group

ad (toward)	**aggre**gate	총합
con (together)	**con**gregate	모이다
	congregation	(예배를 보기 위해 모인) 신도들
se (apart from)	**se**gregate	분리하다, 구분하다
-ous (adj.)	**gre**garious	사교적인
ex (out of)	**e**greg**i**ous	지독한, 매우 나쁜

DAY

32

WORDS TO LEARN

☐ accost	☐ dwindle	☐ insipid	☐ posthumous
☐ anatomy	☐ entrust	☐ kin	☐ predicament
☐ autonomous	☐ expedient	☐ laudable	☐ retrieve
☐ boulder	☐ fickle	☐ lukewarm	☐ scuttle
☐ circumscribe	☐ frigid	☐ memento	☐ secede
☐ condone	☐ gregarious	☐ mundane	☐ steadfast
☐ cower	☐ heresy	☐ obsequious	☐ surly
☐ derivative	☐ hysterical	☐ pamper	☐ token
☐ discredit	☐ indefatigable	☐ physique	☐ unfledged

01

accost
[*uh*-kawst]

v. to approach someone aggressively or confront someone in an inappropriate way
(위협적으로) 다가가 말을 걸다
She was **accosted** by an angry anti-fur activist when she wore her fine fur coat.[1]

syn. approach, confront, address

02

anatomy
[*uh*-nat-*uh*-mee]

n. the study of the structure of the bodies of people or animals
해부, 해부학
Arthur Conan Doyle studied **anatomy** in medical school.[2]

syn. dissection, analysis

03

autonomous
[aw-ton-*uh*-m*uh*s]

adj. subject to its own laws only
자치의, 스스로 다스리는, 독립적인
He works for the IARC, which is an **autonomous** body under the umbrella of the World Health Organization.[3]

syn. self-governing, independent

 예문 해석

01 그녀가 멋진 모피 코트를 입었을 때 화가 난 모피 반대 운동가가 다가왔다.　**02** 아서 코난 도일은 의대 시절 해부학을 공부했다.　**03** 그는 세계보건기구 산하의 국제 암연구소(IARC)에서 일한다.

04 ··

boulder
[bohl-der]

n. a large rounded rock

크고 둥근 암석

He has various rocks that are as small as pebbles or as big as **boulders**.[4]

syn. rock, stone

05 ··

circumscribe
[sur-*kuhm*-skraib]

v. to enclose within bounds

제한하다, 한계를 정하다

In many countries, strikes are legal under a **circumscribed** set of conditions.[5]

syn. limit, restrict, hem in

06 ··

condone
[*kuhn*-dohn]

v. to disregard or overlook

못 본 척 넘어가다

By his silence, he seemed to **condone** their behavior.[6]

syn. overlook, pass over, connive

07 ··

cower
[kou-er]

v. to crouch, as in fear or shame

(겁을 먹고) 몸을 웅크리다

The little mouse **cowered** when a huge, hungry cat approached.[7]

syn. cringe, flinch, recoil

08 ··

derivative
[di-riv-*uh*-tiv]

adj. not original or derived from something else

다른 데서 유래된, 모방한, 독창적이지 않은

Their **derivative** method of solving the problem was not interesting.[8]

syn. copied, unoriginal, imitative

🔖 예문 해석

04 그는 작은 조약돌부터 큰 암석까지 다양한 돌을 가지고 있다. **05** 많은 나라에서 파업은 제한된 조건 아래서는 합법적이다.
06 침묵으로 그는 그들의 행동을 눈감아 주는 듯 보였다. **07** 크고 배고픈 고양이가 다가오자 작은 쥐는 움츠러들었다. **08** 문제
해결을 위한 그들의 유도 방법은 흥미롭지 못했다.

discredit
[dis-kred-it]

v. to injure the credit or blame
평판을 나쁘게 하다, 불명예스럽게 하다
There is no reason to **discredit** people merely because you disagree with their views.[9]

syn. disrepute, defame, disgrace

dwindle
[dwin-dl]

v. to become smaller, weaker, or less in number
줄어들다, 약해지다
The workforce of the company has **dwindled** from over 3,000 to a few hundred.[10]

syn. decrease, decline, diminish

entrust
[en-tr*uh*st]

v. to assign the care of something
책임이나 임무를 맡기다, 위임하다
If parents want to **entrust** their child to the best teacher, they have to travel to the biggest city.[11]

syn. hand over, turn over, confide

expedient
[ik-spee-dee-*uh*nt]

adj. useful or convenient
쓸모 있는, 편리한
The office processed the papers in an **expedient** manner.[12]

syn. convenient, practical, useful

fickle
[fik-*uh*l]

adj. casually changeable
변덕스러운, 변하기 쉬운
Winter in my town is notoriously **fickle**.[13]

syn. capricious, whimsical, fanciful

frigid
[frij-id]

adj. extremely cold
매우 추운
It was hard to adjust to the **frigid** climate.[14]

syn. frosty, glacial, frozen

 예문 해석

09 단지 너와 생각이 다르다고 해서 다른 사람을 폄하할 이유는 없다. **10** 그 회사의 인력은 3,000여 명 이상에서 몇백 명 정도로 줄어들었다. **11** 만약 부모가 자신의 아이를 가장 재능 있는 선생님에게 맡기려 한다면 그들은 가장 큰 도시로 가야 한다. **12** 그 직원은 서류를 빠르게 처리했다. **13** 우리 동네 겨울은 날씨가 변덕스럽기로 악명 높다. **14** 추운 날씨에 적응하는 것은 어려웠다.

gregarious
[gri-gair-ee-*uhs*]

adj. fond of the company of others
사교적인, 사람들과 잘 어울리는
Among his classmates, he was known as a **gregarious** person.[15]

syn. sociable, friendly, affable

heresy
[her-*uh*-see]

n. opinion or doctrine at variance with the orthodox
이교도, 이단
Paul himself fought against that **heresy**.[16]

syn. pagan, infidel

hysterical
[hi-ster-i-k*uhl*]

adj. uncontrollably emotional
과잉 흥분하는, 감정 통제를 못하는 상태의
When his favorite sports team lost a championship, he got **hysterical** and started weeping and screaming all at once.[17]

syn. neurotic, frantic, distraught

indefatigable
[in-di-fat-i-g*uh*-b*uh*l]

adj. incapable of being fatigued
지치지 않는, 질리지 않는, 끈기 있는
He is an **indefatigable** laborer who can work from sunrise to sunset.[18]

syn. unflagging, untiring, inexhaustible

insipid
[in-sip-id]

adj. dull and boring
재미없는, 무미건조한, 김 빠진, 맛 없는
He bored me with **insipid** conversation.[19]

syn. bland, flat, dull

 예문 해석

15 그는 반 친구들 사이에서 사교적인 사람으로 알려져 있었다.   **16** 바울 자신도 이단과 싸웠다.   **17** 자신이 좋아하는 스포츠팀이 우승을 놓치자 히스테리를 부리며 한꺼번에 울며 비명을 지르기 시작했다.   **18** 그는 해 뜰 때부터 해질 때까지 일할 수 있는 지치지 않는 일꾼이었다.   **19** 그는 진부한 대화로 나를 지겹게 만들었다.

kin
[kin]

n. a person having kinship with another or others

친족, 친척

Everyone lived in harmonious relations with all kith and **kin**.[20]

syn. family, relatives, kinsperson

laudable
[law-d*uh*-b*uh*l]

adj. deserve to be praised or admired

칭찬할 만한, 훌륭한

Organizing data was a **laudable** idea.[21]

syn. meritorious, praiseworthy, commendable

lukewarm
[look-wawrm]

adj. having little ardor or enthusiasm

열의 없는, 성의 없는, 미지근한

The editor was **lukewarm** about her script.[22]

syn. halfhearted, tepid

memento
[m*uh*-men-toh]

n. a thing that serves as a reminder of the past

기념물, 추억거리

This **memento** preserves special times spent with treasured friends.[23]

syn. souvenir, keepsake

mundane
[m*uh*n-deyn]

adj. ordinary and boring

평범한, 흔히 있는

She is always willing to do even **mundane** tasks.[24]

syn. everyday, common, routine

obsequious
[*uh*b-see-kwee-*uh*s]

adj. submissively obedient

아첨하는, 비위를 맞추는

The prince did not like **obsequious** servants.[25]

syn. fawning, sycophantic, toadyish

예문 해석

20 모든 사람들이 친구들, 친족들과 함께 조화롭게 살았다. **21** 데이터를 구조화하는 것은 칭찬할만한 아이디어다. **22** 그 편집자는 그녀의 원고에 대해 성의없는 태도를 보였다. **23** 이 기념품은 소중한 친구들과 함께 했던 특별한 시간을 기억하게 해준다. **24** 그녀는 사소한 일이라도 열심히 하려고 한다. **25** 그 왕자는 아첨하는 신하들은 좋아하지 않았다.

26

pamper
[pam-per]

v. to make someone feel comfortable by doing things for them

응석받아주다, 해달라는 대로 해주다

Take the time to **pamper** yourself, even if you can't afford to go anywhere.[26]

syn. indulge, spoil, coddle

27

physique
[fi-zeek]

n. physical or bodily structure, appearance, or development

체격

When he trained for marathons, he took pictures of his **physique** before and after.[27]

syn. shape, structure, build

28

posthumous
[pos-ch*uh*-m*uh*s]

adj. after one's death

사후의

The **posthumous** publication of the author's book had massive success.[28]

syn. postmortem, after death, post-obituary

29

predicament
[pri-dik-*uh*-m*uh*nt]

n. a difficulty, plight or dilemma

곤경, 궁지

He is in a dire **predicament**.[29]

syn. impasse, plight, quandary

30

retrieve
[ri-treev]

v. to get or bring something back again, to recover

되찾다, 복구하다, 만회하다

He **retrieved** his fortunes in the past five years.[30]

syn. recoup, regain

 예문 해석

26 어떤 무슬림 나라든 남자의 1% 미만이 일부다처이다.　**27** 그가 마라톤을 위해 훈련할 때, 그는 운동 전후 체격 사진을 찍었다.　**28** 저자의 사후 출판물은 그의 사망 이후 엄청난 성공을 거두었다.　**29** 그는 비참한 곤경에 처해 있다.　**30** 그는 지난 5년간 잃었던 재산을 되찾았다.

31 ....

scuttle
[sk*uh*t-l]

v. to move quickly with haste
바삐 가다, 황급히 달리다, 허둥지둥 달아나다
Two small children **scuttled** away.[31]

> *syn.* scurry, scamper

32 ....

secede
[si-seed]

v. to withdraw formally from an alliance or association
분리 독립하다
The South wanted to **secede** and become independent during the U.S. Civil War.[32]

> *syn.* split from, separate, break away

33 ....

steadfast
[sted-fast]

adj. fixed in direction
고정된, 흔들리지 않는
He remained **steadfast** in his belief.[33]

> *syn.* steady, loyal, faithful

34 ....

surly
[sur-lee]

adj. abrupt and impolite in manner or speech
무뚝뚝한, 퉁명스러운
He became gruff and **surly** towards me.[34]

> *syn.* gruff, brusque, abrupt

35 ....

token
[toh-k*uh*n]

n. something serving as a sign of something else
상징
She gave a badge as a **token** of her thanks.[35]

> *syn.* sign, symbol, emblem

36 ....

unfledged
[*uh*n-flejd]

adj. young and inexperienced
어리고 경험이 미숙한, 아직 깃털이 채 자라지 않은
I took care of the **unfledged** bird until it could take care of itself.[36]

> *syn.* inexperienced, callow, immature

🦉 예문 해석

31 두 명의 어린아이가 황급히 달려갔다.　**32** 남부는 남북전쟁 동안 분리 독립하기를 원했다.　**33** 그는 자신의 믿음에 흔들림이 없었다.　**34** 그는 나에게 무뚝뚝하고 퉁명스러웠다.　**35** 그녀는 감사의 표시로 배지를 주었다.　**36** 나는 아직 깃털도 나지 않은 아기 새가 스스로 잘 돌볼 수 있을 때까지 돌보았다.

Directions Each of the following questions consists of one word followed by five words or phrases. You are to select the one word or phrase whose meaning is closest to the word in capital letters.

1. ACCOST :
   (A) approach
   (B) resurrect
   (C) gleam
   (D) revolutionize
   (E) scorch

2. AUTONOMOUS :
   (A) disparaging
   (B) frightening
   (C) self-governing
   (D) priceless
   (E) innovative

3. BOULDER :
   (A) tip
   (B) rock
   (C) accolade
   (D) salute
   (E) genuflect

4. CONDONE :
   (A) overlook
   (B) nurture
   (C) restore
   (D) congregate
   (E) glimpse

5. COWER :
   (A) terminate
   (B) cringe
   (C) mumble
   (D) evade
   (E) simulate

6. LUKEWARM :
   (A) halfhearted
   (B) feasible
   (C) pungent
   (D) submissive
   (E) venturesome

7. MEMENTO :
   (A) fury
   (B) souvenir
   (C) roster
   (D) shipment
   (E) armory

8. MUNDANE :
   (A) ashamed
   (B) rowdy
   (C) peculiar
   (D) everyday
   (E) agreeable

9. POSTHUMOUS :
   (A) complaining
   (B) respectful
   (C) delicious
   (D) insolent
   (E) postmortem

10. SECEDE :
   (A) split from
   (B) bounce back
   (C) pass on
   (D) care for
   (E) seize up

"Nothing great was ever achieved without enthusiasm."

— Ralph Waldo Emerson —
U.S. essayist & poet

열정 없이는 어떤 위대한 일도 있을 수 없다.

Greek and Latin Roots & Prefixes 33

★ PHOBIA = fear

akros (topmost)	acro**phobia**	고소 공포증
agora (plaza)	agora**phobia**	광장 공포증
hemo (blood)	hemo**phobia**	혈액 공포증
hydro (water)	hydro**phobia**	물 공포증
claustrum (confined place)	claustro**phobia**	폐소 공포증
ornis (bird)	ornitho**phobia**	조류 공포증
xeno (foreign)	xeno**phobia**	이방인 공포증
zoo (animal)	zoo**phobia**	동물 공포증

DAY

33

WORDS TO LEARN

☐ acrimonious	☐ eager	☐ insolvent	☐ provisional
☐ amnesty	☐ enumerate	☐ isolate	☐ rational
☐ avarice	☐ expedite	☐ launch	☐ recapitulate
☐ boulevard	☐ fidelity	☐ lull[1]	☐ sooty
☐ citadel	☐ frivolous	☐ menace	☐ stealthy
☐ confer	☐ grotesque	☐ municipal	☐ surmise
☐ crevice	☐ histrionic	☐ philanthropy	☐ treason
☐ derive	☐ incidental	☐ prerequisite	☐ unflinching
☐ discrepancy	☐ indelible	☐ propaganda	☐ vital

01

acrimonious
[ak-*ruh*-moh-nee-*uh*s]

adj. caustic, stinging, or bitter in nature, speech, behavior
신랄한

Her tendency to make **acrimonious** remarks alienated her friends.[1]

syn. caustic, stinging, acrid

02

amnesty
[am-n*uh*-stee]

n. a general pardon for offenses against a government
사면

As part of a truce, **amnesty** can be granted to opposition forces in civil disputes.[2]

syn. immunity, pardon, reprieve

03

avarice
[av-er-is]

n. insatiable desire for wealth
탐욕

"**Avarice**, envy, pride, three fatal sparks, have set the hearts of all on fire." - Dante[3]

syn. covetousness, greed, rapacity

예문 해석

01 신랄하게 말하는 성향은 그녀를 친구들과 멀어지게 했다.   **02** 휴전의 일환으로, 민간 분쟁에서 반대 세력에 대한 사면이 허용될 수 있다.   **03** 탐욕과 질투, 자만, 이 치명적인 세 가지 불꽃이 마음을 불구덩이로 만든다.

04

boulevard
[bool-*uh*-vahrd]

n. a broad street in a town or city, especially one lined with trees
넓은 가로수길, 대로
Boulevards usually have areas at the sides or center for trees, grass, or flowers.[4]

syn. street, avenue

05

citadel
[sit-*uh*-dl]

n. a fortified structure designed to provide protection during a battle
요새
The town has the 16th century **citadel**.[5]

syn. fortress, fort, stronghold

06

confer
[k*uh*n-fur]

v. to have a conference in order to talk something over
조언하다
I will **confer** with my lawyer.[6]

syn. advise, consult, counsel

07

crevice
[krev-is]

n. a narrow crack or fissure especially in a rock
갈라진 틈, 균열
Children peeped through a **crevice**.[7]

syn. cleft, rift, fissure, break, fracture, crack

08

derive
[di-raiv]

v. to receive or obtain from a source
끌어내다, 얻다
She **derives** pleasure from helping others.[8]

syn. obtain, gain, attain

예문 해석

04 대로에는 보통 길가나 중간에 나무나 풀, 꽃들을 놓은 공간이 있다. **05** 그 마을에는 16세기 요새가 있다. **06** 내 변호사와 상의해 보겠다. **07** 아이들이 틈으로 들여다 보았다. **08** 그녀는 다른 사람을 돕는 것에서 기쁨을 얻는다.

discrepancy
[di-skrep-*uhn*-see]

n. a difference between two things that should be the same
모순, 불일치, 어긋남
There are **discrepancies** among news media outlets.[9]

syn. inconsistency, disparity, divergence

eager
[ee-ger]

adj. feeling or showing great desire
열망하는, 갈망하는
He was **eager** to talk about life in the Army.[10]

syn. anxious, hungry, ardent, fervent

enumerate
[ih-noo-m*uh*-reyt]

v. to name or list, one by one
한 명씩 대다, 이름을 대다
Can you **enumerate** all the qualities of a skilled scientist? [11]

syn. specify, itemize, count

expedite
[ek-spi-dait]

v. to speed up
진척시키다, 촉진시키다
We tried to help you **expedite** your plans.[12]

syn. accelerate, quicken, speed up

fidelity
[fi-del-i-tee]

n. strict observance of promises or duties
충실, 성실, 충성
I had to promise **fidelity** to the King.[13]

syn. loyalty, faithfulness, reliability

frivolous
[friv-*uh*-lu*h*s]

adj. characterized by lack of seriousness
경박한, 경솔한
His **frivolous** conduct did not allow him to get promoted.[14]

syn. flippant, frolicsome, perky

🔖 예문 해석

09 언론사마다 차이가 있다. **10** 그는 군대 시절 이야기를 매우 하고 싶어했다. **11** 당신은 실력 있는 과학자가 지녀야 할 자질들에 대해 하나씩 말해볼 수 있는가? **12** 우리는 네 계획이 빨리 이루어지도록 노력했다. **13** 나는 왕에게 충성을 맹세해야 했다. **14** 그의 경박한 행동 때문에 그는 승진이 되지 않았다.

grotesque
[groh-tesk]

adj. fantastically ugly

기괴한

The unnatural appearance of a figurine was **grotesque** and scary.[15]

syn. bizarre, eerie, absurd

histrionic
[his-tree-on-ik]

adj. overly dramatic, in behavior or speech.

연극하는 것 같은, 과장된

The musical actor's **histrionic** voice sounded strange in everyday life but is perfect for the stage.[16]

syn. dramatic, flamboyant, overemotional

incidental
[in-si-den-tl]

adj. secondary in time or importance

부수적인, 결과로 따르기 마련인

Her company paid her main expenses when she traveled for business but did not reimburse her for the **incidental** ones.[17]

syn. minor, secondary, related

indelible
[in-del-*uh*-b*uh*l]

adj. that cannot be removed, washed away, or erased

지워지지 않는, 지울 수 없는

Most parents do not want their young children playing with **indelible** ink in the house.[18]

syn. irrevocable, indestructible, irremovable

insolvent
[in-sol-v*uh*nt]

adj. unable to pay debts

파산한. 지불 능력이 없는

The **insolvent** merchant was unable to meet any financial obligations.[19]

syn. bankrupt, indebted, strapped

 예문 해석

15 그 작은 형상의 부자연스러운 모습은 괴기스럽고 추했다. **16** 뮤지컬 배우의 연극적인 목소리는 일상에서는 이상하게 들리지만 무대에서는 안성맞춤이다. **17** 그녀의 회사는 그녀가 출장 갈 때 주요 비용을 지불했지만 부수적인 비용은 그녀에게 변제하지 않았다. **18** 대부분의 부모들은 어린 아이들이 집에서 지워지지 않는 잉크를 가지고 노는 것을 원하지 않는다. **19** 그 파산한 상인은 어떠한 재정적 의무도 이행할 수 없었다.

20

isolate
[ai-*suh*-leyt]

v. to separate from others
격리시키다, 소외시키다
They **isolated** the political prisoners from the other inmates.[20]

syn. separate, detach, seclude

21

launch
[lawnch]

v. to set going
시작하다, 착수하다
Rockets were **launched**.[21]

syn. begin, initiate, commence

22

lull[1]
[l*uh*l]

n. temporary pause
일시적인 고요
There was a **lull** before the storm. [22]

syn. pause, calm, stillness

23

menace
[men-is]

n. a person or thing that causes serious damage
협박, 위협
I think he is a **menace**.[23]

syn. threat, blackmail, intimidation

24

municipal
[myoo-nis-*uh*-p*uh*l]

adj. connected with or belonging to a city
도시의
Large **municipal** areas often have robust public transportation.[24]

syn. civic, public, community

25

philanthropy
[fi-lan-thr*uh*-pee]

n. the act of donating money or time to promote human welfare
자선 활동
These animal shelters need **philanthropy** with large amounts of money.[25]

syn. charity, humanitarianism, altruism

예문 해석

20 정치범들은 다른 죄수들과 격리되었다. **21** 로켓이 발사되었다. **22** 폭풍우가 오기 전에 잠시 잠잠해졌다. **23** 나는 그가 위협이 된다고 생각한다. **24** 큰 도시 지역은 대중교통이 잘 되어 있는 경우가 많다. **25** 이 동물 보호소들은 많은 돈의 자선 활동을 필요로 한다.

26

prerequisite
[pri-rek-w*uh*-zit]

n. a required prior condition

(무엇이 있기 위해서는 꼭 필요한) 전제 조건

A **prerequisite** for French II class is French I.[26]

syn. necessity, condition, qualification

27

propaganda
[prop-*uh*-gan-d*uh*]

n. the spreading of information in support of a specific cause

(보통 거짓의) 정치 선전, 허위 정보

The politician made false **propaganda** to get elected.[27]

syn. disinformation, misleading information, indoctrination

28

provisional
[pr*uh*-vizh-*uh*-nl]

adj. providing for the time being only

임시의, 일시적인

She needs to get a **provisional** license until she passes her actual test.[28]

syn. temporary, tentative, conditional

29

rational
[rash-*uh*-nl]

adj. related to or based on reason or logic

논리적인, 이성적인

He's asking you to come to a **rational** decision.[29]

syn. sensible, sound, wise, reasonable

30

recapitulate
[ree-k*uh*-pich-*uh*-leyt]

v. to summarize briefly

(앞에서 한 말이나 결정 사항을) 정리해 말하다, 요약하다

To **recapitulate** what was said earlier, we need to develop new technology to secure our information.[31]

syn. recap, rehash, go over something again

31

sooty
[soot-ee]

adj. covered, blackened, or smirched with soot.

그을음이 묻은, 시커먼

The chimney sweeper got **sooty** hands after the work.[31]

syn. dingy, blackened, dirty

예문 해석

26 프랑스어 II 수업의 필수 조건은 프랑스어 I 이다. **27** 그 정치인은 당선되기 위해 거짓 선전을 했다. **28** 그녀는 실제 시험을 통과할 때까지 임시 자격증을 취득해야 한다. **29** 그는 당신이 이성적인 판단을 내리기를 요구하고 있다. **30** 앞서 말한 내용을 요약하자면, 우리는 우리의 정보를 보호하기 위해 새로운 기술을 개발할 필요가 있다. **31** 굴뚝 청소부는 작업 뒤 손에 그을음이 묻었다.

32

stealthy
[stel-thee]

adj. acting or done secretly
몰래 하는, 남의 눈을 피해하는
I crept in with **stealthy** footsteps and explored the building.[32]

syn. secretive, furtive, surreptitious

33

surmise
[ser-maiz]

v. to conclude something from the information available
추측하다, 짐작하다
We can only **surmise** what happened.[33]

syn. guess, conjecture

34

treason
[tree-zuhn]

n. the offense of acting to overthrow one's government or to harm or kill its sovereign
반역죄
The rebel was beheaded for **treason** after trying to kill his king.[34]

syn. disloyalty, treachery, sedition

35

unflinching
[uhn-flin-ching]

adj. showing a fearless determination in the face of danger or difficulty
움츠리지 않는, 물러서지 않는, 굽히지 않는
The fireman demonstrated **unflinching** courage when he went into the burning building.[35]

syn. unwavering, constant, steady

36

vital
[vait-l]

adj. very important
매우 중요한, 꼭 필요한
The port is **vital** to our efforts to supply relief supplies to drought victims.[36]

syn. essential, pivotal, crucial

예문 해석

32 나는 살금살금 몰래 기어 들어가 그 건물을 탐험했다. **33** 우리는 무슨 일이 있었는지 추측할 뿐이다. **34** 반란군은 왕을 죽이려다가 반역죄로 참수당했다. **35** 소방관은 불타는 건물 안으로 들어갔을 때 흔들리지 않는 용기를 보였다. **36** 항구는 가뭄으로 고통 받는 사람들에게 줄 구호물자를 전달하는 데 필수적이다.

Directions Each of the following questions consists of one word followed by five words or phrases. You are to select the one word or phrase whose meaning is closest to the word in capital letters.

1. AVARICE :
(A) fragment
(B) foreword
(C) rage
(D) courtesy
(E) covetousness

2. EAGER :
(A) fearless
(B) secret
(C) intact
(D) anxious
(E) persistent

3. ENUMERATE :
(A) push
(B) dawdle
(C) discourage
(D) enroll
(E) specify

4. FIDELITY :
(A) impulsive
(B) suspicious
(C) loyalty
(D) common
(E) necessary

5. FRIVOLOUS :
(A) flippant
(B) feeble
(C) condescending
(D) unruffled
(E) confused

6. PROVISIONAL :
(A) required
(B) temporary
(C) serene
(D) ostentatious
(E) pompous

7. STEALTHY :
(A) experiential
(B) gigantic
(C) academic
(D) secretive
(E) sincere

8. SURMISE :
(A) dictator
(B) honesty
(C) liveliness
(D) guess
(E) faculty

9. UNFLINCHING :
(A) religious
(B) ostentatious
(C) slight
(D) unwavering
(E) feeble

10. VITAL :
(A) similar
(B) refractory
(C) odd
(D) scanty
(E) essential

"Dare to be yourself"

— Andre Gide —
French critic, essayist, & novelist

감히 진실한 너 자신이 되어라.

Greek and Latin Roots & Prefixes 34

★ CIRCUM = round, around

	circuit	순환, 회로
ire (to go)	circuit judge	순회 재판 판사
-ate (v.)	circulate	순환하다
ferre (to carry)	circumference	원주, 원의 둘레
semi (half)	semicircle	반원
kyklos (circle)	cyclone	사이클론 (회오리 폭풍)
	recycle	재활용
spect (to see)	circumspect	신중한, 조심스러운
scribe (to write)	circumscribe	제한하다
venire (to come)	circumvent	피하다, 피해가다

DAY

34

WORDS TO LEARN

☐ acumen	☐ enunciate	☐ itinerant	☐ raucous
☐ androgynous	☐ expenditure	☐ laurel	☐ revenge
☐ averse	☐ fierce	☐ lull[2]	☐ silhouette
☐ bourgeois	☐ frugal	☐ menagerie	☐ slither
☐ cite	☐ gratis	☐ mural	☐ steed
☐ cringe	☐ hiatus	☐ obsessed	☐ surpass
☐ derogatory	☐ immune	☐ paragon	☐ toil
☐ discretion	☐ inexorable	☐ pompous	☐ ungainly
☐ ebb	☐ insolent	☐ propriety	☐ vivid

01

acumen
[*uh*-kyoo-m*uh*n]

n. keen insight

(일에 대한) 감각, 통찰력, 예리함

Capable surgeons with medical **acumen** are valuable to any hospital.[1]

syn. shrewdness, acuity, sharpness

02

androgynous
[an-droj-*uh*-n*uh*s]

adj. being both male and female

양성의, 자웅동체의

A plant that has staminate and pistillate flowers in the same inflorescence is called **androgynous**.[2]

syn. bisexual, hermaphroditic

03

averse
[*uh*-vurs]

adj. having strong feelings of opposition

싫어하는, 꺼리는

He was **averse** to going to the theater.[3]

syn. unwilling, reluctant, disinclined

예문 해석

01 의학적인 안목을 가진 유능한 외과의는 어느 병원에서나 가치가 있다. **02** 암술과 수술이 함께 있는 식물을 자웅동체라고 한다. **03** 그는 극장에 가는 것을 싫어했다.

04

bourgeois
[boor-zhwah]

adj. belonging to the middle class.
중산층의
His **bourgeois** ideas led him to think he was better than most people.[4]

syn. middle-class, conventional, materialistic

05

cite
[sait]

v. to quote (a passage, book, author, etc.), especially as an authority
인용하다, 예를 들다
He **cited** his previous accomplishments in his defense.[5]

syn. quote, mention, exemplify

06

cringe
[krinj]

v. to cower away in fear
겁이 나서 움찔하다, 움츠리다
He **cringed** before the boss.[6]

syn. recoil, cower, flinch, wince

07

derogatory
[di-rog-uh-tawr-ee]

adj. tending to lessen the merit or reputation of a person or thing
경멸하는, 비하하는
Her **derogatory** remark was heard across the room.[7]

syn. disparaging, depreciatory, disdainful

08

discretion
[dih-skresh-uhn]

n. the power or right to decide, or act according to one's own judgment
신중함
He always uses **discretion** and prudence when dealing with others.[8]

syn. prudence, caution, vigilance

예문 해석

04 그의 부르주아 사상은 그가 대부분의 사람들보다 낫다고 생각하게 만들었다. **05** 그는 방어를 위해 자신의 지난 공적들을 예로 들었다. **06** 그는 사장 앞에서 움츠러들었다. **07** 그녀의 경멸적인 말이 방 건너편까지 들렸다. **08** 그는 남을 대할 때 항상 신중하고 또 신중하다.

ebb
[eb]

v. to gradually decrease
썰물이 되다, 서서히 줄어들다
The tide begins to **ebb** at dawn.[9]

syn. recede, dwindle, diminish

enunciate
[i-n*uhn*-see-yet]

v. to state or declare definitely
명확히 발음하다, 명확히 진술하다
He **enunciated** his theory to the field.[10]

syn. articulate, vocalize, state

expenditure
[ik-spen-di-cher]

n. the act of spending money
지출, 지불
Unnecessary **expenditures** include those for luxury items.[11]

syn. spending, expenses, costs

fierce
[feers]

adj. menacingly wild, savage, or hostile
사나운, 잔인한
Lions are **fierce** animals.[12]

syn. ferocious, savage, vicious

frugal
[froo-g*uhl*]

adj. careful particularly in financial matters
절약하는, 검약하는
She lives a **frugal** life.[13]

syn. thrifty, prudent, economical

gratis
[grat-is]

adv. without charge or payment
무료로, 공짜로
She got a ticket for a concert she wanted to go to for **gratis**.[14]

syn. complimentary, free, gratuitous

예문 해석

09 조수는 새벽에 빠지기 시작한다.　**10** 그는 그의 이론을 학계에 명확히 밝혔다.　**11** 불필요한 지출은 명품 지출비를 포함한다.
12 사자는 사나운 동물이다.　**13** 그녀는 절약하는 삶을 산다.　**14** 그녀는 공짜로 가고 싶은 콘서트 티켓을 구했다.

hiatus
[hai-ey-t*uh*s]

n. continuous gap or break
벌어진 틈, 일이나 행동의 중단
She went on a two-week **hiatus** from work.[15]

syn. lull, pause, interruption

immune
[ih-myoon]

adj. protected from a disease by inoculation
(예방접종 등으로 인해) 면역성이 있는, 면역의
I was **immune** to the sickness because of my recent vaccine.[16]

syn. resistant, unsusceptible

inexorable
[in-ek-ser-*uh*-b*uh*l]

adj. not to be placated or appeased
멈출 수 없는, 거침없는
A speeding car with no brakes is **inexorable**; it's not stopping till it crashes.[17]

syn. relentless, stubborn, adamant

insolent
[in-*suh*-lu*h*nt]

adj. rude
건방진, 오만한
I despised listening to his **insolent** replies.[18]

syn. impudent, arrogant, haughty, cocky

itinerant
[ahy-tin-er-*uh*nt]

adj. traveling from place to place to work
돌아다니는, 순회하는
Circuit judges who travel to faraway courtrooms are **itinerant** practitioners. [19]

syn. peripatetic, migratory, ambulatory

 예문 해석

15 그녀는 2주간 일을 쉬었다. **16** 나는 최근의 백신 때문에 질병에 면역이 되었다. **17** 브레이크가 없는 과속 자동차는 거침이 없다. 충돌할 때까지 멈추지 않는다. **18** 나는 그의 무례한 대답을 듣는 것이 싫었다. **19** 먼 법정들로 이동하는 순회 재판관들은 돌아다니는 실무자들이다.

laurel
[lawr-*uhl*]

n. a wreath worn on the head, usually as a symbol of victory

(영예의 상징으로서의) 월계관

The youth's head is framed by a **laurel** tree, representing glory.[20]

syn. distinction, accolade, bays

lull[2]
[l*uh*l]

v. to make one feel calm or sleepy

마음을 진정시키다, 안심시키다

The babysitter **lulled** the crying baby to sleep.[21]

syn. soothe, reassure, comfort

menagerie
[m*uh*-naj-*uh*-ree]

n. a collection of wild animals

서커스 동물들, 동물원, 별난 사람들

"The Glass **Menagerie**" is a play by Tennessee Williams.[22]

syn. zoo, exhibition, collection

mural
[myoor-*uh*l]

n. a picture painted on a wall

벽화

The images of tomb **murals** were duplicated.[23]

syn. wall painting, fresco

obsessed
[*uh*b-sest]

adj. having an obsession

사로잡힌, 집착하는

He was **obsessed** with guilt.[24]

syn. haunted, consumed, preoccupied

paragon
[par-*uh*-gon]

n. an excellent example

모범, 본보기, 귀감

The statue she created was a **paragon** of beauty.[25]

syn. exemplar, epitome, ideal

예문 해석

20 그 젊은이의 머리에는 승리를 상징하는 월계관이 장식되어 있었다. **21** 베이비시터가 우는 아기를 달래 재웠다. **22** "유리 동물원"은 테네시 윌리엄스가 쓴 극작품이다. **23** 그 고분 벽화 이미지들은 복제되었다. **24** 그는 죄책감에 사로잡혀 있었다. **25** 그녀가 만든 동상은 아름다움의 좋은 예였다.

26 ......

pompous
[pom-p*uh*s]

adj. solemnly self-important
잘난 척하는, 과시하는
He was somewhat **pompous**.[26]

syn. pretentious, haughty, gaudy

27 ......

propriety
[pr*uh*-prai-i-tee]

n. correct or appropriate behavior
(도덕적, 사회적으로) 적절함, 예의바름, 예절
He offended her sense of **propriety** by burping loudly at the dinner table.[27]

syn. etiquette, courtesy, decorum

28 ......

raucous
[ra-cus]

adj. sounding loud and rough
요란하고 시끄러운, 소리가 크고 거친
The **raucous** protestors prevented him from being able to concentrate.[28]

syn. rowdy, boisterous, rambunctious

29 ......

revenge
[ri-venj]

n. the act of causing harm to someone who wrongfully hurt someone else
복수
She wanted to take **revenge**.[29]

syn. vengeance, retaliation, reprisal

30 ......

silhouette
[sil-oo-et]

n. a filled-in drawing of the outline of an object
(밝은 바탕을 배경으로 드러나 있는) 검은 윤곽, 실루엣
She only saw the shape of the person through its **silhouette**.[30]

syn. outline, contour, shadow

예문 해석

26 그는 약간 잘난 척하는 경향이 있다. **27** 그는 저녁 식탁에서 큰 소리로 트림을 해서 그녀가 생각하는 매너에 어긋났다. **28** 시끄러운 시위자들이 그가 집중하는 데 방해가 되었다. **29** 그녀는 복수를 하고 싶었다. **30** 그녀는 그 실루엣을 통해서만 그 사람의 모습을 보았다.

slither
[slith-er]

v. to slide along like a snake
(뱀이) 미끄러지듯 나아가다
The snake **slithered** across the path.[31]

syn. slide, move

steed
[steed]

n. an excellent horse
말, 건강한 준마
They always locked the stable door after the **steed** was stolen.[32]

syn. horse

surpass
[ser-pas]

v. to do or be better than somebody
보다 낫다, 능가하다
She **surpasses** me in cooking.[33]

syn. beat, outstrip, excel

toil
[toil]

v. to engage in hard and continuous work
(장시간) 힘들게 일하다
He has **toiled** on roadwork and conservation projects during the Great Depression.[34]

syn. strive, sweat, labor

ungainly
[*uh*n-geyn-lee]

adj. looking awkward or clumsy
꼴사나운, 볼품없는, 다루기 힘든
He swam in his **ungainly** way.[35]

syn. clumsy, awkward, lumbering

vivid
[viv-id]

adj. very clear and detailed
생생한, 선명한
I had a very **vivid** dream last night.[36]

syn. graphic, bright, vibrant

📖 예문 해석

31 그 뱀은 길을 미끄러지듯 지나갔다.　**32** 그들은 항상 말 잃고 마구간 고치는 격이다.('소 잃고 외양간 고친다'는 뜻의 속담)
33 요리에 있어서는 그녀가 나보다 낫다.　**34** 그는 대공황 기간 동안 도로 공사와 보존 사업에서 힘들게 일했다.　**35** 그는 보기 민망하게 수영했다.　**36** 나는 어젯밤 매우 생생한 꿈을 꾸었다.

Directions   Each of the following questions consists of one word followed by five words or phrases.
You are to select the one word or phrase whose meaning is closest to the word in capital letters.

1. **AVERSE :**
   (A) rascal
   (B) similar
   (C) slight
   (D) decorative
   (E) unwilling

2. **BOURGEOIS :**
   (A) upper-class
   (B) middle-class
   (C) hostage
   (D) plebeian
   (E) outcast

3. **CITE :**
   (A) devour
   (B) avoid
   (C) twist
   (D) quote
   (E) burnish

4. **DISCRETION :**
   (A) lookout
   (B) prudence
   (C) disorder
   (D) inconsistency
   (E) chaos

5. **EBB :**
   (A) recede
   (B) apply
   (C) withdraw
   (D) carry out
   (E) restart

6. **FRUGAL :**
   (A) feasible
   (B) confounded
   (C) thrifty
   (D) flabby
   (E) tentative

7. **ITINERANT :**
   (A) pungent
   (B) vague
   (C) aloof
   (D) uproarious
   (E) peripatetic

8. **OBSESSED :**
   (A) excess
   (B) nautical
   (C) haunted
   (D) brief
   (E) breeze

9. **PARAGON :**
   (A) monodrama
   (B) exemplar
   (C) taint
   (D) artifice
   (E) mission

10. **PROPRIETY :**
    (A) latitude
    (B) etiquette
    (C) mystery
    (D) glut
    (E) taint

"Luck is when preparedness meets opportunity."

– Earl Nightingale –
American motivational speaker

운이란 준비가 기회를 만난 것이다.

LESSON

Greek and Latin Roots & Prefixes 35

★ CID = to cut

de (off)	decide	결정하다
herba (grass)	herbicide	제초제
homo (man)	homicide	살인
sui (of oneself)	suicide	자살
rex, regis (king)	regicide	국왕 시해
pre (before)	precise	정확한
in (into)	Incision	절개
ex (out)	excise	잘라내다

DAY

35

WORDS TO LEARN

- ☐ aggregate
- ☐ allude
- ☐ avert
- ☐ boundless
- ☐ clamor
- ☐ crucial
- ☐ culinary
- ☐ descend
- ☐ disdain

- ☐ eccentric
- ☐ ephemeral
- ☐ expert
- ☐ figment
- ☐ fumble
- ☐ grim
- ☐ hibernal
- ☐ immutable
- ☐ indemnify

- ☐ insomnia
- ☐ itinerary
- ☐ lavish
- ☐ lumber
- ☐ mendicant
- ☐ murky
- ☐ obsolete
- ☐ plight
- ☐ ponder

- ☐ prose
- ☐ rave
- ☐ revenue
- ☐ sear
- ☐ slothful
- ☐ surplus
- ☐ topple
- ☐ unnerving
- ☐ vociferous

01

aggregate
[ag-ri-git]

n. a sum or total amount
총합, 합계, 종합
For science class, we combined an **aggregate** of insects to further compare their minute body parts.[1]

syn. sum, total, collection

02

allude
[uh-lood]

v. to refer casually or indirectly
암시하다, 시사하다, 넌지시 말하다
When she **alluded** that her dorm parent was sitting right behind her, her friends stopped talking about their secret party plans.[2]

syn. insinuate, hint at, imply

03

avert
[uh-vurt]

v. to turn away
눈을 돌리다, 외면하다
They **averted** their eyes when the king entered.[3]

syn. turn away, turn from, turn aside

예문 해석

01 과학 시간에 우리는 곤충들의 미세한 신체 부위를 더 비교하기 위해 집합체를 결합했다.　**02** 그녀가 기숙사 사감 선생님이 바로 뒤에 앉아 있다고 암시했을 때, 그녀의 친구들은 그들의 비밀 파티 계획에 대해 이야기하는 것을 멈췄다.　**03** 그들은 왕이 들어왔을 때 눈을 피했다.

04 ·······

boundless
[bound-lis]

adj. having no limit
무한한, 끝없는
His zeal for study was **boundless**.[4]

syn. infinite, limitless

05 ·······

clamor
[klam-er]

n. a loud uproar
시끄러운 외침, 떠들썩함
The **clamor** of the soccer crowd grew louder and louder.[5]

syn. commotion, hubbub, uproar

06 ·······

crucial
[kroo-sh*uh*l]

adj. decisive or critical
중요한, 중대한
This was a **crucial** experiment for him to fully support his thesis.[6]

syn. critical, essential, decisive

07 ·······

culinary
[k*uh*-li-nair-ee]

adj. relating to cooking or the kitchen
요리의, 음식의
The chef created a **culinary** masterpiece that fascinated his patrons.[7]

syn. of cooking, eatable, savory

08 ·······

descend
[di-send]

v. to move downwards
내려가다
Things are cooler as we **descend** to the cellar.[8]

syn. go down, sink, subside

예문 해석

04 학문에 대한 그의 열정은 끝이 없었다. **05** 축구 관중의 함성이 점점 더 커졌다. **06** 이것은 그의 논문을 전적으로 뒷받침하는 중요한 실험이었다. **07** 그 요리사는 손님들을 매료시킨 요리 걸작을 만들었다. **08** 지하실로 내려갈수록 점점 더 시원해졌다.

09

disdain
[dis-deyn]

v. to treat with contempt
경멸하다
He **disdained** being insulted.[9]

> *syn.* despise, scorn, contempt

10

eccentric
[ik-sen-trik]

adj. conspicuously unconventional or unusual
별난, 괴팍한
My friends thought it was **eccentric** to go swimming at night.[10]

> *syn.* unusual, peculiar, erratic

11

ephemeral
[e-fem-er-*uhl*]

adj. lasting a short time
하루살이 목숨의, 짧게 지속되는
The **ephemeral** joys of childhood are fond memories.[11]

> *syn.* transient, transitory, evanescent

12

expert
[ek-spurt]

n. someone with great skill in a particular subject
전문가
An **expert** in calligraphy came to our art class to demonstrate.[12]

> *syn.* authority, maven, connoisseur

13

figment
[fig-m*uh*nt]

n. something imagined or existing only in one's mind
마음속에만 있는 것, 허구
That was only a **figment** of your imagination.[13]

> *syn.* illusion, fiction, production

14

fumble
[f*uh*m-b*uh*l]

v. to feel or grope about clumsily
손으로 더듬어 찾다, 공을 잡았다 놓치다
I **fumbled** in my pocket for the key.[14]

> *syn.* grope, mishandle, botch

예문 해석

09 그는 모욕을 무시해버렸다. **10** 내 친구들은 한밤중에 수영하러 가는 것을 별나다고 생각했다. **11** 어린 시절의 소소한 기쁨들은 좋은 추억이다. **12** 서예 전문가가 우리 미술 수업에 와서 시범을 보여 주었다. **13** 그것은 네 상상력이 만들어 낸 허구일 뿐이야. **14** 나는 주머니를 더듬어 열쇠를 찾았다.

15

grim
[grim]

adj. severe or stern
엄한, 엄격한, 잔인한, 냉혹한
The feud was a **grim** reality.[15]

> *syn.* gloomy, stark, ghastly, somber

16

hibernal
[hai-b*ur*-nl]

adj. of winter
겨울의, 겨울 같은
The bear is in **hibernal** sleep.[16]

> *syn.* wintry, chilly, frigid

17

immutable
[i-myoo-t*uh*-b*uh*l]

adj. never changing or cannot be changed
변경 할 수 없는, 불변의
The **immutable** laws were something that my family despised.[17]

> *syn.* unchangeable, changeless

18

indemnify
[in-dem-n*uh*-fai]

v. to compensate for damage or loss sustained, expense incurred, etc.
배상하다, 보상하다
The insurance company **indemnified** its customers for their loss after the fire.[18]

> *syn.* reimburse, compensate, remit

19

insomnia
[in-som-nee-*uh*]

n. inability to obtain sufficient sleep
불면증
The pill may cause **insomnia** if you take it at night.[19]

> *syn.* sleeplessness, restlessness

20

itinerary
[ai-tin-*uh*-rer-ee]

n. a detailed plan for a journey
여행 일정표
He did not disclose the purpose or **itinerary** of the visit.[20]

> *syn.* travel schedule, route, plan of travel

예문 해석

15 그 불화는 엄연한 현실이었다.　**16** 그 곰은 동면 중이다.　**17** 그 불변의 법칙이란 것들은 우리 가족이 경멸하는 것이었다.
18 그 보험 회사는 화재 후 고객들에게 손해를 배상했다.　**19** 그 약은 밤에 먹으면 불면증을 야기할 수 있다.　**20** 그는 이번 방문 목적이나 여정에 대해 알리지 않았다.

lavish
[lav-ish]

adj. using or giving in great amounts
아낌없이 쓰는, 호화스러운
The media attacked his **lavish** spending and flamboyant life style.[21]

syn. sumptuous, extravagant, prodigal

lumber
[lu*h*m-ber]

v. to walk heavily
쿵쿵 걷다, 육중하게 움직이다
He could hear the elephants **lumber** in the zoo.[22]

syn. walk heavily, trudge, plod

mendicant
[men-di-k*uh*nt]

n. a person who lives by begging
거지, 걸인
The **mendicant** hoped pedestrians would drop some money in his bucket.[23]

syn. beggar, pauper, panhandler

murky
[mur-kee]

adj. dark and unpleasant
어둑어둑한, 탁한
The river was very **murky**, and we couldn't see the fish at all.[24]

syn. dark, foggy, gloomy

obsolete
[ob-s*uh*-leet]

adj. no longer in use
낙후되어서 안 쓰이는, 폐기된, 못쓰게 된
Since the advent of the telephone, telegram service has become **obsolete**[25]

syn. outdated, antiquated, out-of-date

 예문 해석

21 미디어는 그의 큰 지출과 호화로운 라이프 스타일을 비난했다. **22** 그는 동물원에서 코끼리가 터벅터벅 걷는 소리를 들을 수 있었다. **23** 그 탁발사는 보행자들이 그의 양동이에 약간의 돈을 떨어뜨리기를 바랐다. **24** 그 강물은 매우 탁해서 우리는 물고기를 전혀 볼 수 없었다. **25** 전화의 발명 이후 전보는 낙후되어서 더 이상 사용되지 않게 되었다.

plight
[plait]

n. a condition, state, or situation, especially an unfavorable or unfortunate one
역경, 곤경
He couldn't even assume what a **plight** he had to endure.[26]

> *syn.* dilemma, predicament, quandary

ponder
[pon-der]

v. to consider or contemplate something deeply
숙고하다, 곰곰이 생각하다
Ponder over your real nature.[27]

> *syn.* consider, think about, think over

prose
[prohz]

n. the ordinary form of written or spoken language
산문(운문, 시에 반대되는 개념으로)
In college, I studied **prose** and verse.[28]

> *syn.* essay, nonrhythmic literature, composition

rave
[reyv]

adj. extravagantly flattering or enthusiastic
극찬의, 격찬의, 열광적인
His play received **rave** reviews.[29]

> *syn.* flattering, enthusiastic

revenue
[rev-*uhn*-oo]

n. the income of a government or company
수입, 정부의 세입, 수익
The business lost **revenue** because of the inventory shortage.[30]

> *syn.* income, proceeds, profits

sear
[seer]

v. to burn or char the surface of
태우다, 그을리다
The heat from the pizza oven nearly **seared** the cook's eyelashes.[31]

> *syn.* char, burn, scorch

예문 해석

26 그는 자신이 견뎌야 하는 곤경이 얼마나 큰지 짐작조차 할 수 없었다.　**27** 네 본성에 대해 곰곰이 생각해 보아라.　**28** 대학에서 나는 산문과 운문을 공부했다.　**29** 그의 희곡은 극찬을 받았다.　**30** 그 사업은 재고 부족으로 수익을 잃었다.　**31** 피자 오븐에서 나오는 열기는 주방장의 눈썹을 거의 그을릴 정도였다.

32

slothful
[slawth-ful]

adj. disinclined to work or exertion
게으른, 나태한
He punished a **slothful** servant.[32]

syn. sluggardly, idle, indolent

33

surplus
[sur-pl*uh*s]

n. an amount that is extra or more than one needs
잉여, 나머지
The **surplus** population was a tremendous burden to feed.[33]

syn. excess, extra, spare

34

topple
[top-*uh*l]

v. to fall forward
흔들거리다, 넘어뜨리다, 전복시키다
Winds and rain **toppled** trees by the roads.[34]

syn. fall over, collapse, pitch

35

unnerving
[*uh*n-nur-ving]

adj. depriving a person of courage, strength or confidence
불안하게 만드는, 지치게 하는
As an orphan, life was **unnerving** and distressing.[35]

syn. disconcerting, disquieting, unsettling

36

vociferous
[voh-sif-er-*uh*s]

adj. crying out noisily
큰 소리로 고함치는
The resolution was adopted over the **vociferous** objections of the opposition.[36]

syn. clamorous, uproarious, boisterous

 예문 해석

32 그는 게으른 종을 벌 주었다.　**33** 잉여 인구는 먹여 살리기에 엄청난 부담이 되었다.　**34** 바람과 비가 길가의 나무들을 쓰러뜨렸다.　**35** 고아로서 삶은 불안하고 고통스러웠다.　**36** 그 결정은 반대파의 거친 반대 함성에도 불구하고 채택되었다.

Directions   Each of the following questions consists of one word followed by five words or phrases. You are to select the one word or phrase whose meaning is closest to the word in capital letters.

1. AGGREGATE :
(A) sum
(B) bondage
(C) lawsuit
(D) severity
(E) pundit

2. AVERT :
(A) call off
(B) let up
(C) turn away
(D) put on
(E) take off

3. DISDAIN :
(A) untangle
(B) judge
(C) praise
(D) relegate
(E) despise

4. ECCENTRIC :
(A) probable
(B) carefree
(C) exhilarating
(D) unusual
(E) irreversible

5. EPHEMERAL :
(A) lustrous
(B) shapeless
(C) carefree
(D) conclusive
(E) transient

6. FUMBLE :
(A) investigate
(B) grope
(C) commence
(D) liberate
(E) suppress

7. INSOMNIA :
(A) predicament
(B) litigation
(C) instinct
(D) feudalism
(E) sleeplessness

8. LAVISH :
(A) propitious
(B) irritable
(C) sumptuous
(D) pale
(E) absurd

9. MURKY :
(A) accidental
(B) banal
(C) dark
(D) absurd
(E) dissatisfied

10. SURPLUS :
(A) mild
(B) gigantic
(C) curious
(D) excess
(E) parched

"Insist on yourself; never imitate... Every great man is unique."

– Ralph Waldo Emerson –
U.S. essayist & poet

나 자신이길 고집하라, 절대 따라 하지 마라. 모든 위대한 사람은 대신할 것이 없는 존재이다.

Greek and Latin Roots & Prefixes 36

★ PRE = before

cavere (guard)	precaution	예방책
cede (go)	precede	앞서 가다
dict (speak)	predict	예언하다
jud (judge)	prejudice	편견
post (after)	preposterous	터무니없는, 말도 안 되는
textere (weave)	pretext	구실, 핑계
venire (come)	prevent	막다, 예방하다
view (show)	preview	미리보기

DAY

36

WORDS TO LEARN

- ☐ adjudicate
- ☐ antipathy
- ☐ avid
- ☐ bounty
- ☐ clarify
- ☐ confine
- ☐ cryptic
- ☐ descendant
- ☐ disenchanted

- ☐ eclectic
- ☐ epic
- ☐ expertise
- ☐ figurative
- ☐ frolic
- ☐ grimace
- ☐ hideous
- ☐ impart
- ☐ imperious

- ☐ indict
- ☐ jabber
- ☐ lax
- ☐ luminous
- ☐ mentor
- ☐ murmur
- ☐ obstinate
- ☐ pallid
- ☐ ponderous

- ☐ prospective
- ☐ ravenous
- ☐ reverberation
- ☐ seclude
- ☐ sentry
- ☐ slovenly
- ☐ supercilious
- ☐ torrid
- ☐ unwitting

01

adjudicate
[*uh*-joo-di-keyt]

v. to pronounce or decree by judicial sentence
판결을 내리다, 재결하다
The board of trustees will **adjudicate** claims made against faculty.[1]

syn. settle, judge, decide

02

antipathy
[an-tip-*uh*-thee]

n. a natural, basic, or habitual repugnance
반감
The students expressed their **antipathy** for the school by vandalizing the gym.[2]

syn. animosity, disgust, antagonism

03

avid
[av-id]

adj. enthusiastic
열광적인, 열성적인, 탐내는
He is an **avid** fan of baseball.[3]

syn. passionate, covetous, ardent

예문 해석

01 학교 이사회는 교수진을 대상으로 판결을 내릴 것이다.　**02** 학생들은 체육관을 훼손함으로써 학교에 대한 반감을 표현했다.
03 그는 야구광이다.

04

bounty
[boun-tee]

n. a reward or a generous gift
아낌없이 주어진 것, 하사품, 상여금
The **bounty** was plentiful.[4]

syn. present, benefaction, munificence

05

clarify
[klar-*uh*-fai]

v. to make or become clearer
명백하게 설명하다
She **clarified** her position.[5]

syn. clear up, elucidate, explain

06

confine
[k*uh*n-fain]

v. to limit
제한하다, 가두다, 감금하다
Please **confine** your remarks to the facts.[6]

syn. restrict, limit, imprison

07

cryptic
[krip-tik]

adj. mysterious in meaning
난해한, 해석하기 어려운
We worked on solving the **cryptic** message.[7]

syn. puzzling, vague, esoteric

08

descendant
[di-sen-d*uh*nt]

n. a person considered as descended from some ancestor or race
자손, 후예
He is the last **descendant** of his family.[8]

syn. offspring, posterity, progeny

09

disenchanted
[dis-en-chant]

adj. no longer enchanted with
흥미를 잃은, 환멸을 느낀
She was a little **disenchanted** with her new boyfriend.[9]

syn. disillusioned, disappointed

예문 해석

04 현상금은 충분했다.   **05** 그녀는 자신의 입장을 분명히 했다.   **06** 사실만을 말씀해주십시오.   **07** 우리는 수수께끼 같은 메시지를 풀기 위해 노력했다.   **08** 그가 그 집안의 마지막 후손이다.   **09** 그녀는 새 남자친구에게 약간 흥미를 잃었다.

10

eclectic
[i-klek-tik]

adj. drawn from many sources
(많은 것 중에서) 선별된, 폭넓은
The collection includes an **eclectic** mix of music.[10]

> *syn.* assorted, diverse

11

epic
[ep-ik]

n. a long narrative poem telling of heroic acts
(영웅을 노래한) 서사시
Homer's Iliad is an **epic** poem.[11]

> *syn.* heroic poem, legend, tale

12

expertise
[ek-sper-teez]

n. expert skill or knowledge
전문 기술, 전문 지식
He has great **expertise** in making films.[12]

> *syn.* skillfulness, knowledge, know-how

13

figurative
[fig-yer-*uh*-tiv]

adj. metaphorical or not literal
비유적인, 상징적인
Her poetry is highly **figurative**.[13]

> *syn.* metaphorical, allegorical, symbolic

14

frolic
[frol-ik]

v. play boisterously
즐겁게 뛰놀다
The children **frolicked** in the backyard garden.[14]

> *syn.* gambol, make merry, cavort

15

grimace
[grim-*uhs*]

n. a facial expression that indicates disapproval or pain
표정이 일그러짐, 얼굴을 찌푸림
He **grimaced** when he saw all the work he had to do before he could leave.[15]

> *syn.* frown, scowl, wry face

예문 해석

10 그 컬렉션은 다양한 음악을 포함하고 있다.　**11** 호머의 일리아드는 서사시이다.　**12** 그는 영화를 만드는 굉장한 전문 기술을 가지고 있다.　**13** 그녀의 시는 매우 비유적이다.　**14** 아이들은 뒷마당에서 장난을 쳤다.　**15** 그는 떠나기 전 해야 할 많은 일들을 보고 얼굴을 찌푸렸다.

hideous
[hid-ee-*uh*s]

adj. horrible or frightful to the senses
흉측한, 흉물스러운, 끔찍한
The special effects team tries to make the monsters **hideous** in horror movies.[16]

syn. repulsive, abominable, grotesque

impart
[im-pahrt]

v. to make known
전하다, 알리다
The ability to **impart** knowledge is the essential qualification for teachers.[17]

syn. inform, convey, make known

imperious
[im-peer-ee-*uh*s]

adj. presupposing dominance or supremacy
고압적인
The **imperious** boss always gives orders to show he feels superior or more important than other people.[18]

syn. overbearing, arrogant, domineering

indict
[in-dait]

v. to accuse someone
죄를 비난하다, 고발하다
She was **indicted** for possessing cocaine.[19]

syn. accuse, charge, impeach

jabber
[jab-er]

v. to talk or utter rapidly, indistinctly or excitedly
지껄이다, 수다떨다
Because they **jabbered** and took up valuable time, their teacher got angry.[20]

syn. chatter, babble, prattle

예문 해석

16 특수효과팀은 공포영화에 나오는 괴물들을 흉측하게 만들기 위해 노력한다. **17** 지식을 전달하는 능력은 교사들이 반드시 갖춰야 할 자질이다. **18** 거만한 상사는 자신이 다른 사람들보다 우월하거나 더 중요하다고 느낀다는 것을 보여주기 위해 항상 명령을 내린다. **19** 그 지역을 수색하기 위해 군용 헬리콥터가 급파되었다. **20** 그들이 수다를 떨면서 소중한 시간을 허비했기 때문에 선생님은 화가 났다.

21

lax
[laks]

adj. not strict or severe

느슨한, 해이한

Lax security among airport personnel is a huge problem.[21]

syn. slack, slipshod, heedless

22

luminous
[loo-m*uh*-n*uh*s]

adj. full of or giving out light

빛을 내는, 반짝이는

She visited the castle's **luminous** chamber.[22]

syn. bright, shining

23

mentor
[men-tawr]

n. a wise and trusted counselor

현명하고 성실한 조언자, 스승

In high school, the boy had a **mentor** he respected.[23]

syn. adviser, counselor, guru

24

murmur
[mur-mer]

v. to speak in a low tone or indistinctly

속삭이다, 웅얼거리다

They **murmured** quietly to each other.[24]

syn. mumble, mutter, whisper

25

obstinate
[ob-st*uh*-nit]

adj. tenaciously unwilling

완고한, 고집 센

His **obstinate** personality is determined to get accepted into a prestigious university.[25]

syn. dogged, mulish, headstrong

26

pallid
[pal-id]

adj. having a pale complexion

창백한, 핼쑥한

Spending too much time at an indoor laboratory made him **pallid**.[26]

syn. pale, anemic, wan

예문 해석

21 공항 검문의 느슨함이 큰 문제이다. **22** 그녀는 성의 빛나는 방을 방문했다. **23** 고등학교 때, 소년에게는 존경하는 멘토가 있었다. **24** 그들은 조용히 속닥거렸다. **25** 그는 고집 센 성격으로 일류 대학에 합격하기로 마음먹었다. **26** 실내 실험실에서 너무 많은 시간을 보내자 그는 창백해졌다.

ponderous
[pon-der-*uhs*]

adj. slower and less graceful because of weight

크고 육중한

She watched the elephant's **ponderous** progress.[27]

syn. cumbersome, bulky, weighty

prospective
[pr*uh*-spek-tiv]

adj. likely to happen soon

장래의, 미래의, 유망한

The **prospective** student and his family were touring the campus.[28]

syn. future, expected, coming

ravenous
[rav-*uh*-n*uhs*]

adj. extremely hungry

게걸스럽게 먹는, 배고픈

They ate the food with a **ravenous** appetite.[29]

syn. gluttonous, rapacious, voracious

reverberation
[ri-vur-b*uh*-rey-sh*uh*n]

n. a loud noise that continues for some time after it has been produced

반향, 반향음, 반사

Reverberations from the explosion were felt within a ten-mile radius.[30]

syn. echo, sound, noise

seclude
[si-klood]

v. to keep someone away from contact with other people

격리시키다, 떨어뜨려놓다

They were **secluded** from other patients.[31]

syn. isolate, estrange, sequester

 예문 해석

27 그녀는 코끼리의 육중한 전진을 보았다.   **28** 그 예비 학생과 그의 가족은 캠퍼스를 둘러보고 있었다.   **29** 그들은 게걸스럽게 그 음식을 먹었다.   **30** 그 폭발로 인한 반향이 반경 10마일 내에서 감지되었다.   **31** 그들은 다른 환자들로부터 격리되었다.

sentry
[sen-tree]

n. someone who stands guard or watches against some intrusion or unwelcomed activity

보초, 보초병

The wealthy family hired a **sentry** to protect their mansion.[32]

syn. guard, sentinel, watcher

slovenly
[sluhv-uhn-lee]

adj. careless or untidy in appearance

단정치 못한, 게으른

She was irritated by the **slovenly** attitude of her boyfriend.[33]

syn. sloppy, careless, disheveled

supercilious
[soo-per-sil-ee-uhs]

adj. haughtily disdainful or contemptuous

거만한, 남을 얕보는

The **supercilious** attitude of the opposing hockey home team was intimidating.[34]

syn. condescending, arrogant, overbearing

torrid
[tawr-id]

adj. emotionally charged and passionate

열렬한, 타는 듯이 뜨거운

She loved to watch a **torrid** romance in a soap opera.[35]

syn. fervent, fervid, ardent

unwitting
[uhn-wit-ing]

adj. not intentional or deliberate

자신도 모르는, 의식 못하고 있는

They are **unwitting** victims of this economic system.[36]

syn. accidental, inadvertent, unsuspecting

 예문 해석

32 그 부유한 가족은 그들의 저택을 지키기 위해 보초를 고용했다. **33** 그녀는 남자친구의 단정치 못한 행동이 신경쓰였다. **34** 상대 하키 홈팀의 거만한 태도가 위협적이었다. **35** 그녀는 드라마에서 열렬한 로맨스를 보는 것을 좋아했다. **36** 그들은 자기도 모르는 사이에 이 경제 시스템의 희생자들이다.

Directions   Each of the following questions consists of one word followed by five words or phrases. You are to select the one word or phrase whose meaning is closest to the word in capital letters.

1. ADJUDICATE :
(A) apply
(B) pardon
(C) designate
(D) settle
(E) anticipate

2. AVID :
(A) timid
(B) passionate
(C) shocked
(D) common
(E) finicky

3. CONFINE :
(A) overturn
(B) jeer
(C) appear
(D) restrict
(E) advocate

4. CRYPTIC :
(A) compliant
(B) dexterous
(C) puzzling
(D) chary
(E) stern

5. DISENCHANTED :
(A) representative
(B) parched
(C) complaining
(D) mysterious
(E) disillusioned

6. FROLIC :
(A) indulge
(B) harmonize
(C) annoy
(D) gambol
(E) tantalize

7. LAX :
(A) digressive
(B) obligatory
(C) slack
(D) huge
(E) obedient

8. LUMINOUS :
(A) bright
(B) harmonious
(C) varied
(D) inopportune
(E) complaining

9. MENTOR :
(A) pit
(B) quack
(C) adviser
(D) passion
(E) inquiry

10. RAVENOUS :
(A) casual
(B) frail
(C) rambling
(D) arbitrary
(E) gluttonous

Directions Each of the following questions consists of one word followed by five words or phrases. You are to select the one word or phrase whose meaning is closest to the word in capital letters.

1. ANARCHY :
   (A) relief
   (B) diversion
   (C) pagan
   (D) justification
   (E) disorder

2. FRENZY :
   (A) favor
   (B) repartee
   (C) instruction
   (D) bulwark
   (E) fury

3. HEREDITARY :
   (A) farmable
   (B) callous
   (C) polished
   (D) inherited
   (E) cozy

4. MUFFLE :
   (A) mute
   (B) concentrate
   (C) estrange
   (D) profess
   (E) squeeze

5. PALTRY :
   (A) showy
   (B) civic
   (C) submissive
   (D) insignificant
   (E) languid

6. CIRCUMSCRIBE :
   (A) commit
   (B) revere
   (C) adopt
   (D) revise
   (E) limit

7. DWINDLE :
   (A) aim
   (B) survive
   (C) amplify
   (D) stumble
   (E) decrease

8. FICKLE :
   (A) respectable
   (B) slim
   (C) deserted
   (D) capricious
   (E) reasonable

9. PHYSIQUE :
   (A) agony
   (B) luster
   (C) irregularity
   (D) shape
   (E) instinct

10. AMNESTY :
   (A) model
   (B) immunity
   (C) conduct
   (D) neutral
   (E) fragrance

11. **LAUNCH :**
   (A) relieve
   (B) denounce
   (C) spellbind
   (D) begin
   (E) penetrate

12. **PROPAGANDA :**
   (A) destitution
   (B) confidence
   (C) disinformation
   (D) privilege
   (E) courtesy

13. **MENAGERIE :**
   (A) wile
   (B) scenario
   (C) zoo
   (D) decision
   (E) spending

14. **POMPOUS :**
   (A) highest
   (B) pretentious
   (C) furtive
   (D) thin
   (E) brawny

15. **GRIM :**
   (A) common
   (B) gloomy
   (C) capable
   (D) temporary
   (E) abhorrent

16. **OBSOLETE :**
   (A) outdated
   (B) confused
   (C) imaginative
   (D) conscientious
   (E) physical

17. **UNNERVING :**
   (A) haughty
   (B) ridiculous
   (C) disconcerting
   (D) thrifty
   (E) foolish

18. **FIGURATIVE :**
   (A) satirical
   (B) metaphorical
   (C) hypocritical
   (D) wary
   (E) spiteful

19. **SECLUDE :**
   (A) isolate
   (B) adapt
   (C) charge
   (D) consult
   (E) limit

20. **IMPART :**
   (A) exculpate
   (B) advocate
   (C) allure
   (D) overwhelm
   (E) inform

"No one is useless in this world who lightens the burdens of another."

— Charles Dickens —
English novelist

다른 사람의 짐을 덜어 준다면 이 세상에 쓸모 없는 사람이란 없다.

LESSON

Greek and Latin Roots & Prefixes 37

★ POST = after

script (write)	postscript	추신
-ior (adj.)	posterior	뒤의, 후방의
humous (human beings)	posthumous	사후의
mortem (death)	postmortem	사후의, 죽은 뒤의
ponere (put)	postpone	미루다
-ity (n.)	posterity	후손
war (military conflict)	postwar	전쟁 후의

DAY

37

WORDS TO LEARN

☐ acute	☐ ecstatic	☐ intractable	☐ raze
☐ adversity	☐ entrepreneur	☐ jaded	☐ revere
☐ avocation	☐ epidemic	☐ macabre	☐ seditious
☐ belittle	☐ filch	☐ mercenary	☐ sluggish
☐ cardinal	☐ furnish	☐ mutable	☐ steer
☐ conducive	☐ grimy	☐ obtuse	☐ surreptitious
☐ culminate	☐ hind	☐ paramount	☐ torture
☐ deserted	☐ impartial	☐ plaintive	☐ unprecedented
☐ disguise	☐ indifferent	☐ prostrate	☐ voluminous

01

acute
[*uh*-kyoot]

adj. sharp and intense
예리한, 날카로운
The doctor said she developed an **acute** sickness.[1]

syn. shrewd, astute, keen

02

adversity
[ad-vur-si-tee]

n. a state of misfortune or affliction
역경, 고난
Refugees from war-torn countries encounter terrible
adversity.[2]

syn. hardship, mishap, misery

03

avocation
[av-*uh*-key-shu*h*n]

n. something a person does in addition to a principal
occupation, especially for pleasure.
취미, 여가 활동
He enjoys a wide range of **avocations**: tennis, golf, sudoku,
and writing poetry.[3]

syn. hobby, pastime, amusement

예문 해석

01 의사는 그녀가 급성 질환에 걸렸다고 말했다. **02** 전쟁으로 피폐해진 나라에서 온 난민들은 끔찍한 역경에 직면한다. **03** 그는 테니스, 골프, 스도쿠, 시 쓰기 등 다양한 취미를 즐긴다.

04

belittle
[bih-lit-l]

v. cause to seem less serious
하찮게 만들다, 경시하다
The candidate **belittled** his opponent by pointing out that his fellow candidate had an inferior intellect during a press conference.[4]

syn. detract, disparage, depreciate

05

cardinal
[kahr-dn-l]

adj. of prime importance
가장 중요한, 기본적인
Recycling is not an option but a **cardinal** law in this land.[5]

syn. principal, essential, chief

06

conducive
[kuhn-doo-siv]

adj. tending to produce
~에 좋은, ~에 도움이 되는
Darkness is **conducive** to getting sleep.[6]

syn. helpful, contributive, favorable

07

culminate
[kuhl-muh-neyt]

v. to reach a final or climactic stage
정점에 닿다
The argument **culminated** in a fistfight.[7]

syn. climax, come to a climax

08

deserted
[di-zur-tid]

adj. place or building that is no longer used or occupied
버려진, 사람이 살지 않는
The explorers walked through the **deserted** village.[8]

syn. abandoned, forsaken

🧘 **예문 해석**

04 그 후보자는 기자 회견에서 동료 후보가 지능이 떨어진다고 지적함으로써 상대 후보를 경시했다. **05** 재활용은 선택이 아니라 이 땅의 기본법이다. **06** 어둠은 잠을 자는데 도움이 된다. **07** 논쟁은 주먹다짐으로 정점에 다다랐다. **08** 탐험가들은 인적이 드문 마을을 거닐었다.

disguise
[dis-gaiz]

v. to hide the identity of someone by a change of appearance
위장시키다
She was **disguised** in a man's clothes.[9]

syn. camouflage, hide, conceal

ecstatic
[ek-stat-ik]

adj. extremely happy, excited and enthusiastic
황홀한, 무아지경의
She was **ecstatic** when she heard that she passed the entrance examination of a prestigious boarding school.[10]

syn. euphoric, exhilarated, rapturous

entrepreneur
[ahn-truh-pruh-nur]

n. a person who organizes and manages any enterprise
(특히 모험적인) 사업가
She has been a successful **entrepreneur** for the last ten years in the tech field.[11]

syn. administrator, executive, businessperson

epidemic
[ep-i-dem-ik]

adj. extremely prevalent
급속도로 퍼지는, 전염성이 강한
People were taking precautions because of the flu **epidemic**.[12]

syn. widespread, rampant, prevalent

filch
[filch]

v. to steal especially something of small value
좀도둑질하다, 훔치다
He **filched** ashtrays from restaurants.[13]

syn. pilfer, steal

 예문 해석

09 그녀는 남자로 위장하고 있었다. **10** 명문 기숙학교 입학시험에 합격했다는 소식을 들었을 때 그녀는 황홀했다. **11** 그녀는 지난 10년간 기술 분야에서 성공한 기업인이었다. **12** 유행성 독감 때문에 사람들은 예방 조치를 취하고 있었다. **13** 그는 레스토랑에서 재떨이를 좀도둑질 해왔다.

14

furnish
[fur-nish]

v. to provide a place with furniture
설비를 갖추다
Many luxurious hotels try to **furnish** their rooms with antiques.[14]

syn. supply, provide, equip

15

grimy
[grai-mee]

adj. dirty
때 묻은, 더러운
She held his **grimy** hand.[15]

syn. soiled, filthy, stained

16

hind
[haind]

adj. situated in the rear or at the back
뒤의
The bear bellowed and stood on its **hind** legs.[16]

syn. posterior, rear, behind

17

impartial
[im-pahr-sh*uh*l]

adj. free from undue bias or preconceived opinions
공정한, 공평한
The newspaper boasted about its **impartial** reporting.[17]

syn. fair, neutral, unbiased

18

indifferent
[in-dif-r*uh*nt]

adj. lacking interest
무관심한, 냉담한
People have become **indifferent** to the suffering of others.[18]

syn. uncaring, aloof, phlegmatic

19

intractable
[in-trak-t*uh*-b*uh*l]

adj. difficult to manage or mold
다루기 힘든, 고집센
His **intractable** little brother won't do what anyone says.[19]

syn. unmanageable, intransigent, stubborn

예문 해석

14 많은 고급 호텔들이 고가구로 설비를 갖추려 하고 있다. **15** 그녀는 그의 지저분한 손을 잡아주었다. **16** 그 곰은 울부짖으며 뒷다리로 섰다. **17** 그 신문은 공정한 보도를 자랑했다. **18** 사람들은 다른 사람의 고통에 무관심해져 왔다. **19** 그의 고집센 남동생은 누가 시키는 대로 하지 않을 것이다.

jaded
[jey-did]

adj. tired and bored, because you had too much of something

지칠 대로 지친, 질린

Sometimes I feel a little **jaded** about the human race.[20]

syn. exhausted, bored, tired

macabre
[muh-kah-bruh]

adj. gruesome and horrifying

(죽음에 관련되어) 섬뜩한, 으스스한

His mom forbids him to watch the **macabre** contents on the web.[21]

syn. frightening, ghastly, horrible

mercenary
[mur-suh-ner-ee]

adj. working or acting merely for money or other reward

용병의, 보수를 목적으로 하는, 탐욕스러운

He was a **mercenary** soldier.[22]

syn. greedy, acquisitive, unscrupulous

mutable
[myoo-tuh-buhl]

adj. liable or subject to change

변덕스러운, 변하기 쉬운

We had to plan our day around the **mutable** weather.[23]

syn. changeable, fickle, inconstant

obtuse
[uhb-toos]

adj. slow to understand something

둔한, 무딘

The **obtuse** man didn't understand the joke.[24]

syn. unintelligent, dull, dense

paramount
[par-uh-mount]

adj. of supreme importance

주요한, 탁월한, 훌륭한

The child's welfare must be seen as **paramount**.[25]

syn. foremost, supreme

예문 해석

20 나는 가끔 인간들에게 질려버릴 때가 있다. **21** 그의 엄마는 그가 웹에서 끔찍한 내용을 보는 것을 금지한다. **22** 그는 용병이었다. **23** 우리는 변덕스러운 날씨에 맞춰 하루를 계획해야 했다. **24** 그 둔한 남자는 그 농담을 이해하지 못했다. **25** 아이들의 복지가 최우선으로 여겨져야 한다.

26

plaintive
[pleyn-tiv]

adj. expressing sorrow or melancholy
애처로운, 구슬픈
Her **plaintive** words showed the sorrow and remorse that she felt.[26]

syn. mournful, heartrending, sorrowful

27

prostrate
[pros-treyt]

adj. lying on the ground and facing downwards
엎드린
He was lying **prostrate**.[27]

syn. flat, face down, horizontal

28

raze
[reyz]

v. to destroy or demolish completely
완전히 파괴하다, 무너뜨리다
The bomb **razed** the building to the ground.[28]

syn. annihilate, demolish, pulverize

29

revere
[ri-veer]

v. to feel or show great respect or reverence for someone or something
숭배하다, 경외하다, 존경하다
The child **revered** her parents.[29]

syn. worship, admire, venerate

30

seditious
[si-dish-uhs]

adj. encouraging people to rebel against higher authority
선동적인, 치안 방해의
The speaker staked out a position that was not merely offensive, but quite **seditious**.[30]

syn. rebellious, defiant, disloyal

 예문 해석

26 그녀의 애처로운 말에는 그녀가 느꼈던 슬픔과 회한이 묻어났다. **27** 그는 엎드려 있었다. **28** 그들은 음식을 게걸스럽게 먹었다. **29** 그 아이는 부모를 공경했다. **30** 연설자는 단지 불쾌할 뿐 아니라 꽤 선동적인 입장을 취했다.

31

sluggish
[sl*uh*g-ish]

adj. not acting or working with full vigor

둔한, 느린, 늘어진

Circulation is much more **sluggish** in the feet than in the hands.[31]

syn. lethargic, slow, listless

32

steer
[steer]

v. to guide or control the direction of a vehicle or vessel

키를 잡다, 방향을 조정하다

The driver needed to concentrate on **steering** the wheel instead of being distracted by his phone.[32]

syn. guide, turn, maneuver

33

surreptitious
[sur-*uh*p-tish-*uh*s]

adj. done secretly or quickly

비밀의, 내밀의, 몰래 하는, 은밀한

He made a **surreptitious** entrance to the basement.[33]

syn. furtive, sneaky, clandestine

34

torture
[tawr-cher]

n. the act of inflicting excruciating pain

고문, 심한 고통

Many people were forced to serve in the military and suffered **torture**.[34]

syn. torment, abuse

35

unprecedented
[*uh*n-pres-i-den-tid]

adj. not known to have ever happened before

전례가 없는, 전에 없던, 공전의

Such a move is rare but not **unprecedented**.[35]

syn. unparalleled, extraordinary

36

voluminous
[v*uh*-loo-m*uh*-n*uh*s]

adj. very large or containing a lot of things

부피가 큰, 용적이 큰, 방대한, 풍부한

Many believe that the FBI kept **voluminous** data on aliens.[36]

syn. vast, ample, extensive

예문 해석

31 손보다 발의 혈액순환이 훨씬 더 느리다. **32** 운전자는 전화기에 정신이 팔리는 대신 운전대를 잡는 데 집중해야 했다. **33** 그는 지하실로 통하는 비밀 문을 만들었다. **34** 많은 사람들이 군대로 강제 징집되거나 고문을 받았다. **35** 이러한 움직임은 드물지만 전례가 없는 것은 아니다. **36** 많은 사람들이 FBI가 외계인에 대한 방대한 양의 자료를 보유하고 있을 것이라 생각한다.

Directions   Each of the following questions consists of one word followed by five words or phrases. You are to select the one word or phrase whose meaning is closest to the word in capital letters.

1. **ACUTE :**
   (A) obsolete
   (B) anxious
   (C) fidgety
   (D) shrewd
   (E) frank

2. **AVOCATION :**
   (A) fragility
   (B) spite
   (C) hobby
   (D) apex
   (E) courage

3. **CARDINAL :**
   (A) insane
   (B) principal
   (C) imminent
   (D) secondary
   (E) pretentious

4. **CONDUCIVE :**
   (A) impulsive
   (B) fruitless
   (C) insignificant
   (D) helpful
   (E) obedient

5. **DISGUISE :**
   (A) shake
   (B) restrain
   (C) camouflage
   (D) mystify
   (E) slide

6. **JADED :**
   (A) daring
   (B) exhausted
   (C) unruffled
   (D) muffled
   (E) required

7. **MACABRE :**
   (A) magistrate
   (B) inherited
   (C) frightening
   (D) well-known
   (E) haphazard

8. **MERCENARY :**
   (A) greedy
   (B) rapacious
   (C) ardent
   (D) uncanny
   (E) exacting

9. **PLAINTIVE :**
   (A) foolish
   (B) nimble
   (C) mournful
   (D) furious
   (E) spirited

10. **REVERE :**
    (A) contort
    (B) isolate
    (C) entice
    (D) strike
    (E) worship

"We make a living by what we get. We make a life by what we give."

— Winston Churchill —
British politician

우리는 받는 것으로 삶을 유지하고 주는 것으로 진정한 삶을 살게 된다.

Greek and Latin Roots & Prefixes 38

★ MONO = one, alone

logos (speech)	monologue	독백
arkhein (to rule)	monarch	고독 공포증
polein (to sell)	monopoly	독점
monotonos (of one tone)	monotonous	단조로운
khroma (color)	monochrome	흑백의, 단색으로 된
oculus (eye)	monocle	한 알로 된 안경
gamy (mate)	monogamy	일부일처제
lithos (stone)	monolith	하나로 된 거대한 암석
terion (place)	monastery	수도원

DAY

38

WORDS TO LEARN

☐ abolish	☐ ecumenical	☐ instigate	☐ recalcitrant
☐ adamant	☐ exculpate	☐ jar	☐ reverie
☐ arbiter	☐ explicable	☐ lean	☐ secrete
☐ brandish	☐ fecund	☐ lunge	☐ sly
☐ cleave	☐ furor	☐ merchandise	☐ stern
☐ confiscate	☐ grin	☐ muddle	☐ surveillance
☐ cunning	☐ hierarchy	☐ obviate	☐ tantamount
☐ desist	☐ impassive	☐ pending	☐ unremitting
☐ disinterested	☐ indigenous	☐ probation	☐ vile

01

abolish
[*uh*-bol-ish]

v. to get rid of
(법률이나 제도를) 폐지하다, 없애다
Abolitionists wanted to **abolish** slavery before the Civil War.[1]

syn. annul, cancel, nullify

02

adamant
[ad-*uh*-m*uh*nt]

adj. utterly unyielding in attitude or in opinion
단호한, 확고한
I am quite **adamant** that you should leave at once.[1]

syn. unyielding, determined, resolute

03

arbiter
[ahr-bi-ter]

n. someone selected to judge and settle a dispute
결정권자
The food critic was considered to be an **arbiter** of modern fusion cuisine.[3]

syn. mediator, umpire, judge

🔖 예문 해석

01 노예제 폐지론자들은 남북전쟁 이전에 노예제도를 폐지하기를 원했다.　**02** 나는 네가 즉시 떠나야 한다는 점에서는 확고하다.
03 그 음식 평론가는 현대 퓨전 요리의 결정권자로 여겨졌다.

04 ·······

brandish
[bran-dish]

v. to hold a weapon in a threatening way
(무기를 위협적으로) 휘두르다
He **brandishes** his gun, waving it in the air, yelling for the crowd to stay back.[4]

syn. wield, flaunt, swing around

05 ·······

cleave
[kleev]

v. to split or to divide
자르다, 나누다, 쪼개다
He could **cleave** the log with one giant swing of the ax.[5]

syn. split, separate, divide

06 ·······

confiscate
[kon-*fuh*-skeyt]

v. to seize as forfeited to the public domain
몰수하다, 압수하다
The teacher **confiscated** his backpack after he swung it at his friend.[6]

syn. seize, forfeit, appropriate

07 ·······

cunning
[k*uh*n-ing]

adj. showing or made with ingenuity
교활한, 교묘한
He is remembered as a **cunning** man but also as a man with a strong will to pursue his dream.[7]

syn. crafty, sly, wily

08 ·······

desist
[di-zist]

v. to stop
그만두다, 단념하다
She never **desisted** from trying to persuade her family to move to America.[8]

syn. cease, resign, abstain

🔖 **예문 해석**

04 그는 총을 공중으로 휘두르며 사람들에게 물러서라고 소리쳤다.   **05** 그는 도끼를 크게 한 번 휘둘러 통나무를 쪼갤 수 있었다.
06 선생님은 그가 친구에게 가방을 던지자 가방을 압수했다.   **07** 그는 교활한 사람으로 기억되지만 자신의 꿈을 쫓는 강인한 의지가 있는 사람으로 여겨지기도 한다.   **08** 그녀는 가족들에게 미국으로 가자고 설득하는 것을 절대 단념하지 않았다.

09

disinterested
[dis-in-t*uh*-res-tid]

adj. unbiased by personal interest or advantage

관심이 없는, 사심이 없는

His teacher chastised him for being **disinterested** in class.[9]

syn. impartial, neutral, unbiased

10

ecumenical
[ek-yoo-men-i-k*uh*l]

adj. of worldwide scope or applicability

세계적인, 전반적인, 보편적인

The **ecumenical** approach gained many followers.[10]

syn. universal, ubiquitous, cosmopolitan

11

exculpate
[ek-sk*uh*l-peyt]

v. to find someone not guilty of criminal charges

무죄를 입증하다

He was wrongly accused of homicide, and he hoped a judge would **exculpate** him.[11]

syn. forgive, absolve, acquit

12

explicable
[ek-spli-k*uh*-b*uh*l]

adj. capable of being explained

설명할 수 있는, 설명될 수 있는

Her eccentric behavior is only **explicable** in terms of her depression.[12]

syn. understandable, fathomable

13

fecund
[fee-k*uh*nd]

adj. capable of producing offspring or vegetation

비옥한, 다산의

All that lives returns to dust in due season, making the earth **fecund** with life.[13]

syn. fertile, fruitful, productive

14

furor
[fyoor-awr]

n. a general outburst of excitement or indignation

격렬한 감정, 열광적인 반응

The superintendent's motivational speech created a **furor**.[14]

syn. enthusiasm, fervor, zeal

예문 해석

09 그의 선생님은 수업에 관심이 없다고 그를 꾸짖었다.　**10** 전기독교적인 접근법은 많은 추종자들을 얻었다.　**11** 그는 살인죄로 잘못 기소되었고, 판사가 그를 무죄로 해주길 바랐다.　**12** 그녀의 이상한 행동은 우울증으로만 설명될 수밖에 없다.　**13** 모든 생명체는 때가 되면 먼지로 돌아가, 지구를 생명체로 가득 채운다.　**14** 교육감의 동기부여 연설은 분노를 불러일으켰다.

grin
[grin]

v. to smile broadly
(이를 드러내고) 싱긋 웃다
The boy **grinned** at the girl.[15]

syn. smile, smirk, beam

16

hierarchy
[hai-*uh*-rahr-kee]

n. an organization that classifies people in order of rank
계층제, 계급제
With a rigid **hierarchy**, workers and managers had strictly defined duties.[16]

syn. strata, caste, class

17

impassive
[im-pas-iv]

adj. without emotion
무감정한, 냉담한
When the normally **impassive** Sarah was invited the party, her eyes filled with tears.[17]

syn. apathetic, unmoved, indifferent

18

indigenous
[in-dij-*uh*-n*uh*s]

adj. belonging to the region, rather than coming from another country
토착의, 그 지역 고유의
The **indigenous** people had a great history in their region.[18]

syn. native, aboriginal

19

instigate
[in-sti-geyt]

v. to cause by incitement
자극하다, 부추기다, 조장하다
He **instigated** a fight with his brother.[19]

syn. foment, incite, provoke

 예문 해석

15 소년이 소녀를 보고 싱긋 웃었다. **16** 엄격한 계급제로 상사와 직원들은 명확히 구분되는 임무가 있다. **17** 평소 무표정하던 사라가 파티에 초대되었을 때 그녀의 눈에는 눈물이 가득했다. **18** 원주민들은 그들의 지역에서 위대한 역사를 가지고 있었다. **19** 그는 형에게 시비를 걸었다.

jar
[jahr]

v. to move with a fairly hard shaking movement
덜컹덜컹 흔들리다, 삐걱거리다
As the storm came in, the boat **jarred** a little.[20]

syn. jolt, jerk, bash, bump

lean
[leen]

adj. without much fat
마른
Lean red meat fits in well with a healthy diet.[21]

syn. lanky, angular, slender

lunge
[luhnj]

v. to move in a certain direction suddenly
갑자기 돌진하다
He **lunged** at me and grabbed me violently.[22]

syn. thrust, pounce

merchandise
[mur-chuhn-daiz]

n. manufactured goods
상품
General **merchandise** was sold at the department store.[23]

syn. goods, commodities, products

muddle
[muhd-l]

v. to mix up in a confused manner
뒤죽박죽을 만들다, 헝클어뜨리다
Her **muddled** room looks like a hurricane just hit it.[24]

syn. clutter, disorganize, befuddle

obviate
[ob-vee-eyt]

v. to prevent or remove a potential problem in advance
미리 막다, 방지하다
E-mail has **obviated** the need for fax machines.[25]

syn. preclude, forestall, prevent

예문 해석

20 폭풍이 들이닥치자 배가 약간 덜컹거렸다. **21** 지방이 적은 붉은 살코기는 건강한 식단에 적합하다. **22** 그는 갑자기 달려들어 나를 거칠게 붙잡았다. **23** 백화점에서 잡화를 팔았다. **24** 그녀의 어수선한 방은 마치 허리케인이 덮친 것 같다. **25** 이메일은 팩스 사용을 필요 없게 만든다.

pending
[pen-ding]

adj. awaiting conclusion or confirmation
미결정인, 결정을 기다리는 중인
The score report was not released yet; it is **pending**.[26]

syn. undecided, awaiting, hanging

probation
[proh-bey-shuhn]

n. the testing or trial of a person's conduct or qualifications
보호 관찰, 수습 기간, 근신 기간
On **probation**, the criminal was not in jail, but he had to do certain things demanded by the court.[27]

syn. apprenticeship, trial, test period

recalcitrant
[ri-kal-si-truhnt]

adj. resisting authority or control
저항하는, 다루기 힘든
The **recalcitrant** teenager gets into trouble every day.[28]

syn. disobedient, fractious, rebellious

reverie
[rev-uh-ree]

n. a state of dreamy meditation
공상, 몽상, 환상곡
He was jolted out of his **reverie** as the door opened.[29]

syn. daydream, illusion, fantasy, fancy

secrete
[si-kreet]

v. to produce a liquid substance
분비하다
The copperhead snake **secretes** venom to kill its prey.[30]

syn. generate, emit, discharge

sly
[slai]

adj. acting in a secret way
교활한, 음흉한
She is **sly** and manipulative.[31]

syn. cunning, crafty, wily

예문 해석

26 성적표는 아직 공개되지 않았다. 보류 중이다. **27** 보호 관찰 기간 동안 범인은 감옥에 있지 않았지만, 법원에서 요구하는 특정한 일들을 해야만 했다. **28** 고집불통인 그 십대는 매일 말썽을 부린다. **29** 그는 문이 열리자 몽상에서 갑자기 깨어났다. **30** 구리머리 뱀은 먹이를 죽이기 위해 독을 분비한다. **31** 그녀는 음흉하고 사람을 잘 다룬다.

stern
[sturn]

adj. extremely strict
가혹한, 용서 없는, 엄격한
He issued a **stern** warning to those who persist in violence.[32]

syn. strict, grim, rigid

surveillance
[ser-vey-luhns]

n. a close watch over something
감시, 감독
He demanded round-the-clock **surveillance** over his new business.[33]

syn. observation, supervision, vigilance

tantamount
[tan-*tuh*-mount]

adj. being essentially equal to something
～와 마찬가지의, ～에 상당하는
If she resigned, it would be **tantamount** to admitting that she was guilty.[34]

syn. commensurate, same, identical

unremitting
[*uh*n-ri-mit-ing]

adj. uninterrupted in time and indefinitely long
끊임없이 노력하는
Children need **unremitting** attention from parents.[35]

syn. unending, perpetual, unceasing

vile
[vail]

adj. morally reprehensible
극도로 불쾌한, 나쁜
I complained about the **vile** smell and demanded to switch the room.[36]

syn. disgusting, offensive, horrible

 예문 해석

32 그는 폭력을 고집하는 사람에게는 엄한 경고를 내렸다.   **33** 그는 새 사업에 대해 24시간 감시할 것을 요구했다.   **34** 그녀가 사직한다면 그것은 자신이 유죄임을 인정하는 것과 마찬가지가 될 것이었다.   **35** 아이들은 부모의 지속적인 관심이 필요하다.
36 나는 끔찍한 악취에 대해 불평하고 방을 바꿔 달라고 요구했다.

Directions   Each of the following questions consists of one word followed by five words or phrases. You are to select the one word or phrase whose meaning is closest to the word in capital letters.

1. ABOLISH :
(A) insinuate
(B) discourage
(C) annul
(D) topple
(E) curtail

2. ADAMANT :
(A) rascal
(B) lethargic
(C) unyielding
(D) composed
(E) notorious

3. ARBITER :
(A) warlock
(B) quack
(C) authority
(D) impostor
(E) mediator

4. BRANDISH :
(A) initiate
(B) compensate
(C) sort
(D) wield
(E) flatter

5. CONFISCATE :
(A) seize
(B) annul
(C) leap
(D) evade
(E) suppress

6. CUNNING :
(A) insane
(B) forceful
(C) entrenched
(D) crafty
(E) dilapidated

7. EXCULPATE :
(A) wander
(B) disguise
(C) deceive
(D) forgive
(E) smother

8. JAR :
(A) disrepute
(B) specify
(C) jolt
(D) pulverize
(E) annoy

9. MUDDLE :
(A) degenerate
(B) abandon
(C) commence
(D) reject
(E) clutter

10. RECALCITRANT :
(A) level
(B) horrifying
(C) digressive
(D) enchanting
(E) disobedient

"Kind words can be short and easy to speak, but their echoes are truly endless."

— Mother Teresa —
Saint

친절한 말은 짧고 말하기 쉽지만 그 말의 울림은 진정 끝이 없다.

Greek and Latin Roots & Prefixes 39

★ POLY = many

gon (angles)	polygon	다각형
morph (shape)	polymorphous	다양한 형태의
glot (tongue)	polyglot	여러 언어를 구사하는
the (god)	polytheism	다신론
Khroma (color)	polychromatic	다색의, 다양한 색으로 된
gamy (mate)	polygamy	일부다처제
graph (drawing)	polygraph	거짓말탐지기

DAY

39

WORDS TO LEARN

☐ adept   ☐ edible   ☐ integrate   ☐ rejuvenate

☐ animosity   ☐ epitaph   ☐ jargon   ☐ revert

☐ babble   ☐ explicit   ☐ magnate   ☐ secular

☐ brash   ☐ finesse   ☐ merger   ☐ smack

☐ circumvent   ☐ furtive   ☐ mutter   ☐ stifle

☐ cull   ☐ glib   ☐ ordinance   ☐ susceptible

☐ cupidity   ☐ hitherto   ☐ parry   ☐ towering

☐ desolate   ☐ impeach   ☐ portal   ☐ unruly

☐ dismantle   ☐ indignant   ☐ prosaic   ☐ vulnerable

01

adept
[*uh*-dept]

adj. skilfull at doing something
숙련된, 숙달된
He is an **adept** surgeon.[1]

syn. skillful, skilled, expert, dexterous

02

animosity
[an-*uh*-mos-i-tee]

n. a strong dislike or hatred
악의, 증오
There's a long history of **animosity** between the two nations.[2]

syn. hostility, hatred, loathing, enmity

03

babble
[bab-*uh*l]

v. to talk or say something quickly
불명료한 소리를 내다, 웅얼거리다
The child started to **babble**.[3]

syn. jabber, prattle

 예문 해석

01 그는 숙련된 외과의사이다.   **02** 두 나라 간에는 오랜 앙숙의 역사가 있다.   **03** 아이가 웅얼거리며 말하기 시작했다.

04

brash
[brash]

adj. confident in an aggressive way
성급한, 경솔한
She seems hard, **brash**, and uncompromising.[4]

syn. cocky, impudent, rude

05

circumvent
[sur-*kuh*m-vent]

v. to go around or bypass
(어려움이나 법 등을) 피하다
When he finds a clever way around rules or barriers, he
dares to **circumvent** them.[5]

syn. sidestep, avoid, evade

06

cull
[*kuh*l]

v. to select and remove from a group, especially to discard
or destroy as inferior
(특정 동물의 수를 제한하기 위해) 골라내다.
The entrance exam is administered, so the school can **cull**
the best students for admission.[6]

syn. select, pick out, winnow

07

cupidity
[kyoo-pid-i-tee]

n. excessive desire
탐욕
His **cupidity** can never be satiated.[7]

syn. greed, avarice, covetousness

08

desolate
[des-*uh*-lit]

adj. barren or laid waste
황폐한
During our road trip, we saw a **desolate** landscape.[8]

syn. dreary, barren, bleak

 예문 해석

04 그녀는 대하기 어렵고, 성급하며, 고집 센 것처럼 보인다. **05** 그는 규칙이나 장벽을 우회하는 영리한 방법을 찾았을 때, 과감히 그것들을 피한다. **06** 입학 시험은 학교가 최고의 학생들을 선발할 수 있도록 실행된다. **07** 그의 탐욕은 끝이 없다. **08** 자동차 여행 중에 우리는 황량한 풍경을 보았다.

dismantle
[dis-man-tl]

v. to take apart
철거하다, 해체하다, 부수다
The wind **dismantled** the ship.[9]

> *syn.* break apart, demolish, disassemble

edible
[ed-*uh*-b*uh*l]

adj. suitable to eat
먹을 수 있는, 식용의
The **edible** mushrooms were tasteful when prepared properly.[10]

> *syn.* eatable, comestible, able to be eaten

epitaph
[ep-i-taf]

n. a commemorative inscription on a tomb
비문, 묘비글
His **epitaph** reads, "seize the day."[11]

> *syn.* inscription, engraving, etching

explicit
[ik-splis-it]

adj. fully and clearly expressed
진술 등이 명백한, 뚜렷한
I gave **explicit** instructions to the substitute teacher.[12]

> *syn.* specific, obvious, clear

finesse
[fi-ness]

n. tact and poise in handling situations
술책, 책략, 수완
He showed great **finesse** in dealing with his opponents.[13]

> *syn.* gimmick, maneuver, guile

furtive
[fur-tiv]

adj. secretive or hidden
몰래 하는, 남의 눈을 속이는, 은밀한
The man gave a **furtive** glance to his coworker.[14]

> *syn.* stealthy, secretive, sly

예문 해석

09 바람이 배를 부서뜨렸다.　**10** 그 식용 곰팡이는 적절하게 준비되면 맛이 있었다.　**11** 그의 묘비에는 '오늘을 충실히 살아라'라고 쓰여 있다.　**12** 나는 대리 교사에게 명확한 지시를 내렸다.　**13** 그는 반대 세력을 다루는 뛰어난 수완을 보였다.　**14** 그 남자는 동료에게 슬쩍 눈길을 보냈다.

15

glib
[glib]

adj. artfully persuasive in speech
구변 좋은, 말을 잘 하는
The HR manager thought Ben was **glib** and insincere when she was reading his pretentious resume.[15]

syn. slick, smooth-talking, slippery

16

hitherto
[hith-er-too]

adv. up to this point; until the present time
지금까지는, 그때까지
A very shy girl in his math class who was **hitherto** totally silent finally spoke up today and asked a brilliant mathematical question.[16]

syn. until now, up to this point

17

impeach
[im-peech]

v. to accuse a public or government official of misconduct while in office
탄핵하다
A National Assembly vote on whether to **impeach** the president is expected tomorrow.[17]

syn. incriminate, accuse, charge

18

indignant
[in-dig-n*uh*nt]

adj. shocked and angry
분개한, 분노한
I could read the **indignant** expression on her face.[18]

syn. choleric, enraged, furious

19

integrate
[in-ti-greyt]

v. make into a whole or make part of a whole
통합시키다, 통합되다
It is important to **integrate** new students, so they can feel a part of the class.[19]

syn. combine, merge, mix

 예문 해석

15 인사 담당자는 벤의 가식적인 이력서를 읽으면서 그가 말만 잘하고 진실되지 못하다고 생각했다.   **16** 그의 수학 수업에서 지금까지 완전히 침묵하고 있던 매우 수줍은 소녀가 오늘 마침내 말을 꺼내서 훌륭한 수학적 질문을 했다.   **17** 대통령에 대한 탄핵 표결을 내일 국회에서 갖기로 예정되어 있다.   **18** 나는 그녀의 분노한 표정을 읽을 수 있었다.   **19** 신입생들을 반의 일원이라 느낄 수 있도록 그들을 통합하는 것이 중요하다.

jargon
[jahr-g*uh*n]

n. terminology that relates to a specific activity, profession or group

은어, 전문어

Try to avoid using too much medical **jargon** when you have a conversation with your patient.[20]

syn. terminology, language, vernacular

magnate
[mag-neyt]

n. a very wealthy or powerful businessperson

거물, 왕

He was a hugely successful businessperson and a wealthy oil **magnate**.[21]

syn. mogul, tycoon, businessperson

merger
[mer-jer]

n. the joining together of two separate companies

합병

The **merger** between two of Britain's biggest trade unions was quite an accomplishment.[22]

syn. amalgamation, union, combination

mutter
[m*uh*t-er]

v. to speak indistinctly or in a low tone

궁시렁거리다, 투덜거리다

Workers continued to **mutter** about the supervisor.[23]

syn. murmur, grumble, mumble

ordinance
[awr-dn-*uh*ns]

n. an authoritative rule

조례, 법령

This city passed **ordinances** making it mandatory for pet owners to curb their dogs.[24]

syn. law, decree, command

예문 해석

20 환자와 이야기할 때 너무 많은 의학 전문용어를 쓰는 것을 피하도록 하라. **21** 그는 매우 성공한 사업가이자 부유한 석유 재벌이었다. **22** 영국의 가장 큰 두 노동조합 간의 합병은 상당한 성과였다. **23** 작업자들은 감독관에 대해 계속해서 투덜거렸다. **24** 이 도시는 애완동물 주인들이 그들의 개를 통제하는 것을 의무화하는 법을 통과시켰다.

25

parry
[par-ee]

v. to ward off
받아넘기다. 슬쩍 피하다
It is difficult to block with a shield or **parry** with a weapon.[25]

syn. avert, evade, dodge

26

portal
[pawr-tl]

n. a door, gate, or entrance
현관, 정문
Google is one of the world's largest Internet **portals**.[26]

syn. gate, doorway, gateway

27

prosaic
[proh-zey-ik]

adj. commonplace or dull
평범한, 따분한
She led a **prosaic** everyday life without anything adventurous.[27]

syn. unimaginative, mundane, drab

28

rejuvenate
[ri-joo-v*uh*-neyt]

v. to make young again
다시 젊어 보이게 하다, 활기를 되찾게 하다
He **rejuvenated** a dying plant, bringing it back to health with water and nutritional supplements.[28]

syn. revitalize, reinvigorate, regenerate

29

revert
[ri-vurt]

v. to go back to a previous stage
원상태로 돌아가다, 복귀하다
He **reverted** to the original topic of conversation.[29]

syn. degenerate, regress, turn back

30

secular
[se-kyoo-l*uh*r]

adj. not connected with spiritual or religious matters
속세의, 이승의, 세속적인
Her grandparents were extremely religious, and they did not want her to listen to **secular** music.[30]

syn. earthy, worldly, materialistic

예문 해석

25 방패로 막거나 무기로 받아치는 것은 쉽지 않다.　**26** 구글은 세계에서 가장 큰 인터넷 포털 중 하나이다.　**27** 그녀는 모험적인 일은 전혀 하지 않고 매일 평범하게 살았다.　**28** 그는 죽어가는 식물에 물과 영양 보충제로 건강하게 만들어 활기를 되찾아 주었다.　**29** 그는 원래 대화 주제로 돌아갔다.　**30** 그녀의 조부모는 매우 신앙심이 깊어, 그녀가 세속적인 음악을 듣는 것을 원하지 않았다.

smack
[smak]

v. to strike sharply, especially with the hand or a flat object
찰싹 치다, 탁 소리가 나게 치다
He **smacked** his hand down on the table.[31]

syn. strike, spank

stifle
[stai-*fuhl*]

v. to die because there is no air to breathe
숨을 막다, 질식시키다
I felt **stifled** in the airless room.[32]

syn. suffocate, choke, smother

susceptible
[suh-sep-tuh-buhl]

adj. very likely to be influenced, harmed or affected
민감한, 영향을 받기 쉬운
Young people are the most **susceptible** to advertisements.[33]

syn. responsive, sensitive, receptive

towering
[tou-er-ing]

adj. extremely tall or high
우뚝 솟은, 매우 높은
A **towering** pine tree stood next to my home.[34]

syn. colossal, gigantic, imposing

unruly
[*uh*n-roo-lee]

adj. disobedient or disorderly
말 안 듣는, 복종하지 않는
It's not good enough just to blame the **unruly** children.[35]

syn. recalcitrant, refractory

vulnerable
[v*uh*l-ner-*uh*-b*uh*l]

adj. easily hurt or harmed, either physically or emotionally
약한, 위약한, 쉽게 공격 당하는
Babies are particularly **vulnerable** to viruses.[36]

syn. susceptible, pregnable

📖 **예문 해석**

31 그는 탁자를 손으로 내리쳤다. **32** 나는 공기가 희박한 방에서 숨이 막혔다. **33** 젊은이들은 광고에 가장 민감하다. **34** 우리 집 옆에 우뚝 솟은 소나무가 서 있었다. **35** 말 안 듣는 아이를 야단치기만 하는 것만으로는 충분하지 않다. **36** 아기들은 바이러스에 특히 취약하다.

Directions   Each of the following questions consists of one word followed by five words or phrases.
You are to select the one word or phrase whose meaning is closest to the word in capital letters.

1. ADEPT :
  (A) exhausted
  (B) fierce
  (C) awkward
  (D) unintentional
  (E) skillful

2. BABBLE :
  (A) decipher
  (B) jabber
  (C) gather
  (D) swarm
  (E) discern

3. CULL :
  (A) annoy
  (B) control
  (C) devalue
  (D) select
  (E) appall

4. DESOLATE :
  (A) dreary
  (B) flippant
  (C) sublime
  (D) impoverished
  (E) placid

5. DISMANTLE :
  (A) side with
  (B) object to
  (C) make up for
  (D) spur on
  (E) break apart

6. ORDINANCE :
  (A) law
  (B) roster
  (C) climax
  (D) atrocity
  (E) conduct

7. PARRY :
  (A) horrify
  (B) avert
  (C) camouflage
  (D) evacuate
  (E) topple

8. PORTAL :
  (A) homage
  (B) courier
  (C) salute
  (D) gate
  (E) starvation

9. REJUVENATE :
  (A) fumble
  (B) recede
  (C) ensnare
  (D) revitalize
  (E) hibernate

10. REVERT :
  (A) heed
  (B) gobble
  (C) ignite
  (D) embody
  (E) degenerate

"Education is the most powerful weapon which you can use to change the world."

— Nelson Mandela—
South. African black civil rights leader

교육은 세상을 변화시키는 데 사용할 수 있는 가장 강력한 무기이다.

Greek and Latin Roots & Prefixes 40

★ CO, COM = together

-er (n.)	coexist	공존하다
-et (n.)	combine	결합하다
haerere (to stick)	cohesive	화합하는
-ant (n.)	coincidence	우연의 일치
mittere (to release)	commission	수수료, 위원회
miserari (to pity)	commiserate	위로하다
memorare (to remind)	commemorate	기념하다
operari (to work)	cooperate	협동하다
pati (to suffer)	compatible	사이 좋게 지낼 수 있는, 양립하는

DAY

40

WORDS TO LEARN

☐ adhere	☐ edict	☐ instinct	☐ rebuff
☐ annex	☐ epoch	☐ jaunt	☐ revile
☐ badger	☐ exploit	☐ kleptomaniac	☐ sedative
☐ bravado	☐ flowery	☐ lure	☐ smolder
☐ clench	☐ futile	☐ mercurial	☐ stigma
☐ confront	☐ grisly	☐ mutual	☐ sustain
☐ cursory	☐ hilarious	☐ occupy	☐ toxic
☐ despicable	☐ impeccable	☐ partial	☐ unscathed
☐ disposable	☐ indiscreet	☐ protrude	☐ yearn

01

adhere
[ad-heer]

v. to stick to something
(물리적으로) 둘러붙다, 부착하다 (규칙등을) 준수하다, 지키다
She used glue to **adhere** the paper to the board.[1]

syn. stick, cling

02

annex
[uh-neks]

v. to attach or add to something more important
덧붙이다, 부가하다, 합병하다
In the late 1830s, the United States was hesitant to **annex** Texas for fear of provoking a war with Mexico.[2]

syn. add, append, attach

03

badger
[baj-er]

v. to ask again and again
귀찮게 하다, 괴롭히다
She kept phoning and **badgering** me.[3]

syn. pester, irritate, annoy, vex

예문 해석

01 그녀는 풀을 사용해 게시판에 종이를 붙였다. **02** 1830년대 후반 미국은 멕시코와의 전쟁이 일어날 것을 우려해 텍사스를 합병하는 것에 주저했다. **03** 그녀는 계속 전화를 해서 나를 귀찮게 했다.

04

bravado
[bruh-vah-doh]

n. a display of confidence or daring, often a boastful and insincere one

허세, 허풍

He said it with **bravado**.[4]

syn. bluster, boldness

05

clench
[klench]

v. to tighten up

이를 악물다, 주먹을 꽉 쥐다

He **clenched** his fists in anger.[5]

syn. clinch, grasp

06

confront
[kuhn-fruhnt]

v. to face in hostility or defiance

직면하다, 마주하다

The candidates **confronted** each other during a televised debate.[6]

syn. challenge, face, oppose

07

cursory
[kur-suh-ree]

adj. going rapidly over something

서두르는, 대충하는, 엉성한

Cursory inspection fails to reveal the flaws of construction.[7]

syn. hasty, superficial, careless

08

despicable
[des-pi-kuh-buhl]

adj. deserving to be despised

경멸할 만한, 비열한

They thought her actions were **despicable**.[8]

syn. contemptible, detestable, loathsome

예문 해석

04 그는 허세를 부리며 말했다. **05** 그는 분노로 주먹을 꽉 쥐었다. **06** 후보자들은 TV 토론회에서 서로 마주쳤다. **07** 엉성한 조사로는 건축의 결함을 찾을 수 없다. **08** 그들은 그녀의 행동이 비열하다고 생각했다.

09

disposable
[dih-spoh-*zuh*-buh*l*]

adj. an item that can be thrown away after it has been used
일회용의, 사용 후 버리게 되어 있는
The famous female inventor Marion Donovan invented **disposable** diapers.[9]

syn. dispensable, removable, unimportant

10

edict
[ee-dikt]

n. an order issued by any authority
명령, 국왕의 포고
The royal **edict** proved to be beneficial to the wealthy rather than the poor.[10]

syn. order, decree, command

11

epoch
[ep-*uhk*]

n. a particular period of time
시대, 기간
During my history studies, we studied various **epochs**.[11]

syn. era, period, generation

12

exploit
[ek-sploit]

v. to utilize for profit
착취하다, 개발하다
He was not an employer who **exploited** his workers.[12]

syn. abuse, misuse

13

flowery
[flou-*uh*-ree]

adj. rhetorically ornate or precious
(글의) 꾸밈이 심한, 미사여구가 많은
His English teacher dislikes **flowery** language when it comes to writing.[13]

syn. ornate, fancy, grandiloquent

14

futile
[fyoo-tail]

adj. producing no result or effect
쓸모없는, 부질없는
It was a **futile** attempt.[14]

syn. useless, pointless, fruitless

 예문 해석

09 유명한 여성 발명가 마리온 도노반은 일회용 기저귀를 발명했습니다. **10** 그 법은 가난한 사람보다 부유한 사람들에게 이로운 것으로 판명되었다. **11** 역사를 공부하는 동안 우리는 다양한 시대를 연구했다. **12** 그는 종업원을 착취하는 고용주는 아니었다. **13** 그의 영어 선생님은 글쓰기에 관한 한 상투적인 언어를 싫어하신다. **14** 그것은 헛된 시도였다.

grisly
[griz-lee]

adj. shockingly repulsive and horrible
소름 끼치게 하는, 무서운
She closed her eyes at the movie theater during the **grisly** scene.[15]

> *syn.* gruesome, ghastly, alarming

hilarious
[hi-lair-ee-*uhs*]

adj. extremely funny
매우 재미있는, 우스운
I thought it was **hilarious** when I first saw it.[16]

> *syn.* jolly, humorous

impeccable
[im-pek-*uh*-b*uh*l]

adj. free from fault or error
결점 없는, 완벽한
His record is **impeccable**.[17]

> *syn.* faultless, flawless, perfect

indiscreet
[in-di-skreet]

adj. lacking prudence or good judgment
무분별한, 지각 없는
That was an **indiscreet** remark.[18]

> *syn.* imprudent, foolhardy, rash

instinct
[in-stingkt]

n. a natural or innate impulse, inclination, or tendency
본능, 직감
He has an **instinct** for business.[19]

> *syn.* intuition, gut feeling, hunch

jaunt
[jawnt]

n. a short trip, usually for pleasure
짧고 즐거운 여행, 소풍
Brief **jaunts** were okay, but he didn't like to travel much.[20]

> *syn.* excursion, short trip, expedition

예문 해석

15 그녀는 영화관에서 그 끔찍한 장면이 나오는 동안 눈을 감았다.　**16** 나는 그것을 처음 보고 너무 웃기다고 생각했다.　**17** 그의 성적은 완벽하다.　**18** 그것은 경솔한 발언이었다.　**19** 그는 사업에 천부적인 감각이 있다.　**20** 짧은 여행은 괜찮았지만, 그는 여행을 그다지 좋아하지는 않았다.

kleptomaniac
[klep-t*uh*-mey-nee-ak]

n. someone with an irrational urge to steal in the absence of an economic motive

도벽이 있는 사람

A **kleptomaniac** has a mental disorder that compels the person to steal.[21]

syn. thief, stealer, pilferer

lure
[loor]

v. to provoke someone to do something through persuasion

유혹하다, 꾀다

He **lured** her into the parking lot, but her friends soon came looking for her.[22]

syn. entice, attract, cajole

mercurial
[mer-kyoor-ee-*uh*l]

adj. liable to sudden unpredictable change

변덕스러운

Because she is taking a new medication, her moods have become quite **mercurial** and changeable.[23]

syn. volatile, fickle, changeable

mutual
[myoo-choo-*uh*l]

adj. shared or interactive

상호간의

We can collaborate for our **mutual** benefit.[24]

syn. reciprocal, shared, common

occupy
[ok-y*uh*-pai]

v. to be in or fill time or space

자리나 시간을 차지하다, 살다

Our company **occupies** a special niche in this field.[25]

syn. inhabit, live in, dwell in

예문 해석

21 도벽이 있는 사람은 훔치도록 강요하는 정신 장애를 가지고 있다. **22** 그는 그녀를 주차장으로 유인했지만, 그녀의 친구들이 곧 그녀를 찾으러 왔다. **23** 그녀가 새로운 약을 먹고 있기 때문에, 그녀의 기분은 꽤 변덕스러워졌다. **24** 우리는 상호 간의 이익을 위해 함께 협동할 수 있다. **25** 우리 회사는 이 분야에서 특별한 위치를 차지하고 있다.

26

partial
[pahr-sh*uh*l]

adj. favoring one side or person unfairly
일부의, 편파적인
He was **partial** to extreme sports.[26]

syn. unfair, biased, prejudiced

27

protrude
[proh-trood]

v. to stick out
앞으로 튀어나오다, 불쑥 튀어나오다
His belly is **protruding**.[27]

syn. bulge, swell, jut out

28

rebuff
[ri-b*uh*f]

n. an unexpected and blunt refusal or rejection
거절, 퇴짜
They were met with a **rebuff**.[28]

syn. refusal, rejection, snub

29

revile
[ri-vail]

v. to speak of abusively
매도하다, 헐뜯다
He is **reviled** as a murderous tyrant.[29]

syn. vilify, castigate, berate

30

sedative
[sed-*uh*-tiv]

n. any agent, especially a drug, that has a calming effect
진정제
They used opium as a **sedative**.[30]

syn. tranquilizer, narcotic, downer

31

smolder
[smohl-der]

v. to burn without flame
연기만 피운 채 타다
He **smoldered** with rage.[31]

syn. simmer, burn, boil

🧘 예문 해석

26 그는 유달리 격한 운동을 좋아한다.   **27** 그의 배는 불룩 튀어나왔다.   **28** 그들은 갑작스러운 거절을 당했다.   **29** 그는 흉악한 독재자라는 욕을 먹고 있었다.   **30** 그들은 아편을 진정제로 사용했다.   **31** 그는 분노로 이글거렸다.

32

stigma
[stig-m*uh*]

n. a mark of disgrace or infamy
치욕, 오명, 오점, 불명예
There's no **stigma** attached any more.[32]

> *syn.* dishonor, disgrace, shame

33

sustain
[suh-steyn]

v. to provide enough of what someone needs in order to
live or exist
지탱하다, 지속하다, 버티다
We had enough food to **sustain** us for a week.[33]

> *syn.* maintain, continue, carry on

34

toxic
[tok-sik]

adj. containing poison
유독성의, 치명적인
The **toxic** smoke burned my throat as I breathed.[34]

> *syn.* poisonous, deadly, lethal

35

unscathed
[*uh*n-skeythd]

adj. not hurt
다치지 않은, 손상되지 않은
She emerged **unscathed**.[35]

> *syn.* undamaged, unharmed, intact

36

yearn
[yurn]

v. to have an earnest or strong desire
갈망하다, 동경하다
When she was pregnant, all she did was **yearn** for chocolate
and steaks.[36]

> *syn.* long, covet, crave

🔖 **예문 해석**

32 이젠 더 이상의 오명은 없다. **33** 우리는 일주일을 버틸 충분한 식량이 있었다. **34** 숨쉴 때 마다 유독한 연기에 목이 따끔따
끔했다. **35** 그녀는 멀쩡하게 나타났다. **36** 그녀는 임신했을 때 초콜릿과 스테이크를 간절히 원했다.

Directions   Each of the following questions consists of one word followed by five words or phrases. You are to select the one word or phrase whose meaning is closest to the word in capital letters.

1. ADHERE :
   (A) contain
   (B) enchant
   (C) kindle
   (D) stick
   (E) lessen

2. BADGER :
   (A) advocate
   (B) pester
   (C) sidestep
   (D) improve
   (E) scavenge

3. CONFRONT :
   (A) ooze
   (B) challenge
   (C) trudge
   (D) ban
   (E) procure

4. CURSORY :
   (A) hasty
   (B) pious
   (C) flawless
   (D) intimate
   (E) mortal

5. DESPICABLE :
   (A) thorough
   (B) diurnal
   (C) wary
   (D) contemptible
   (E) aloof

6. EDICT :
   (A) cleft
   (B) ratio
   (C) order
   (D) synopsis
   (E) plagiarism

7. EPOCH :
   (A) surfeit
   (B) repartee
   (C) era
   (D) fleet
   (E) satellite

8. REBUFF :
   (A) vessel
   (B) recluse
   (C) starvation
   (D) refusal
   (E) omen

9. REVILE :
   (A) recur
   (B) vilify
   (C) contemplate
   (D) quench
   (E) enroll

10. UNSCATHED :
   (A) mute
   (B) ravenous
   (C) profuse
   (D) undamaged
   (E) petrified

"No one can make you feel inferior without your consent."

— Eleanor Roosevelt —
U.S. diplomat & reformer

당신 자신의 동의 없이 아무도 당신이 열등감을 갖게할 수 없다.

LESSON

Greek and Latin Roots & Prefixes 41

★ UNI = one

cornus (horn)	unicorn	유니콘, 일각수
form (shape)	uniform	획일적인, 다 같은
-fy (v.)	unify	통합하다, 통일하다
-it (n.)	unit	구성 단위, 한 개
-ity (n.)	unity	통합, 통일
the (god)	union	연방, 연합
que (adj.)	unique	유일무이한, 독특한
wer (turn)	universe	은하계, 우주

DAY

41

WORDS TO LEARN

☐ adjacent	☐ edifice	☐ insufficient	☐ rebuke
☐ annihilate	☐ equanimity	☐ jaunty	☐ reminiscence
☐ baleful	☐ expunge	☐ laudatory	☐ sedentary
☐ brawl	☐ foible	☐ lurk	☐ smug
☐ cliché	☐ gale	☐ meritorious	☐ stray
☐ conjecture	☐ groan	☐ myriad	☐ swoop
☐ curtail	☐ hinder	☐ opus	☐ tether
☐ debunk	☐ impede	☐ partisan	☐ unseemly
☐ disparage	☐ indiscriminate	☐ prudence	☐ waft

01

adjacent
[uh-jey-suhnt]

adj. lying near or close
이웃의, 인접한
The family moved to a house **adjacent** to good schools.[1]

syn. adjoining, neighboring, contiguous

02

annihilate
[uh-nai-*uh*-leyt]

v. to destroy completely
전멸시키다
New intelligence systems will **annihilate** those terrorist groups.[2]

syn. pulverize, raze, destroy

03

baleful
[beyl-fuhl]

adj. expressing anger and hate
악의적인, 해로운
The cat gave the mouse a **baleful** look.[3]

syn. malevolent, pernicious, evil

예문 해석

01 그 가족은 좋은 학교들 근처로 이사했다. **02** 새로운 첩보 시스템이 테러리스트 그룹을 전멸시킬 것이다. **03** 고양이는 쥐를 사악하게 쳐다보았다.

04 ·······

brawl
[brawl]

n. a noisy quarrel or fight, especially in public
말다툼, 싸움
He had been in a drunken **brawl**.[4]

syn. quarrel, wrangle, spat, tiff

05 ·······

cliché
[klee-shey]

n. a trite, stereotyped expression
진부한 표현, 상용화된 문구
'Strong as an ox' is a common example of a **cliché**.[5]

syn. platitude, stereotype, banality

06 ·······

conjecture
[k*uh*n-jek-cher]

n. expression of an opinion without sufficient evidence
추측, 추측성 발언
Mere **conjectures** are to be avoided in debates. Facts need to support opinions.[6]

syn. surmise, guess, inference

07 ·······

curtail
[ker-teyl]

v. to cut short
줄이다, 자르다
They decided to **curtail** the budget for next year.[7]

syn. reduce, shorten, abridge

08 ·······

debunk
[dih-b*uh*ngk]

v. to expose as being pretentious or false
(생각이나 믿음 등이) 틀렸음을 밝히다
The famous magician has **debunked** the idea that magic is anything other than a very clever illusion.[8]

syn. disprove, demystify, ridicule

📖 예문 해석

04 그는 술 취해 말다툼하는 데 끼어들게 되었다. **05** '황소처럼 힘센'이란 표현은 진부한 상용구의 일반적인 예다. **06** 토론에서는 단순한 추측은 피해야 한다. 사실들이 의견을 뒷받침할 필요가 있다. **07** 그들은 내년 예산을 감축하기로 결정했다. **08** 그 유명한 마술사는 마술이 매우 영리한 환상과는 다른 것이라는 생각을 밝혀냈다.

disparage
[di-spar-ij]

v. to speak of someone or something with contempt
얕보다, 깔보다
He tends to **disparage** literature.[9]

> *syn.* belittle, despise, underrate

edifice
[ed-*uh*-fis]

n. a building, especially a large impressive one
대 건축물
The magnificent **edifice** was a tourist spot.[10]

> *syn.* structure, construction

equanimity
[ee-kwuh-nim-i-tee]

n. calmness of temper
평정, 침착, 태연
When the doctor informed the patient of her fatal diagnosis, he was surprised by her **equanimity** concerning the matter.[11]

> *syn.* aplomb, composure, calmness

expunge
[ik-spuhnj]

v. to strike or blot out
지우다, 삭제하다
Because the court has decided to **expunge** his criminal record, there will be no evidence of his past misdeeds.[12]

> *syn.* erase, abolish, obliterate

foible
[foi-b*uh*l]

n. a minor weakness or failing of character
기벽, 약점
Jason tolerated Emma's **foible** because her many admirable qualities covered it.[13]

> *syn.* defect, flaw, eccentricity

예문 해석

09 그는 문학을 얕보는 경향이 있다. **10** 그 웅장한 건물은 관광지였다. **11** 의사가 환자에게 그녀의 치명적인 진단을 알렸을 때, 그는 그 문제에 대한 그녀의 태연함에 놀랐다. **12** 법원이 그의 전과 기록을 말소하기로 결정했기 때문에, 그의 과거 악행의 증거는 없을 것이다. **13** Emma의 많은 존경할 만한 자질이 작은 단점들을 덮었기 때문에 Jason은 그녀의 단점을 용인했다.

14

gale
[geyl]

n. a very strong wind
돌풍, 강한 바람
The fierce **gales** were causing difficulty for the captain to sail his ship.[14]

syn. gust, storm, tempest

15

groan
[grohn]

v. to utter a deep, mournful sound expressive of pain or grief
신음하다, 괴로워하다
The patient **groaned** with pain.[15]

syn. moan, whine, whimper

16

hinder
[hin-der]

v. to cause delay or interruption
방해하다
The snowstorm **hindered** our progress.[16]

syn. block, prevent, deter

17

impede
[im-peed]

v. to obstruct something
방해하다
Environmentally-healthy policies could **impede** industrial development.[17]

syn. obstruct, hinder, hamper

18

indiscriminate
[in-di-skrim-uh-nit]

adj. not discriminating
무차별의, 닥치는 대로의, 분별 없는
The **indiscriminate** player picked his teammates randomly, and it tended to bother his teammates.[18]

syn. haphazard, random, slapdash

19

insufficient
[in-suh-fish-uhnt]

adj. lacking in what is necessary or required
불충분한, 부족한
There was an **insufficient** supply of fuel.[19]

syn. inadequate, scanty, deficient

예문 해석

14 사나운 바람 때문에 선장은 배를 항해하는 데 어려움을 겪고 있었다.   **15** 그 환자는 고통으로 신음했다.   **16** 눈보라가 우리의 진척을 방해했다.   **17** 환경친화정책이 산업 발전에 방해가 될 수 있다.   **18** 그 무차별한 선수는 팀원들을 무작위로 뽑아서 팀원들을 괴롭히는 경향이 있었다.   **19** 연료 공급이 부족했다.

jaunty
[jawn-tee]

adj. easy and sprightly in manner or bearing
쾌활한, 명랑한, 멋진
The child walked with a **jaunty** step.[20]

syn. buoyant, jolly, sprightly

laudatory
[law-*duh*-tawr-ee]

adj. containing or expressing praise
칭찬하는, 감탄하는
The president issued a **laudatory** speech celebrating the nation's team's Olympic victory.[21]

syn. acclamatory, complimentary, flattering

lurk
[lurk]

v. to wait somewhere secretly
잠복하다, 숨어 기다리다
The fugitive **lurked** in the darkness.[22]

syn. skulk, sneak, prowl, ambush

meritorious
[me-ri-taw-ree-us]

adj. deserving praise
공적이 있는, 칭찬할 만한, 가치있는
She rendered **meritorious** service to the community.[23]

syn. praiseworthy, honorable, commendable

myriad
[mir-ee-*uh*d]

adj. of an indefinitely great number
무수한, 막대한, 1만의
The **myriad** of stars was unfathomable.[24]

syn. innumerable, countless, infinite

opus
[oh-p*uh*s]

n. a musical work that has been created
(유명 작곡가의 번호가 매겨진) 작품
Magnum **opus** refers to one's most remarkable music work.[25]

syn. music piece, composition, magnum opus

예문 해석

20 아이는 쾌활한 발걸음으로 걸었다.　**21** 대통령은 자국 팀의 올림픽 승리를 축하하는 축사를 발표했다.　**22** 도망자는 어둠 속에서 숨어 기다렸다.　**23** 그녀는 지역사회에 칭찬할 만한 봉사를 했다.　**24** 무수한 별들은 헤아릴 수 없었다.　**25** 매그넘 오푸스란 한 사람의 가장 주목할 만한 음악 작품을 말한다.

26

partisan
[pahr-t*uh*-z*uh*n]

n. an adherent or supporter of a person or group
열렬한 지지자, 일당
He was groomed to be a **partisan** of a specific political party because of his indoctrinated upbringing.[26]

syn. devotee, follower, zealot

27

prudence
[prood-ns]

n. sensible decisions about everyday life
신중, 사려 분별, 조심, 빈틈없음
He has enough **prudence** to spend his money wisely.[27]

syn. discretion, vigilance, caution

28

rebuke
[ri-byook]

v. to speak severely to someone because they have done wrong
비난하다, 꾸짖다
The teacher **rebuked** him for his bad attitude.[28]

syn. reprimand, censure, castigate

29

reminiscence
[rem-*uh*-nis-*uh*ns]

n. the act of recalling past experiences or events
추억, 회상
A visit to her old school flooded her brain with **reminiscences**.[29]

syn. memory, recollection, remembrance

30

sedentary
[sed-n-ter-ee]

adj. accustomed to sitting or resting a great deal or to exercise little
앉아 있는, 앉아서 일하는
A **sedentary** lifestyle causes heart diseases and obesity.[30]

syn. fixed, immobile, inactive, stationary

31

smug
[sm*uh*g]

adj. contentedly confident of one's ability
잘난 척하는, 점잖은 척하는
His **smug** look meant he'd beaten his rival at chess again.[31]

syn. complacent, pompous, snobbish

 예문 해석

26 그는 세뇌된 교육을 받았기 때문에 특정 정당의 열렬한 신봉자가 되도록 키워졌다. **27** 그는 돈을 현명하게 쓸 만큼 신중하다. **28** 선생님은 그의 나쁜 태도를 꾸짖었다. **29** 그녀가 다니던 학교를 방문하자 그녀의 머릿속은 추억으로 가득 찼다. **30** 앉아만 있는 생활은 심장 질환과 비만을 초래한다. **31** 그의 잘난 척하는 듯한 모습은 그가 체스에서 라이벌을 또 이겼다는 것을 뜻했다.

32

stray
[strey]

v. to deviate from the direct course or leave the proper place
(자기도 모르게) 제 위치를 벗어나다, 옆길로 새다
Little Red Riding Hood strayed from the path and ended up getting eaten by the Big Bad Wolf. [32]

syn. get lost, wander, roam

33

swoop
[swoop]

v. to sweep through the air, as a bird or a bat, especially down upon prey
급강하하다, 위에서 덮치다
The bird **swoops** down in the air, making an arc or loop.[33]

syn. plummet, dive, pounce

34

tether
[teth-er]

v. to fasten or keep things tied together
(동물이 멀리 가지 못하게 말뚝에) 묶다
When astronauts go outside the space station, they **tether** themselves to the station using wires and a hook.[34]

syn. moor, bind, fasten

35

unseemly
[uhn-seem-lee]

adj. not becoming or fitting
예의 없는, 어울리지 않는
It would be **unseemly** for the CEO to receive pay increases when others are having to tighten their belts.[35]

syn. improper, inappropriate, indecent

36

waft
[waft]

v. to move, or make something move gently through the air
풍기게 하다, 감돌게 하다
A coffee aroma **wafted** in from the kitchen.[36]

syn. carry, drift, float

 예문 해석

32 빨간 모자는 길을 벗어나 나쁜 늑대에게 먹히고 말았다.　**33** 그 새는 호나 고리 모양을 그리며 공중으로 하강한다.　**34** 우주 비행사들이 우주 정거장 밖으로 나갈 때, 그들은 줄과 고리를 사용하여 정거장에 스스로를 묶는다.　**35** 다른 이들은 모두 허리띠를 조이는데 회사 대표만 봉급을 올리는 것은 보기 좋지 않다.　**36** 좋은 커피 향이 부엌에서부터 풍겨왔다.

Directions   Each of the following questions consists of one word followed by five words or phrases.
You are to select the one word or phrase whose meaning is closest to the word in capital letters.

1. ANNIHILATE :
   (A) pulverize
   (B) monitor
   (C) grovel
   (D) intimidate
   (E) foretell

2. BRAWL :
   (A) quarrel
   (B) glee
   (C) fanatic
   (D) sequence
   (E) option

3. CONJECTURE :
   (A) felicity
   (B) hierarchy
   (C) surmise
   (D) incentive
   (E) finale

4. CURTAIL :
   (A) embark
   (B) peddle
   (C) approach
   (D) reduce
   (E) lengthen

5. DEBUNK :
   (A) disprove
   (B) entice
   (C) dawdle
   (D) enlarge
   (E) misinform

6. EDIFICE :
   (A) deluge
   (B) aplomb
   (C) structure
   (D) fortress
   (E) harangue

7. FOIBLE :
   (A) idiosyncrasy
   (B) exemption
   (C) trickery
   (D) defect
   (E) stance

8. MERITORIOUS :
   (A) deficient
   (B) irrevocable
   (C) gluttonous
   (D) skillful
   (E) praiseworthy

9. MYRIAD :
   (A) unparalleled
   (B) confidential
   (C) staunch
   (D) innumerable
   (E) mournful

10. REMINISCENCE :
    (A) prompt
    (B) annals
    (C) disintegration
    (D) theme
    (E) memory

"An investment in knowledge always pays the best interest."

— Benjamin Franklin —
U.S. author, diplomat, inventor, physicist, politician & printer

지식에 투자하는 것은 언제나 최고의 이익을 가져다 준다.

Greek and Latin Roots & Prefixes 42

★ BI = two

annus (year)	biannual	1년에 2번씩
annus (year)	biennial	2년마다
lingua (language)	bilingual	두 개 언어를 구사하는
-ity (n.)	bicycle	자전거
ped (foot)	biped	두 발 동물
weik (to bend)	biweekly	격주의
cuspidem (point)	bicuspid	두 부분이 뾰족한

DAY

42

WORDS TO LEARN

☐ adjourn	☐ edify	☐ jettison	☐ rebuttal
☐ annotation	☐ expound	☐ legacy	☐ revoke
☐ balk	☐ fissure	☐ lush	☐ seep
☐ brazen	☐ gallantry	☐ mesmerize	☐ snag
☐ climactic	☐ groove	☐ mystical	☐ stink
☐ connoisseur	☐ hoard	☐ odor	☐ swindle
☐ curb	☐ impending	☐ pastoral	☐ transcend
☐ despondent	☐ indisputable	☐ posterity	☐ unswerving
☐ disparate	☐ insular	☐ provincial	☐ wail

01

adjourn
[*uh*-jurn]

v. to delay or postpone to a later time
연기하다, 미루다
They **adjourned** the meeting.[1]

syn. defer, postpone, put off

02

annotation
[an-*uh*-tey-sh*uh*n]

n. an explanatory note or comment
주석
Many articles are provided below, along with extensive **annotations**.[2]

syn. footnote, commentary, notes

03

balk
[bawk]

v. to stop and refuse to proceed
갑자기 서다, 망설이다
She **balked** at the price.[3]

syn. hesitate, desist, evade

예문 해석

01 그들은 회의를 연기했다.　**02** 많은 기사가 방대한 주석과 함께 제공되고 있다.　**03** 그녀는 가격을 보고 망설였다.

04

brazen
[brey-zuhn]

adj. very bold and not caring
뻔뻔스러운, 철면피한
It was one of the largest and most **brazen** corporate financial frauds in history.[4]

syn. shameless, impudent, audacious

05

climactic
[klai-mak-tik]

adj. coming to a climax
클라이맥스의, 절정의, 피크의
That is the **climactic** scene of this play.[5]

syn. decisive, critical, paramount

06

connoisseur
[kon-uh-sur]

n. one who has exceptional knowledge and skills of the subject
전문가, 감정가, 감식가
The instructor was a **connoisseur** of classical ballet.[6]

syn. expert, specialist, veteran

07

curb
[kurb]

v. to control as with a curb
(좋지 못한 것을) 억제하다, 제한하다
She had to learn to **curb** her ill-temper.[7]

syn. restrain, check, constrain

08

despondent
[di-spon-duhnt]

adj. lacking in resolution
기가 죽은, 의기소침한
I felt **despondent** when my offer was rejected.[8]

syn. dejected, discouraged, depressed

예문 해석

04 그것은 역사상 가장 크고 뻔뻔한 기업 금융 사기 중 하나였다. **05** 그것이 이 연극의 가장 절정인 장면이다. **06** 그 강사는 고전 발레의 전문가였다. **07** 그녀는 자신의 성질을 억제하는 법을 배워야 했다. **08** 내 제안이 거절당했을 때 나는 의기소침해 졌다.

disparate
[dis-per-it]

adj. completely different
본질적으로 다른, 공통점이 없는
Our **disparate** interests will never make this friendship work.[9]

syn. dissimilar, discrepant

edify
[ed-*uh*-fai]

v. to instruct or benefit morally or spiritually
교화하다, 계몽하다
Religious paintings **edify** the viewer.[10]

syn. enlighten, inform, educate

expound
[ik-spound]

adj. to give a clear and detailed explanation
명확하게 설명하다
He **expounded** his theories.[11]

syn. explain, talk about, elucidate

fissure
[fish-er]

n. a long narrow crack
갈라진 틈
The ground opened in **fissures**.[12]

syn. crack, crevice, opening

gallantry
[gal-uhn-tree]

n. the qualities of a hero or heroine
용감함, 용기
His **gallantry** was conspicuous.[13]

syn. bravery, daring, valor

groove
[groov]

n. a long narrow channel especially one cut with a tool
(문턱이나 레코드 판 등의) 홈, 바퀴 자국
I saw the man hollow out a **groove**.[14]

syn. furrow, channel, trench

예문 해석

09 우리는 본질적으로 다른 관심사 때문에 친구가 되기는 힘들 것 같다.   **10** 종교적인 그림들은 보는 사람을 교화시킨다.   **11** 그는 그의 이론을 명확하게 설명했다.   **12** 땅은 갈라져 있었다.   **13** 그의 용기는 눈에 띄게 두드러졌다.   **14** 나는 그 남자가 홈을 파내는 것을 보았다.

15

hoard
[hohrd]

v. to store or gather
저장하다, 몰래 축적하다
They **hoarded** food during the famine.[15]

syn. stockpile, accumulate, amass

16

impending
[im-pen-ding]

adj. likely to happen in the near future
임박한, 급박한
He had a sense of **impending** danger.[16]

syn. imminent, looming

17

indisputable
[in-di-spyoo-tuh-buhl]

adj. beyond doubt
논란의 여지가 없는, 명백한
It is **indisputable** that the evidence was tampered with.[17]

syn. unquestionable, certain, clear

18

insular
[in-suh-ler]

adj. unwilling to meet new people or to consider new ideas
배타적인, 편협한
It is an **insular** country, with little outside influence.[18]

syn. narrow-minded, provincial, illiberal

19

jettison
[jet-uh-suhn]

v. to cast goods overboard in order to lighten a vessel or aircraft
(무게를 줄이기 위해) 버리다
When the airplane ran out of fuel, they could buy more time by **jettisoning** cargo.[19]

syn. dump, abandon, discard

🧘 **예문 해석**

15 그들은 기근 동안 식량을 비축했다.　**16** 그는 급박한 위기를 감지했다.　**17** 증거가 조작되었다는 것은 논란의 여지가 없다.
18 그곳은 외부 영향을 거의 받지 않는 섬나라였다.　**19** 비행기 연료가 떨어졌을 때, 그들은 화물을 버림으로써 더 많은 시간을 벌
수 있었다.

20

legacy
[leg-*uh*-see]

n. something handed down by a past owner

유산, 유물, 물려받은 것

You could have a huge influence on someone's life by leaving them a generous **legacy**.[20]

syn. inheritance, bequest, heritage

21

lush
[lu*h*sh]

adj. fresh and abundant

싱싱한, 싱싱하고 푸르른

The **lush** garden, in the back of his house, has a lot of flowers and trees.[21]

syn. verdant, luxuriant, succulent

22

mesmerize
[mez-m*uh*-raiz]

v. to hypnotize someone

매혹시키다, 최면술을 걸다

I was absolutely **mesmerized** by Pavarotti's voice.[22]

syn. hypnotize, captivate, enthrall

23

mystical
[mis-ti-k*uh*l]

adj. mystic and spiritual

신비로운, 불가사의한

Watching the sun rise over the horizon was an almost **mystical** experience.[23]

syn. cryptic, enigmatic, mystic

24

odor
[oh-der]

n. a particular and distinctive smell

냄새, 향기, 악취

The herb has a characteristic taste and **odor**.[24]

syn. smell, scent, aroma

25

pastoral
[pas-ter-*uh*l]

adj. pertaining to the country or to country life

전원 생활의, 목가적인

I memorized a **pastoral** poem for class.[25]

syn. idyllic, rural, rustic

예문 해석

20 많은 유산을 남김으로써 다른 사람들의 삶에 큰 영향을 줄 수도 있다.　**21** 그의 집 뒤편에 있는 푸른 정원에는 많은 꽃과 나무들이 있었다.　**22** 나는 파바로티의 목소리에 완전히 매료되었다.　**23** 바다 위로 해가 떠오르는 것을 바라보는 것은 거의 신비한 경험이었다.　**24** 그 허브는 특징적인 맛과 향내를 가진다.　**25** 나는 수업 시간에 목가시를 외웠다.

26 ·····

posterity
[po-ster-i-tee]

n. future generations
자손, 후손
His father recorded the scene on video for **posterity**.[26]

syn. brood, offspring

27 ·····

provincial
[pruh-vin-shuhl]

adj. relating to the parts of a country away from the capital
지방의, 시골의
My family has a distinct **provincial** accent.[27]

syn. regional, state, local

28 ·····

rebuttal
[ri-buht-l]

n. opposing evidence to disprove or refute
반박, 반증
They are preparing their own **rebuttal**.[28]

syn. refutation, disproof, confutation

29 ·····

revoke
[ri-vohk]

v. to cancel or make no longer valid
취소하다, 폐지하다, 무효로 하다
They **revoked** her driver's license after receiving many
traffic violations.[29]

syn. cancel, repeal, rescind

30 ·····

seep
[seep]

v. to flow or ooze gradually through a porous substance
새어 나오다, 스며 나오다
The light **seeped** through the opening.[30]

syn. ooze, exude, leak

31 ·····

snag
[snag]

n. a problem or drawback
예상 밖의 문제, 곤란한 일
Efforts to reach an agreement to terminate the nuclear
weapons program again have hit a **snag**.[31]

syn. drawback, problem, difficulty

예문 해석

26 그의 아버지가 후손을 위해 그 장면을 영상으로 기록해 두었다. **27** 우리 가족은 독특한 지역 사투리를 가지고 있다. **28** 그들은 그들만의 반박을 준비하고 있다. **29** 그녀가 교통 법규를 여러 번 위반한 뒤에, 그들은 그녀의 운전면허를 취소했다. **30** 틈새로 불빛이 새어 나왔다. **31** 핵 무기 종결 합의를 위한 노력이 또 다시 암초에 부딪쳤다.

32

stink
[stingk]

v. to have a strong offensive smell
악취를 풍기다
This rotten fish **stinks**.[32]

> *syn.* reek, smell

33

swindle
[swin-dl]

v. to cheat or trick someone in order to obtain money from them
속이다, 사기 치다
He **swindled** investors out of millions of dollars.[33]

> *syn.* cheat, con, trick, deceive

34

transcend
[tran-send]

v. to be beyond the limits, scope, or range
초월하다, 능가하다
Their new idea **transcended** the limits of conventional thought.[34]

> *syn.* exceed, surpass, overreach

35

unswerving
[*uhn*-swur-ving]

adj. not deviating from a belief or aim
변함없는, 흔들림 없는, 충성스러운
The knights pledged **unswerving** loyalty to the monarchy.[35]

> *syn.* undeviating, unwavering, steadfast

36

wail
[weyl]

v. to emit long loud cries
울부짖다
After the baby fell off the bed, she began to **wail**.[36]

> *syn.* weep, grieve, lament, howl

 예문 해석

32 썩은 물고기에서 악취가 난다. **33** 그는 투자자들에게 수백 달러의 사기를 쳤다. **34** 그들의 새로운 아이디어는 관습적인 생각의 한계를 뛰어넘는 것이었다. **35** 기사들은 군주에게 변함없는 충성을 맹세했다. **36** 아기가 침대에서 떨어진 후 울기 시작했다.

Directions   Each of the following questions consists of one word followed by five words or phrases. You are to select the one word or phrase whose meaning is closest to the word in capital letters.

1. ANNOTATION :
   (A) margin
   (B) hostility
   (C) convention
   (D) footnote
   (E) leftover

2. BRAZEN :
   (A) insincere
   (B) shameless
   (C) thoughtful
   (D) risky
   (E) concise

3. CLIMACTIC :
   (A) articulate
   (B) volatile
   (C) clumsy
   (D) pompous
   (E) decisive

4. CURB :
   (A) restrain
   (B) circumscribe
   (C) banish
   (D) harmonize
   (E) swerve

5. DESPONDENT :
   (A) dejected
   (B) profitable
   (C) lacking
   (D) clever
   (E) deceptive

6. LEGACY :
   (A) inheritance
   (B) declamation
   (C) motivation
   (D) hermit
   (E) progeny

7. PASTORAL :
   (A) hygienic
   (B) profitable
   (C) idyllic
   (D) celestial
   (E) bountiful

8. PROVINCIAL :
   (A) gloomy
   (B) everlasting
   (C) belated
   (D) regional
   (E) submissive

9. REBUTTAL :
   (A) illusion
   (B) defect
   (C) refutation
   (D) gourmet
   (E) remuneration

10. SNAG :
   (A) bias
   (B) aqueduct
   (C) placebo
   (D) passion
   (E) drawback

Directions   Each of the following questions consists of one word followed by five words or phrases.
You are to select the one word or phrase whose meaning is closest to the word in capital letters.

1. **ADVERSITY :**
   (A) aristocracy
   (B) courtesy
   (C) illiteracy
   (D) hardship
   (E) proverb

2. **CULMINATE :**
   (A) climax
   (B) impair
   (C) control
   (D) imply
   (E) grieve

3. **RAZE :**
   (A) persevere
   (B) specify
   (C) propel
   (D) saturate
   (E) annihilate

4. **FILCH :**
   (A) accelerate
   (B) encircle
   (C) pilfer
   (D) repel
   (E) plod

5. **INSTIGATE :**
   (A) foment
   (B) quell
   (C) understand
   (D) solicit
   (E) resurrect

6. **PENDING :**
   (A) undecided
   (B) infinite
   (C) suave
   (D) tepid
   (E) industrious

7. **SURVEILLANCE :**
   (A) premonition
   (B) observation
   (C) agenda
   (D) stealthy
   (E) tact

8. **FINESSE :**
   (A) rhetoric
   (B) deeds
   (C) allocation
   (D) gimmick
   (E) tenacity

9. **GLIB :**
   (A) illegitimate
   (B) slick
   (C) quaint
   (D) astonishing
   (E) intact

10. **MAGNATE :**
   (A) token
   (B) deadlock
   (C) vivacity
   (D) compensation
   (E) tycoon

11. PRUDENCE :
    (A) discretion
    (B) zeal
    (C) gala
    (D) blackout
    (E) wrath

12. FLOWERY :
    (A) mellow
    (B) ornate
    (C) inquisitive
    (D) baneful
    (E) sociable

13. FUTILE :
    (A) useless
    (B) cruel
    (C) bleak
    (D) amicable
    (E) vigorous

14. HILARIOUS :
    (A) vague
    (B) jolly
    (C) bashful
    (D) ridiculous
    (E) industrious

15. IMPECCABLE :
    (A) insufficient
    (B) urbane
    (C) faultless
    (D) trepid
    (E) immortal

16. PARTISAN :
    (A) hypothesis
    (B) deceit
    (C) evacuation
    (D) feudalism
    (E) devotee

17. EDIFY :
    (A) denounce
    (B) recompense
    (C) revive
    (D) taint
    (E) enlighten

18. GALLANTRY :
    (A) bravery
    (B) implication
    (C) strata
    (D) souvenir
    (E) revenue

19. REVOKE :
    (A) repel
    (B) cancel
    (C) pretend
    (D) emphasize
    (E) define

20. UNSWERVING :
    (A) inopportune
    (B) scrupulous
    (C) undeviating
    (D) infrequent
    (E) reminiscent

"Success is not final, failure is not fatal; it is the courage to continue that counts."

– Winston Churchill –
British politician

성공은 결승점이 아니며, 실패는 치명적인 것이 아니다. 중요한 것은 계속해서 할 수 있는 용기이다.

Greek and Latin Roots & Prefixes 43

★ TRI = three

angulus (corner)	triangle	삼각형
athlon (contest)	triathlon	철인 3종 경기
-io (n.)	trio	3중주, 3인조
logos (story)	trilogy	3부작
weik (to bend)	tripod	삼발이, 삼각대
let (small thing)	triplet	세쌍둥이, 셋잇단음표
sek (to cut)	trisect	3등분 하다

DAY

43

WORDS TO LEARN

☐ adjunct	☐ ensign	☐ jeer	☐ recede
☐ anonymous	☐ equilibrium	☐ liaison	☐ revolve
☐ banal	☐ exponential	☐ luster	☐ seethe
☐ bowdlerize	☐ fruitful	☐ memoir	☐ snicker
☐ clinch	☐ gallop	☐ notify	☐ stingy
☐ conscience	☐ hoax	☐ odyssey	☐ suave
☐ daring	☐ imperative	☐ opulence	☐ swivel
☐ dictator	☐ indoctrinate	☐ postulate	☐ unveil
☐ disparity	☐ insulate	☐ quarantine	☐ waive

01

adjunct
[aj-*uh*ngkt]

n. something added to another thing but not essential to it
부가물, 부속물
He was not a full-time preofessor; he was an **adjunct**.[1]

syn. accessory, addition, help

02

anonymous
[*uh*-non-*uh*-mu*h*s]

adj. not named or identified
익명의, 작자 미상의
The donor wishes to remain **anonymous**.[2]

syn. unknown, nameless, unidentified

03

banal
[b*uh*-nal]

adj. devoid of freshness or originality
진부한, 뻔한
They did not want a **banal** advertisement phrase for their product.[3]

syn. hackneyed, trite, cliché

📖 **예문 해석**

01 그는 풀타임 정교수가 아니라 부교수이다. **02** 그 기부자는 익명으로 남길 바랬다. **03** 그들은 그들의 제품에 진부한 광고 문구를 원하지 않았다.

04

bowdlerize
[bohd-luh-raiz]

v. to expurgate a written work by removing or modifying passages considered vulgar or objectionable
(부적절한 부분을) 삭제하다
The editor had no wish to **bowdlerize** the established female writer's work because he loved her ways and words.[4]

syn. censor, expurgate, redact

05

clinch
[klinch]

v. to settle a matter decisively
확정짓다, 결말짓다, 확보하다
Her home run **clinched** the victory.[5]

syn. decide, determine, nail, settle

06

conscience
[kon-shuhns]

n. an inner sense of right and wrong
양심, 양심의 가책
Let your **conscience** be your guide.[6]

syn. compunction, qualm, scruple

07

daring
[dair-ing]

adj. bold or courageous
대담한, 용감한
It was **daring** to attempt the escape at midday.[7]

syn. undaunted, reckless, adventurous

08

dictator
[dik-tey-ter]

n. a king with absolute power
독재자, 폭군
The possession of unlimited power will make a **dictator** of almost any man.[8]

syn. despot, tyrant, autocrat

예문 해석

04 편집자는 그 유명한 여성 작가의 작품 방식과 그녀의 언어를 사랑했기 때문에 그녀의 작품을 검열하여 삭제하고 싶지 않았다. **05** 그녀의 홈런이 승리를 확정지었다. **06** 당신의 양심에 따라 행동하라. **07** 한낮에 탈출을 시도한 것은 대담한 일이었다. **08** 무한한 권력을 소유하게 되면 어느 누구나 폭군이 될 것이다.

09

disparity
[di-spar-i-tee]

n. great or fundamental difference
불균형, 불일치
There were great economic **disparities** between East and West Germany.[9]

syn. difference, inequality, discrepancy

10

ensign
[en-sahyn]

n. a flag or banner, as a military or naval standard used to indicate nationality
(국적이나 소속을 나타내는) 기, 깃발
The ship displayed the Korean **ensign**.[10]

syn. flag, banner, emblem

11

equilibrium
[ee-kw*uh*-lib-ree-*uh*m]

n. a stable situation in which forces cancel one another
평형상태, 마음의 평정
The pressures of the situation caused her to lose her **equilibrium**.[11]

syn. stability, equality, composure

12

exponential
[ek-spoh-nen-sh*uh*l]

adj. rising or expanding at a steady, rapid rate.
기하급수적인
Prices have increased at an **exponential** rate.[12]

syn. aggressive, epidemic, rampant

13

fruitful
[froot-f*uh*l]

adj. producing good results
생산적인, 유익한
Her business is **fruitful**, creating profits and expanding.[13]

syn. successful, productive, profitable

14

gallop
[gal-*uh*p]

v. to ride at full speed
전속력으로 질주하다
The horses **galloped** away.[14]

syn. bolt, race, speed

 예문 해석

09 동독과 서독 사이에는 큰 경제적 차이가 있었다. **10** 그 배는 한국 국기를 게양했다. **11** 상황에서 오는 압박감에 그녀는 평정을 잃었다. **12** 물가가 기하급수적으로 올랐다. **13** 그녀의 사업은 생산적이고, 수익을 창출하며, 확장되고 있다. **14** 말들은 질주하여 가버렸다.

15

hoax
[hohks]

n. something intended to deceive or defraud

속임수

The Piltdown Man was a famous scientific **hoax**.[15]

> *syn.* fraud, deception, fake

16

imperative
[im-per-*uh*-tiv]

adj. absolutely necessary or required

피할 수 없는, 명령의

In order to do well on the final exam, it is absolutely **imperative** to study thoroughly.[16]

> *syn.* compulsory, obligatory, necessary

17

indoctrinate
[in-dok-tr*uh*-neyt]

v. to teach uncritically

주입하다, 가르치다

They were **indoctrinated** into believing that their race was superior.[17]

> *syn.* brainwash, infuse, instill, imbue

18

insulate
[in-s*uh*-leyt]

v. to place in an isolated situation or condition

고립시키다, 절연시키다

Heat can be retained in the house with **insulated** window coverings.[18]

> *syn.* segregate, seclude, sequester

19

jeer
[jeer]

v. to say rude and insulting things

조롱하다, 야유하다

Don't **jeer** unless you can do better.[19]

> *syn.* boo, sneer, mock, scoff, scorn

예문 해석

15 필트다운인 사건(1912년 영국 Sussex주 Piltdown에서 두개골이 발견되었으나, 후에 가짜로 판명된 사건)은 유명한 과학 사기극이다.   **16** 기말고사를 잘 치르기 위해서는 공부를 철저히 하는 것이 절대적으로 필요하다.   **17** 그들은 자신의 민족이 가장 우수하다고 믿도록 세뇌 받았다.   **18** 열기는 단열 창문 덮개로 유지될 수 있다.   **19** 네가 더 잘 할 수 없으면 비난하지 말아라.

20

liaison
[lee-ey-zawn]

n. a channel for communication between groups
(두 조직 간의) 연락 담당자
She became a double spy, and the **liaison** lasted till she died.[20]

syn. contact, communication, link

21

luster
[luhs-ter]

n. the state of shining by reflecting light
광택, 윤
The mineral has a bright metallic **luster**.[21]

syn. glitter, sparkle, gloss, sheen

22

memoir
[mem-wahr]

n. an account of the author's personal experiences
회고록, 전기
My father penned a **memoir** about a thirty-year veteran in the military.[22]

syn. biography, chronicle, recollection

23

notify
[noh-tuh-fai]

v. to inform somebody of something
알리다, 통지하다
I shall **notify** you as soon as she arrives.[23]

syn. announce, declare, alert

24

odyssey
[od-uh-see]

n. a long and adventurous journey
장기간의 방랑, 길고 힘든 여행
This **odyssey** will lead him into self discovery.[24]

syn. trek, wandering, roaming

25

opulence
[op-yuh-luhns]

n. wealth as evidenced by sumptuous living
풍요, 부유함
Protection is the first necessity of **opulence** and luxury.[25]

syn. wealth, affluence, riches

 예문 해석

20 그녀는 이중 스파이가 되었고, 그녀가 죽을 때까지 연락은 계속되었다. **21** 그 광물은 밝은 금속성 광택을 띤다. **22** 아버지는 군대에서 30년간 복무한 군인에 대한 회고록을 쓰셨다. **23** 그녀가 도착하는 대로 너에게 알려줄게. **24** 이 길고 힘든 여행은 그 스스로를 돌아보게 할 것이다. **25** 보호는 풍요와 사치의 첫 번째 필요이다.

26

postulate
[pos-ch*uh*-leyt]

v. to hypothesize
(당연한 일로) 가정하다
Freud **postulated** that we all have a death instinct as well as a life instinct.[26]

syn. assume, guess

27

quarantine
[kwawr-*uh*n-teen]

n. isolation to prevent the spread of infectious disease
(전염병 확산을 막기 위한) 격리
If you contract pinkeye, please **quarantine** yourself so that you don't infect others with it.[27]

syn. isolation, seclusion, sequestration

28

recede
[ri-seed]

v. to move gradually away
뒤로 멀어지다, 물러나다
As she **receded**, he waved goodbye.[28]

syn. retreat, recede, move away

29

revolve
[ri-volv]

v. to move or turn
돌다, 회전하다
The electrons **revolve** around the nucleus.[29]

syn. rotate, twirl, swivel

30

seethe
[seeth]

v. to surge or foam as if boiling
끓어 오르다
She **seethed** with severe jealousy.[30]

syn. boil, bubble, ferment

31

snicker
[snik-er]

v. to laugh in a quiet, unpleasant way
킥킥거리다, 숨죽여 웃다
We **snickered** at him.[31]

syn. giggle, chortle, chuckle

🧘 **예문 해석**

26 프로이트는 우리가 생존의 본능처럼 죽음의 본능도 가지고 있다고 가정했다.　**27** 유행성 결막염에 걸리면 다른 사람에게 감염되지 않도록 격리해 주세요.　**28** 그녀가 멀어지자 그는 손을 흔들어 작별 인사를 했다.　**29** 전자는 핵 주위를 돈다.　**30** 그녀는 질투로 속이 끓어 올랐다.　**31** 우리는 그를 보고 킥킥거렸다.

stingy
[stin-jee]

adj. not given or giving willingly
인색한, 구두쇠의
He was a **stingy** man.[32]

syn. miserly, parsimonious

suave
[swahv]

adj. having a sophisticated charm
정중한, 상냥한
He is **suave** and debonair like a gentleman riding horses on the covers of romance novels.[33]

syn. courteous, smooth, charming

swivel
[swiv-*uhl*]

v. to turn or pivot on a swivel
회전하다, 돌다
His chairs can **swivel**, but they can't move up or down.[34]

syn. spin, rotate, revolve, gyrate, twirl

unveil
[*uh*n-veyl]

v. to remove a cover or curtain
베일을 벗기다, 폭로하다, 밝히다
The detective tried to **unveil** the secret.[35]

syn. expose, reveal, debunk

waive
[weyv]

v. to voluntarily give up a right
(권리나 주장을) 포기하다, 철회하다
The accused **waived** his right to a trial.[36]

syn. relinquish, surrender, give up

🔖 예문 해석

32 그는 매우 인색한 사람이었다. **33** 그는 로맨스 소설 표지의 말을 탄 신사처럼 우아하고 멋지다. **34** 그의 의자들은 회전할 수는 있지만 위아래로 움직일 수는 없다. **35** 탐정은 비밀을 밝히려 애썼다. **36** 그 피고인은 재판을 받을 수 있는 권리를 포기했다.

Directions Each of the following questions consists of one word followed by five words or phrases. You are to select the one word or phrase whose meaning is closest to the word in capital letters.

1. BANAL :
(A) hackneyed
(B) disrespectful
(C) reckless
(D) reverent
(E) mysterious

2. BOWDLERIZE :
(A) burnish
(B) accuse
(C) lament
(D) glimpse
(E) censor

3. CONSCIENCE :
(A) outcast
(B) tumult
(C) compunction
(D) intention
(E) fragility

4. DICTATOR :
(A) tyro
(B) despot
(C) fraud
(D) quack
(E) copyist

5. DISPARITY :
(A) communication
(B) deliverance
(C) composure
(D) difference
(E) advertisement

6. EQUILIBRIUM :
(A) circumlocution
(B) elasticity
(C) resilience
(D) stability
(E) gourmand

7. JEER :
(A) boo
(B) souvenir
(C) partisan
(D) pundit
(E) query

8. LIAISON :
(A) extremity
(B) contact
(C) carcass
(D) nonchalance
(E) effectiveness

9. MEMOIR :
(A) reflection
(B) gardening
(C) momentum
(D) obstruction
(E) biography

10. OPULENCE :
(A) dearth
(B) fragrance
(C) delusion
(D) wealth
(E) distinction

"Appearances often are deceiving."

— Aesop —
Greek slave & fable author

외모는 종종 우리를 속인다.

Greek and Latin Roots & Prefixes 44

★ QUAD = four

-er (n.)	quarter	4분의 1
-et (n.)	quartet	4중주, 4인조
-ant (n.)	quadrant	4분면
lingua (language)	quadrilingual	4개 언어를 구사하는
latus (side)	quadrilateral	4변형, 4각형
ped (foot)	quadruped	네발 동물

DAY

44

WORDS TO LEARN

- ☐ adroit
- ☐ annul
- ☐ banish
- ☐ banter
- ☐ cling
- ☐ consent
- ☐ debonair
- ☐ destitute
- ☐ dispassionate

- ☐ editorial
- ☐ equitable
- ☐ exquisite
- ☐ flagrant
- ☐ galvanize
- ☐ gross
- ☐ hoist
- ☐ imperil
- ☐ indolent

- ☐ insurgent
- ☐ jeopardy
- ☐ legible
- ☐ methodical
- ☐ modify
- ☐ naive
- ☐ officiate
- ☐ posture
- ☐ provoke

- ☐ receptive
- ☐ rhetoric
- ☐ segregate
- ☐ sober
- ☐ stint
- ☐ sycophant
- ☐ transient
- ☐ unwieldy
- ☐ vanity

---

01 ·······

adroit
[*uh*-droit]

adj. skillful in action or thought
노련한, 능숙한
An **adroit** sculptor turned a lump of clay into an object of great beauty.[1]

syn. ingenious, adept, skillful

---

02 ·······

annul
[*uh*-*nuhl*]

v. to cancel officially
취소하다
They **annulled** the contract.[2]

syn. nullify, repeal, revoke

---

03 ·······

banish
[ban-ish]

v. to expel, as if by official decree
추방하다
He was **banished** to the arid desert.[3]

syn. exile, expel, deport

예문 해석

01 한 노련한 조각가는 점토 덩어리 하나를 아주 아름다운 조각으로 만들었다.   **02** 그들은 계약을 취소했다.   **03** 그는 메마른 사막으로 추방되었다.

04

banter
[ban-ter]

v. to tease lightly
(정감 어린) 농담을 주고받다
Good friends usually **banter** back and forth easily.[4]

syn. tease, taunt, joke

05

cling
[kling]

v. to hold firmly
달라붙다, 지지하다
The children love her and just **cling** to her.[5]

syn. adhere, stick

06

consent
[kuhn-sent]

v. to agree
동의하다
He finally **consented** to go with me.[6]

syn. assent, accord, concur, comply

07

debonair
[deb-uh-nair]

adj. having a sophisticated charm
세련되고 멋진
Her **debonair** son has good manners, wit, and style.[7]

syn. elegant, suave, charming

08

destitute
[des-ti-toot]

adj. extremely poor
결핍한, 극도로 가난한
He was a **destitute** child who lived on the streets.[8]

syn. needy, indigent, impoverished

예문 해석

04 좋은 친구들은 농담을 편하게 주고 받는다.　**05** 아이들은 그녀를 좋아해서 그녀에게 달라붙어 있었다.　**06** 그는 결국 나와 같이 가는 것에 동의했다.　**07** 그녀의 아들은 매너, 재치, 스타일이 좋다.　**08** 그는 거리에 사는 극도로 가난한 아이였다.

dispassionate
[dis-pash-*uh*-nit]

adj. devoid of personal feeling
냉정한, 공정한
Prosecutors must try to be **dispassionate** about the cases.[9]

syn. unbiased, unprejudiced, impartial

editorial
[ed-i-tawr-ee-*uh*l]

n. an article that presents the opinion of the editors
사설, 논설
He has been on the **editorial** staff of 'The New York Times' since 1977.[10]

syn. opinion, perspective

equitable
[ek-wi-t*uh*-b*uh*l]

adj. fair and reasonable
공정한, 공평한
Inner-city students are often not afforded the same **equitable** academic outcomes.[11]

syn. reasonable, fair, impartial

exquisite
[ik-skwiz-it]

adj. extraordinarily fine or admirable
매우 아름다운
We walked through the National Art Museum in D.C. to see the **exquisite** artwork.[12]

syn. finely detailed, beautiful, excellent

flagrant
[fley-gr*uh*nt]

adj. extremely bad or shocking in a very obvious way
명백한, 뻔뻔한
That was a **flagrant** violation of the UN charter.[13]

syn. blatant, glaring, obvious

예문 해석

09 검사들은 사건에 있어 감정적이지 않도록 노력해야 한다. **10** 그는 1977년부터 뉴욕타임즈의 논설위원이었다. **11** 도심 지역 학생들은 종종 평등한 학업 결과를 얻지 못한다. **12** 우리는 아름다운 예술 작품을 보기 위해 워싱턴에 있는 국립 미술관을 걸었다. **13** 그것은 명백한 UN 헌장의 위반이었다.

14

galvanize
[gal-*vuh*-naiz]

v. to stimulate by administering a shock
전기가 통한 듯이 갑자기 활기를 띠게 하다
The team's stunning performance **galvanized** the whole country.[14]

syn. invigorate, stimulate, energize

15

gross
[grohs]

n. total with no deductions
총합, 전체
Before buying a home, it is essential to know your **gross** income.[15]

syn. total, sum

16

hoist
[hoist]

v. to lift or raise up something with a piece of equipment
(장비를 이용하여) 들어올리다
The cargo was **hoisted** aboard by crane.[16]

syn. lift, heave

17

imperil
[im-per-*uhl*]

v. to put in danger
위험에 처하게 하다, 위태롭게 하다
Greenhouse gases **imperil** the future of the Earth.[17]

syn. endanger, jeopardize

18

indolent
[in-dl-*uhnt*]

adj. disinclined to work or exertion
게으른, 나태한
He is the most **indolent** person I've ever seen.[18]

syn. idle, shiftless, sluggish

19

insurgent
[in-sur-j*uh*nt]

n. someone who takes up arms against the authorities
반란을 일으킨 사람, 반역자
The platoon would shoot any enemy **insurgent** on sight.[19]

syn. mutineer, radical, rebel

예문 해석

14 팀의 놀라운 실력은 온 나라를 자극시켰다.   **15** 집을 사기 전에 자신의 총소득을 아는 것이 중요하다.   **16** 그 화물은 크레인으로 실렸다.   **17** 온실 가스가 지구의 미래를 위험에 빠뜨린다.   **18** 내가 본 사람 중에 그가 가장 게으르다.   **19** 그 소대는 어떤 반란군이라도 보이는 즉시 사살할 것이다.

jeopardy
[jep-er-dee]

n. a source of danger

위험, 위험성

Drinking ten cups of coffee every day could put your health in **jeopardy**.[20]

syn. peril, trouble, danger

legible
[lej-*uh*-bu*h*l]

adj. clear enough to read

알아볼 수 있게 쓰여진

Write **legible** notes.[21]

syn. readable, neat, lucid

methodical
[m*uh*-thod-i-k*uh*l]

adj. done in a careful and logical way

체계적인, 논리적인

It is essential to work in a **methodical** way.[22]

syn. systematic, organized, logical

modify
[mod-*uh*-fai]

v. to change but only slightly

(더 알맞도록) 수정하다, 변경하다

His coach tried to improve his shooting average by **modifying** his aiming technique.[23]

syn. alter, change, adjust

naïve
[nah-eev]

adj. easy to be deceived

순진한, 천진난만한, 잘 속는

It's **naïve** to think that teachers are always tolerant.[24]

syn. credulous, gullible, easily fooled

officiate
[*uh*-fish-ee-eyt]

v. to act in an official capacity

직무를 행하다

He **officiated** as the chairperson.[25]

syn. serve, function

예문 해석

20 하루에 10잔의 커피를 마시는 것은 당신의 건강을 위태롭게 할 수 있다. **21** 알아볼 수 있도록 써라. **22** 일을 체계적으로 하는 것은 필수적이다. **23** 코치는 조준 기술을 수정해 평균 슈팅을 높이려 했다. **24** 선생님들이 항상 참아줄 것이라고 생각하는 것은 순진한 생각이다. **25** 그는 의장으로서의 직무를 수행했다.

26

posture
[pos-cher]

n. the way one holds one's body while standing, sitting or walking

자세, 포즈

He is recognizable by his body **posture**.[26]

syn. stance, attitude, circumstance

27

provoke
[pruh-vohk]

v. to annoy and try to make someone act aggressively

자극하다, 선동하다

They **provoked** a confrontation.[27]

syn. incite, instigate, hassle

28

receptive
[ri-sep-tiv]

adj. willing to listen to or to accept new ideas or suggestions

수용하는, 새로운 의견이나 아이디어를 잘 받아들이는

She is **receptive** to new ideas from others.[28]

syn. open, amenable, accessible

29

rhetoric
[ret-er-ik]

n. the art of speaking and writing well

수사학, 웅변술, 미사여구

What is required is immediate action, not **rhetoric**.[29]

syn. oratory, public speaking, speech-making

30

segregate
[seg-ri-geyt]

v. to keep apart

격리시키다, 떨어뜨려 놓다

The pupils **segregated** by grade.[30]

syn. divide, insulate, sequester

31

sober
[soh-ber]

adj. not intoxicated or drunk

술 취하지 않은, 올바른 정신의

I am stone-cold **sober**.[31]

syn. sane, temperate, moderate

예문 해석

26 그는 그의 자세로 알아볼 수 있다. **27** 그들은 대립을 야기시켰다. **28** 그녀는 다른 사람들의 새로운 아이디어를 잘 받아들이는 편이다. **29** 지금 필요한 것은 화려한 말이 아니라 당장의 행동이다. **30** 학생들은 학년에 따라 구분되었다. **31** 난 절대 취하지 않았어.

32

stint
[stint]

v. to provide only a small amount
아까워하다, 인색하게 굴다
She never **stints** on the wine at her parties.[32]

syn. scrimp, economize, hold back

33

sycophant
[sik-*uh*-fuh*nt*]

n. someone who flatters in a servile way
추종자, 아첨꾼
The dictator was surrounded by **sycophants**, frightened to
tell him what he may not like to hear.[33]

syn. adulator, toady, fawner, flatterer

34

transient
[tran-sh*uh*nt]

adj. lasting only a short time
잠시 동안만 지속되는, 덧없는, 일시적인
Military families have a **transient** lifestyle causing them to
move often during the spouse's military career.[34]

syn. fleeting, transitory, ephemeral

35

unwieldy
[*uh*n-weel-dee]

adj. difficult to move or control because of size, shape or
weight
다루기 힘든, 무겁고 부피가 큰
It was a bit **unwieldy** and difficult to handle in the wind.[35]

syn. awkward, heavy, bulky

36

vanity
[van-i-tee]

n. feelings of excessive pride
자만심, 허영심
She has **vanity** in her appearance, refusing to work that
might dirty her clothes or mess up her hair.[36]

syn. conceit, egotism, arrogance

예문 해석

32 그녀는 파티에 와인을 내놓은 것에 인색하지 않았다.　**33** 독재자는 그가 싫어할 소리를 하는 것을 두려워하는 아첨꾼들에게 둘러싸여 있었다.　**34** 군인 가족은 배우자의 군대 경력 동안 자주 이사를 다니는 일시적인 생활 방식을 가진다.　**35** 바람이 불어 다루기가 약간 버겁고 어려웠다.　**36** 그녀는 외모에 심한 자만심이 있어, 옷을 더럽히거나 머리를 흐트러뜨릴 수 있는 일을 거부했다.

Directions   Each of the following questions consists of one word followed by five words or phrases. You are to select the one word or phrase whose meaning is closest to the word in capital letters.

1. **ADROIT :**
   (A) ingenious
   (B) sullen
   (C) ridiculous
   (D) queer
   (E) sloping

2. **ANNUL :**
   (A) humiliate
   (B) deceive
   (C) cross
   (D) waste
   (E) nullify

3. **BANISH :**
   (A) demand
   (B) charge
   (C) exile
   (D) reveal
   (E) amass

4. **CLING :**
   (A) describe
   (B) dash
   (C) insert
   (D) adhere
   (E) descend

5. **DEBONAIR :**
   (A) destitute
   (B) elegant
   (C) bombastic
   (D) confounded
   (E) extravagant

6. **GALVANIZE :**
   (A) penetrate
   (B) introduce
   (C) invigorate
   (D) stoop
   (E) quote

7. **INSURGENT :**
   (A) onlooker
   (B) hobo
   (C) mutineer
   (D) gawker
   (E) bystander

8. **LEGIBLE :**
   (A) inexperienced
   (B) illicit
   (C) miserly
   (D) readable
   (E) tattered

9. **MODIFY :**
   (A) refuge
   (B) repudiate
   (C) alter
   (D) pretend
   (E) disperse

10. **NAIVE :**
    (A) credulous
    (B) onerous
    (C) bottomless
    (D) relentless
    (E) instructive

"Early to bed and early to rise makes a man healthy, wealthy, and wise."

— Benjamin Franklin —
U.S. author, diplomat, inventor, physicist, politician, & printer

일찍 자고 일찍 일어나는 것은 사람을 건강하고 부유하며 현명하게 만든다.

LESSON

Greek and Latin Roots & Prefixes 45

★ SUR, SUPER = above, beyond

bheue (to be)	superb	최고의, 최상의
eme (to situate)	supreme	최고의, 최대의
impose (to put in)	superimpose	겹쳐놓다, 덧붙이다
-or (n.)	superior	우수한, 상급자
intendere (to direct)	superintendent	관리자
videre (to see)	supervisor	감독관
plus (more)	surplus	과잉, 잉여
realis (actual)	surreal	비현실적인
weid (to see)	survey	설문조사
face (face)	surface	표면

DAY

45

WORDS TO LEARN

- ☐ affirmative
- ☐ antagonist
- ☐ barge
- ☐ blasphemy
- ☐ clique
- ☐ consecutive
- ☐ daydream
- ☐ detached
- ☐ dispatch

- ☐ efface
- ☐ equity
- ☐ fair
- ☐ flamboyant
- ☐ gentility
- ☐ grove
- ☐ hollow
- ☐ impermeable
- ☐ indubitable

- ☐ intact
- ☐ jest
- ☐ legion
- ☐ magnanimous
- ☐ meticulous
- ☐ narcissistic
- ☐ olfactory
- ☐ pathetic
- ☐ potable

- ☐ prowess
- ☐ recondite
- ☐ relish
- ☐ sinister
- ☐ sociable
- ☐ stipend
- ☐ translucent
- ☐ unwilling
- ☐ wane

01

affirmative
[*uh*-fur-m*uh*-tiv]

adj. expressing agreement or approval
긍정의, 긍정하는
The cast's director gave them an **affirmative** nod after their performance.[1]

syn. positive, approving, supporting

02

antagonist
[an-tag-*uh*-nist]

n. an opponent or enemy
적대자, 경쟁자, 라이벌
An **antagonist** is a character who represents the opposition to the protagonist.[2]

syn. rival, adversary, opponent, foe

03

barge
[bahrj]

v. to rudely interrupt
무례하게 끼어들다, 주제넘게 참견하다
He **barged** into our private conversation.[3]

syn. intrude, interrupt

예문 해석

01 출연진 감독은 공연이 끝난 후 긍정적인 의미로 고개를 끄덕였다. **02** 악역은 주인공과 대적하는 역할이다. **03** 그는 우리의 사적인 대화에 무례하게 끼어들었다.

04

blasphemy
[blas-*fuh*-mee]

n. impious utterance or action concerning God or sacred things

신성 모독

They accused him of **blasphemy** by saying terrible about a god.[4]

syn. irreverence, desecration, heresy

05

clique
[kleek]

n. a small, exclusive group of people

한무리, 그룹, 파벌

A **clique** of girls stared at him as he passed by.[5]

syn. inner circle, coterie, set

06

consecutive
[k*uh*n-sek-y*uh*-tiv]

adj. following one after the other

연속되는

The manager had worked late for two **consecutive** days.[6]

syn. successive, following

07

daydream
[dey-dreem]

n. pleasant thoughts indulged in while awake

백일몽, 공상

He **daydreamed** in class instead of listening to the teacher.[7]

syn. fantasy, vision, imagination

08

detached
[di-tacht]

adj. no longer connected or joined

사심 없는, 공평한

He tried to remain emotionally **detached** from the prisoners.[8]

syn. disinterested, impartial, equitable

🧘 **예문 해석**

04 그들은 그가 신에 대해 끔찍한 말을 해서 신성모독했다고 비난했다.　**05** 한 무리의 여자 아이들이 그가 지나가자 그를 빤히 쳐다보았다.　**06** 매니저는 이틀 연속 야근을 했다.　**07** 그는 수업 시간에 선생님의 말씀을 듣지 않고 공상에 빠졌다.　**08** 그는 죄수들과 감정적으로 떨어지려 노력했다.

dispatch
[di-spach]

v. to send someone for a particular reason
급파하다
He **dispatched** scouts ahead of the group.[9]

syn. send off, send out, post

efface
[i-feys]

v. to wipe out
지우다, 말살하다
He tried to **efface** his unhappy memories.[10]

syn. expunge, remove, obliterate

equity
[ek-wi-tee]

n. fair or just conditions or treatment
공평, 공정, 정당
It is believed that through **equity**, equality is achievable.[11]

syn. fairness, impartiality, justice

fair
[fair]

adj. very pleasing to the eye
아름다운, 매력적인
She was a **fair** lady and wise scholar.[12]

syn. beautiful, sightly, comely

flamboyant
[flam-boi-*uh*nt]

adj. marked by ostentation but often tasteless
현란한, 화려한
She delivered a **flamboyant** speech about her success.[13]

syn. bombastic, extravagant, theatrical

gentility
[jen-til-i-tee]

n. elegance by virtue of fineness of manner and expression
고상함, 품위, 세련됨
In the small town, his family was known for their **gentility**.[14]

syn. propriety, sophistication, elegance

예문 해석

09 그는 정찰대를 먼저 급파했다. **10** 그는 자신의 안 좋았던 기억을 지우려 애썼다. **11** 평등은 형평성을 통해 달성될 수 있다고 믿어진다. **12** 그녀는 아름다운 숙녀였고 현명한 학자였다. **13** 그녀는 자신의 성공에 대해 (미사여구를 많이 쓴) 연설을 했다. **14** 그의 가족은 그 작은 마을에서 품위 있기로 유명했다.

15

grove
[grohv]

n. a small group of trees

작은 숲

For a peaceful getaway, the landscaper wanted the vacation home to be surrounded by **groves**.[15]

syn. forest, woods, orchard

16

hollow
[hol-oh]

adj. having a space or cavity inside

속이 빈, 움푹 패인

The bird made its nest inside the **hollow** tree.[16]

syn. vacant, unfilled, empty

17

impermeable
[im-pur-mee-*uh*-b*uh*l]

adj. not allowing fluid to pass through

액체가 스며들지 않는, 불침투성의

The life jacket is made from an **impermeable** material.[17]

syn. impenetrable, hermetic, airtight

18

indubitable
[in-doo-bi-t*uh*-b*uh*l]

adj. patently evident or certain

의심할 여지 없는, 확실한

Rousseau explained that the only thing he admired in Voltaire was his **indubitable** genius.[18]

syn. undoubted, unquestionable, certain

19

intact
[in-takt]

adj. remaining uninjured, sound, or whole

손대지 않은, 손상되지 않은

The vase remained **intact** despite the war.[19]

syn. untouched, undamaged, unscathed

20

jest
[jest]

v. to joke

농담하다

He enjoyed **jesting** with his close friends.[20]

syn. joke, kid, tease

예문 해석

15 평화로운 휴가를 위해, 조경사는 별장이 숲으로 둘러싸여 있기를 원했다.   **16** 새는 속이 빈 나무 안에 둥지를 틀었다.   **17** 그 구명조끼는 방수 재질로 만들어졌다.   **18** 볼테르에 대해 칭찬할 만한 유일한 한 가지는 거의 의심할 여지 없는 천재성 뿐이라고 루소는 말했다.   **19** 그 화병은 전쟁에도 온전히 남아 있었다.   **20** 그는 친한 친구들과 농담하는 것을 즐겼다.

21

legion
[lee-j*uh*n]

n. a multitude or great number
특정 유형의 많은 사람들, 군단
Her **legions** of followers gathered around the stadium exit, hoping to catch a glimpse of their favorite movie star.[21]

syn. throng, mass, multitude

22

magnanimous
[mag-nan-*uh*-m*uh*s]

adj. kind and forgiving
마음이 넓은, 관대한
They are **magnanimous** toward their enemies.[22]

syn. generous, benevolent, liberal

23

meticulous
[m*uh*-tik-y*uh*-l*uh*s]

adj. very carefully and with great attention to detail
꼼꼼한, 세심한
He was **meticulous** about everything.[23]

syn. careful, fastidious, exacting

24

narcissistic
[nahr-s*uh*-sis-tik]

adj. having an undue fascination with oneself
자기 도취증에 빠진, 자기애가 심한
His **narcissistic** friend couldn't stop talking about herself and was constantly obsessing about how she looked.[24]

syn. egotistic, self-centered, self-absorbed

25

olfactory
[ol-fak-t*uh*-ree]

adj. of or pertaining to the sense of smell
후각의
When it comes to odors, dogs have more **olfactory** receptors than humans.[25]

syn. odorous, aromatic, olfactive

26

pathetic
[p*uh*-thet-ik]

adj. causing or evoking pity, sympathetic sadness
불쌍한, 안된
The group of onlookers presented a **pathetic** sight.[26]

syn. pitiful, sad, feeble

예문 해석

21 그녀의 많은 추종자들이 그들이 좋아하는 영화배우의 모습을 잠깐이라도 볼 수 있을까 바라는 마음에 스타디움 출구 옆에 모여 있었다. **22** 그들은 적들에게 관대하다. **23** 그는 매사에 매우 꼼꼼했다. **24** 그의 자아도취적인 친구는 자기 자신에 대한 이야기를 멈출 수 없었고 자신의 외모에 대해 끊임없이 집착했다. **25** 냄새에 관한 한 개는 사람보다 후각 수용체가 더 많다. **26** 몇몇 지나가는 구경꾼들이 그 불쌍한 광경을 보았다.

27

potable
[poh-t*uh*-b*uh*l]

adj. suitable for drinking

마실 수 있는

I bought a specific straw for a hike that allowed water to become **potable**.[27]

syn. drinkable, clean, filtered

28

prowess
[prou-is]

n. great skill at doing something

용기, 실력

He's always bragging about his **prowess**.[28]

syn. skill, caliber, ability

29

recondite
[rek-*uh*n-dait]

adj. difficult to understand

많이 알려지지 않은, 난해한

These philosophy books seemed **recondite** and made him confused.[29]

syn. profound, esoteric, abstruse

30

relish
[rel-ish]

v. get enjoyment from

(대단히) 즐기다, 좋아하다

After each bite at a dinner party, he showed just how much he **relished** the meal.[30]

syn. enjoy, appreciate, delight in

31

sinister
[sin-*uh*-ster]

adj. threatening or portending evil or harm

불길한, 해로운

After a moment of **sinister** silence, she heard the sound of footsteps running.[31]

syn. ominous, malevolent, nasty

 예문 해석

27 나는 하이킹을 위해 물을 가지고 다니며 마실 수 있는 특별한 빨대를 구입했다.   **28** 그는 항상 자신의 실력을 자랑한다.   **29** 이 철학 책들은 난해해 보이고, 그를 혼란스럽게 했다.   **30** 저녁 파티에서 한 입 한 입 먹은 후, 그는 그가 얼마나 맛있게 먹었는지 보여주었다.   **31** 잠시 불길한 침묵이 흐른 후, 그녀는 달리는 발자국 소리를 들었다.

32 ·······

sociable
[soh-shuh-buhl]

adj. friendly or agreeable in company
사교적인, 사람들과 잘 어울리는
She is outgoing and **sociable**.[32]

> *syn.* gregarious, outgoing, convivial

33 ·······

stipend
[stai-pend]

n. a sum of money allotted on a regular basis
수당, 급료, 봉급
For every business trip she took, her company gave her a travel **stipend**.[33]

> *syn.* salary, wage, allowance

34 ·······

translucent
[trans-loo-suhnt]

adj. allowing light to pass diffusely
반투명의
Frosted window glass is **translucent** but not transparent.[34]

> *syn.* see-through, clear, crystalline

35 ·······

unwilling
[uhn-wil-ing]

adj. unfavorably inclined
꺼려하는, 내키지 않는
She was **unwilling** to participate in the math competition.[35]

> *syn.* reluctant, grudging, averse

36 ·······

wane
[weyn]

v. to become gradually weaker
작아지다, 쇠약해지다, 감퇴하다
While his interest in baseball began to **wane**, a passion for football developed.[36]

> *syn.* decline, weaken, diminish, fail

 예문 해석

32 그녀는 외향적이며 사교적이다.　**33** 그녀가 출장 갈 때마다 회사에서 여행 수당을 주었다.　**34** 서리 낀 창문은 반투명이지 완전 투명하지는 않다.　**35** 그녀는 수학 경시에 참여하고 싶지 않았다.　**36** 야구에 대한 관심이 점차 줄어들면서 그는 축구에 열정이 타올랐다.

Directions   Each of the following questions consists of one word followed by five words or phrases. You are to select the one word or phrase whose meaning is closest to the word in capital letters.

1. **AFFIRMATIVE :**
   (A) alternative
   (B) well-bred
   (C) thoughtful
   (D) voluntary
   (E) positive

2. **BARGE :**
   (A) char
   (B) renounce
   (C) intrude
   (D) weaken
   (E) captivate

3. **CLIQUE :**
   (A) social bias
   (B) comprehensive view
   (C) inner circle
   (D) penitent sinner
   (E) sumptuous meal

4. **CONSECUTIVE :**
   (A) successive
   (B) agile
   (C) renowned
   (D) curious
   (E) inopportune

5. **DAYDREAM :**
   (A) praise
   (B) attendants
   (C) poise
   (D) fantasy
   (E) euphoria

6. **DETACHED :**
   (A) disinterested
   (B) industrious
   (C) steadfast
   (D) vital
   (E) reserved

7. **JEST :**
   (A) pitch
   (B) joke
   (C) hydrate
   (D) jar
   (E) approach

8. **METICULOUS :**
   (A) spiteful
   (B) advantageous
   (C) careful
   (D) plentiful
   (E) irritated

9. **NARCISSISTIC :**
   (A) overbearing
   (B) egotistic
   (C) amiable
   (D) offensive
   (E) unnerving

10. **OLFACTORY :**
    (A) obedient
    (B) furtive
    (C) sensible
    (D) odorous
    (E) irritable

"Genius without education is like silver in the mine."

— Benjamin Franklin —
U.S. author, diplomat, inventor, physicist, politician, & printer

교육 없는 천재는 광산의 은과 같다.

Greek and Latin Roots & Prefixes 46

★ SUB = under

com (thoroughly) + scire (to know)	subconscious	잠재의식적인
ducere (to lead)	subdue	진압하다
ject (to throw)	subject	(무력으로) 지배하에 두다
mare (sea)	submarine	잠수함
mergere (to immerse)	submerge	잠수하다, 물 속에 잠기다
ordo (rank)	subordinate	부하, 하급자
wegh (to go)	subway	지하철, 지하도

DAY

46

WORDS TO LEARN

- ☐ admonish
- ☐ anticlimax
- ☐ barbaric
- ☐ broach
- ☐ clumsy
- ☐ comely
- ☐ consensus
- ☐ detain
- ☐ dispel

- ☐ efficacy
- ☐ equivalent
- ☐ exterminate
- ☐ flammable
- ☐ gape
- ☐ grovel
- ☐ holistic
- ☐ impetus
- ☐ inducement

- ☐ intangible
- ☐ jocose
- ☐ legislation
- ☐ magnificent
- ☐ metropolitan
- ☐ nascent
- ☐ ominous
- ☐ pariah
- ☐ potent

- ☐ proximity
- ☐ reciprocal
- ☐ self-conscious
- ☐ soiled
- ☐ stipulation
- ☐ synthesize
- ☐ travail
- ☐ unyielding
- ☐ warp

01

admonish
[ad-mon-ish]

v. to scold gently
조용히 타이르다, 경고하다
"**Admonish** thy friends in secret, praise them openly." - Publilius Syrus [1]

syn. warn, caution, scold

02

anticlimax
[an-ti-klai-maks]

n. something that is less dramatic or important than expected
예상과 달리 실망스러운 결말
Travelling in Africa was an **anticlimax**. [2]

syn. letdown, ineffective conclusion, disappointment

03

barbaric
[bahr-bar-ik]

adj. without civilizing influences
야만적인
His parents have different opinions about hunting — for his dad, it's a way of life, and for mom, it's **barbaric**. [3]

syn. savage, inhuman, uncivilized

예문 해석

01 친구를 나무랄 때는 조용히 타이르고, 칭찬할 때는 공공연히 칭찬하라.　**02** 아프리카 여행은 생각과 달리 실망스러웠다.　**03** 그의 부모님은 사냥에 대해 다른 의견을 가지고 있다. 그의 아버지에게는 사냥이 삶의 방식이고 어머니에게는 야만적인 일이다.

04

broach
[brohch]

v. to mention or suggest for the first time
언급하다, 처음으로 이야기를 꺼내다
He **broached** the subject in the meeting.[4]

> *syn.* introduce, mention, address

05

clumsy
[kl*uh*m-zee]

adj. awkward
꼴사나운, 어색한, 서투른
Don't make a **clumsy** excuse.[5]

> *syn.* crude, unskillful, ungainly

06

comely
[k*uh*m-lee]

adj. pleasing in appearance
예쁜, 매력적인
He has **comely** manners knowing the right way to act to put people at ease.[6]

> *syn.* attractive, fair, beautiful

07

consensus
[k*uh*n-sen-s*uh*s]

n. general agreement
일치, 합의
The **consensus** of the group was that they should end this war.[7]

> *syn.* concord, harmony, agreement

08

detain
[di-teyn]

v. to take into custody
못가게 붙들다, 감금하다
He was **detained** for questioning.[8]

> *syn.* confine, restrict

예문 해석

04 그가 회의에서 처음으로 그 문제에 대해 이야기를 꺼냈다.   **05** 말도 안 되는 핑계 대지 마라.   **06** 그는 사람들을 편안하게 하기 위한 올바른 행동 방법을 아는 매력적인 매너를 가지고 있다.   **07** 사람들의 일치된 의견은 이 전쟁을 끝내야 한다는 것이었다. **08** 그는 심문을 위해 구류되었다.

dispel
[di-spel]

v. to make a feeling disappear
쫓아 버리다, 흩뜨리다
She could **dispel** her fears with music.[9]

syn. disperse, dissipate

efficacy
[ef-i-k*uh*-see]

n. capacity for producing a desired result or effect
효능, 효력
The **efficacy** of her business plan was monumental in its growth.[10]

syn. effectiveness

equivalent
[i-kwiv-*uh*-lu*h*nt]

adj. being essentially comparable to something
동등한, 같은
Silence is **equivalent** to an admission of guilt.[11]

syn. equal, identical

exterminate
[ik-stur-m*uh*-neyt]

v. to destroy totally
근절하다, 완전히 없애다
They tried to **exterminate** the cockroaches that were in their house.[12]

syn. eliminate, eradicate, annihilate

flammable
[flam-*uh*-b*uh*l]

adj. easily set on fire
불이 잘 붙는, 가연성의, 불안정한
Petrol is a **flammable** liquid.[13]

syn. inflammable, combustible, volatile

gape
[geyp]

v. to stare with open mouth as in wonder
(놀람이나 감탄으로) 입을 탁 벌리다, 입을 벌리고 멍하니 바라보다
They **gaped** at him in amazement.[14]

syn. glare, gaze, stare

 예문 해석

09 그녀는 음악으로 두려움을 떨칠 수 있었다.　**10** 그녀의 사업 계획의 효과는 그 성장에 있어 기념비적인 것이었다.　**11** 침묵은 죄를 인정하는 것과 같다.　**12** 그들은 집에 있는 바퀴벌레를 모조리 없애려 노력하였다.　**13** 석유는 가연성이 높은 액체이다.
14 그들은 놀라서 입을 딱 벌리고 그를 바라보았다.

15

grovel
[gr*uhv-uh*l]

v. to cringe or humble yourself in great fear or humility
기다, 비굴하게 굴다
He was so embarrassed about his mistake, he **groveled** at his boss.[15]

syn. abase, demean oneself, beseech

16

holistic
[hoh-lis-tik]

adj. encompassing the whole of a thing, not just the part
전체론의, 전체론적인
The **holistic** approach in education addresses the entirety of a student's mind, emotional, behavioral, and academic growth.[16]

syn. complete, whole, comprehensive

17

impetus
[im-pi-t*uh*s]

n. the force or energy with which something moves
움직이게 하는 힘, 원동력, 충동
We need a new **impetus** to spur growth.[17]

syn. momentum, impulsion

18

inducement
[in-doos-m*uh*nt]

n. something that motivates or persuades
유인, 유도하게 만드는 것
They offer every **inducement** to foreign businesses to invest in their country.[18]

syn. incentive, encouragement

19

intangible
[in-tan-j*uh*-b*uh*l]

adj. incapable of being perceived by the sense of touch
손으로 만질 수 없는, 실체가 없는, 막연한
Confidence is an **intangible** asset within oneself.[19]

syn. impalpable

예문 해석

15 그는 자신의 실수에 너무 당황해서 상사에게 굽실거렸다.   **16** 교육의 총체적 접근은 학생의 정신, 정서, 행동 및 학업 성장을 전체적으로 다루는 것이다.   **17** 우리는 성장을 자극할 새로운 힘이 필요하다.   **18** 그들은 외국 회사들이 자신의 나라에 투자하도록 다양한 유인책을 제공했다.   **19** 자신감은 보이지 않는 자산이다.

20

jocose
[joh-kohs]

adj. given to or characterized by joking
익살스러운, 유머러스한
His **jocose** manner was inappropriate for such a solemn occasion.[20]

syn. jesting, humorous, cheerful

21

legislation
[lej-is-ley-shuhn]

n. the act of making or enacting laws
법률제정
They introduced **legislation** for the new tax.[21]

syn. enactment, lawmaking, legislating

22

magnificent
[mag-nif-uh-suhnt]

adj. making a splendid appearance or show
수려한, 화려한, 아름다운
I went to Broadway to watch the **magnificent** show first hand.[22]

syn. superb, grand, marvelous

23

metropolitan
[me-truh-pol-i-tn]

adj. belonging or relating to a large city
주요 도시의, 대도시의
The Seoul **Metropolitan** Police Agency is urging citizens not to use their cars.[23]

syn. municipal, urban

24

nascent
[nas-uhnt]

adj. in the early stages of development
초기의, 발생 초기 단계의
During the first year of the university's program, the professor contributed greatly to the **nascent** business program.[24]

syn. budding, incipient

25

ominous
[om-uh-nuhs]

adj. portending evil or harm
나쁜 징조의, 불길한
There was an **ominous** silence at the other end of the phone.[25]

syn. threatening, warning, worrying

예문 해석

20 그의 익살스러운 태도는 그런 엄숙한 자리에는 적절하지 않았다.　**21** 그들은 새로운 세금 제도에 대한 법률을 제정했다.　**22** 나는 그 웅장한 쇼를 직접 보기 위해 브로드웨이에 갔다.　**23** 서울 경찰청은 시민들에게 자가용 이용 자제를 당부했다.　**24** 그 대학 프로그램의 첫 해 동안, 그 교수는 비즈니스 프로그램 초기에 크게 기여했다.　**25** 수화기 저편에서는 불길한 침묵이 흘렀다.

26

pariah
[puh-rai-uh]

n. a person who is rejected from society or community
추방자, 버림받은 사람
People did not dislike **pariahs**; they avoided them at all costs.[26]

> *syn.* outcast, vagabond, outsider

27

potent
[poht-nt]

adj. very effective and powerful
강력한, 효과적인, 센
The most **potent** weapon is education.[27]

> *syn.* powerful, effective, strong

28

proximity
[prok-sim-i-tee]

n. closeness in space or time
공간이나 시간적으로 가까움
She's constantly talking to him in very close **proximity**.[28]

> *syn.* nearness, closeness, immediacy

29

reciprocal
[ri-sip-ruh-kuhl]

adj. given or felt by each toward the other
상호간의, (수학에서) 역수의
Their success was based on their **reciprocal** respect.[29]

> *syn.* exchanged, alternate, mutual

30

self-conscious
[self-kon-shuhs]

adj. excessively aware of being observed by others
다른 사람의 시선을 의식하는, 수줍어하는, 자의식이 강한
I felt a bit **self-conscious** in my swimsuit.[30]

> *syn.* nervous, anxious, embarrassed

31

soiled
[soild]

adj. likely to soil with dirt or grime
더러워진
They had to change from their **soiled** clothes into clean ones.[31]

> *syn.* smeared, sullied, dirty

예문 해석

26 사람들은 추방자들을 좋아하지 않았던 것이 아니다. 무슨 수를 써서라도 그들을 피했다.　**27** 가장 강력한 무기는 교육이다.
28 그녀는 계속해서 아주 가까운 거리에서 그와 이야기했다.　**29** 그들의 성공은 그들의 상호 존중에 바탕을 두고 있었다.　**30** 수영복을 입은 나는 다른 사람의 시선에 신경이 쓰였다.　**31** 그들은 더러워진 옷을 깨끗한 것으로 갈아입어야 했다.

32 ··

stipulation
[stip-*yuh*-ley-sh*uh*n]

n. a condition, demand, or promise in an agreement or contract

(필요 조건을 구체적으로) 명시, 조건, 단서

There was a **stipulation** that both costs would be shared equally.[32]

syn. condition, proviso, specification

33 ··

synthesize
[sin-th*uh*-saiz]

v. to combine and form a complex whole

합성하다

These days, many doctors are likely to **synthesize** Eastern and Western approaches to medicine.[33]

syn. incorporate, blend, combine

34 ··

travail
[tr*uh*-veyl]

n. painfully difficult or burdensome work; toil.

고생, 고역

He shed blood, sweat, and tear and endured significant **travail**.[34]

syn. toil, tribulation, woe

35 ··

unyielding
[*uh*n-yeel-ding]

adj. unable to bend or be penetrated under pressure

완고한, 단호한

His parents were **unyielding** on the wedding issue.[35]

syn. obdurate, unbending, obstinate

36 ··

warp
[wawrp]

v. to bend or twist out of shape

휘다, 구부리다

The book cover was **warped** by moisture.[36]

syn. distort, twist, bend

 예문 해석

32 양쪽이 비용을 똑같이 부담한다는 조항이 있었다. **33** 요즘 많은 의사들이 의학에 대한 동서양의 접근법을 종합할 가능성이 높다. **34** 그는 피와 땀과 눈물을 흘렸고 상당한 고통을 견디냈다. **35** 그의 부모님은 결혼 문제에 있어서는 매우 완고했다. **36** 책 표지가 습기 때문에 휘었다.

Directions   Each of the following questions consists of one word followed by five words or phrases. You are to select the one word or phrase whose meaning is closest to the word in capital letters.

1. **ADMONISH :**
   (A) claim
   (B) incite
   (C) refer
   (D) urge
   (E) warn

2. **ANTICLIMAX :**
   (A) recession
   (B) salute
   (C) decision
   (D) letdown
   (E) greeting

3. **BROACH :**
   (A) introduce
   (B) chant
   (C) admonish
   (D) defame
   (E) rip

4. **COMELY :**
   (A) remarkable
   (B) common
   (C) attractive
   (D) dreadful
   (E) unfledged

5. **EQUIVALENT :**
   (A) hygienic
   (B) paramount
   (C) unfair
   (D) equal
   (E) grimy

6. **FLAMMABLE :**
   (A) reckless
   (B) required
   (C) soiled
   (D) inflammable
   (E) elegant

7. **HOLISTIC :**
   (A) frown
   (B) applaud
   (C) complete
   (D) slum
   (E) disguise

8. **MAGNIFICENT :**
   (A) breeze
   (B) superb
   (C) blue
   (D) meritorious
   (E) conclusive

9. **OMINOUS :**
   (A) metaphorical
   (B) threatening
   (C) infinitesimal
   (D) impenetrable
   (E) titular

10. **TRAVAIL :**
   (A) locomotive
   (B) attendants
   (C) compunction
   (D) metropolitan
   (E) toil

"The greatest thing in life is to keep your mind young."

— Henry Ford —
American industrialist & business magnate

삶에서 가장 중요한 것은 마음을 젊게 유지하는 것이다.

Greek and Latin Roots & Prefixes 47

★ INTRA = within, inside

cella (small room)	intracellular	가로막다, 가로채다
galaxia (milky way)	intragalactic	은하 내의
murus (wall)	intramural	교내의
nasal (nose)	intranasal	코 안의, 비강 내의
ocular (eye)	intraocular	눈 안의, 안구 내의
persona (person)	intrapersonal	개인 내의
psykhe (soul, mind, life)	intrapsychic	정신 내부의
vena (vein)	intravenous	정맥으로 들어가는, 정맥 주사의
net (network)	intranet	인트라넷, 내부 전산망

DAY

47

WORDS TO LEARN

☐ adorn	☐ egocentric	☐ integrity	☐ prudent
☐ apex	☐ equivocal	☐ jolly	☐ reckless
☐ aplomb	☐ extol	☐ legitimate	☐ rickety
☐ brood	☐ flicker	☐ magnitude	☐ snobbish
☐ conscript	☐ gait	☐ midst	☐ sojourn
☐ consort	☐ grudging	☐ natal	☐ symmetry
☐ dearth	☐ homogeneous	☐ omit	☐ transmute
☐ deter	☐ implant	☐ patron	☐ upheaval
☐ disperse	☐ induction	☐ pine	☐ wary

01

adorn
[*uh*-dawrn]

v. to decorate
꾸미다, 장식하다
"Know, first, who you are; and then **adorn** yourself accordingly." - Epictetus[1]

syn. ornament, embellish, garnish

02

apex
[ey-peks]

n. the tip, point, or vertex
꼭대기, 정점
At the **apex** of feudalism sits a king of a nation.[2]

syn. pinnacle, summit, top

03

aplomb
[*uh*-plom]

n. imperturbable self-possession, poise, or assurance
침착함
She was enraged without her usual **aplomb**.[3]

syn. poise, composure, calmness

예문 해석

01 네 자신이 누구인지 먼저 잘 알고, 그에 맞게 꾸며라. **02** 봉건제도의 정점에 한 나라의 왕이 앉아 있다. **03** 그녀는 평소의 침착함이 없이 격분했다.

04

brood
[brood]

n. a breed, species, group, or kind
종족, 품종, 한 어미에서 난 새끼들
History includes a culmination of **brood** wars.[4]

syn. breed, clan, family

05

conscript
[k*uh*n-skript]

v. to draft for military or naval service
징집하다
Ukraine has started **conscripting** reservists aged 18-60
following a decree by their President.[5]

syn. draft, induct, recruit

06

consort
[kon-sawrt]

n. a husband or wife
(통치자의) 배우자
She was choosing a **consort** based on their accomplishments
and stature in society.[6]

syn. spouse, mate

07

dearth
[durth]

n. an inadequate supply
부족, 결핍
There was a **dearth** of potable water at the campsite.[7]

syn. lack, scarcity, deficiency, shortage

08

deter
[di-tur]

v. to discourage
방해하다
The large tree **deterred** trespassers.[8]

syn. impede, hamper, hinder

🔖 예문 해석

04 역사는 종족간 전쟁들의 정점을 포함한다.   **05** 우크라이나는 대통령의 명령에 따라 18세에서 60세 사이의 예비군 징집을 시작
했다.   **06** 그녀는 그들의 업적과 사회적 위상을 바탕으로 배우자를 고르고 있었다.   **07** 캠프장에는 마실 수 있는 물이 부족했다.
08 큰 나무가 지나가는 사람들을 방해했다.

09

disperse
[di-spurs]

v. to move away from each other
흩어지게 하다, 사라지게 하다
The police **dispersed** the mob.[9]

syn. scatter, dissipate, spread out

10

egocentric
[ee-goh-sen-trik]

adj. interested in oneself only
자기 중심의, 이기적인
He is **egocentric**.[10]

syn. self-centered, self-absorbed, selfish

11

equivocal
[i-kwiv-*uh*-k*uh*l]

adj. of doubtful meaning
모호한, 확실치 않은, 분명치 않은
Research results are somewhat **equivocal**.[11]

syn. ambiguous, vague, dim

12

extol
[ik-stohl]

v. to praise enthusiastically
극찬하다, 크게 칭찬하다
Now experts are **extolling** his new invention.[12]

syn. praise, admire

13

flicker
[flik-er]

v. to burn unsteadily
깜박거리다
A fluorescent light **flickers** for a while before it starts working.[13]

syn. blink, gleam, shimmer

14

gait
[geyt]

n. a manner of walking
걸음걸이
As he strode through the hallway, everyone could tell by his **gait** that he was the leader of this group.[14]

syn. bearing, stride, tread

 예문 해석

09 경찰이 군중을 해산시켰다. **10** 그는 이기적이다. **11** 리서치 결과는 약간 모호했다. **12** 전문가들은 이제 그의 발견을 극찬하고 있다. **13** 형광등이 잠시 깜박이다가 작동을 시작한다. **14** 그가 복도를 성큼성큼 걸어가자 걸음걸이로 그가 이 그룹의 리더임을 알 수 있었다.

15

grudging
[gruhj-ing]

adj. displaying reluctance or unwillingness
꺼려하는, 내키지 않는
The team broke into a **grudging** trot as the coach shouted.[15]

syn. afraid, reluctant, unwilling

16

homogeneous
[hoh-muh-jee-nee-uhs]

adj. composed of parts or elements that are all of the same kind
동종의, 동질의
The research study's sample size was based on a **homogeneous** ethnic group.[16]

syn. identical, similar, comparable

17

implant
[im-plant]

v. to fix or plant something securely
꽂아 넣다, 박다
We need to **implant** sound principles in a child's mind.[17]

syn. insert, embed

18

induction
[in-duhk-shuhn]

n. the act or process of inducting or being inducted
도입, 유도, 시작
She attended the **induction** course in May 2008.[18]

syn. initiation, introduction, inaugural

19

integrity
[in-teg-ri-tee]

n. honesty and firmness
진실성, 정직함, 완전함
He was regarded as a man of **integrity**.[19]

syn. uprightness, honesty

20

jolly
[jol-ee]

adj. in good spirits or happy
즐거운, 행복한
At the grandfather's funeral, he was remembered by others as a **jolly** old man.[20]

syn. merry, gay, blithe, convivial

예문 해석

15 코치가 소리치자 그 팀은 내키지 않아 하며 뛰기 시작했다.   **16** 이 연구의 표본 크기는 단일 민족 집단을 기반으로 했다.   **17** 우리는 아이에게 건전한 정신을 심어줄 필요가 있다.   **18** 그녀는 2008년 신입사원 연수에 참석하였다.   **19** 그는 정직한 사람으로 여겨졌다.   **20** 그 할아버지의 장례식에서 그는 다른 사람들에게 유쾌한 노인으로 기억되었다.

legitimate
[li-jit-*uh*-mit]

adj. acceptable according to the law
합법적인, 적법의, 정당한
He took over the throne by force and was not considered the **legitimate** king.[21]

syn. lawful, legal, licit

magnitude
[mag-ni-tood]

n. great in size or importance
크기, 크고 작음
That would make our power the same order of **magnitude** as theirs.[22]

syn. scale, size, extent

midst
[midst]

n. the location of something surrounded by other things
중앙, 한가운데, 한복판
In the **midst** of life's busyness, sometimes it is hard to stop and take a break.[23]

syn. middle, core, center

natal
[neyt-l]

adj. related to birth
출생의, 태어나면서부터의
Scientific studies have determined that many sea animals such as turtles and seals often return to their **natal** location to give birth.[24]

syn. inherent, inborn

omit
[oh-mit]

v. to fail to do something
빠뜨리다, 생략하다
We had to apologize for **omitting** his name from this article.[25]

syn. leave out, pass over, skip

예문 해석

21 그는 무력으로 왕위를 물려받았고 합법적인 왕으로 간주되지 않았다. **22** 그렇게 되면 우리의 힘이 그들에 버금가게 될 것이다. **23** 바쁜 삶 속에서 멈춰 쉬기가 힘들 때가 있다. **24** 과학 연구들은 거북이나 바다표범과 같은 많은 바다 동물들이 종종 출산을 위해 태어난 장소로 돌아온다는 것을 밝혀냈다. **25** 이 기사에서 그의 이름을 빠뜨린 것에 대해 우리는 사과해야 했다.

patron
[pey-tru*hn*]

n. a person who supports, with money or efforts, an artist or charity

(예술가나 자선단체 등의) 후원자

He was always a **patron** of the arts, and when he died, he donated all of his money to the local art charity.[26]

syn. sponsor, benefactor, backer

pine
[pain]

v. have a desire for something or someone who is not present

애타게 그리워하다, 갈망하다

Ben had been **pining** for Emma, desperately wanting to see her.[27]

syn. long for, crave, yearn

prudent
[prood-nt]

adj. wise or careful in conduct

신중한, 조심스러운, 절약하는

They asked the Assembly for a **prudent** approach to the issue.[28]

syn. sagacious, discreet, sensible

reckless
[rek-lis]

adj. very careless and rash

앞뒤를 가리지 않는, 무모한

His **reckless** driving almost caused an accident on his way home from work.[29]

syn. brash, careless, thoughtless

rickety
[rik-i-tee]

adj. likely to fall or collapse

흔들흔들하는, 곧 무너질 것 같은

The **rickety** raft almost sank.[30]

syn. shaky, ramshackle, decrepit

예문 해석

26 그는 항상 예술의 후원자였고, 그가 죽었을 때, 그는 그의 모든 돈을 지역 예술 자선 단체에 기부했다. **27** 벤은 애타게 엠마를 보고 싶어했다. **28** 그들은 국회에서 그 문제에 대한 신중한 접근을 요구했다. **29** 그의 난폭운전으로 퇴근길에 사고가 날 뻔했다. **30** 흔들흔들하던 뗏목은 거의 가라앉을 뻔했다.

31

snobbish
[snob-ish]

adj. characteristic of those who rebuff the advances of people considered inferior
속물적인, 고상한 척하는, 우월감에 젖어 있는
His **snobbish** friend refuses to borrow his coat because it looks so cheap.[32]

> *syn.* conceited, condescending, haughty

32

sojourn
[soh-jurn]

n. a temporary visit or stay
일시적인 체류
We will make a **sojourn** in Paris.[31]

> *syn.* visit, brief travel, stopover

33

symmetry
[sim-i-tree]

n. balance among the parts of something
대칭, 균형
I was fascinated with the incredible beauty and **symmetry** of a snowflake.[33]

> *syn.* balance, proportion, equilibrium

34

transmute
[trans-myoot]

v. to change or alter in form, appearance, or nature
바꾸다, 변형시키다
Alchemists attempted to **transmute** lead into gold.[34]

> *syn.* change, alter, convert

35

upheaval
[*uh*p-hee-v*uh*l]

n. strong or violent change or disturbance
대변동, 격변, 들어 올림, 융기
The nation suffered another **upheaval** in 1882 due to a war.[35]

> *syn.* disaster, major change, catastrophe

36

wary
[wair-ee]

adj. careful when dealing with something
조심성 있는, 경계하는
You should teach your children to be **wary** of strangers.[36]

> *syn.* chary, watchful, cautious

 예문 해석

31 그의 속물 친구는 코트가 너무 싸 보여서 빌리기를 거부한다. **32** 그 아이는 우유를 스푼으로 휘저었다. **33** 나는 눈송이의 놀라운 아름다움과 대칭미에 반해버렸다. **34** 연금술사들은 납을 금으로 변화시키려 했다. **35** 그 나라는 전쟁으로 인해 1882년 또 다른 대격변을 겪었다. **36** 당신은 아이들이 낯선 사람을 경계하도록 가르쳐야 한다.

Directions Each of the following questions consists of one word followed by five words or phrases. You are to select the one word or phrase whose meaning is closest to the word in capital letters.

1. ADORN :
   (A) censor
   (B) ornament
   (C) strive
   (D) confirm
   (E) endeavor

2. APEX :
   (A) pinnacle
   (B) luster
   (C) momentum
   (D) distinction
   (E) caliber

3. APLOMB :
   (A) glee
   (B) onomatopoeia
   (C) hypocrisy
   (D) rapport
   (E) poise

4. CONSCRIPT :
   (A) recoil
   (B) scorn
   (C) postpone
   (D) draft
   (E) shiver

5. DEARTH :
   (A) abundance
   (B) deputy
   (C) plot
   (D) lack
   (E) salvation

6. EQUIVOCAL :
   (A) daring
   (B) ambivalent
   (C) convenient
   (D) obligatory
   (E) flippant

7. LEGITIMATE :
   (A) lawful
   (B) excess
   (C) secret
   (D) biting
   (E) grand

8. PATRON :
   (A) sarcasm
   (B) sponsor
   (C) wanderer
   (D) outcast
   (E) refuge

9. PRUDENT :
   (A) tranquil
   (B) disembarked
   (C) sagacious
   (D) insincere
   (E) ostentatious

10. SNOBBISH :
   (A) awkward
   (B) enunciate
   (C) dormant
   (D) rowdy
   (E) conceited

"If you judge people, you have no time to love them."

— Mother Teresa —
Saint

당신이 다른 사람을 비판만 하면 그들을 사랑할 시간이 없다.

Greek and Latin Roots & Prefixes 48

★ PAX = peace

-fy (to make)	pacify	진정시키다, 달래다
-ist (person)	pacifist	평화주의자, 반전주의자
Romana (Rome)	Pax Romana	로마의 지배에 의한 평화
ad (toward)	appease	달래다

★ BELLUM = war

gerere (to bear)	belligerent	적대적인, 공격적인
cose (inclined)	bellicose	호전적인, 싸우기 좋아하는
ant (before)	antebellum	(미국 남북) 전쟁 전의
post (after)	postbellum	(미국 남북) 전쟁 후의
re (against)	rebel	반란을 일으키다, 반역자
	rebellion	반란, 모반

DAY

48

WORDS TO LEARN

☐ antidote	☐ egregious	☐ jolt	☐ reckon
☐ arboreal	☐ era	☐ leisurely	☐ rife
☐ bashful	☐ extort	☐ maintenance	☐ sensible
☐ brook	☐ greed	☐ manifold	☐ solace
☐ clutch	☐ grumble	☐ munificent	☐ stoic
☐ conspicuous	☐ hoodwink	☐ omnipresent	☐ sympathy
☐ deafening	☐ implausible	☐ patronizing	☐ tier
☐ deteriorate	☐ indulge	☐ precipitate	☐ uproar
☐ disposition	☐ integral	☐ pseudo	☐ wholesome

01

antidote
[an-ti-doht]

n. something that stops a poison from working
해독제
Quick, get the **antidote**! [2]

syn. antitoxin, cure, remedy

02

arboreal
[ahr-bawr-ee-*uhl*]

adj. relating to trees
나무의, 수목의, 나무에서 사는
The rings of a tree are an indication of its **arboreal** age. [2]

syn. relating to trees, arborous, branchy

03

bashful
[bash-f*uhl*]

adj. diffident and easily embarrassed
숫기 없는, 수줍어하는, 부끄러워 하는
He has a crush on Emma and is uncharacteristically **bashful** in her presence. [3]

syn. shy, timid, sheepish

예문 해석

01 빨리 해독제 좀 가져 와! **02** 나무의 나이테는 나무의 나이를 나타낸다. **03** 그는 엠마에게 반해서 그녀가 있으면 이상하게 수줍음을 탄다.

04

brook
[brook]

n. small stream
작은 시내, 개울
The **brook** dried up every summer.[4]

syn. creek, rivulet

05

clutch
[kl*uh*ch]

v. to grip or hold tightly or firmly
꽉 쥐다, 꽉 잡다, 매달리다
She **clutches** her child's hand as they crossed the street.[5]

syn. hold, grip, catch

06

conspicuous
[k*uh*n-spik-yoo-*uh*s]

adj. easily seen or noticed
눈에 띄는
The school advertisement needed to be placed in a
conspicuous spot.[6]

syn. remarkable, noticeable, prominent

07

deafening
[def-*uh*-ning]

adj. extremely loud
귀가 멀 정도로 큰소리의
The sound is **deafening**.[7]

syn. earsplitting, roaring, thunderous

08

deteriorate
[di-teer-ee-*uh*-reyt]

v. to become worse
악화시키다, 저하시키다
His condition **deteriorated** rapidly.[8]

syn. exacerbate, aggravate, degenerate

09

disposition
[dis-p*uh*-zish-*uh*n]

n. the way one tends to behave or feel
성질, 성격
She has a sunny **disposition**.[9]

syn. nature, character

예문 해석

04 그 작은 개울은 매해 여름이 되면 말라 버렸다.   **05** 그녀는 길을 건너면서 아이의 손을 꽉 잡았다.   **06** 학교 광고는 눈에 띄는 곳에 배치되어야 했다.   **07** 그 소리에 귀청이 찢어질 것 같았다.   **08** 그의 상태는 점점 악화되었다.   **09** 그녀는 밝고 명랑한 성격이다.

10 ·······

egregious
[i-gree-j*uh*s]

adj. conspicuously bad

악명 높은, 지독한, 엄청난

His theme was marred by a number of **egregious** errors in spelling.[10]

syn. atrocious, outrageous, vicious

11 ·······

era
[eer-*uh*]

n. a period of time

시대

The **era** of the Roman Empire was long-standing due to their leaders, laws, and foresight.[11]

syn. epoch, period

12 ·······

extort
[ik-stawrt]

v. to obtain money or information by threats or violence

강제로 빼앗다

Corrupt government officials were **extorting** money from him.[12]

syn. blackmail, coerce, cheat

13 ·······

greed
[greed]

n. insatiable desire for wealth or money

탐욕, 욕심

Watching people grabbing for cash furiously, he was surprised at their **greed**.[13]

syn. avarice, rapacity, covetousness

14 ·······

grumble
[gr*uh*m-b*uh*l]

v. to murmur or mutter in discontent

투덜거리다, 불평하다

He **grumbled** constantly.[14]

syn. complain, grouch

예문 해석

10 수많은 오타가 그의 주장을 망쳐 놓았다. **11** 로마 제국 시대는 그들의 지도자들, 법들, 그리고 선견지명 때문에 오래 지속되었다. **12** 부패한 정부 관리는 그에게 돈을 요구했다. **13** 그는 사람들이 현금을 마구 움켜쥐는 것을 보고는 그들의 욕심에 놀랐다. **14** 그는 끊임없이 불평했다.

15

hoodwink
[hood-wingk]

v. to deceive
속이다, 눈가림하다
Do not think you can **hoodwink** people.[15]

syn. mislead, hoax, swindle

16

implausible
[im-plaw-*zuh*-b*uh*l]

adj. not likely to be true
사실 같지 않은, 믿기 어려운
His **implausible** alibi did not hold well in court.[16]

syn. impossible, improbable

17

indulge
[in-d*uh*lj]

v. to yield to an inclination or desire
욕망이나 환락에 빠지다, 탐닉하다
I'm going to **indulge** in all kinds of desserts.[17]

syn. yield, cater, gratify

18

integral
[in-ti-gr*uh*l]

adj. necessary to the completeness of the whole
없어서는 안 될, 꼭 필요한
A library is an **integral** part of a school.[18]

syn. vital, essential, indispensable

19

jolt
[johlt]

v. to shake up roughly and suddenly
갑자기 세게 흔들다, 덜커덩거리다
The bus gave a sudden **jolt**.[19]

syn. jar, lurch, jerk

20

leisurely
[lee-zher-lee]

adj. relaxed and unhurried
느긋한, 유유한, 여유로운
Brunch was a **leisurely** affair.[20]

syn. unhurried, easy

예문 해석

15 사람들을 눈속임 할 수 있을 것이라 생각하지 말아라.　**16** 그의 사실 같지 않은 알리바이는 법정에서 잘 성립되지 않았다. **17** 나는 모든 종류의 디저트를 다 즐길 것이다.　**18** 도서관은 학교에서 반드시 필요한 공간이다.　**19** 버스가 갑자기 세게 흔들렸다.　**20** 브런치는 느긋하게 먹는 것이다.

maintenance
[meyn-t*uh*-n*uh*ns]

n. the act of keeping something in good condition
관리, 유지, 점검
His company is in charge of **maintenance** of the country's road system.[21]

syn. sustenance, perpetuation, care

manifold
[man-*uh*-fohld]

adj. of many kinds
많은, 여러 가지의
The **manifold** household chores seem like they are never-ending.[22]

syn. numerous, varied, abundant

munificent
[myoo-nif-*uh*-s*uh*nt]

adj. very generous
대단히 후한
The wealthy patron always gives the charities **munificent** donations.[23]

syn. beneficent, charitable, lavish

omnipresent
[om-n*uh*-prez-*uh*nt]

adj. present everywhere at the same time
어디에나 있는
The sound of sirens was **omnipresent** in New York.[24]

syn. ubiquitous, common

patronizing
[pey-tr*uh*-nai-zing]

adj. indicative of an offensively condescending manner
드러내어 선심을 쓰는, 은인인 체 하는
I was only trying to explain; I didn't want to sound **patronizing**.[25]

syn. snobbish, condescending, pretentious

예문 해석

21 그의 회사는 나라의 도로를 관리하는 일을 맡고 있다.   **22** 다양한 집안일이 끝이 없는 것처럼 보인다.   **23** 그 부유한 후원자는 자선단체에 항상 아낌없는 기부를 한다.   **24** 뉴욕에서는 사이렌 소리가 어디에서나 들린다.   **25** 나는 단지 설명하려는 것뿐이야. 선심 쓰는 척 들리기는 싫다고.

precipitate
[pri-sip-i-teyt]

v. to hasten the occurrence of
(특히 나쁜 일을) 촉발시키다
Indifference to violence **precipitates** another violence.[26]

syn. hurry, speed, accelerate

pseudo
[soo-doh]

adj. not genuine but having the appearance of
가짜의, 허위의
Pseudo-science is an activity resembling science but based on fallacious assumptions.[27]

syn. artificial, counterfeit, fake

reckon
[rek-*uhn*]

v. to expect, believe, or suppose
세다, 계산하다, 가늠하다
Her mother **reckoned** the cost of the trip at $1,000.[28]

syn. think, guess, imagine

rife
[rahyf]

adj. (usually said of something unfavorable) very common or frequently occurring
나쁜 것이 만연한, 많이 퍼진
Crime is **rife** in the slum areas.[29]

syn. prevalent, widespread, common

sensible
[sen-*suh-buh*l]

adj. having reasonableness and good judgment
지각 있는, 상식적인, 똑똑한
She was a **sensible** young lady.[30]

syn. level-headed, wise, reasonable

solace
[sol-is]

n. comfort in time of disappointment or sorrow
위로, 위안
I found **solace** in writing.[31]

syn. consolation, condolence

예문 해석

26 폭력에 대한 무관심은 또 다른 폭력을 촉발한다. **27** 사이비 과학은 과학을 닮았지만 잘못된 가정에 기반을 둔 활동이다. **28** 그녀의 어머니는 여행 경비를 1,000달러로 계산했다. **29** 슬럼가에는 범죄가 만연하다. **30** 그녀는 분별력 있는 아가씨였다. **31** 나는 글을 쓰면서 위안을 얻었다.

stoic
[stoh-ik]

adj. not affected by or showing passion or feeling
극기의, 금욕의, 냉담한
The martinet had a **stoic** expression on his face.[32]

syn. impassive, indifferent, aloof

sympathy
[sim-p*uh*-thee]

n. the feeling of being sorry for someone
공감, 동정, 동감
She's not looking for **sympathy**.[33]

syn. compassion, kindness, understanding

tier
[teer]

n. a level or a layer
(여러 줄·단으로 이뤄진 것의 어느 한) 줄, 단, 단계
He was the most popular and well-known actor. He was considered part of the top **tier**, getting all the best parts.[34]

syn. level, layer, category

uproar
[*uh*p-rawr]

n. an outbreak of noisy and boisterous behavior
소란, 거세고 시끄러운 소동
The announcement caused an **uproar** in the crowd.[35]

syn. chaos, pandemonium, upheaval

wholesome
[hohl-s*uh*m]

adj. conducive to moral or general well-being
건강에 좋은, 건전한
Wholesome foods are the ones that help you stay healthy.[36]

syn. salutary, beneficial, healthy

🧘 **예문 해석**

32 규율에 엄격한 그 사람은 냉담한 표정을 하고 있었다.　**33** 그녀는 동정은 바라지 않는다.　**34** 그는 가장 유명하고 잘 알려진 배우였다. 그는 최고의 파트를 모두 손에 넣으며 최고 등급의 일원으로 여겨졌다.　**35** 그 발표는 군중들의 소란을 야기했다.　**36** 건강에 좋은 음식은 당신이 건강하게 지내도록 도와준다.

Directions   Each of the following questions consists of one word followed by five words or phrases. You are to select the one word or phrase whose meaning is closest to the word in capital letters.

1. **ANTIDOTE :**
   (A) antibiotic
   (B) delegate
   (C) principle
   (D) antitoxin
   (E) glut

2. **ARBOREAL :**
   (A) relating to animals
   (B) relating to birds
   (C) relating to trees
   (D) relating to virtues
   (E) relating to weather

3. **BASHFUL :**
   (A) irate
   (B) shy
   (C) cuddly
   (D) solitary
   (E) biased

4. **CONSPICUOUS :**
   (A) remarkable
   (B) unconquerable
   (C) docile
   (D) wary
   (E) mammoth

5. **EGREGIOUS :**
   (A) carefree
   (B) atrocious
   (C) illustrious
   (D) costly
   (E) dogged

6. **ERA :**
   (A) timepiece
   (B) pageantry
   (C) epoch
   (D) lighthouse
   (E) latitude

7. **MUNIFICENT :**
   (A) appeasing
   (B) intimate
   (C) satirical
   (D) beneficent
   (E) resolute

8. **PATRONIZING :**
   (A) remote
   (B) loyalty
   (C) venerable
   (D) wasted
   (E) snobbish

9. **SENSIBLE :**
   (A) debatable
   (B) level-headed
   (C) mulish
   (D) dejected
   (E) sincere

10. **SOLACE :**
    (A) consolation
    (B) paradigm
    (C) records
    (D) nomad
    (E) vacuum

Directions   Each of the following questions consists of one word followed by five words or phrases.
You are to select the one word or phrase whose meaning is closest to the word in capital letters.

1. ANONYMOUS :
(A) distinguishing
(B) enduring
(C) civic
(D) unknown
(E) diseased

2. FRUITFUL :
(A) compulsory
(B) hybrid
(C) successful
(D) irrevocable
(E) finicky

3. GALLOP :
(A) consult
(B) discern
(C) eliminate
(D) associate
(E) jolt

4. HOAX :
(A) monodrama
(B) deceit
(C) bogus
(D) prose
(E) verse

5. BANTER :
(A) grovel
(B) tease
(C) entangle
(D) grove
(E) amend

6. JEOPARDY :
(A) offspring
(B) velocity
(C) exemption
(D) arrangement
(E) peril

7. METHODICAL :
(A) systematic
(B) persistent
(C) bisexual
(D) nautical
(E) brazen

8. POSTURE :
(A) zenith
(B) present
(C) plea
(D) stance
(E) retribution

9. SEGREGATE :
(A) smite
(B) appeal
(C) comfort
(D) divide
(E) satirize

10. DISPATCH :
(A) dive into
(B) walk over
(C) send off
(D) fall behind
(E) turn around

11. FAIR :
   (A) enormous
   (B) docile
   (C) reticent
   (D) undaunted
   (E) beautiful

12. RELISH :
   (A) push
   (B) accommodate
   (C) glimpse
   (D) revive
   (E) enjoy

13. SOCIABLE :
   (A) transient
   (B) sinister
   (C) compliant
   (D) distinguished
   (E) gregarious

14. SOILED :
   (A) passionate
   (B) gullible
   (C) complaining
   (D) nervous
   (E) smeared

15. STIPULATION :
   (A) total
   (B) condition
   (C) pundit
   (D) deference
   (E) letdown

16. EXTOL :
   (A) gaze
   (B) debunk
   (C) praise
   (D) retard
   (E) loiter

17. FLICKER :
   (A) endorse
   (B) blink
   (C) scurry
   (D) pierce
   (E) evict

18. SOJOURN :
   (A) impart
   (B) visit
   (C) leap
   (D) abstain
   (E) scavenge

19. INTEGRAL :
   (A) vital
   (B) capricious
   (C) galactic
   (D) haughty
   (E) enthusiastic

20. SYMPATHY :
   (A) repartee
   (B) heritage
   (C) device
   (D) compassion
   (E) deliverance

"If we are together nothing is impossible. If we are divided, all will fail."

— Winston Churchill —
British politician

우리가 함께 힘을 합치면 불가능한 일이 없다. 만약 우리가 분열하면 우리 모두는 실패할 것이다.

Greek and Latin Roots & Prefixes 49

★ OB = in the way of, toward

jacio (to throw)	object	반대하다
sequor (to follow)	obsequious	아부하는, 아첨하는
servo (to keep)	observe	관찰하다, 주시하다
teneo (to hold)	obtain	얻다, 존재하다
curro (to run)	occur	일어나다, 발생하다
positus (arrangement)	oppose	반대하다, 겨루다
pono (to arrange)	opponent	경쟁자, 반대자
facio (to make)	office	사무소
fero (to bear)	offer	제의, 제안
sedere (to sit)	obsess	～에 집착하게 하다

DAY

49

WORDS TO LEARN

- [ ] aboriginal
- [ ] adversary
- [ ] batch
- [ ] bent
- [ ] clutter
- [ ] conspiracy
- [ ] debilitated
- [ ] dejected
- [ ] disprove

- [ ] egress
- [ ] eradicate
- [ ] extenuate
- [ ] extract
- [ ] garish
- [ ] grumpy
- [ ] hospitality
- [ ] implement
- [ ] indulgent

- [ ] intemperate
- [ ] jostle
- [ ] lengthy
- [ ] makeshift
- [ ] milestone
- [ ] mint
- [ ] onset
- [ ] pragmatic
- [ ] prolong

- [ ] reclaim
- [ ] rigid
- [ ] ruffle
- [ ] solemn
- [ ] stolid
- [ ] synchronize
- [ ] trauma
- [ ] urbane
- [ ] waver

01

aboriginal
[ab-*uh*-rij-*uh*-nl]

adj. having existed from the beginning
원주민의, 토착의
In Canada, Inuits and Métis were considered **aboriginals**.[1]

syn. original, native, indigenous

02

adversary
[ad-ver-ser-ee]

n. an opponent
적, 적수
She didn't consider him her **adversary**, but he wasn't her friend, either.[2]

syn. enemy, antagonist, foe

03

batch
[bach]

n. a group of things or people
한 차례 굽는 양, 1회분, 한 묶음
The office manager always brought us a **batch** of cookies every Monday morning.[3]

syn. group, lot, set

예문 해석

01 캐나다에서는 이누이트 족과 메티 족이 원주민으로 여겨졌다.   **02** 그녀는 그를 적으로 여기지는 않았지만 그렇다고 친구인 것도 아니었다.   **03** 사무실 매니저는 매주 월요일 아침마다 우리에게 쿠키를 한 묶음씩 가져다 주었다.

04

bent
[bent]

n. a strong inclination to react to something in a specific manner

취향, 성향

Because he had a strong scientific **bent**, he found reports of witnessing aliens, UFOs, and even Loch Ness monsters interesting.[4]

syn. inclination, proclivity, tendency

05

clutter
[kl*uht*-er]

v. to make untidy

어지르다

The floor was **cluttered** with toys.[5]

syn. jumble, disarray, strew

06

conspiracy
[k*uh*n-spir-*uh*-see]

n. the act of plotting in secret

음모, 공모

The three men are accused of **conspiracy**.[6]

syn. collusion, plot, scheme

07

debilitated
[di-bil-i-teyt]

adj. lacking strength or vigor

쇠약해진

Alzheimer's was the illness that **debilitated** Reagan for the last 10 years of his life.[7]

syn. infirm, enervated, sapped

08

dejected
[dih-jek-tid]

adj. marked by low spirits

낙담한, 실망한

Because he was ejected from an important game due to his injury, he felt deeply **dejected**.[8]

syn. despondent, depressed, blue

예문 해석

04 그가 강한 과학적 취향을 가졌기 때문에, 그는 외계인, UFO, 그리고 심지어 네스호의 괴물을 목격했다는 보고들을 재미있게 생각했다.   **05** 바닥은 장난감으로 어지럽혀져 있었다.   **06** 세 명의 사람들이 음모를 꾸민 혐의로 기소되었다.   **07** 알츠하이머는 레이건의 마지막 10년 인생을 쇠약하게 만든 병이다.   **08** 그는 부상으로 중요한 경기에서 퇴장당해 허탈감이 컸다.

disprove
[dis-proov]

v. to prove something to be false or wrong
잘못되었음을 증명하다, 논박하다
I **disproved** his claim.[9]

syn. refute, confute, contradict

---

egress
[ee-gres]

n. a way out
출구, 나가는 길
There was an **egress** out of the swamp, but only a few familiar with the territory knew of it.[10]

syn. exit, passage out, doorway

---

eradicate
[i-rad-i-keyt]

v. to get rid of something completely
뿌리를 뽑다, 박멸하다, 근절하다
Since they are attempting to **eradicate** crime, they are significantly increasing security measures in the local area.[11]

syn. root up, eliminate, exterminate

---

extenuate
[ik-sten-yoo-yet]

v. to make less of something or try to minimize its importance
(죄나 벌을) 경감하다, 정상을 참작하다
His penalty was **extenuated** when his teacher knew why he showed up late.[12]

syn. diminish, lessen, mitigate

---

extract
[ik-strakt]

v. to take out
뽑다, 밖으로 끌어내다, 추출하다
I went to the dentist, and they had to **extract** a tooth.[13]

syn. withdraw, wrest

 예문 해석

09 나는 그의 주장의 잘못된 부분을 증명했다. **10** 늪에서 빠져나오는 출구가 있었지만, 그 지역을 잘 아는 소수의 사람들만이 그것을 알고 있었다. **11** 그들은 범죄 근절을 위해 노력하고 있기 때문에, 지역의 치안 대책을 대폭 강화하고 있다. **12** 그의 선생님이 그가 왜 늦게 나타났는지를 알았을 때 그의 처벌은 경감되었다. **13** 나는 치과에 가서 이를 뽑아야 했다.

garish
[gair-ish]

adj. unpleasantly bright or colorful
지나치게 번쩍거리는
He doesn't like the restaurant's **garish**, illuminated signs.[14]

syn. glaring, flashy, ostentatious

grumpy
[gr*uh*m-pee]

adj. annoyed and irritable
퉁명스러운, 투덜대는
Scrooge was a **grumpy** old man.[15]

syn. grouch, surly, ill-tempered

hospitality
[hos-pi-tal-i-tee]

n. the friendly reception and treatment of guests
호의, 환대
Thank you for your **hospitality**.[16]

syn. friendliness, neighborliness, accommodation

implement
[im-pl*uh*-m*uh*nt]

v. to apply in a manner consistent with its purpose or design
시행하다, 실행하다, 구현하다
This program is much easier to **implement** in most types of businesses.[17]

syn. put into action, carry out, realize

indulgent
[in-d*uh*l-j*uh*nt]

adj. benignly lenient or permissive
제멋대로 하게 두는, 봐 주는
His **indulgent** mother was willing to let him do anything he wanted.[18]

syn. lenient, giving, tolerant

intemperate
[in-tem-per-it]

adj. not controlled or restrained
절제하지 않는, 과도한
His **intemperate** habits were a disadvantage for him in the workplace.[19]

syn. immoderate, unbalanced, extreme

예문 해석

14 그는 레스토랑의 지나치게 화려하고 번쩍거리는 간판을 싫어했다.   **15** 스크루지는 퉁명스러운 노인이었다.   **16** 당신의 호의에 감사드립니다.   **17** 이 프로그램은 대부분의 기업에서 구현하기가 훨씬 쉽다.   **18** 응석을 다 받아주는 그의 어머니는 그가 원하는 대로 두었다.   **19** 그의 무절제한 습관은 직장에서 그에게 불리했다.

20

jostle
[jos-*uhl*]

v. to push roughly against somebody in a crowd
밀치다, 떠밀다
The crowd **jostled** him into the subway.[20]

> *syn.* shove, push, bump

21

lengthy
[lengk-thee]

adj. relatively long in duration
길고 장황한
The agreement came after **lengthy** negotiations.[21]

> *syn.* extended, long, tedious

22

makeshift
[meyk-shift]

adj. done or made using whatever is available
임시방편의
The boxes were **makeshift** shelters of the homeless.[22]

> *syn.* improvised, temporary, provisional

23

milestone
[mahyl-stohn]

n. a significant event or stage in the life or development
이정표, (인생이나 역사의) 획기적인 사건
Her study will set a new **milestone** in the Education Technology.[23]

> *syn.* landmark, achievement, breakthrough

24

mint
[mint]

n. a plant where money is coined by authority of the government
조폐국, 화폐를 만드는 곳
The Royal **Mint** was located within the walls of the Tower of London for many centuries.[24]

> *syn.* coin plant

25

onset
[on-set]

n. an assault or attack
시작, 습격
During the battle, the **onset** of the enemy did not take them by surprise.[25]

> *syn.* assault, attack, onslaught

예문 해석

20 많은 사람들이 그를 밀치며 지하철 안으로 밀어 넣었다.　**21** 합의는 오랜 협상 끝에 이루어진 것이다.　**22** 그 박스들은 홈리스들의 임시 보금자리였다.　**23** 그녀의 연구는 교육 공학에 역사적인 획을 그을 것이다.　**24** 왕립 조폐국은 수세기 동안 런던 탑의 벽 안에 있었다.　**25** 전투 중에 적의 습격은 그들을 놀라게 하지 않았다.

pragmatic
[prag-mat-ik]

adj. solving problems in a practical and sensible way
실용적인, 실용주의의
He was a **pragmatic** leader, and his subordinates enjoyed following him.[26]

syn. practical, realistic, down-to-earth

prolong
[pru*h*-lawng]

v. to lengthen in time
연장시키다, 연장하다
She decided to **prolong** her stay in this attractive city.[27]

syn. extend, continue, lengthen

reclaim
[ree-kleym]

v. to seek to regain possession of something
(권리나 소유물의) 반환을 요구하다, 되찾다
They **reclaimed** their lost lands.[28]

syn. retrieve, regain

rigid
[rij-id]

adj. very strict and difficult to change
엄격한, 단단한
Several schools have **rigid** rules about student conduct.[29]

syn. stiff, severe, strict

ruffle
[ru*hf-uh*l]

v. to disturb the smoothness of
(사람의 마음을) 산란하게 만들다, 흐트러뜨리다
Spreading lousy news would **ruffle** public composure.[30]

syn. fluster, mess up, rumple

solemn
[sol-*uh*m]

adj. done, made or carried out in earnest and seriousness
엄숙한, 진지한, 무게 있는
The wedding ceremony allows the bride and groom to make a **solemn** pledge to one another.[31]

syn. earnest, sincere, serious

예문 해석

26 그는 현실적인 지도자였고 그의 부하들은 그를 따르는 것을 좋아했다.   **27** 그녀는 이 매력적인 도시에서 더 오래 머물기로 결심했다.   **28** 그들은 잃어버린 땅을 되찾았다.   **29** 몇몇 학교는 학생 행동에 대한 엄격한 규칙이 있다.   **30** 나쁜 소식을 퍼뜨리는 것은 대중의 평정을 어지럽힐 것이다.   **31** 결혼식은 신랑과 신부가 서로에게 엄숙한 서약을 할 수 있게 해준다.

stolid
[stol-id]

adj. not easily stirred or moved mentally
둔감한, 무신경한, 무덤덤한
He responded to her constant demands with **stolid** indifference.[32]

syn. unemotional, impassive, blank

synchronize
[sing-kruh-nahyz]

v. to happen or cause to happen at the exact same time
(정확한 순간에) 동시에 일어나다, 일치하여 일어나다
It is fascinating to watch **synchronized** swimming.[33]

syn. coordinate, harmonize, orchestrate

trauma
[trou-muh]

n. an experience that produces psychological injury
정신적 외상, 복구되기 어려운 큰 정신적 충격
A victim's videotaped testimony can be used in court, sparing him from the **trauma** of the accident.[34]

syn. shock, agony, pang

urbane
[ur-beyn]

adj. notably polite or polished in manner
도시적인, 세련된, 교양 있는
He was known for his novels of witty and **urbane** observations of contemporary life.[35]

syn. sophisticated, refined, debonair

waver
[wey-ver]

v. to move to and fro
흔들리다, 동요하다, 주저하다, 망설이다
Foliage **wavers** in the breeze.[36]

syn. sway, hesitate, oscillate, vacillate

예문 해석

32 그는 그녀의 계속되는 요구에 무덤덤한 무관심으로 일관했다.   **33** 싱크로나이즈드 스위밍을 보는 것은 흥미롭다.   **34** 비디오로 촬영된 피해자의 증언을 법정에서 사용할 수 있어, 피해자의 정신적 고통을 덜어줄 수 있다.   **35** 그는 오늘날의 삶에 대한 위트 있고 교양 있는 관찰을 한 소설들로 유명하다.   **36** 나뭇잎이 산들바람에 흔들렸다.

Directions   Each of the following questions consists of one word followed by five words or phrases. You are to select the one word or phrase whose meaning is closest to the word in capital letters.

1. **ABORIGINAL** :
   (A) abhorrent
   (B) obvious
   (C) original
   (D) atypical
   (E) philanthropic

2. **ADVERSARY** :
   (A) foundation
   (B) enemy
   (C) gap
   (D) abode
   (E) benefactor

3. **BENT** :
   (A) diary
   (B) final offer
   (C) animosity
   (D) thankfulness
   (E) inclination

4. **CLUTTER** :
   (A) astound
   (B) reject
   (C) withdraw
   (D) jumble
   (E) charge

5. **DEBILITATED** :
   (A) sensible
   (B) troubled
   (C) infirm
   (D) conclusive
   (E) answerable

6. **DEJECTED** :
   (A) transitory
   (B) despondent
   (C) obvious
   (D) astute
   (E) gigantic

7. **INTEMPERATE** :
   (A) loquacious
   (B) immoderate
   (C) indecent
   (D) artless
   (E) lustrous

8. **LENGTHY** :
   (A) slack
   (B) elusive
   (C) determined
   (D) extended
   (E) artless

9. **RECLAIM** :
   (A) flourish
   (B) exfoliate
   (C) stroll
   (D) retrieve
   (E) embellish

10. **SOLEMN** :
    (A) fabulous
    (B) eminent
    (C) idealistic
    (D) earnest
    (E) flippant

"Courage is going from failure to failure without losing enthusiasm."

— Winston Churchill —
British politician

용기란 열정을 잃지 않고 실패에서 실패로 가는 것이다.

LESSON

Greek and Latin Roots & Prefixes 50

★ MICRO = little, short, small

spek (to observe)	microscope	현미경
	microscopic	미세한, 현미경으로 봐야만 보이는
bios (life)	microbe	미생물
	microbiology	미생물학
weigh (to go)	microwave	전자렌지
kosmos (world)	microcosm	소우주
phone (sound)	microphone	마이크
metron (to measure)	micrometer	마이크로미터, 100만분의 1미터
finis (to end)	microfinance	소액금융

DAY

50

WORDS TO LEARN

☐ advent	☐ elapse	☐ intriguing	☐ renounce
☐ antithesis	☐ erode	☐ jovial	☐ rigorous
☐ battalion	☐ extraneous	☐ karma	☐ sentiment
☐ buoyant	☐ fledgling	☐ malady	☐ solicitous
☐ coalesce	☐ garland	☐ mill	☐ stout
☐ cohort	☐ guile	☐ nauseous	☐ syndicate
☐ defamation	☐ hostility	☐ onerous	☐ traverse
☐ discriminating	☐ implicate	☐ porous	☐ usurp
☐ disgruntled	☐ industrious	☐ pry	☐ wax

01

advent
[ad-vent]

n. arrival that has been awaited
출현, 도래
The **advent** of drones opened a whole new era for photography.[1]

syn. arrival, coming, onset

02

antithesis
[an-tith-*uh*-sis]

n. opposition or contrast
대비, 대조, 정반대
Love is the **antithesis** of the desire to control that other's life.[2]

syn. opposite, contrast, opposition

03

battalion
[b*uh*-tal-y*uh*n]

n. a large number of persons or things
두 개 중대 이상으로 편성된 대대, 큰 부대
There are several **battalions** in the army.[3]

syn. army, squadron, legion

예문 해석

01 드론의 등장은 사진술의 완전히 새로운 시대를 열었다. **02** 사랑은 다른 사람의 삶을 통제하고 싶어하는 욕구의 반대이다.
03 군대에는 몇 개의 대대가 있다.

04 ·

buoyant
[boi-*uh*nt]

adj. not easily depressed
자신감에 차 있는, 활발한
Her **buoyant** friend is always fun to be around, laughs a lot, smiles, and cheers other people up.[4]

syn. perky, cheerful, chirpy

05 ·

coalesce
[koh-*uh*-les]

v. to mix together different elements
합동하다, 하나로 섞다
Several different cultures **coalesced**.[5]

syn. unite, combine, fuse, merge

06 ·

cohort
[koh-hawrt]

n. a group of persons sharing a particular statistical or demographic characteristic
(통계적으로 동일한 특색이나 행동 양식을 공유하는) 집단
Baby boomers are the demographic **cohort** following the Silent Generation and preceding Generation X.[6]

syn. company, band, group

07 ·

defamation
[def-*uh*-mey-sh*uh*n]

n. an abusive attack on a person's character or good name
명예 훼손, 중상모략
The newspaper was sued for **defamation** after publishing unfounded gossips about a celebrity.[7]

syn. libel, slander, calumny

08 ·

discriminating
[dih-skrim-*uh*-ney-ting]

adj. showing careful judgement and discernment
안목 있는, 분별할 수 있는
She is a **discriminating** wine connoisseur who can distinguish between good wines and incredible great vintages.[8]

syn. astute, discerning, critical

예문 해석

04 그녀의 활발한 친구는 함께 있으면 항상 즐겁고, 많이 웃고, 다른 사람들을 격려한다.　**05** 몇몇의 다른 문화가 융합되었다.
06 베이비붐 세대는 침묵 세대와 X세대 사이의 인구 통계학적 집단이다.　**07** 그 신문은 연예인에 대한 근거 없는 험담을 게재했다가 명예훼손으로 고소당했다.　**08** 그녀는 좋은 와인과 믿을 수 없을 정도로 훌륭한 와인을 구별할 수 있는 분별력 있는 와인 전문가이다.

disgruntled
[dis-gr*uh*n-tld]

adj. displeased and discontented
불만스러워 하는, 언짢은
He was **disgruntled** when his boss stole all his best ideas without giving him a raise.[9]

syn. discontented, sulky, peevish

elapse
[i-laps]

v. to pass by
시간이 경과하다, 지나가다
Twenty-four hours have **elapsed** since his arrest.[10]

syn. pass by, slip away, go by

erode
[i-rohd]

v. to destroy by slow consumption
침식시키다, 서서히 가치를 떨어뜨리다
Inflation **erodes** the value of money.[11]

syn. wear away, wear down, corrode

extraneous
[ik-strey-nee-*uh*s]

adj. not relevant or essential
관계없는, 외부의
Extraneous remarks should be avoided while the professor is instructing the class.[12]

syn. irrelevant, unrelated, external

fledgling
[flej-ling]

n. an inexperienced person baby bird
풋내기, 깃털이 갓난 새
In Hawaii, I saw an injured **fledgling** on the ground after falling out of its nest, so I nursed it back to health.[13]

syn. novice, beginner, neophyte

garland
[gahr-l*uh*nd]

n. a wreath of flowers or leaves
화관, 화환
During Christmas time, **garlands** can be seen hanging off of every corner of the house.[14]

syn. wreath, swag, festoon

예문 해석

09 그는 상사가 월급도 올려 주지 않고 좋은 아이디어를 모두 가져가버리자 화가 났다.　**10** 그가 체포된 뒤 24시간이 흘렀다.
11 인플레이션은 돈의 가치를 천천히 떨어뜨린다.　**12** 교수님이 강의하는 동안에는 도를 넘는 발언은 피해야 한다.　**13** 나는 하와이에서 둥지에서 떨어져 땅바닥에 있던 아기새를 보고, 건강을 되찾을 수 있도록 간호했다.　**14** 크리스마스 기간 동안 화환이 집 여기저기 매달려 있는 것을 볼 수 있다.

15

guile
[gahyl]

n. the ability to deceive or trick

교활, 음흉함, 엉큼함

She was trusted among all because of her lack of **guile**.[15]

syn. duplicity, cunning, deceit

16

hostility
[ho-stil-i-tee]

n. unfriendly aggressive behavior

적대감, 적의

There has been a serious rise in the levels of racism and **hostility** among different ethnic groups.[16]

syn. enmity, antagonism, animosity

17

implicate
[im-pli-keyt]

v. to connect or involve in something

관련시키다, 연루시키다

Prosecutors alleged that he was **implicated** in the crime.[17]

syn. involve, imply, associate

18

industrious
[in-*duhs*-tree-*uhs*]

adj. working energetically and devotedly

열심히 일하는, 근면한

She was an **industrious** worker.[18]

syn. assiduous, studious, conscientious

19

intriguing
[in-tri-ging]

adj. capable of arousing interest or curiosity

흥미로운, 관심을 끄는

The astronomer found the night sky **intriguing** and enjoyed pondering the infinity of the universe at an early age.[19]

syn. interesting, captivating, fascinating

20

jovial
[joh-vee-*uhl*]

adj. very cheerful and friendly

명랑한, 즐거운, 유쾌한

He appeared to be in a **jovial** mood.[20]

syn. convivial, cheerful, jolly

예문 해석

15 그녀는 남을 속이는 일이 없어 모두에게 신임을 받았다. **16** 민족들 간의 인종차별과 적대감이 심각한 수위로 상승했다. **17** 검찰은 그가 범죄에 연루되었다고 주장했다. **18** 그녀는 열심히 일하는 직원이다. **19** 그 천문학자는 밤하늘이 흥미롭다는 것을 발견했고 어린 나이에 우주의 무한함에 대해 생각하는 것을 즐겼다. **20** 그는 기분이 좋아보였다.

21 ··

karma
[kahr-m*uh*]

n. the effects of a person's actions that determine one's destiny either in this life or in a reincarnation
카르마, 업보
My aunt always told me a phrase about **karma**. She said, "you reap what you sow." [21]

> *syn.* fate, destiny

22 ··

malady
[mal-*uh*-dee]

n. impairment of normal physiological function
병, 질병
The king offered a reward to anybody who could heal his daughter, who suffered from a strange **malady**.[22]

> *syn.* illness, ailment, disease, disorder

23 ··

mill
[mil]

n. a factory used for making and processing materials such as steel, wool, or cotton
제분기, 분쇄기, 방앗간
The class took a field trip to a cotton **mill** to understand the process better.[23]

> *syn.* grinder, crusher, quern

24 ··

nauseous
[naw-sh*uh*s]

adj. causing nausea or sickening
속이 메스꺼운, 구역질나게 하는
She felt **nauseous**.[24]

> *syn.* queasy, revolting, disgusting

25 ··

onerous
[on-er-*uh*s]

adj. burdensome, oppressive, or troublesome
아주 힘든, 부담되는
The king's duties seemed much more **onerous**.[25]

> *syn.* toilsome, laborious, tough

 예문 해석

21 숙모는 항상 나에게 업보에 대한 말을 해주셨다. 그녀는 "뿌린 대로 거둔다"라고 말하셨다. **22** 왕은 희귀한 질병으로 고통받는 딸을 치료해 주는 사람에게 큰 상을 내리기로 했다. **23** 학생들은 그 과정을 더 잘 이해하기 위해 목화 공장으로 현장 답사를 갔다. **24** 그녀는 토할 것 같았다. **25** 왕의 의무는 훨씬 힘들어 보였다.

porous
[pawr-*uhs*]

adj. allowing passage in and out
구멍이 많은, 다공성의, 투과가 가능한
The interior designer chose a **porous** floor to complete a more natural design.[26]

syn. permeable, absorbent, penetrable

pry
[prahy]

v. to inquire impertinently or unnecessarily into something
캐묻다, 엿보다
He might think she was **prying**.[27]

syn. peep, peer, nose

renounce
[ri-nouns]

v. to give up formally and publicly
공식적으로 포기하다, 공개적으로 부인하다
He **renounced** the title.[28]

syn. repudiate, relinquish, abandon

rigorous
[rig-er-*uhs*]

adj. severely exact or accurate
엄격한, 혹독한
Only three of them have met the **rigorous** standards of membership.[29]

syn. severe, harsh, precise

sentiment
[sen-t*uh*-m*uh*nt]

n. an attitude or opinion
감정, 의견
The public **sentiment** judges the officials.[30]

syn. emotion, belief, feeling

solicitous
[s*uh*-lis-i-t*uh*s]

adj. anxious or concerned
걱정하는, 염려하는
The **solicitous** cards and notes she received while in the hospital buoyed her spirits.[31]

syn. mindful, regardful, attentive

예문 해석

26 인테리어 디자이너는 좀 더 자연스러운 디자인으로 완성하기 위해 다공질 바닥을 선택했다. **27** 그는 그녀가 캐묻는다고 생각했을 수도 있다. **28** 그는 그 타이틀을 공개적으로 버렸다. **29** 그들 중 세 명 만이 엄격한 맴버십 기준을 통과했다. **30** 국민 정서가 공직자를 심판한다. **31** 병원에 있는 동안 받은 염려의 카드와 메시지들로 그녀는 기분이 좋아졌다.

stout
[stout]

adj. rather fat and strong
뚱뚱한, 풍채가 당당한, 튼튼한
He was a tall, **stout** man with brown hair.[32]

syn. overweight, robust, brawny

syndicate
[sin-di-kit]

n. a group of people or companies who work together in order to achieve a particular aim
신디케이트, 조직, 연합
There was a violent **syndicate** located in the city.[33]

syn. association, cabinet

traverse
[trav-ers]

v. to go across or through something
가로지르다, 건너다, 방해하다
I **traversed** the narrow pedestrian bridge.[34]

syn. pass over, cross, travel across

usurp
[yoo-surp]

v. to take possession of power or authority by force, without right or unjustly
왕위를 찬탈하다, 정당하지 않은 방법으로 빼앗다
Richard publicly declared his claim to the throne, and on June 26 he **usurped** it.[35]

syn. take over, appropriate, seize

wax
[waks]

v. to increase in size, strength or power
커지다, 늘어나다
The moon **waxed**.[36]

syn. expand, increase, enlarge

🧘 예문 해석

32 그는 갈색머리를 한 키가 크고 풍채가 좋은 사람이었다.   **33** 그 도시에 폭력 조직이 있었다.   **34** 나는 좁은 보행자용 다리를 가로질러 갔다.   **35** 리처드는 왕권을 공식적으로 주장했고, 6월 26일 그는 왕위를 찬탈했다.   **36** 달이 차올랐다.

Directions   Each of the following questions consists of one word followed by five words or phrases. You are to select the one word or phrase whose meaning is closest to the word in capital letters.

1. **ANTITHESIS :**
   (A) justice
   (B) betrayer
   (C) opposite
   (D) faculty
   (E) mystery

2. **BUOYANT :**
   (A) feeble
   (B) nosy
   (C) exact
   (D) cheerful
   (E) formal

3. **COHORT :**
   (A) wrath
   (B) foreboding
   (C) frontier
   (D) company
   (E) clamor

4. **DEFAMATION :**
   (A) unfairness
   (B) mob
   (C) libel
   (D) progeny
   (E) dungeon

5. **FLEDGLING :**
   (A) impasse
   (B) novice
   (C) avalanche
   (D) leeway
   (E) blizzard

6. **GUILE :**
   (A) prose
   (B) duplicity
   (C) inundation
   (D) treachery
   (E) eddy

7. **POROUS :**
   (A) dismal
   (B) permeable
   (C) experienced
   (D) mute
   (E) corpulent

8. **PRY :**
   (A) enrage
   (B) divert
   (C) peep
   (D) topple
   (E) disentangle

9. **RIGOROUS :**
   (A) mysterious
   (B) stringent
   (C) indomitable
   (D) plentiful
   (E) puzzling

10. **STOUT :**
   (A) deadly
   (B) overweight
   (C) learned
   (D) inviolable
   (E) deceptive

"Life's tragedy is that we get old too soon and wise too late."

— Benjamin Franklin —
U.S. author, diplomat, inventor, physicist, politician, & printer

인생의 비극은 우리가 너무 빨리 늙고 너무 늦게 지혜로워진다는 것이다.

Greek and Latin Roots & Prefixes 51

★ MACRO = large, great

spek (to observe)	macroscopic	육안으로 보이는, 거시적인
bios (life)	macrobiotic	자연식의, 건강식의
oikonomia (household management)	macroeconomics	거시경제학
mania (madness, frenzy)	macromania	과대망상광
kosmos (world)	macrocosm	대우주

★ MEGA = big, great

ton (measure of weight)	megaton	메가톤 (TNT 100만톤 상당)
phone (sound)	megaphone	메가폰, 확성기
mania (madness, frenzy)	megalomania	과대망상증

DAY

51

WORDS TO LEARN

☐ anecdote	☐ elastic	☐ intent	☐ pugnacious
☐ apathetic	☐ erratic	☐ jubilant	☐ relate
☐ batter	☐ extravagant	☐ laconic	☐ sanguine
☐ bulwark	☐ fleet	☐ malfunction	☐ sentinel
☐ coarse	☐ garment	☐ mendacious	☐ straightforward
☐ consummate	☐ gullible	☐ nautical	☐ synopsis
☐ decant	☐ hone	☐ onslaught	☐ treacherous
☐ detest	☐ implication	☐ pecuniary	☐ utilize
☐ disrespectful	☐ ineffable	☐ primitive	☐ wilt

---

01 ....

anecdote
[an-ik-doht]

n. short account of an incident
일화, 재미있는 이야기
This figure has many secret and private **anecdotes** that are not fit for print and are unreliable.[1]

syn. episode, short story, tale

---

02 ....

apathetic
[ap-*uh*-thet-ik]

adj. feeling or showing little or no emotion
무감각한, 냉담한
Even the most **apathetic** students are beginning to sit up and listen.[2]

syn. nonchalant, aloof, indifferent

---

03 ....

batter
[bat-er]

v. to strike or hit something or someone hard and often, or continuously
난타하다, 강타하다
The angry mob **battered** the thief with sticks and stones.[3]

syn. hit, strike, beat

예문 해석

01 이 인물은 인쇄하기에 적합하지 않고 신뢰할 수 없는 비밀스럽고 사적인 일화가 많다. **02** 가장 냉담한 학생들조차 자리에 앉아 귀를 기울이기 시작했다. **03** 화난 군중들은 도둑을 막대기와 돌맹이로 때렸다.

04

bulwark
[bool-werk]

n. a wall built as a defense

요새

They built a new **bulwark** for the upcoming attack.[4]

syn. bastion, stronghold, fortress

05

coarse
[kawrs]

adj. lacking in fineness or delicacy

거친, 상스러운

The beach had rough, **coarse** sand.[5]

syn. rough, crude, vulgar

06

consummate
[k*uh*n-s*uh*m-it]

adj. complete or perfect

완벽의, 최고의

He was a **consummate** master of the violin.[6]

syn. flawless, impeccable, superb

07

decant
[dih-kant]

v. to pour a liquid from one container to another

따르다, 붓다

Decant oil and store in a cool dark place.[7]

syn. pour out, pour off, drain

08

detest
[di-test]

v. to dislike intensely

싫어하다, 혐오하다

She **detested** his rudeness.[8]

syn. loathe, abominate, abhor

09

disrespectful
[dis-ri-spekt-f*uh*l]

adj. lacking courtesy or esteem

무례한, 실례되는

The student made a **disrespectful** remark to the teacher, so he was sent to the principal's office.[9]

syn. impolite, discourteous, impertinent

예문 해석

04 그들은 곧 있을 공격에 대비해 새로운 요새를 지었다.　**05** 그 해안은 거친 모래로 이루어져 있었다.　**06** 그는 최고의 바이올리니스트다.　**07** 오일을 따라내고, 어둡고 서늘한 곳에 보관하세요.　**08** 그녀는 그의 무례함을 혐오했다.　**09** 그 학생은 선생님께 무례한 말을 해서 교장실로 보내졌다.

elastic
[ih-las-tik]

adj. capable of returning to its original length or shape after being stretched

탄력 있는, 탄성 있는

By carefully stretching the **elastic** band between his thumb and index finger, he could easily hit the target.[10]

syn. resilient, stretchy, pliant

erratic
[ih-rat-ik]

adj. deviating from the usual or proper course in conduct or opinion

산만한, 변덕스러운, 엉뚱한

The jet was taking an **erratic** flight path.[11]

syn. irregular, eccentric, unpredictable

extravagant
[ik-strav-*uh*-g*uh*nt]

adj. spending much more than necessary

낭비하는, 사치스러운

Her **extravagant** spending has to stop.[12]

syn. lavish, prodigal, profuse

fleet
[fleet]

n. the largest organized unit of naval ships

함대

Magellan's **fleet** set sail for Brazil on a southwest course.[13]

syn. armada, flotilla

garment
[gahr-m*uh*nt]

n. any article of clothing

의류

Dresses, suits, and other **garments** are sold at this department store.[14]

syn. attire, costume, apparel

 예문 해석

10 고무줄을 엄지와 검지 손가락 사이에 조심스럽게 걸고 그는 목표물을 쉽게 맞출 수 있었다. **11** 그 제트기는 이상한 비행 코스로 이동하고 있었다. **12** 그녀의 과소비는 멈춰져야 한다. **13** 마젤란의 함대는 남서쪽 항로로 브라질을 향했다. **14** 이 백화점에서는 드레스, 정장, 기타 의류를 판매한다.

15 ....

gullible
[guhl-uh-buhl]

adj. easily deceived
잘 속는, 사람을 쉽게 믿는
Gullible tourists are easily tricked into buying counterfeit goods.[15]

syn. naive, credulous, trusting

16 ....

hone
[hohn]

v. to sharpen skills
연마하다, 날카롭게 하다
He is **honing** his skills as a hockey coach by working in the regional community league.[16]

syn. sharpen, whet, grind

17 ....

implication
[im-pli-key-shuhn]

n. the state of being implied
함축, 내포, 암시
Their reluctance has profound **implications**.[17]

syn. suggestion, hint, inkling

18 ....

ineffable
[in-ef-uh-buhl]

adj. incapable of being described in words
말로 표현할 수가 없는
She felt **ineffable** joy at the sight of her children.[18]

syn. inexpressible, unutterable, indescribable

19 ....

intent
[in-tent]

adj. determined and resolved
몰두하는, 전념하는
He was so **intent** on doing his work that he didn't notice the time.[19]

syn. determined, resolute, decided

20 ....

jubilant
[joo-buh-luhnt]

adj. extremely happy because of success
승리에 기뻐하는
We were **jubilant** over our victory.[20]

syn. triumphant, overjoyed, exultant

예문 해석

15 잘 속는 관광객들은 복제품을 쉽게 속아 산다. **16** 그는 지역 사회 리그에서 일하며 하키 코치로서의 기량을 연마하고 있다. **17** 그들이 꺼리는 것은 시사하는 바가 크다. **18** 그녀의 아이들을 보고 그녀는 말로 표현할 수 없는 기쁨을 느꼈다. **19** 그는 일에 몰두하느라 시간 가는 줄 몰랐다. **20** 우리는 승리에 환호했다.

laconic
[lu*h*-kon-ik]

adj. brief and to the point
말을 많이 하지 않는, 할 말만 하는
The valedictorian delivered a **laconic** speech, contrary to the salutatorian's lengthy speech.[21]

syn. concise, pithy, terse

malfunction
[mal-f*uh*ngk-sh*uh*n]

n. failure to function properly
오작동, 고장
There was a **malfunction** in the satellite causing an upheaval of confusion.[22]

syn. breakdown, failure, disorder

mendacious
[men-dey-sh*uh*s]

adj. telling lies habitually
거짓인, 진실을 말하지 않는
He always gives me **mendacious** excuses when he is late.[23]

syn. untruthful, dishonest, deceitful

nautical
[naw-ti-k*uh*l]

adj. relating to ships or navigation
선박의, 바다의, 해상의
He sailed hundreds of **nautical** miles with no chart.[24]

syn. maritime, seafaring, marine

onslaught
[on-slawt]

n. an onset, assault, or attack
맹습, 맹공격
The rebels resisted an **onslaught** from the military.[25]

syn. attack, assault, ambush

pecuniary
[pi-kyoo-nee-er-ee]

adj. relating to, concerning or consisting of money
재정상의, 돈의
Gaining **pecuniary** advantage was at the forefront of his mind.[26]

syn. financial, fiscal, monetary

 예문 해석

21 내빈 환영사를 하는 차석 대표의 긴 연설에 비해 졸업생 수석 대표의 고별사는 짧고 간결했다. **22** 위성에 고장이 나서 혼란이 있었다. **23** 그는 지각하면 항상 나에게 거짓 변명을 늘어놓는다. **24** 그는 차트 없이 수백 해리를 항해했다. **25** 반란군들은 군대의 맹공격에 저항했다. **26** 금전적 이익을 얻는 것이 그의 머릿속 가장 중요한 것이었다.

primitive
[prim-i-tiv]

adj. belonging to an early stage of technical development
원시 사회의, 원시적인
The museum displayed **primitive** tools used by the Aztecs.[27]

syn. ancient, original, primordial

28

pugnacious
[puhg-ney-shuhs]

adj. having a strong desire to argue or fight with other people
싸움하기 좋아하는, 호전적인
Korean players are known for a wild, **pugnacious** style of play.[28]

syn. belligerent, bellicose, combative

29

relate
[ri-leyt]

v. to give an account of
~에 대하여 이야기 하다, 이야기를 들려주다
She **related** the details of her trip to Norway.[29]

syn. tell, describe, impart

30

sanguine
[sang-gwin]

adj. cheerfully optimistic
자신감이 넘치는, 낙관적인
She was **sanguine** about her miserable situation, which meant that she thought everything would work out fine.[30]

syn. optimistic, confident, ruddy

31

sentinel
[sen-tn-l]

n. someone posted on guard
보초, 파수꾼
He was standing **sentinel**.[31]

syn. sentry, guard, lookout

예문 해석

27 그 박물관은 아즈텍인들이 사용했던 원시적인 도구들을 전시했다.　**28** 한국 선수들은 거칠고 호전적인 플레이로 유명하다. **29** 그녀는 노르웨이 여행의 세부 사항을 이야기했다.　**30** 그녀는 자신의 비참한 상황에 대해 낙관적이었고, 그것은 모든 것이 잘 될 것이라고 생각했다는 것을 의미했다.　**31** 그는 보초를 서는 중이었다.

straightforward
[streyt-fawr-werd]

adj. direct, not roundabout
똑바른, 솔직한, 직설적인
She prefers a **straightforward** approach to problems.[32]

> *syn.* outspoken, frank, candid

synopsis
[si-nop-sis]

n. a condensed outline
줄거리, 대의, 강령
I don't need to know every detail; just give me a **synopsis** of the movie.[33]

> *syn.* abstract, summary, compendium

treacherous
[trech-er-*uhs*]

adj. likely to betray and cannot be trusted
배반할 것 같은, 믿을 수 없는
He committed a **treacherous** deed that caused others to rebel against him.[34]

> *syn.* unfaithful, disloyal, deceitful

utilize
[yoot-l-ahyz]

v. to make use of
사용하다
Minerals can be absorbed and **utilized** by the body in a variety of different forms.[35]

> *syn.* use, make use of, exploit

wilt
[wilt]

v. to become limp and drooping
(식물이) 시들다, 축 처지다
People also start to **wilt** at a certain age physically.[36]

> *syn.* shrivel, shrink, wither

📖 예문 해석

32 그녀는 문제에 직접적으로 부딪쳐 해결하는 것을 좋아한다. **33** 나는 모든 세세한 것들을 알고 싶은 것이 아니야, 영화의 줄거리만 알려줘. **34** 그는 다른 사람들이 그에게 반항하게 만드는 배신적인 행위를 저질렀다. **35** 미네랄은 몸에 흡수되어 다양한 형태로 사용될 수 있다. **36** 사람들은 또한 특정한 나이에 육체적으로 쇠약해지기 시작합니다.

Directions   Each of the following questions consists of one word followed by five words or phrases. You are to select the one word or phrase whose meaning is closest to the word in capital letters.

1. APATHETIC :
   (A) lenient
   (B) nonchalant
   (C) enunciate
   (D) irascible
   (E) respectable

2. DECANT :
   (A) topple
   (B) stoop
   (C) illuminate
   (D) heed
   (E) pour

3. DETEST :
   (A) trick
   (B) loathe
   (C) grope
   (D) coax
   (E) mend

4. ELASTIC :
   (A) clear
   (B) resistant
   (C) mild
   (D) distinguishing
   (E) resilient

5. GULLIBLE :
   (A) ordinary
   (B) infectious
   (C) supple
   (D) pious
   (E) naïve

6. IMPLICATION :
   (A) farce
   (B) sum
   (C) suggestion
   (D) knack
   (E) gourmet

7. LACONIC :
   (A) judicious
   (B) kinetic
   (C) terse
   (D) flimsy
   (E) ingenious

8. NAUTICAL :
   (A) obvious
   (B) provisional
   (C) timely
   (D) postmortem
   (E) maritime

9. ONSLAUGHT :
   (A) onset
   (B) pariah
   (C) ramble
   (D) crevice
   (E) insomnia

10. RELATE :
   (A) mar
   (B) soil
   (C) stimulate
   (D) tell
   (E) sell

"We must learn to live together as brothers or perish together as fools."

– Martin Luther King Jr. –
U.S. civil rights leader & clergyman

우리 모두 형제로서 더불어 사는 것을 배워야 한다. 아니면 우리 모두가 바보로서 함께 멸망할 것이다.

Greek and Latin Roots & Prefixes 52

★ PAN = all

doron (gift)	pandora	판도라 (모든 선물을 받은 사람)
demos (people)	pandemic	전세계 유행병
horama (sight)	panorama	전경, 파노라마
akos (cure)	panacea	만병통치약
the (god)	pantheon	(모든 신들을 위한) 만신전, 판테온
	pantheism	다신교, 범신론
mimos (imitator)	pantomime	무언극
daemonium (evil spirit)	pandemonium	대혼란

DAY

52

WORDS TO LEARN

☐ advocate	☐ elated	☐ judicial	☐ refined
☐ appease	☐ erroneous	☐ lethal	☐ refute
☐ bear	☐ extricate	☐ malice	☐ sequel
☐ bungle	☐ fleeting	☐ mingle	☐ solitude
☐ coin	☐ garnish	☐ nebulous	☐ strain
☐ contagious	☐ haggard	☐ ooze	☐ tacit
☐ deception	☐ hovel	☐ pedantic	☐ tread
☐ detour	☐ implicit	☐ prattle	☐ vacillate
☐ disrupt	☐ injection	☐ pulverize	☐ wispy

---

01 ···

advocate
[ad-*vuh*-keyt]

v. to speak or write in favor of
옹호하다, 지지하다
He **advocated** higher salaries for doctors.[1]

syn. champion, support, recommend

02 ···

appease
[*uh*-peez]

v. to satisfy or relieve
진정시키다, 고통을 줄여주다
The queen tried to **appease** her angry king.[2]

syn. ease, pacify, soothe

03 ···

bear
[bair]

v. to carry or to have within
나르다, 가지고 다니다, (무기, 표정, 흔적 등을) 몸에 지니다
They thought every citizen had a right to **bear** arms in
defense of himself and the state.[3]

syn. have, carry, bring

예문 해석

01 그는 의사들이 높은 급여를 받는 것을 지지했다. **02** 여왕은 화난 왕을 진정시키려 애썼다. **03** 그들은 모든 시민은 자신과
주를 방어하기 위해 무기를 가지고 다닐 권리가 있다고 생각했다.

04

bungle
[b*uh*ng-g*uh*l]

v. to do something carelessly or badly
망치다, 실수하다
The prisoners **bungled** the escape.[4]

syn. mess up, blow, ruin

05

coin
[koin]

v. to make up a new way to say something
말을 만들다, 새로운 낱말 어구를 만들다
William Shakespeare **coined** over one thousand words and phrases into the English language.[5]

syn. create, invent, contrive

06

contagious
[k*uh*n-tey-j*uh*s]

adj. infectious
전염되는, 전염성의
Laughter is **contagious**.[6]

syn. infectious, catching, communicable

07

deception
[di-sep-sh*uh*n]

n. an act of deceiving or the state of being deceived
속임, 사기
"War is based on deception." - Sun–Tzu [7]

syn. trickery, fraud, deceit

08

detour
[di-toor]

n. a roundabout road
우회로, 둘러 가는 길
Because of the road work, the road constructors set a sign directing drivers to take a **detour**.[8]

syn. indirect course, roundabout, deviation

🧘 예문 해석

04 죄수들은 탈출에 실패했다. **05** 윌리엄 셰익스피어는 천 개가 넘는 단어와 구절을 영어로 만들었다. **06** 웃음은 전염된다.
07 전쟁은 속임수를 기반으로 한다. **08** 도로 공사 때문에 도로 공사자들은 운전자들이 우회할 수 있도록 안내 표지판을 설치했다.

disrupt
[dis-*ruh*pt]

v. to throw into disorder
붕괴시키다, (통신, 전기를) 두절시키다
Our electricity was **disrupted** for hours.[9]

syn. break, interrupt, stop

elated
[i-ley-tid]

adj. very happy or proud
마냥 행복해하는, 신이 난
She became an **elated** winner at the science fair contest.[10]

syn. jubilant, triumphant

erroneous
[*uh*-roh-nee-*uh*s]

adj. containing or characterized by error
잘못된, 틀린
Her **erroneous** assumptions resulted in poor outcomes.[11]

syn. inaccurate, untrue, false

extricate
[ek-stri-keyt]

v. to free someone or something from difficulties
위험이나 곤란에서 구해내다, 탈출시키다
He **extricated** her from a dangerous situation.[12]

syn. disentangle, extract, free

fleeting
[flee-ting]

adj. passing swiftly
(시간이) 휘리릭 지나가는, 한순간의, 덧없는
Life is **fleeting**.[13]

syn. vanishing, transient, ephemeral

garnish
[gahr-nish]

v. to decorate especially for foods
장식하다, 요리를 장식하다
They **garnish** fish with green vegetables.[14]

syn. adorn, embellish, decorate

예문 해석

09 우리 집 전기가 몇 시간 동안 끊겼었다.　**10** 그녀는 과학 박람회 대회에서 행복한 우승자가 되었다.　**11** 그녀의 잘못된 추측은 좋지 않은 결과를 낳았다.　**12** 그는 그녀를 위험에서 구해 주었다.　**13** 인생은 눈 깜짝할 사이 지나간다.　**14** 그들은 생선 요리에 야채를 곁들였다.

haggard
[hag-erd]

adj. having a gaunt, wasted or exhausted appearance
초췌한
He looked **haggard** after a long, harrowing ordeal of getting lost in the woods for days.[15]

syn. drawn, worn, weakened

hovel
[huhv-uhl]

n. a small hut
오두막
They lived in a squalid **hovel** for two years.[16]

syn. hut, shack, shed

implicit
[im-plis-it]

adj. implied, rather than expressly stated
암묵적인, 함축적인
I regretted having an **implicit** agreement rather than a written contract.[17]

syn. implied, inferred, understood

injection
[in-jek-shuhn]

n. a shot or a dose of medicine given by way of a syringe and a needle
주사, (액체의) 주입
The medical **injection** forces a small amount of a drug under the skin by a syringe.[18]

syn. dose, needle, inoculation

judicial
[joo-dish-uhl]

adj. of or pertaining to a judge
사법의, 재판의, 판사의
The U.S. **judicial** system is critical in assuring the balance of power within the Federal Government.[19]

syn. juridical, legal, judiciary

예문 해석

15 그는 며칠 동안 숲에서 길을 잃고 처참한 시련을 겪은 후 초췌해 보였다. **16** 그들은 더러운 오두막에서 2년간 살았다. **17** 나는 서면 계약서보다 암묵적인 합의를 한 것을 후회했다. **18** 그 의료 주사는 주사기로 피부 밑에 소량의 약물을 강제로 넣는 것이다. **19** 미국 사법 시스템은 연방 정부 내에서 힘의 균형을 보장하는 데 매우 중요하다.

20

lethal
[lee-th*uh*l]

adj. causing death
치명적인, 죽일 수도 있는
The robber at the gas station had a **lethal** tone as he demanded money.[20]

> *syn.* deadly, fatal, mortal

21

malice
[mal-is]

n. the desire or intention to harm or hurt another or others
악의, 앙심, 원한
I don't bear any **malice** towards you.[21]

> *syn.* hatred, spite, malevolence

22

mingle
[ming-g*uh*l]

v. to become or make something become blended or mixed
섞다, 섞이다
He **mingled** throughout the crowd at the party.[22]

> *syn.* mix, blend, come together

23

nebulous
[neb-y*uh*-lu*h*s]

adj. lacking distinct shape
흐린, 불투명한, 모호한
Nebulous concepts are difficult to understand.[23]

> *syn.* hazy, obscure, vague

24

ooze
[ooz]

v. to overflow with a quality or feeling
새어 나오다, 흘러 나오다
Blood is **oozing** from the cut on my finger.[24]

> *syn.* leak, exude, seep

25

pedantic
[p*uh*-dan-tik]

adj. ostentatious in one's learning
아는 체 하는, 학자인 체 하는
Perhaps I'm being somewhat **pedantic**, but that makes a difference to me.[25]

> *syn.* bookish, precise

예문 해석

20 주유소의 강도는 돈을 요구하면서 위협적인 어조로 말했다. **21** 당신에게 아무런 원한이 없다. **22** 그는 파티에서 사람들과 섞였다. **23** 모호한 개념들은 이해하기 어렵다. **24** 손가락이 베인 곳에서 피가 배어 나왔다. **25** 내가 아는 체 하는 것일지는 몰라도 그것은 내게는 엄연히 다르다.

26

prattle
[prat-l]

v. to chatter or utter childishly or foolishly
(쓸데없이 마구) 지껄이다, 쓸데없는 말을 하다
The teacher is used to hearing the loud **prattle** of children
in the lunch hall.[26]

syn. babble, jabber, chatter

27

pulverize
[p*uh*l-v*uh*-rahyz]

v. to crush or crumble to dust or powder
가루로 만들다, 부수다
They **pulverized** their enemy.[27]

syn. shatter, smash, destroy

28

refined
[ri-fahynd]

adj. having well-bred taste
교양 있는, 세련된, 품위 있는
He had a **refined** taste in art, knowing how to judge what is
good and why.[28]

syn. cultured, genteel, cultivated

29

refute
[ri-fyoot]

v. to prove to be false or erroneous
논박하다, 반박하다
When the suspect swore he wasn't there at the crime scene,
the detective **refuted** his claim by presenting the security
camera picture of him.[29]

syn. rebut, discredit, counter

30

sequel
[see-kw*uh*l]

n. anything that follows on from a previous event
속편, 후편
She is currently writing a **sequel** to her best-selling novel.[30]

syn. follow-up, continuation

31

solitude
[sol-i-tood]

n. the state of being alone or secluded
고독, 홀로됨
He enjoyed his moments of **solitude**.[31]

syn. loneliness, isolation

예문 해석

26 선생님은 식당 홀에서 아이들이 떠드는 시끄러운 소리를 듣는 데 익숙하다.   **27** 그들은 적들을 격파했다.   **28** 그는 무엇이 좋고 왜 좋은지 판단하는 법을 아는 세련된 예술 취향을 가지고 있었다.   **29** 용의자가 범행 현장에 없었다고 단언하자 형사는 CCTV 사진을 제시하며 그의 주장을 반박했다.   **30** 그녀는 현재 베스트셀러 소설의 속편을 쓰고 있다.   **31** 그는 고독한 순간을 즐겼다.

strain
[str-eyn]

v. to try to make something do more than it is able to do
한계에 이르게 하다, 무리를 주다
Their complaints were **straining** my patience.[32]

> *syn.* stretch, tense, extend

tacit
[tas-it]

adj. understood but not actually stated
무언의, 암묵적인
He had the **tacit** approval of his father.[33]

> *syn.* silent, unspoken, implied

tread
[tred]

v. to set down the foot or feet in walking
밟다, 걷다
The yellow flag with a snake that states, "Don't **tread** on me," is from the American Revolutionary War time symbolizing freedom from tyranny.[34]

> *syn.* step, walk

vacillate
[vas-*uh*-leyt]

v. to change opinions or decisions frequently
결정을 자꾸 바꾸다, 주저하다, 망설이다
She **vacillates** between two men.[35]

> *syn.* waver, oscillate, hesitate

wispy
[wispee]

adj. used to describe something physically or an idea that is not substantial
(촘촘하지 못하고) 몇 가닥으로 된, 어설픈
His **wispy** explanation didn't help his teacher understand his reasons. [36]

> *syn.* flimsy, thin, vague

 예문 해석

32 그들의 불만들은 내 인내심에 한계를 가져왔다. **33** 그는 아버지의 암묵적인 승인을 받았다. **34** 나를 밟지 말라고 적힌 뱀이 그려진 노란 깃발은 자유를 상징하는 미국 독립전쟁 시대의 것이다. **35** 그녀는 두 명의 남자 사이에서 망설이고 있었다. **36** 그의 어설픈 설명은 선생님이 그의 이유를 이해하는 데 도움이 되지 않았다.

Directions   Each of the following questions consists of one word followed by five words or phrases. You are to select the one word or phrase whose meaning is closest to the word in capital letters.

1. ADVOCATE :
- (A) tap
- (B) blend
- (C) amalgamate
- (D) champion
- (E) implore

2. COIN :
- (A) create
- (B) anatomize
- (C) droop
- (D) obstruct
- (E) terminate

3. CONTAGIOUS :
- (A) incurable
- (B) pertinent
- (C) infectious
- (D) rowdy
- (E) dishonest

4. DETOUR :
- (A) next episode
- (B) chaotic disorder
- (C) disgraceful infamy
- (D) unforgivable sin
- (E) indirect course

5. ELATED :
- (A) laden
- (B) jubilant
- (C) threadbare
- (D) infinite
- (E) profuse

6. MALICE :
- (A) game
- (B) hatred
- (C) abstinence
- (D) onset
- (E) clamor

7. NEBULOUS :
- (A) worn
- (B) hazy
- (C) irrelevant
- (D) fruitless
- (E) pallid

8. OOZE :
- (A) vend
- (B) leak
- (C) suppress
- (D) enchant
- (E) recompense

9. PULVERIZE :
- (A) shatter
- (B) afford
- (C) repudiate
- (D) pacify
- (E) expend

10. REFINED :
- (A) offense
- (B) gullible
- (C) cultured
- (D) sluggardly
- (E) dreadful

"Content makes poor men rich; discontentment makes rich men poor."

— Benjamin Franklin —
U.S. author, diplomat, inventor, physicist, politician, & printer

만족은 가난한 사람을 부자로 만들고, 불만족은 부자를 가난하게 만든다.

Greek and Latin Roots & Prefixes 53

★ DYS = ill, bad, diseased

lexis (word)	dyslexia	난독증, 독서 장애
topos (place)	dystopia	우울한 미래상, 디스토피아
function (performance)	dysfunction	기능장애
plassein (to mold)	dysphasia	실어증
pherein (to carry)	dysphoria	불쾌감
keie (to set in motion)	dyskinesia	운동장애

DAY

53

WORDS TO LEARN

☐ aegis	☐ elicit	☐ intercept	☐ pun
☐ attenuate	☐ erudite	☐ judicious	☐ repartee
☐ bedlam	☐ exuberant	☐ lethargic	☐ roam
☐ coerce	☐ flick	☐ malicious	☐ sequence
☐ constitution	☐ garner	☐ minuscule	☐ somber
☐ contempt	☐ grudge	☐ nomenclature	☐ taciturn
☐ decimate	☐ ignorant	☐ opaque	☐ treaty
☐ detract	☐ implore	☐ pedestal	☐ venerable
☐ dissect	☐ inept	☐ preamble	☐ wheedle

01

aegis
[ee-jis]

n. protection or support

보호, 지원

Many cultural institutions were under the imperial **aegis**.[1]

syn. patronage, protection, sponsorship

02

attenuate
[*uh*-ten-yoo-wey-t]

v. to become weaker, in strength, value, or magnitude

약화시키다, 희석시키다

This tanning process tends to **attenuate** the horse hide, making it softer.[2]

syn. debilitate, weaken, vitiate

03

bedlam
[bed-l*uh*m]

n. a scene of wild uproar and confusion

대소동, 소란한 곳

The **bedlam** in the classroom perplexed the new teacher.[3]

syn. clamor, din, chaos

예문 해석

01 많은 문화 기관이 황실의 보호 아래 있었다. **02** 이 태닝 과정은 말의 가죽을 약하게 하여 부드럽게 만드는 경향이 있다. **03** 교실 안의 난리법석에 새로 온 선생님은 당황했다.

04

coerce
[koh-urs]

v. to compel by force or intimidation
강요하다, 압박하다
They **coerced** him into signing the document.[4]

syn. impel, compel, force

05

constitution
[kon-sti-too-sh*uh*n]

n. the physical makeup of a person
체질
Because he had a strong **constitution**, he didn't get sick very often.[5]

syn. health, nature, structure

06

contempt
[k*uh*n-tempt]

n. the state of being despised
경멸, 조롱
He has **contempt** for lazy people.[6]

syn. mockery, disdain, scorn

07

decimate
[des-*uh*-meyt]

v. to kill or destroy in large number
(특정 지역의 동식물이나 사람들을) 대량으로 죽이다
The oil spill of the tanker **decimated** the wildlife along the coast.[7]

syn. exterminate, annihilate, slaughter

08

detract
[di-trak]

v. to take away apart from quality
손상시키다, 떨어뜨리다
His bad manners **detract** from his good character.[8]

syn. take away, lessen, decry

예문 해석

04 그들은 그에게 문서에 서명하도록 강요했다. **05** 그는 강한 체질이었기 때문에 자주 아프지 않았다. **06** 그는 게으른 사람들을 경멸한다. **07** 유조선의 기름 유출로 해안가의 야생 동물이 대량으로 살상되었다. **08** 나쁜 매너가 좋은 이미지를 손상시킨다.

dissect
[di-sekt]

v. to examine minutely part by part
해부하다, 상세히 분석하다
The animal was **dissected** in the science lab.[9]

syn. anatomize, analyze

elicit
[i-lis-it]

v. to cause something to happen
도출하다, 유도해내다
I hoped my request would **elicit** a positive response.[10]

syn. bring about, cause, derive

erudite
[er-yoo-dahyt]

adj. showing or having a great deal of knowledge
학식 있는, 박학한
He was **erudite** and well informed.[11]

syn. learned, scholarly

exuberant
[ig-zoo-ber-*uh*nt]

adj. lavishly abundant
넘치고 충만한
New Hampshire's autumn foliage displays **exuberant** colors.[12]

syn. profuse, lush, effusive

flick
[flik]

v. to strike lightly with a whip or the finger
(채찍이나 손가락 등으로) 가볍게 치다, 털어내다, 튕기다
I **flick** dust from my coat sleeve.[13]

syn. tap, strike, hit

garner
[gahr-ner]

v. to assemble or get together
(정보나 지지를) 얻다, 모으다
We put up posters to **garner** interest in our club fundraiser.[14]

syn. earn, collect, gather

예문 해석

09 동물은 과학실에서 해부되었다. **10** 나는 내 제안이 긍정적인 결과를 낳길 바랐다. **11** 그는 학식 있고 지적이다. **12** 뉴햄프셔의 가을 단풍은 화려한 색채를 보여준다. **13** 나는 코트 소매의 먼지를 털어냈다. **14** 우리는 동아리 모금 행사에 관심을 끌기 위해 포스터를 붙였습니다.

15

grudge
[gruhj]

n. a feeling of ill will or resentment

원한, 유감

The boy is harboring a **grudge** against the bully.[15]

syn. antipathy, animosity, hard feeling

16

ignorant
[ig-ner-uhnt]

adj. lacking in knowledge

무지한, 무식한

When he made an **ignorant** comment, people laughed at him.[16]

syn. unaware, unknowing, illiterate

17

implore
[im-plawr]

v. to beg

애원하다

They **implored** forgiveness.[17]

syn. beseech, plead, entreat, solicit

18

inept
[in-ept]

adj. without skill or aptitude

실력 없는, 솜씨 없는

She is **inept** at mechanical tasks.[18]

syn. incompetent, awkward, clumsy

19

intercept
[in-ter-sept]

v. to stop or check

가로채다, 도중에서 잡다

They **intercepted** a messenger.[19]

syn. cut off, catch, interrupt

20

judicious
[joo-dish-uhs]

adj. wise and careful

분별력 있는, 현명한

It would be **judicious** to remain silent.[20]

syn. discreet, prudent, sagacious

예문 해석

15 그 소년은 그 불량배에게 원한을 품고 있다. **16** 그가 무식한 발언을 하자 사람들은 그를 비웃었다. **17** 그들은 용서를 간절히 빌었다. **18** 그녀는 기계를 다루는 일에는 솜씨가 없다. **19** 그들은 전령을 도중에서 붙잡았다. **20** 잠자코 있는 것이 현명할 것이다.

lethargic
[luh-thahr-jik]

adj. not having any energy or enthusiasm
늘어진, 무기력한
He felt **lethargic** after running a marathon.[21]

syn. sluggish, torpid, drowsy, indolent

malicious
[muh-lish-uhs]

adj. having or showing hatred and a desire to harm somebody
악의 있는, 심술궂은
That might merely have been some **malicious** gossip.[22]

syn. vicious, spiteful, malevolent

minuscule
[min-uh-skyool]

adj. extremely small
매우 작은, 소립자의
The exhibition was held for a **minuscule** amount of time.[23]

syn. minute, tiny, very small

nomenclature
[noh-muhn-kley-cher]

n. a set or system of words used to name things in a discipline
(학술적) 이름, 명명법
He had trouble understanding the **nomenclature** when adjusting to the new study field.[24]

syn. vocabulary, glossary, terminology

opaque
[oh-peyk]

adj. not allowing light to pass through or not transparent
불투명한, 빛을 통과시키지 않는
You can use **opaque** glass if you want to block a street view.[25]

syn. dim, dark, dull

예문 해석

21 그는 마라톤을 한 후 무기력함을 느꼈다.   **22** 그것은 악의적인 소문이었을지도 모른다.   **23** 그 전시회는 아주 짧게 열렸다.
24 그는 새로운 연구 분야에 적응할 때 명명법을 이해하는 데 어려움을 겪었다.   **25** 창밖의 시선을 피하고 싶다면 불투명한 유리를 사용하면 된다.

26

pedestal
[ped-*uh*-stl]

n. the base on which a statue is placed or mounted

받침대

The statue rests on a **pedestal**.[26]

syn. podium, support, foundation

27

preamble
[pree-am-b*uh*l]

n. introduction

서문, 머리말, 서론

Without any **preamble**, the principal launched into an explanation of the new project.[27]

syn. preface, foreword, prologue

28

pun
[p*uh*n]

n. a form of joke consisting of the use of a word or phrase

말장난, 동음이의어로 만든 익살

No **pun** intended![28]

syn. wordplay, quip, joke

29

repartee
[rep-er-tee]

n. a quick, witty reply

재치 있는 응답, 재치 있는 응수

He was renowned for his witty **repartee**.[29]

syn. retort, banter, answer

30

roam
[rohm]

v. to walk, go, or travel without a fixed purpose or direction

정처 없이 떠돌다, 어슬렁거리다

He **roamed** about the world.[30]

syn. meander, drift, wander

31

sequence
[see-kw*uh*ns]

n. order of succession

연속, 순열

She listened to the telephone messages in **sequence**.[31]

syn. series, order, array

예문 해석

26 그 동상은 받침대 위에 놓여 있었다.　**27** 어떤 서론도 없이 교장은 바로 새 프로젝트에 대한 설명을 시작했다.　**28** 말장난 아님!　**29** 그는 위트 있는 응수로 유명하다.　**30** 그는 전세계를 떠돌았다.　**31** 그녀는 전화 메시지를 순서대로 들었다.

32 ....

somber
[som-ber]

adj. serious or sad

우울한, 슬픈

They were in a **somber** mood.[32]

> *syn.* dismal, gloomy, bleak

33 ....

taciturn
[tas-i-turn]

adj. quiet and uncommunicative

과묵한, 말수가 적은

He was a **taciturn** man; he replied to my questions in monosyllables.[33]

> *syn.* reticent, silent, reserved

34 ....

treaty
[tree-tee]

n. a formal agreement between states or governments

협정, 조약

A **treaty** is often used to promote peace and support both signing states or governments.[34]

> *syn.* pact, contract, agreement

35 ....

venerable
[ven-er-*uh-buh*l]

adj. profoundly honored

깊이 존경받는, 덕망 있는

Saint Bede is a **venerable** scholar called the Father of English History.[35]

> *syn.* revered, respected, august

36 ....

wheedle
[hweed-l]

v. to persuade someone by flattery

감언이설로 꾀이다, 속이다

The impostor **wheedled** him out of money.[36]

> *syn.* coax, cajole, inveigle

 예문 해석

32 그들은 우울해 했다. **33** 그는 과묵한 사람이어서 내 질문에 한 음절로 대답했다. **34** 조약은 종종 평화를 촉진하고 서명국이나 정부를 지원하기 위해 사용된다. **35** 성 베다는 영국 역사의 아버지라고 불리는 깊이 존경받는 학자이다. **36** 사기꾼은 감언이설로 유혹하여 그에게 돈을 빼앗았다.

Directions   Each of the following questions consists of one word followed by five words or phrases.
You are to select the one word or phrase whose meaning is closest to the word in capital letters.

1. **AEGIS :**
   (A) caution
   (B) patronage
   (C) masquerade
   (D) emotion
   (E) meditation

2. **ATTENUATE :**
   (A) trudge
   (B) anatomize
   (C) lengthen
   (D) debilitate
   (E) whip

3. **CONSTITUTION :**
   (A) suggestion
   (B) center
   (C) domicile
   (D) health
   (E) motivation

4. **CONTEMPT :**
   (A) caliber
   (B) mockery
   (C) hike
   (D) enigma
   (E) fortress

5. **DECIMATE :**
   (A) fabricate
   (B) exterminate
   (C) hoist
   (D) awaken
   (E) perplex

6. **ELICIT :**
   (A) get in
   (B) bring about
   (C) call on
   (D) put off
   (E) let up

7. **JUDICIOUS :**
   (A) discreet
   (B) indecent
   (C) towering
   (D) affecting
   (E) lavish

8. **LETHARGIC :**
   (A) sluggish
   (B) narcissistic
   (C) smooth
   (D) prodigious
   (E) deceptive

9. **NOMENCLATURE :**
   (A) abstract
   (B) novice
   (C) vocabulary
   (D) disinformation
   (E) wickedness

10. **REPARTEE :**
    (A) odium
    (B) condition
    (C) retort
    (D) mission
    (E) episode

"Do not go where the path may lead,
go instead where there is no path and leave a trail."

— Ralph Waldo Emerson —
US essayist & poet

길이 이끄는 곳으로 가지 말고, 길이 없는 곳으로 가서 길을 만들라.

Greek and Latin Roots & Prefixes 54

★ AUTOS = self

matos (thinking)	automaton	난독증, 독서 장애
hentes (doer, being)	authentic	진본인, 진짜인
nomos (law)	autonomous	자주적인, 자치의
kratos (power)	autocrat	전제 군주, 독재자
graphein (to write)	autograph	서명, 싸인
bios (life) + graphein (to write)	autobiography	자서전
mobilis (easy to move)	automobile	자동차
ismos (action)	autism	자폐증

DAY

54

WORDS TO LEARN

☐ aesthetic	☐ effervescent	☐ jumble	☐ repel
☐ appliance	☐ elongate	☐ liable	☐ robust
☐ beguile	☐ exude	☐ malleable	☐ sequester
☐ burgeon	☐ flinch	☐ minute	☐ sonorous
☐ commute	☐ garrulous	☐ negate	☐ stratagem
☐ contemplation	☐ huddle	☐ opportune	☐ tackle
☐ decree	☐ immaterial	☐ pedestrian[1]	☐ trek
☐ detrimental	☐ inequity	☐ precarious	☐ valedictory
☐ disseminate	☐ interim	☐ pungent	☐ whet

01

aesthetic
[es-thet-ik]

adj. able to appreciate beauty
예술적인, 미의, 심미적인
"It's asking a great deal that things should appeal to your reason as well as your sense of the **aesthetic**."
- W. Somerset Maugham[1]

syn. artistic, decorative, ornamental

02

appliance
[*uh*-plahy-*uh*ns]

n. a machine designed to do things in the house
가전제품, 전자 제품, 기계
Electrical **appliances** in the house include the vacuum cleaner, the TV set, and the freezer.[2]

syn. device, instrument, gadget

03

beguile
[bih-gahyl]

v. to entertain and convince by flattery
속이다, 기만하다, 속여 빼앗다
He was **beguiled** by her beauty.[3]

syn. fool, deceive, entice

예문 해석

01 미적인 측면 뿐 아니라 이성적인 면에서도 흥미를 불러일으키기는 쉽지 않은 일이다.   **02** 가전제품에는 진공 청소기, TV, 냉장고 등이 포함된다.   **03** 그는 그녀의 미모에 현혹되었다.

04

burgeon
[bur-*juh*n]

v. to grow or flourish
급증하다, 급성장하다
Hope **burgeoned** in his heart as the charming girl walked toward him.[4]

syn. bloom, prosper, sprout

05

commute
[*kuh*-myoot]

n. a regular journey to and from one's place of work
통근
He immensely enjoyed the subway **commute** because it gave him lots of time to read.[5]

syn. travel to work, go back and forth

06

contemplation
[kon-t*uh*m-pley-sh*uh*n]

n. thoughtful observation
심사숙고, 명상
After serious **contemplation**, they decided to move to another state that would better meet the needs of their family.[6]

syn. meditation, deliberation

07

decree
[di-kree]

n. a judicial decision or order
명령
The people were hesitant to obey the Emperor's **decree**.[7]

syn. mandate, fiat, order

08

detrimental
[de-tr*uh*-men-tl]

adj. causing harm or injury
해로운, 불리한
It's probably **detrimental** to your health to eat too much ice cream.[8]

syn. injurious, harmful, pernicious

예문 해석

04 매력적인 여자아이가 자기에게 다가오자 그의 마음은 희망으로 부풀었다.   **05** 그는 지하철 출퇴근이 책을 읽을 수 있는 많은 시간을 주었기 때문에 매우 즐거워했다.   **06** 심사숙고 끝에 그들은 가족의 요구에 더 잘 맞는 다른 주로 이사하기로 결정했다.   **07** 백성들은 황제의 명령을 따르는 것을 주저했다.   **08** 아이스크림을 너무 많이 먹는 것은 건강에 해로울 것이다.

disseminate
[di-sem-*uh*-neyt]

v. to cause to become widely known
흩뿌리다, 퍼뜨리다
They **disseminated** anti-government propaganda.[9]

syn. diffuse, dissipate, disperse

effervescent
[ef-er-ves-*uh*nt]

adj. marked by high spirits or excitement like giving off bubbles
열광하는, 기운이 넘치는, 거품이 나는
The college town was full of **effervescent** young people.[10]

syn. vivacious, merry, lively

elongate
[ih-lawng-geyt]

v. to increase in length
연장하다, 늘이다
The fairy is able to **elongate** her entire body like a snake.[11]

syn. lengthen, extend

exude
[ig-zood]

v. to come out gradually in drops
흘러 나오다, 새어 나오다
The factory **exuded** a pungent smell.[12]

syn. secrete, ooze, leak

flinch
[flinch]

v. to withdraw or shrink from or as if from pain
(고통이나 불쾌함으로) 주춤하다, 움찔하다
The criminal **flinched** when a policeman tapped him on the shoulder.[13]

syn. wince, recoil, withdraw

garrulous
[gar-*uh*-lu*h*s]

adj. excessively talkative
매우 수다스러운
She hates **garrulous** people.[14]

syn. loquacious, talkative, verbose

예문 해석

09 그들은 반정부 선전을 퍼뜨렸다.   **10** 대학가에는 활기가 넘치는 젊은이들로 가득했다.   **11** 그 요정은 몸을 늘려 마치 뱀처럼 만들 수 있었다.   **12** 그 공장에서는 심한 냄새가 풍겨 나왔다.   **13** 그 범죄자는 경찰관이 그의 어깨를 두드리자 움찔했다.   **14** 그녀는 수다스러운 사람들을 싫어한다.

15 ....

huddle
[huhd-l]

v. to gather or crowd together in a close mass
되는 대로 모아넣다, 떼지어 모여들다
The boys **huddled** toys into a box.[15]

syn. crouch, press close

16 ....

immaterial
[im-*uh*-teer-ee-*uh*l]

adj. lacking importance
중요하지 않은, 무의미한
When the testimony or evidence is meaningless or beside the point, the attorney says, "It's **immaterial**!"[16]

syn. inconsequential, irrelevant, extraneous

17 ....

inequity
[in-ek-wi-tee]

n. injustice by virtue of not conforming with standards
불공정, 불공평
Favoritism caused every **inequity** that exists in today's society.[17]

syn. unfairness, injustice, iniquity

18 ....

interim
[in-ter-*uh*m]

adj. not intended to be final or to last
당분간의, 임시의
The **interim** music teacher started teaching at the school during the last quarter.[18]

syn. acting, temporary, provisional

19 ....

jumble
[j*uh*m-b*uh*l]

v. to mix up
마구 뒤섞다, 난잡하게 엉클어놓다
At the restaurant, they **jumbled** our orders.[19]

syn. disarrange, muddle

 예문 해석

15 소년들은 장난감을 박스에 마구 주워담았다.　**16** 증언이나 증거가 무의미하거나 요점을 벗어나면 변호사는 "그건 중요하지 않아!"라고 말한다.　**17** 편파 성향이 오늘날 사회에 존재하는 모든 불평등을 야기했다.　**18** 그 임시 음악 선생님은 지난 분기부터 그 학교에서 가르치기 시작했다.　**19** 레스토랑에서 그들은 우리의 주문을 뒤죽박죽으로 만들었다.

liable
[lahy-*uh*-bu*h*l]

adj. legally responsible
법적 책임이 있는
After driving into the neighbor's fence, he was held **liable** for fixing it.[20]

syn. answerable, responsible, accountable

---

malleable
[mal-ee-*uh*-bu*h*l]

adj. capable of being extended or shaped
두들겨 펼 수 있는, 온순한, 유순한
Clay is **malleable** and easy to work with.[21]

syn. adaptable, tractable, pliable

---

minute
[my-noot]

adj. very small
매우 작은, 하찮은
Only a **minute** amount is needed.[22]

syn. minuscule, tiny, microscopic

---

negate
[ni-geyt]

v. to cancel the effect of something
부정하다, 취소하다
Pessimists always **negate** the possibility of success.[23]

syn. undo, cancel, nullify

---

opportune
[op-er-toon]

adj. suitable and timely
때가 좋은, 타이밍이 좋은, 시기가 좋은
The timing was **opportune**.[24]

syn. timely, appropriate, favorable

---

pedestrian[1]
[p*uh*-des-tree-*uh*n]

n. a person who is walking
보행자
Drivers need to be aware of **pedestrians** crossing.[25]

syn. walker, ambler, perambulator

예문 해석

20 이웃집 울타리로 차를 몰고 들어간 후, 그는 울타리를 고쳐야 할 책임이 생겼다.　**21** 점토는 잘 변형되고 작업하기 쉽다.　**22** 아주 적은 양만 필요하다.　**23** 염세주의자들은 항상 성공 가능성을 부정한다.　**24** 타이밍이 좋았다.　**25** 운전자들은 횡단보도를 건너는 보행자들을 주의해야 한다.

26 ·······························

precarious
[pri-kair-ee-*uhs*]

adj. dependent on circumstances beyond one's control
불확실한, 믿을 수 없는, 불안정한
Our financial situation was **precarious**.[26]

syn. insecure, uncertain, unstable

27 ·······························

pungent
[p*uhn*-j*uh*nt]

adj. cleverly caustic or biting
(혀나 코를) 강하게 자극하는, 신랄한
As she walked past the dumpster, she could smell a **pungent** odor.[27]

syn. piquant, sharp, biting

28 ·······························

repel
[ri-pel]

v. to force or drive something or someone back or away
쫓아버리다, 물러서게 하다
They **repelled** an invasion successfully.[28]

syn. keep away, fend off, drive back

29 ·······························

robust
[roh-b*uh*st]

adj. strong and healthy
건강하고 튼튼한
They were **robust** young men.[29]

syn. healthy, vigorous, hearty

30 ·······························

sequester
[si-kwes-ter]

v. to take control of someone's property or assets until a debt has been paid
압류하다, 떨어뜨려놓다
Everything he owned was **sequestered**.[30]

syn. confiscate, seize, appropriate

31 ·······························

sonorous
[son-er-*uhs*]

adj. having a full deep sound
소리가 잘 울려퍼지는, 낭랑한
The **sonorous** metal bell resounded through the hall.[31]

syn. resonant, vibrant, resounding

예문 해석

26 우리의 재정 상황은 불확실했다. **27** 쓰레기통을 지날 때 그녀는 심하게 자극적인 냄새를 맡을 수 있었다. **28** 그들은 성공적으로 침략군을 격퇴시켰다. **29** 그들은 건강하고 튼튼한 젊은이들이었다. **30** 그가 가진 모든 것이 압류되었다. **31** 금속 종소리가 복도에 울려 퍼졌다.

stratagem
[strat-*uh*-ju*h*m]

n. a plan, scheme, or trick for surprising or deceiving an enemy

책략, 술수

In every war, there are conceived **stratagems** in order to achieve victory.[32]

syn. plan, scheme, trick

tackle
[tak-*uh*l]

v. to undertake to handle

(일이나 문제에) 달려들다, 붙들고 씨름하다

She **tackled** a difficult problem.[33]

syn. grip, grapple, approach

trek
[trek]

v. to take a long, hard walk lasting several days or weeks

길고 고된 여행을 하다

They had to **trek** across vast stretches of desert.[34]

syn. hike, odyssey

valedictory
[val-i-dik-t*uh*-ree]

n. any farewell address or oration

고별사, 졸업 연설

She delivered the **valedictory** at her graduation in 2011.[35]

syn. address, oration

whet
[wet]

v. to sharpen a bladed tool by rubbing it against stone

칼 등을 갈다, 갈아서 날카롭게 하다

He **whets** a scythe on the stone.[36]

syn. hone, sharpen, file

📖 예문 해석

32 모든 전쟁에는 승리를 얻기 위해 고안된 전략이 있다.   **33** 그녀는 어려운 문제를 붙잡고 늘어졌다.   **34** 그들은 길고 힘든 사막 횡단을 해야 했다.   **35** 그녀는 2011년 졸업식 때 졸업 연설을 했다.   **36** 그는 큰 낫을 돌로 갈았다.

Directions Each of the following questions consists of one word followed by five words or phrases. You are to select the one word or phrase whose meaning is closest to the word in capital letters.

1. AESTHETIC :
   (A) illiterate
   (B) legible
   (C) flabby
   (D) artistic
   (E) untiring

2. BEGUILE :
   (A) confound
   (B) plagiarize
   (C) fool
   (D) attack
   (E) confine

3. BURGEON :
   (A) stimulate
   (B) propel
   (C) accumulate
   (D) bloom
   (E) scamper

4. CONTEMPLATION :
   (A) curb
   (B) perseverance
   (C) meditation
   (D) impiety
   (E) massacre

5. DECREE :
   (A) abode
   (B) tribute
   (C) mandate
   (D) beginning
   (E) mound

6. DISSEMINATE :
   (A) diffuse
   (B) petrify
   (C) rebut
   (D) obtain
   (E) encircle

7. JUMBLE :
   (A) coax
   (B) disarrange
   (C) grope
   (D) evade
   (E) acquire

8. LIABLE :
   (A) answerable
   (B) fidgety
   (C) religious
   (D) copied
   (E) panicked

9. NEGATE :
   (A) affirm
   (B) condole
   (C) undo
   (D) horrify
   (E) scamper

10. PUNGENT :
   (A) submissive
   (B) experienced
   (C) gullible
   (D) piquant
   (E) hazy

Directions   Each of the following questions consists of one word followed by five words or phrases.
You are to select the one word or phrase whose meaning is closest to the word in capital letters.

1. DISPROVE :
   (A) refute
   (B) provoke
   (C) sharpen
   (D) enroll
   (E) amass

2. EGRESS :
   (A) exit
   (B) drama
   (C) consolation
   (D) boulder
   (E) conflict

3. ERADICATE :
   (A) root up
   (B) get off
   (C) speed up
   (D) dry out
   (E) cut down

4. RUFFLE :
   (A) insinuate
   (B) droop
   (C) hone
   (D) fluster
   (E) begin

5. HOSTILITY :
   (A) enmity
   (B) adversity
   (C) debacle
   (D) echo
   (E) family

6. IMPLICATE :
   (A) ransack
   (B) tell
   (C) exemplify
   (D) involve
   (E) expel

7. SOLICITOUS :
   (A) titular
   (B) digressive
   (C) secured
   (D) mindful
   (E) supple

8. SYNDICATE :
   (A) association
   (B) apparel
   (C) clamor
   (D) rejection
   (E) duplicity

9. WAX :
   (A) unveil
   (B) expand
   (C) bewilder
   (D) condone
   (E) debunk

10. ERRATIC :
    (A) sharp
    (B) cultured
    (C) irregular
    (D) eternal
    (E) outrageous

11. **SANGUINE :**
    (A) imaginative
    (B) forceful
    (C) minuscule
    (D) optimistic
    (E) skeptical

12. **SYNOPSIS :**
    (A) resentment
    (B) gourmet
    (C) abstract
    (D) hangar
    (E) ratio

13. **BEAR :**
    (A) brighten
    (B) have
    (C) shove
    (D) quote
    (E) forsake

14. **MINGLE :**
    (A) repel
    (B) mix
    (C) absorb
    (D) amass
    (E) scold

15. **REFUTE :**
    (A) disguise
    (B) shorten
    (C) exterminate
    (D) rebut
    (E) conquer

16. **GARNISH :**
    (A) improve
    (B) gaze
    (C) impel
    (D) adorn
    (E) begrudge

17. **TREAD :**
    (A) falter
    (B) chatter
    (C) step
    (D) humiliate
    (E) enlarge

18. **DISSECT :**
    (A) captivate
    (B) recede
    (C) designate
    (D) scamper
    (E) anatomize

19. **OPPORTUNE :**
    (A) condescending
    (B) timely
    (C) discriminating
    (D) blameworthy
    (E) laudable

20. **PRECARIOUS :**
    (A) delicious
    (B) insecure
    (C) disloyalty
    (D) relevant
    (E) taciturn

"Nothing can bring you peace but yourself."

— Winston Churchill —
British politician

너 자신 말고는 아무도 너에게 평화를 줄 수 없다.

Greek and Latin Roots & Prefixes 55

★ EPI = among

demos (people)	epidemic	유행의
dermis (skin)	epidermis	표피
gramma (drawn)	epigram	경구, 짧은 풍자시
logos (word)	epilogue	끝맺는 말
hodos (path)	episode	시간
tome (remains of)	epitome	완벽한 본보기, 전형
skopeo (to look)	episcopal	주교의, 감독 교회의

DAY

55

WORDS TO LEARN

☐ affable	☐ eloquence	☐ interloper	☐ repent
☐ apt	☐ escalate	☐ junction	☐ rod
☐ behold	☐ factitious	☐ mammoth	☐ serendipity
☐ burnish	☐ flippant	☐ mire	☐ specious
☐ coherent	☐ gasp	☐ negligible	☐ stratify
☐ contend	☐ hackneyed	☐ omniscient	☐ tactful
☐ decrepit	☐ hue	☐ pedestrian[2]	☐ valiant
☐ devastate	☐ imposing	☐ precede	☐ vie
☐ dissent	☐ inert	☐ puny	☐ whimsical

01

affable
[af-*uh*-b*uh*l]

adj. diffusing warmth and friendliness
친근한, 상냥한
She greeted the guests with an **affable** smile.[1]

syn. amiable, agreeable, congenial

02

apt
[apt]

adj. perfectly appropriate, clever and well-suited
~를 잘하는, ~하는 경향이 있는
She is **apt** to ignore matters she considers irrelevant.[2]

syn. Inclined, disposed, prone

03

behold
[bi-hohld]

v. to see with attention
보다, 바라보다
Beauty is in the eye of the **beholder**.[3]

syn. look at, regard, see

예문 해석

01 그녀는 상냥한 미소로 손님들을 맞이했다.   **02** 그녀는 무관하다고 생각하는 일을 잘 무시한다.   **03** 아름다움은 보는 사람에
따라 다르다.

04

burnish
[bur-nish]

v. to make smooth and bright
윤내다, 광내다
She **burnished** the pan until she could see her reflection in the bottom.[4]

syn. polish, smooth, shine

05

coherent
[koh-heer-*uh*nt]

adj. logically connected
조리 있는, 논리적인
The parents checked his language was **coherent** after the boy fell and hit his head.[5]

syn. logical, rational, consistent

06

contend
[k*uh*n-tend]

v. to compete for something
논쟁하다, 강하게 주장하다
The two opponents are **contending** for the ultimate title.[6]

syn. argue, compete, dispute

07

decrepit
[di-krep-it]

adj. weakened by old age
노쇠한, 약한
He became a **decrepit** man who could hardly walk.[7]

syn. weakened, infirm, feeble

08

devastate
[dev-*uh*-steyt]

v. to cause extensive destruction or ruin utterly
파괴하다
The fire **devastated** large parts of the city.[8]

syn. demolish, ravage, dilapidate

예문 해석

04 그녀는 바닥에 자기의 모습이 비칠 때까지 냄비를 문질러 광을 냈다.   **05** 소년이 넘어져서 머리를 부딪힌 후 그의 부모는 그의 언어가 일관성이 있는지 확인했다.   **06** 두 상대는 최종 우승을 놓고 경쟁하고 있다.   **07** 그는 제대로 걷지도 못하는 노쇠한 사람이 되었다.   **08** 화재는 도시의 많은 부분을 파괴했다.

dissent
[di-sent]

v. to be of different opinions
의견을 달리하다, 반대하다
Only one of the 30 members **dissented**.[9]

syn. disagree, differ, demur

eloquence
[el-*uh*-kw*uh*ns]

n. the art or power of using speech to impress, move or persuade
웅변, 능변
She was renowned for her **eloquence**.[10]

syn. fluency, expressiveness, oratory

escalate
[es-k*uh*-leyt]

v. to increase or be increased rapidly in scale or degree
단계적으로 확대되다, 점차적으로 올라가다
The dispute could **escalate**.[11]

syn. heighten, increase, intensify

factitious
[fak-tish-*uhs*]

adj. not produced by natural forces
(진짜처럼 보이도록) 꾸며낸, 인위적인
He created a **factitious** diamond out of plastic.[12]

syn. unnatural, artificial, fake

flippant
[flip-*uh*nt]

adj. not serious enough about grave matters
경박한, 경솔한
Don't be **flippant**! This is serious.[13]

syn. frivolous, disrespectful, irreverent

gasp
[gasp]

v. to catch one's breath
헐떡거리다, (공포나 놀람으로) 숨이 막히다
At his last **gasp**, he confessed to the crime.[14]

syn. draw breath, choke, snort

예문 해석

09 삼십 명의 일원 중 단 한 명만이 반대했다.　**10** 그녀는 달변으로 유명했다.　**11** 논쟁은 점점 심해질 수 있다.　**12** 그는 플라스틱으로 가짜 다이아몬드를 만들었다.　**13** 장난치지 마, 심각하다고!　**14** 마지막 숨을 몰아 쉬며 그는 그 죄를 고백했다.

15 ······

hackneyed
[hak-need]

adj. made commonplace or trite
진부한, 상투적인
The teacher doesn't like **hackneyed** phrases.[15]

syn. trite, unoriginal, banal

16 ······

hue
[hyoo]

n. the quality of a color determined by its dominant wavelength
색, 색채
The same **hue** looks different in different light.[16]

syn. color, shade, tinge

17 ······

imposing
[im-poh-zing]

adj. very impressive
인상적인, 당당한, 훌륭한
He lived in a grand and **imposing** mansion.[17]

syn. impressive, dignified, majestic

18 ······

inert
[in-urt]

adj. having no inherent power of action
스스로 움직일 힘이 없는, 늘어진, 둔한
The man appears to be rendered **inert** by the cold.[18]

syn. inactive, dormant, listless

19 ······

interloper
[in-ter-lohp-uhr]

n. a person who intrudes into some region without a proper license
남의 일에 참견하고 나서는 사람, 참견꾼
She regarded us as **interlopers**.[19]

syn. intruder, trespasser, meddler

20 ······

junction
[juhngk-shuhn]

n. an intersection of two roads
접합점, 교차점
Change lanes if you want to turn off at the next **junction**.[20]

syn. intersection, connection, confluence

예문 해석

15 그 선생님은 상투적인 문구를 싫어하셨다. **16** 같은 색깔도 조명에 따라 달라 보인다. **17** 그는 크고 웅장한 저택에 살았다.
18 그 남자는 추위 때문에 움직이지 못하게 된 것처럼 보인다. **19** 그녀는 우리를 참견꾼 취급했다. **20** 다른 교차점에서 빠져나가려면 차선을 바꿔라

21

mammoth
[mam-*uh*th]

adj. exceedingly extensive as to suggest a mammoth
큰, 거대한
It will be the **mammoth** task to relocate the headquarters.[21]

syn. enormous, tremendous, gigantic

22

mire
[mai*uh*r]

v. a tract or area of wet, swampy ground
진흙탕, 수렁, 곤경
His car sank deeper into the **mire**.[22]

syn. bog, marsh, quagmire

23

negligible
[neg-li-j*uh*-b*uh*l]

adj. unimportant enough to ignore
무시해도 좋은, 하찮은, 사소한
The employees' stipends were **negligible**.[23]

syn. paltry, trivial, insignificant

24

omniscient
[om-nish-*uh*nt]

adj. knowing, seeing, or understanding everything
모든 것을 다 아는, 전지의
Many religions have a god who is omnipotent and
omniscient.[24]

syn. all-knowing, all-seeing, almighty

25

pedestrian[2]
[p*uh*-des-tree-*uh*n]

adj. ordinary and not at all interesting
평범한
His style is so **pedestrian**.[25]

syn. mundane, common, ordinary

26

precede
[pri-seed]

v. to go or be before someone or something, in time, order,
position, rank or importance
앞서다, 우선하다
Preceding the exam, students began to immerse
themselves in studying.[26]

syn. predate, presage, foreshadow

예문 해석

21 본부를 이전하는 것은 엄청난 일이 될 것이다.　**22** 그의 차는 수렁에 깊이 가라앉았다.　**23** 직원들이 받은 임금은 너무 작았다.　**24** 많은 종교에는 모든 것이 가능하고, 모든 것을 아는 신이 있다.　**25** 그의 스타일은 매우 평범했다.　**26** 시험을 앞두고 학생들은 공부에 몰두하기 시작했다.

puny
[pyoo-nee]

adj. very small or weak
약한, 보잘 것 없는, 작은
He gave a **puny** excuse to the teacher about why he cheated on the test.[27]

syn. petty, meager, trivial, trifling

repent
[ri-pent]

v. to feel great sorrow or regret for something one has done
후회하다, 뉘우치다, 회개하다
Those who refuse to **repent**, he said, will be punished.[28]

syn. deplore, rue, atone

rod
[rod]

n. a long slender stick or bar of wood, metal, etc.
막대기, 지팡이
I was given a fishing **rod** gift for Christmas one year.[29]

syn. pole, stick, bar

serendipity
[ser-*uhn*-dip-i-tee]

n. the fact of something interesting or pleasant happening by chance
우연히 좋은 일이 일어남
Serendipity may hand you something pleasant that you hadn't thought of.[30]

syn. chance, happy accident

specious
[spee-sh*uhs*]

adj. plausible but fake
허울만 그럴듯한, 거짓의
His **specious** argument seems good, correct, and logical but is not so.[31]

syn. misleading, deceptive, erroneous

예문 해석

27 그는 선생님께 시험에서 부정행위를 한 이유에 대해 하찮은 변명을 했다. **28** 회개하지 않으려는 사람들은 벌 받을 것이라고 그는 말했다. **29** 나는 어느 해 크리스마스에 낚싯대 선물을 받았다. **30** 우연한 좋은 일이 일어나 당신에게 생각지도 못한 즐거움을 줄 수 있다. **31** 그의 그럴듯한 주장은 좋고, 옳고, 논리적으로 보이지만 그렇지 않다.

32 ···

stratify
[strat-*uh*-fai]

v. to classify or arrange things into different grades, levels or social classes
층을 형성하다, 계급을 나누다
India is a highly **stratified** society.[32]

syn. classify, categorize, sort

33 ···

tactful
[takt-*fuhl*]

adj. careful not to say or do anything that will annoy or upset other people
재치 있는, 빈틈없는, 능수능란한
He had been extremely **tactful** in dealing with the financial question.[33]

syn. diplomatic, discreet, sensitive

34 ···

valiant
[val-*yuh*nt]

adj. very brave and determined
용감한, 대담한
Despite **valiant** resistance, the rebel army was subdued.[34]

syn. intrepid, undaunted, unflinching

35 ···

vie
[vai]

v. to compete for something
(어떤 것을 차지하기 위해) 다투다, 경쟁하다
Marathoners from many nations were **vying** for the title.[35]

syn. compete, contend, strive

36 ···

whimsical
[hwim-zi-*kuh*l]

adj. given to whimsy or fanciful notions
변덕스러운, 마음이 잘 변하는
His wife doesn't like his **whimsical** side.[36]

syn. fanciful, fickle, capricious

 예문 해석

32 인도는 매우 계층화된 사회이다. **33** 재정 문제를 다룰 때 그는 굉장히 능수능란한 사람이었다. **34** 용감한 저항에도 불구하고 반란군은 진압되었다. **35** 많은 나라에서 온 마라토너들이 타이틀을 놓고 경쟁하고 있었다. **36** 그의 부인은 그의 변덕스러운 면을 좋아하지 않았다.

Directions   Each of the following questions consists of one word followed by five words or phrases. You are to select the one word or phrase whose meaning is closest to the word in capital letters.

1. AFFABLE :
(A) inadequate
(B) perilous
(C) inharmonious
(D) bulky
(E) amiable

2. APT :
(A) elastic
(B) disorganized
(C) feasible
(D) vague
(E) inclined

3. BURNISH :
(A) disprove
(B) anticipate
(C) polish
(D) generate
(E) restart

4. CONTEND :
(A) nurture
(B) imprison
(C) argue
(D) push
(E) contemplate

5. DECREPIT :
(A) weakened
(B) delicious
(C) convenient
(D) brief
(E) arrogant

6. DISSENT :
(A) disagree
(B) enroll
(C) scorch
(D) accelerate
(E) condole

7. JUNCTION :
(A) locomotive
(B) intersection
(C) refuge
(D) haven
(E) disgust

8. OMNISCIENT :
(A) dazzling
(B) all-knowing
(C) intact
(D) pungent
(E) slight

9. PEDESTRIAN :
(A) cumbersome
(B) mundane
(C) ceaseless
(D) gust
(E) queer

10. REPENT :
(A) deplore
(B) accumulate
(C) snuggle
(D) diverge
(E) achieve

"Keep your face always toward the sunshine,
and shadows will fall behind you."

— Walt Whitman —
American poet

항상 해를 바라보아라, 그러면 그림자는 너의 뒤로 떨어질 것이다.

Greek and Latin Roots & Prefixes 56

★ VENIO = arrive

ad (toward)	advent	출현, 도래
circum (around)	circumvent	피하다, 면하다
contra (against)	contravene	위반하다
con (together)	convene	소집하다, 화합하다
	convention	관습, 관례
	convenient	편리한, 간편한
inter (between)	intervene	개입하다, 끼어들다
pre (before)	prevent	막다, 예방하다

DAY

56

WORDS TO LEARN

☐ affectation	☐ elucidate	☐ interlude	☐ puritanical
☐ aggrandize	☐ eschew	☐ juncture	☐ repertoire
☐ belie	☐ fabricate	☐ leverage	☐ serene
☐ belligerent	☐ ferocious	☐ managerial	☐ sophisticated
☐ cohesion	☐ fulfill	☐ mirthful	☐ streak
☐ contented	☐ heritage	☐ negligent	☐ tactile
☐ decry	☐ humanities	☐ optimum	☐ trenchant
☐ deviate	☐ impostor	☐ phlegmatic	☐ validate
☐ dissertation	☐ indigent	☐ purge	☐ willful

01

affectation
[af-ek-tey-sh*uh*n]

n. an effort to appear to have a quality not really possessed
그런 척함, 뽐냄
In their first meeting, he found her quiet, proper and without **affectation**.[1]

syn. feint, pretense

02

aggrandize
[*uh*-gran-dahyz]

v. to increase the scope, power or importance
크게 하다, 확대하다
He **aggrandized** his job title to make it sound greater than it is.[2]

syn. magnify, glorify, augment

03

belie
[bih-lahy]

v. to show to be false
착각하게 만들다, 거짓임을 보여주다
Her looks **belie** her 60 years.[3]

syn. contradict, negate, misrepresent

예문 해석

01 그들이 처음 만났을 때, 그는 그녀가 조용하고 예의 바르며 꾸밈없다고 생각했다. **02** 그는 자신의 직함을 과장해서 실제보다 더 대단한 것처럼 들리게 했다. **03** 그녀의 외모로 봐서는 60세가 아닌 것 처럼 보인다.

04

belligerent
[b*uh*-lij-er-*uh*nt]

adj. aggressively hostile
호전적인
The long-standing war was in need of a peace treaty
between the **belligerent** nations.[4]

syn. hostile, warlike, bellicose

05

cohesion
[koh-hee-zh*uh*n]

n. the tendency to unite or stick together
결합, 응집력
Wet sand has more **cohesion** than dry sand.[5]

syn. combination, union, fusion

06

contented
[k*uh*n-ten-tid]

adj. satisfied or showing satisfaction
만족한
He **contented** himself with his position.[6]

syn. satisfied, content, fulfilled

07

decry
[di-krai]

v. to speak disparagingly of
비난하다, 헐뜯다
People **decried** the political campaign as a waste of money.[7]

syn. reprove, reproach, denounce

08

deviate
[dee-vee-ate]

v. to turn aside
빗나가다, 일탈하다
Do not **deviate** from them, for any reason.[8]

syn. diverge, stray

예문 해석

04 호전적인 나라들 사이의 평화협정　**05** 젖은 모래가 마른 모래보다 잘 점착된다.　**06** 그는 자신의 위치에 만족했다.　**07** 사람들은 그 정치 캠페인이 돈 낭비라고 비난했다.　**08** 그들로부터 절대 떨어지지 말아라. 어떤 이유에서든.

09

dissertation
[dis-er-tey-shuhn]

n. a long essay forming part of a higher education degree course

학술 논문

He wrote his **dissertation** on the Civil War.[9]

syn. treaty, thesis

10

elucidate
[i-loo-si-deyt]

v. to make clear or explain, to shed light on something

명료하게 하다, 밝히다, 해명하다

She gave a plausible explanation that **elucidated** his recent strange behavior.[10]

syn. clarify, explicate, expound

11

eschew
[es-choo]

v. to abstain from

의도적으로 피하다, 멀리하다, 삼가다

They tried to **eschew** evil.[11]

syn. shun, avoid, forgo

12

fabricate
[fab-ri-keyt]

v. to invent or make up

거짓말을 꾸며내다, 문서를 위조하다

They **fabricated** evidence.[12]

syn. falsify, concoct, contrive

13

ferocious
[fuh-roh-shuhs]

adj. marked by extreme and violent energy

맹렬한, 격렬한

The family had to endure the **fierce** wind, trembling with fear during the hurricane.[13]

syn. barbaric, brutal, savage

 예문 해석

09 그는 남북전쟁에 대한 논문을 썼다.   **10** 그녀는 요즘 그가 보이는 이상한 행동에 대해 그럴듯한 설명을 했다.   **11** 그들은 악을 멀리하려 했다.   **12** 그들은 증거를 거짓으로 만들었다.   **13** 그 가족은 허리케인이 부는 동안 두려움에 떨며 사나운 바람을 견뎌야 했다.

14

fulfill
[fuhl-fil]

v. to bring to completion
(의무나 약속을) 수행하다, 완료하다
She realized that she could **fulfill** herself in her career.[14]

syn. accomplish, achieve, complete

15

heritage
[her-i-tij]

n. that which is inherited
(국가나 사회의) 유산
This area has a Korean traditional rich musical **heritage**.[15]

syn. legacy, inheritance, bequest

16

humanities
[hyoo-man-i-teez]

n. studies intended to provide general knowledge and skills
인문학, 역사, 철학, 문학 등 인간의 사상과 문화를 연구하는 학문
Studying the **humanities** gives him general knowledge but not a practical aspect.[16]

syn. liberal arts, philosophy, languages

17

imposter
[im-pos-ter]

n. a person who practices deception
사기꾼, 협잡꾼
He was an **imposter**, disguised as a doctor.[17]

syn. charlatan, swindler, quack

18

indigent
[in-di-juhnt]

adj. poor enough to need help from others
궁핍한, 가난한
He is an **indigent** person lacking the primary resources of everyday life.[18]

syn. destitute, impoverished, needy

19

interlude
[in-ter-lood]

n. a short period of time when an activity stops
사이, 막간, 중간
The Broadway play had a musical **interlude** in between the three acts.[19]

syn. interval, intermission

🧘 **예문 해석**

14 그녀는 자신의 일에서 자신이 해낼 수 있다는 것을 깨달았다.　**15** 이 지역은 한국의 전통 음악 유산이 풍부하다.　**16** 인문학을 공부하는 것은 그에게 일반적인 지식을 주지만 실용적인 측면은 아니다.　**17** 그는 의사로 위장한 사기꾼이었다.　**18** 그는 일상생활의 주요 자원이 부족한 가난한 사람이다.　**19** 브로드웨이 연극은 3막 사이에 음악적인 막간을 두었다.

20

juncture
[ju*h*ngk-cher]

n. a serious state of affairs
중대한 시기, 위기, 고비
The six-party talks are at a crucial **juncture**.[20]

syn. turning point, crisis, crux

21

leverage
[lev-er-ij]

n. power or ability to act or to influence people, events, decisions, etc.
영향력
Relatively small groups can often exert immense political **leverage**.[21]

syn. influence, sway, weight

22

managerial
[man-i-jeer-ee-*uh*l]

adj. relating to the work of a manager
관리자의, 관리 업무에 관한
The union's demand is a challenge to **managerial** rights.[22]

syn. executive, supervisory, directorial

23

mirthful
[murth-f*uh*l]

adj. full of or showing high-spirited merriment
즐거운, 유쾌한
Their **mirthful** laughs were heard throughout the movie theater.[23]

syn. gay, jolly, merry

24

negligent
[neg-li-j*uh*nt]

adj. failing to give something enough care or attention
부주의한, 태만한, 소홀한
The jury found the defendant **negligent**.[24]

syn. inattentive, careless, heedless

25

optimum
[op-t*uh*-m*uh*m]

adj. best or most favorable
최적의, 가장 알맞은
Do some physical activity three times a week for **optimum** conditioning.[25]

syn. best possible, optimal

예문 해석

20 6자 회담은 중요한 국면에 놓여 있다. **21** 상대적으로 작은 집단이 종종 엄청난 정치적 영향력을 행사할 수도 있다. **22** 노조의 요구는 경영권에 대한 도전이다. **23** 그들의 즐거운 웃음소리가 영화관 전체에 들렸다. **24** 배심원들은 피고가 태만했다는 것을 알았다. **25** 최적의 컨디션을 위해 일주일에 3회 운동을 하십시오.

phlegmatic
[fleg-mat-ik]

adj. showing no emotion, composed
침착한, 냉정한
The **phlegmatic** palace guards wearing red coats and big hats show absolutely no expression on their faces.[26]

syn. undemonstrative, indifferent, apathetic

purge
[purj]

v. to rid of whatever is impure or undesirable
축출하다, 제거하다, 정화하다
The principal wanted to **purge** the school of troublesome students.[27]

syn. cleanse, purify, expunge

puritanical
[pyoor-i-tan-i-k*uh*l]

adj. morally rigorous and strict
철저한 금욕주의자의, 청교도적인
She is **puritanical**, overly rigid in her beliefs, and not much fun to be around.[28]

syn. strait-laced, prudish, rigid

repertoire
[rep-er-twahr]

n. the list of plays, dances or pieces that one can perform
연주 가능한 목록, 레퍼토리
The singer has a thousand songs in her **repertoire**.[29]

syn. collection, repertory, range

serene
[s*uh*-reen]

adj. calm and cloudless
고요한, 잔잔한
She wanted to go on a vacation surrounded by a **serene** landscape.[30]

syn. placid, tranquil, peaceful

 예문 해석

26 붉은 외투를 입고 큰 모자를 쓴 냉담해 보이는 궁정의 보초들은 전혀 표정이 없다.　**27** 교장은 문제 있는 학생들을 몰아내고 싶어 했다.　**28** 그녀는 청교도적이고, 신앙이 지나치게 엄격하며, 재미가 별로 없다.　**29** 그녀는 천여 곡의 레퍼토리를 가지고 있다.　**30** 그녀는 고요한 풍경으로 둘러싸인 휴가를 떠나고 싶었다.

sophisticated
[*suh*-fis-ti-key-tid]

adj. reflecting educated taste and worldly knowledge
세련된, 순진하지 않은
The **sophisticated** lady pointed out every little flaw.[31]

syn. cosmopolitan, cultured, refined

streak
[streek]

n. a long, narrow mark
줄, 줄무늬, 선
A **streak** of light appeared.[32]

syn. line, band, stripe

tactile
[tak-til]

adj. perceptible to the sense of touch
촉각으로 알 수 있는
Babies who sleep with their parents receive much more **tactile** stimulation than babies who sleep in a cradle.[33]

syn. tangible, palpable, perceptible

trenchant
[tren-ch*uh*nt]

adj. expressed strongly and effectively in a clear way
직설적인, 신랄한
Her comment was short but **trenchant**.[34]

syn. incisive, cutting, penetrating

validate
[val-i-deyt]

v. to make something valid
정당성을 입증하다, 유효하게 해주다
The reception staff can **validate** your parking receipt.[35]

syn. authenticate, legalize

willful
[wil-f*uh*l]

adj. unreasonably stubborn or headstrong
제 마음대로의, 고집 센
Willful neglect could cause serious harm to a whole group.[36]

syn. arbitrary, headstrong, stubborn, obstinate

예문 해석

31 까다로운 아가씨는 작은 잘못도 다 지적해 냈다.　**32** 한줄기 빛이 나타났다.　**33** 요람에서 자는 아기보다 부모랑 함께 자는 아기가 촉각적인 감각 자극을 많이 받는다.　**34** 그녀의 언급은 짧지만 신랄했다.　**35** 리셉션에 있는 직원이 주차 도장을 찍어드릴 겁니다.　**36** 고의적 태만은 전체 그룹에 심각한 해를 야기할 수 있다.

Directions   Each of the following questions consists of one word followed by five words or phrases.
You are to select the one word or phrase whose meaning is closest to the word in capital letters.

1. **AFFECTATION :**
   (A) apprenticeship
   (B) expedition
   (C) attendant
   (D) feint
   (E) agreement

2. **BELLIGERENT :**
   (A) derisive
   (B) detrimental
   (C) untiring
   (D) hostile
   (E) enunciate

3. **DEVIATE :**
   (A) mar
   (B) diverge
   (C) conquer
   (D) arbitrate
   (E) contain

4. **FABRICATE :**
   (A) falsify
   (B) contemplate
   (C) shred
   (D) ban
   (E) inhabit

5. **HERITAGE :**
   (A) judge
   (B) legacy
   (C) avalanche
   (D) inundation
   (E) disgrace

6. **MIRTHFUL :**
   (A) gay
   (B) prejudiced
   (C) roaming
   (D) brief
   (E) conflicting

7. **PHLEGMATIC :**
   (A) cumbersome
   (B) undemonstrative
   (C) carnivorous
   (D) slack
   (E) paltry

8. **PURGE :**
   (A) categorize
   (B) accomplish
   (C) cleanse
   (D) redeem
   (E) ponder

9. **PURITANICAL :**
   (A) initial
   (B) strait-laced
   (C) insipid
   (D) wanton
   (E) adolescent

10. **TACTILE :**
    (A) ceaseless
    (B) initial
    (C) latent
    (D) negligent
    (E) tangible

"I do not think much of a man who is not wiser today
than he was yesterday."

— Abraham Lincoln —
16th president of the U.S.

어제보다 오늘 더 현명해지지 못하는 사람을 나는 대단하게 여기지 않는다.

Greek and Latin Roots & Prefixes 57

★ HYPER = above, excessive

ballo (to throw)	hyperbole	과장법
kirtes (to judge)	hypercritical	혹평하는
gramma (drawn)	hyperactive	과잉 행동의
logos (word)	hypertension	고혈압

★ HYPO = under

demos (people)	hypothesis	가설, 추측
kirtes (to judge)	hypocritical	위선적인, 가식적인
	hypocrite	위선자
derma (skin)	hypodermic	피하의, 피부 아래쪽의
teinein (to stretch)	hypotenuse	(직각 삼각형의) 빗변

DAY

57

WORDS TO LEARN

☐ affection	☐ esoteric	☐ jurisdiction	☐ replenish
☐ ardor	☐ façade	☐ liability	☐ retribution
☐ benefactor	☐ flounder	☐ magistrate	☐ semblance
☐ cache	☐ gaunt	☐ mandate	☐ souvenir
☐ contentious	☐ hail	☐ nip	☐ strenuous
☐ deduce	☐ humiliate	☐ nonpartisan	☐ taint
☐ deprive	☐ impoverished	☐ pedigree	☐ trespass
☐ diviation	☐ incredulous	☐ plague	☐ valor
☐ elusive	☐ interminable	☐ punitive	☐ wily

01

affection
[*uh*-fek-sh*uh*n]

n. a feeling of love or strong liking
애정, 사랑
A kiss can express **affection**.[1]

syn. fondness, liking, love

02

ardor
[ahr-der]

n. great warmth of feeling
열정, 정열, 열심
He's full of **ardor** about their relationship, so he writes her love poems every day.[2]

syn. fervor, enthusiasm, eagerness

03

benefactor
[ben-*uh*-fak-ter]

n. a person who gives help, especially financial help
후원자
In his old age he became a **benefactor** of the arts.[3]

syn. patron, sponsor, supporter

예문 해석

01 입맞춤으로 애정을 표현할 수 있다. **02** 그는 그들의 관계에 대한 열정으로 가득 차서 매일 그녀에게 연애시를 쓴다. **03** 노년에 가서 그는 예술 후원자가 되었다.

04 ....

cache
[kash]

n. a hiding-place
은닉처, 저장소
A huge arms **cache** was discovered by police.[4]

syn. hideout, hoard, stash

05 ....

contentious
[kuhn-ten-shuhs]

adj. causing argument
논란의 여지가 많은
This is the one of the most **contentious** issues.[5]

syn. quarrelsome, disputatious, combative

06 ....

deduce
[di-doos, -dyoos]

v. to think out and make a conclusion
추론하다
He had **deduced** that his father was the author of the novel.[6]

syn. infer, derive

07 ....

deprive
[dih-praiv]

v. to remove or withhold something from possession
(물건이나 권리를) 빼앗다
Because Mark got hyper every time he ate sweets, his parents **deprived** him of candies. [7]

syn. dispossess, rob, divest

08 ....

deviation
[dee-vee-ey-shuhn]

n. the act of deviating
탈선, 벗어남
"Without **deviation** from the norm, progress is not possible."
- Frank Zappa[8]

syn. aberration, anomaly, divergence

🧘 예문 해석

04 거대한 비밀 무기고가 경찰에 의해 발견되었다. **05** 이것은 가장 논란의 여지가 많은 이슈 중 하나이다. **06** 그는 소설을 쓴 사람이 그의 아버지라는 사실을 추론해갔다. **07** 마크는 사탕을 먹을 때마다 흥분했기 때문에 그의 부모님은 그에게서 캔디를 빼앗았다. **08** 규범에서 벗어나지 않고서는 진보란 불가능하다.

09

elusive
[i-loo-siv]

adj. difficult to find or catch
교묘히 피하는
Late-night taxis are **elusive**.[9]

> syn. slippery, evasive, shifty

10

esoteric
[es-*uh*-ter-ik]

adj. secret or mysterious
난해한, 비밀의
He thinks poetry is full of **esoteric** allusions.[10]

> syn. abstruse, arcane, obscure

11

façade
[*fuh*-sahd]

n. a superficial appearance or illusion of something
(실제와는 다른) 표면, 허울
She managed somehow to maintain a **façade** of great wealth.[11]

> syn. deceptive appearance, front, exterior

12

flounder
[floun-der]

v. to struggle with stumbling or plunging movements
버둥거리다, 허우적거리다
He saw the child **floundering** about in the water.[12]

> syn. struggle, falter, stumble

13

gaunt
[gawnt]

adj. extremely thin and bony
매우 마르고 수척한
He looks **gaunt** and tired.[13]

> syn. haggard, emaciated, bony

14

hail
[heyl]

v. to attract attention by shouting or making gestures
손짓이나 소리쳐 부르다, 환호하다
She **hailed** a taxi.[14]

> syn. call to, yell for, signal

예문 해석

09 심야 택시는 잘 잡히지 않는다. **10** 그는 시라는 것은 난해한 암시로 가득 차 있다고 생각한다. **11** 그녀는 어떻게든 엄청난 부자인 척을 유지할 수 있었다. **12** 그는 물속에서 허우적대는 아이를 보았다. **13** 그는 수척하고 피곤해 보인다. **14** 그녀는 택시를 불렀다.

15 ··

humiliate
[hyoo-mil-ee-yet]

v. to cause someone a painful loss of pride, self-respect, or dignity
굴욕감을 주다, 창피하게 만들다
The teacher didn't want to **humiliate** her in front of her friends.[15]

syn. mortify, dishonor, disgrace

16 ··

impoverished
[im-pov-er-isht]

adj. reduced to poverty
가난한, 피폐해진
The **impoverished** country was left in ruins after a tsunami overtook it.[16]

syn. penurious, indigent, insolvent

17 ··

incredulous
[in-krej-*uh*-luhs]

adj. not to be persuaded or changed
쉽게 믿지 않는, 못 믿겠다는 듯한
They gave an **incredulous** look when he told about those aliens and UFO he saw last night.[17]

syn. skeptical, doubtful, dubious

18 ··

interminable
[in-tur-m*uh*-nuh-b*uh*l]

adj. without an end
끝없는, 한없는
The **interminable** meeting felt like an eternity.[18]

syn. endless, ceaseless, incessant

19 ··

jurisdiction
[joor-is-dik-sh*uh*n]

n. the right or authority to apply laws
사법권, 재판권, 권한이 미치는 범위
The police have no **jurisdiction** to investigate over foreign bank accounts.[19]

syn. extent of power, area of authority, control

 예문 해석

15 선생님은 그녀의 친구들 앞에서 그녀를 망신시키고 싶지 않았다. **16** 그 가난한 나라는 쓰나미가 덮친 후 폐허가 되었다. **17** 그가 지난 밤에 본 외계인과 UFO에 대해 말했을 때 그들은 믿을 수 없다는 표정을 지었다. **18** 끝없는 만남이 영원처럼 느껴졌다. **19** 경찰은 해외 계좌에 대해서는 수사 권한이 없다.

liability
[lai-*uh*-bil-i-tee]

n. the state of being legally obliged and responsible
법적 책임, 채무, 빚
He had massive **liability** as a mortgage.[20]

syn. answerability, responsibility, debt

magistrate
[maj-*uh*-streyt]

n. a lay judge or civil authority who administers the law
치안 판사
Minor offenses are often brought before a **magistrate**.[21]

syn. judge, civil office, civil authority

mandate
[man-deyt]

n. a command or authorization to act in a particular way
명령, 지령, 지시
The royal **mandate** was heavily discussed.[22]

syn. command, order, decree

nip
[nip]

v. to squeeze or compress tightly between two surfaces or points
살짝 꼬집다, 살짝 물다
Her terrier always **nips** at her guests' ankles.[23]

syn. bite, nibble, pinch

nonpartisan
[non-pahr-t*uh*-zuhn]

adj. free from party affiliation or bias
초당파적인, 공정한, 공평한
A **nonpartisan** bill will not be good just for one party: it would be good for the whole country.[24]

syn. independent, neutral, impartial

pedigree
[ped-i-gree]

n. a record of lineage
족보, 가계, 혈통
He is a nobleman by **pedigree**.[25]

syn. lineage, ancestry

📖 **예문 해석**

20 그는 담보 대출로 막대한 부채를 지고 있었다. **21** 경미한 범죄는 흔히 치안 판사 앞에 서게 된다. **22** 왕실의 위임은 심각하게 논의되었다. **23** 그녀의 테리어 개는 항상 그녀의 손님들의 발목을 살짝 문다. **24** 초당파적인 법안은 한 정당에만 좋은 것이 아니라 나라 전체에 좋을 것이다. **25** 그는 귀족 태생이다.

26

plague
[pleyg]

n. any large-scale calamity especially when thought to be sent by God

전염병, 페스트, 큰 재앙

The **plague** was a contagious illness that spread like wildfire through Europe in the Middle Ages, killing millions of people.[26]

syn. pestilence, contagion, pandemic

27

punitive
[pyoo-ni-tiv]

adj. inflicting punishment

가혹한, 처벌을 위한

The **punitive** effect of higher taxes will be detrimental to the middle class.[27]

syn. punishing, vindictive, retaliatory

28

replenish
[ri-plen-ish]

v. to fill up or make complete again

재충전하다

You should **replenish** supplies.[28]

syn. refill, refresh, restore

29

retribution
[re-truh-byoo-shuhn]

n. a justly deserved penalty

응징, 징벌, 보복

"An eye for an eye" is a commandment found in the Book of Exodus 21:23–27 expressing the principle of **retribution**.[29]

syn. retaliation, compensation, punishment

30

semblance
[sem-bluhns]

n. outward aspect or appearance

외관, 겉모습

She hoped her claims would have a **semblance** of authenticity.[30]

syn. aura, appearance, pretense

예문 해석

26 페스트는 중세 유럽 전역에 들불처럼 번져 수백만 명의 목숨을 앗아간 전염병이었다.   **27** 높은 세금으로 인한 징벌적 효과는 중산층에 해가 될 것이다.   **28** 당신은 공급을 보충해 놓을 필요가 있다.   **29** "눈에는 눈"은 출애굽기 21장 23절~27절에서 볼 수 있는 보복의 원리를 표현한 계명이다.   **30** 그녀는 자신의 주장이 진실처럼 보이기를 바랐다.

31 ·········

souvenir
[soo-v*uh*-neer]

n. a reminder of a place, person, occasion
기념품
He kept the record as a **souvenir**.[31]

syn. memento, reminder, keepsake

32 ·········

strenuous
[stren-yoo-*uh*s]

adj. needing great effort or energy
분투의, 힘들게 노력하는
Avoid **strenuous** exercise in the evening.[32]

syn. tiring, arduous, exhausting

33 ·········

taint
[teynt]

v. to affect with something bad or offensive
더럽히다, 오염시키다, 망치다
He hoped that the fight with his best friend wouldn't **taint** their relationship.[33]

syn. sully, contaminate, spoil

34 ·········

trespass
[tres-p*uh*s]

v. to enter someone else's property without the right or permission
침입하다, 권리를 침해하다
The police arrested the man for **trespassing**.[34]

syn. infringe, intrude, encroach

35 ·········

valor
[val-er]

n. boldness or determination in facing great danger
용기, 대담함
Discretion is the better part of **valor**.[35]

syn. courage, bravery, spirit

36 ·········

wily
[wai-lee]

adj. marked by skill in deception
꾀가 많은, 약삭빠른, 책략을 쓰는, 교활한
The **wily** scheme was unable to deceive the police officer.[36]

syn. artful, crafty, sly

 예문 해석

31 그는 레코드판을 기념으로 간직하고 있었다. **32** 저녁 시간 너무 힘든 운동은 피하십시오. **33** 그는 가장 친한 친구와의 싸움으로 관계가 나빠지지 않기를 바랐다. **34** 경찰은 침입 혐의로 그 남자를 체포했다. **35** 신중함이 용기의 핵심이다. **36** 그 교활한 계략은 경찰관을 속일 수 없었다.

Directions   Each of the following questions consists of one word followed by five words or phrases. You are to select the one word or phrase whose meaning is closest to the word in capital letters.

1. AFFECTION :
(A) speed
(B) memento
(C) fondness
(D) stealthy
(E) barrier

2. ARDOR :
(A) quarrel
(B) prose
(C) fervor
(D) beginning
(E) stature

3. ELUSIVE :
(A) transitory
(B) barbaric
(C) inconsolable
(D) slippery
(E) inborn

4. ESOTERIC :
(A) obvious
(B) dramatic
(C) opinionated
(D) enormous
(E) abstruse

5. FLOUNDER :
(A) compete
(B) brighten
(C) struggle
(D) deter
(E) mimic

6. GAUNT :
(A) bashful
(B) dramatic
(C) assuring
(D) enduring
(E) haggard

7. LIABILITY :
(A) answerability
(B) salvation
(C) incision
(D) deadlock
(E) smudge

8. MANDATE :
(A) bungalow
(B) dishonor
(C) illusion
(D) command
(E) hybrid

9. NONPARTISAN :
(A) independent
(B) wan
(C) neurotic
(D) clamorous
(E) overbearing

10. PEDIGREE :
(A) confusion
(B) dissection
(C) impetus
(D) shrewdness
(E) lineage

"Winners never quit, and quitters never win."

– Vince Lombardi –
U.S. football coach

승자는 결코 중도에 그만두지 않고, 중도에 그만두는 자는 결코 승자가 되지 못한다.

Greek and Latin Roots & Prefixes 58

★ META = beyond, change, after

wer (to turn)	metaverse	가상 공간, 사이버 스페이스
morphe (shape)	metamorphosis	탈바꿈, 변형, 변태
phora (a carrying)	metaphor	은유
physica (natural things)	metaphysics	형이상학
	metaphysical	철학적인, 추상적인, 난해한
ballo (to throw)	metabolic	생물의 신진대사의
histani (to place)	metastasis	(병이나 암의) 전이

DAY

58

WORDS TO LEARN

- ☐ aftermath
- ☐ apprehensive
- ☐ blockade
- ☐ cacophony
- ☐ collaborate
- ☐ contort
- ☐ deem
- ☐ dilettante
- ☐ dissipate

- ☐ emanate
- ☐ esteem
- ☐ facet
- ☐ flourish
- ☐ haggle
- ☐ hunch
- ☐ impregnable
- ☐ infallible
- ☐ intermission

- ☐ juvenile
- ☐ liberal
- ☐ maneuver
- ☐ miserable
- ☐ nemesis
- ☐ opulent
- ☐ pernicious
- ☐ preclude
- ☐ profuse

- ☐ recoil
- ☐ roster
- ☐ savor
- ☐ sovereign
- ☐ stride
- ☐ tangible
- ☐ trickery
- ☐ vanquish
- ☐ wince

01

aftermath
[af-ter-math]

n. something that results or follows from an event
여파, 결과
In the **aftermath** of the Korean war, Korea was divided along the 38th parallel.[1]

syn. consequence, impact, outcome

02

apprehensive
[ap-ri-hen-siv]

adj. uneasy or fearful about something that might happen
걱정되는, 불안한
Because he lived near a busy intersection with no stop signs, he was **apprehensive** about crossing the street.[2]

syn. concerned, anxious, fearful

03

blockade
[blo-keyd]

n. a war measure isolating an area of importance to the enemy
봉쇄, 차단
They built a **blockade** to confine their enemies and isolate them.[3]

syn. barrier, barricade, encirclement

예문 해석

01 한국 전쟁의 결과로 한국은 38선을 따라 나뉘었다.　**02** 그는 정지 표지판이 없는 번화한 교차로 근처에 살았기 때문에, 길을 건너는 것이 걱정되었다.　**03** 그들은 적을 감금하고 고립시키기 위해 봉쇄를 구축했다.

04

cacophony
[kuh-kof-uh-nee]

n. a harsh, unpleasant sound

불협화음

That blaring **cacophony** was the school marching band tuning their instruments.[4]

syn. discord, noise

05

collaborate
[kuh-lab-uh-reyt]

v. to work together

함께 일하다, 공동 연구하다

The three authors **collaborated** to create a popular novel.[5]

syn. cooperate, get together

06

contort
[kuhn-tawrt]

v. to twist and press out of shape

비틀어서 일그러뜨리다, 왜곡시키다

His face **contorted**.[6]

syn. bend, distort, garble

07

deem
[deem]

v. to judge, think, or consider

생각하다, 간주하다

I was **deemed** to be a competent consultant.[7]

syn. regard, consider

08

dilettante
[dil-i-tahnt]

n. a person who takes up an art, activity, or subject merely for amusement, especially in a desultory or superficial way

아마추어, 호사가, 취미로 조금씩 해보는 사람

He is a stereotypical **dilettante** who pretends to be very knowledgeable.[8]

syn. dabbler, amateur, beginner

예문 해석

04 시끄러운 불협화음은 학교 밴드가 악기 튜닝을 하는 소리였다.   **05** 그 세 작가는 공동으로 인기 소설을 만들었다.   **06** 그의 얼굴이 일그러졌다.   **07** 나는 능력 있는 컨설턴트로 여겨졌다.   **08** 그는 박식한 척 하는 전형적인 아마추어였다.

dissipate
[dis-*uh*-peyt]

v. to separate and scatter

(슬픔이나 공포가) 없어지다, (재산을) 탕진하다

The tension in the room had **dissipated** with his humor.[9]

syn. dispel, disperse, dissolve

10

emanate
[em-*uh*-neyt]

v. to send forth

나오다, 발산하다, 퍼지다

The traveller **emanated** a faint odor of sawdust and straw.[10]

syn. give off, emerge, exude

11

esteem
[i-steem]

n. the condition of being honored

존경, 경외

He is held in high **esteem** by colleagues in the IT industry.[11]

syn. respect, admiration, regard

12

facet
[fas-it]

n. the different aspects of something

다면체, 자른 면

She wanted to explore every **facet** of life through travel.[12]

syn. aspect, phase

13

flourish
[flur-ish]

v. to grow vigorously

번성하다

The plant **flourishes** particularly well in a slightly arid climate.[13]

syn. thrive, prosper, burgeon

14

haggle
[hag-*uhl*]

v. to wrangle (over a price)

(특히 물건 값을 두고) 실랑이를 벌이다, 흥정을 하다

Because he wanted a great deal on a used TV, he tried to **haggle** with the sellers to see if they would bring the price down.[14]

syn. wrangle, bargain, bicker

예문 해석

09 그의 유머로 방의 긴장이 사라졌다. **10** 그 여행자에게는 톱밥과 지푸라기 냄새가 희미하게 났다. **11** 그는 IT업계에서 동료들의 높은 존경을 받고 있다. **12** 그녀는 여행을 통해 삶의 모든 면을 탐험하고 싶었다. **13** 이 식물은 약간 건조할 때 특히 더 잘 자란다. **14** 그는 중고 TV를 많이 사고 싶었기 때문에, 판매자들과 가격을 낮출 수 있는지 흥정하려고 했다.

15

hunch
[huhnch]

n. a feeling that something is going to happen, often something unpleasant
(특히 불길한) 예감
My **hunch** had been right.[15]

syn. gut feeling, instinct, intuition

16

impregnable
[im-preg-nuh-buhl]

adj. strong enough to resist or withstand attack
무적의, 난공불락의
The soldiers surrounded the **impregnable** fort.[16]

syn. invulnerable, invincible, unconquerable

17

infallible
[in-fall-uh-buhl]

adj. absolutely trustworthy or sure
절대 오류가 없는, 절대 확실한
She wanted to buy an **infallible** dress to wear at the pageant.[17]

syn. unerring, certain, unfailing

18

intermission
[in-ter-mish-uhn]

n. a short break between two parts of a film, concert, or show
휴식 시간, 막간
The play went on for three hours without an **intermission**.[18]

syn. recess, break, lull

19

juvenile
[joo-vuh-nl]

adj. of young persons
소년소녀의, 어린, 청소년의
He was young when he committed the crime, so he was sent to a **juvenile** detention center.[19]

syn. adolescent, junior, young

20

liberal
[lib-er-uhl]

adj. showing or characterized by broad-mindedness
관대한, 편견이 없는, 자유주의의
She was a **liberal** giver.[20]

syn. giving, generous, prodigal

예문 해석

15 내 예감이 맞았다. **16** 병사들은 난공불락의 요새를 포위했다. **17** 그녀는 대회에서 입을 완벽한 드레스를 사고 싶었다. **18** 그 공연은 세 시간 동안 쉬는 시간 없이 계속 되었다. **19** 그는 범행 당시 나이가 어렸기 때문에 소년원에 보내졌다. **20** 그녀는 아낌없이 베푸는 사람이다.

maneuver
[m*uh*-noo-ver]

n. a planned and regulated movement

책략, 술책

We were on a **maneuver** for two months.[21]

syn. stratagem, operation, exercise

miserable
[miz-er-*uh*-b*uh*l]

adj. wretchedly unhappy

불쌍한, 비참한

The company compensated each with $100 million for their **miserable** working conditions.[22]

syn. wretched, pitiable, lamentable

nemesis
[nem-*uh*-sis]

n. punishment that is deserved, or an unconquerable opponent

이길 수 없는 상대, 네메시스(복수의 여신)

The test seems to be my **nemesis**.[23]

syn. adversary, bane, affliction

opulent
[op-yuh-lu*h*nt]

adj. very wealthy

부유한, 호화로운

He tried to make the interior of his mansion look as **opulent** as possible.[24]

syn. luxurious, wealthy, lavish

pernicious
[per-nish-*uh*s]

adj. exceedingly harmful

치명적인, 악의에 찬

Pernicious poison gas causes illness in those exposed to it over the years.[25]

syn. detrimental, malicious, lethal

 예문 해석

21 우리는 두 달간 작전에 참여했다.   **22** 그 회사는 열악한 작업환경에 대한 보상으로 각각 1억 원씩 배상했다.   **23** 그 테스트는 이길 수 없는 상대처럼 보인다.   **24** 그는 자신의 대저택 내부를 최대한 호화스럽게 하려 했다.   **25** 유해한 독가스는 수년간 그것에 노출된 사람들에게 질병을 유발한다.

26

preclude
[pri-klood]

v. to prevent the presence
일어나지 않게 하다, 사전에 막다
Opening a dialogue with an adversary does not **preclude** continued conflict.[26]

syn. inhibit, avert, deter

27

profuse
[pr*uh*-fyoos]

adj. growing in extreme abundance
많은, 다량의
If a person is bleeding **profusely**, be on the lookout for symptoms of shock.[27]

syn. copious, abundant, excessive

28

recoil
[re-koil]

v. to shrink back as in alarm, horror, or disgust
움찔하다, 흠칫 놀라다
The **recoil** of a gun is a backward movement caused by momentum.[28]

syn. flinch, shrink, cower

29

roster
[ros-ter]

n. a list or roll of people's names
근무 표, 당번 리스트, 선수 명단
I had a **roster** of all the attendees at the auction.[29]

syn. list, inventory, table

30

savor
[sey-ver]

v. taste appreciatively
맛을 느끼다. 풍미를 즐기다.
She **savored** her chocolate tart, eating it slowly, bit by bit, deliberately picking every last crumb off the plate.[30]

syn. relish, taste, flavor

예문 해석

26 적과 공개적으로 대화를 트는 것이 계속되는 충돌을 막아주지는 않는다. **27** 출혈이 심할 경우 쇼크 증상을 주의하도록 하라. **28** 총의 반동은 추진력에 의해 발생하는 후진 운동이다. **29** 나는 경매에 나온 모든 참가자들의 명단이 있었다. **30** 그녀는 초콜릿 타르트를 음미하며 천천히 조금씩 먹으며, 신중하게 접시에 남은 마지막 부스러기까지 모두 떠먹었다.

sovereign
[sov-rin]

n. a king, queen, or other royal ruler of a country

통치자, 군주

The American colonies sought to break ties with their **sovereign** king.[31]

syn. ruler, monarch, supreme ruler

stride
[strahyd]

v. to walk with long steps

큰 걸음으로 걷다, 성큼성큼 걷다

He **strode** down the garden path.[32]

syn. march, stalk, tread

tangible
[tan-*juh*-*buh*l]

adj. clear enough to be easily seen, felt, or noticed

형체가 있는, 구체적인, 만질 수 있는

There should be some **tangible** evidence that he is the criminal.[33]

syn. real, concrete, palpable

trickery
[trik-*uh*-ree]

n. an act, instance, or the practice, of deceiving or cheating

속임수, 사기

There's a smell of **trickery** about it.[34]

syn. chicanery, deceit, deception

vanquish
[vang-kwish]

v. to defeat or overcome someone

정복하다, 패배시키다

The hero **vanquished** the dragon.[35]

syn. defeat, conquer, crush

wince
[wins]

v. to shrink back

주춤하다, 꽁무니 빼다, 질겁하다, 움츠리다, 겁내다

He **winced** in pain.[36]

syn. cower, cringe, recoil

예문 해석

31 미국 식민지는 주권자인 왕과의 관계를 끊으려고 했다. **32** 그는 정원 길을 성큼성큼 걸었다. **33** 그가 범인이라는 것을 증명하기 위한 구체적인 증거가 필요하다. **34** 무언가 속임수의 냄새가 난다. **35** 영웅이 용을 쓰러뜨렸다. **36** 그는 고통으로 움찔했다.

Directions   Each of the following questions consists of one word followed by five words or phrases.
You are to select the one word or phrase whose meaning is closest to the word in capital letters.

1. **AFTERMATH :**
   (A) consequence
   (B) precedence
   (C) boulevard
   (D) feint
   (E) enigma

2. **APPREHENSIVE :**
   (A) flammable
   (B) concerned
   (C) obese
   (D) dazzling
   (E) complimentary

3. **CACOPHONY :**
   (A) disposition
   (B) companion
   (C) persistence
   (D) discord
   (E) prudence

4. **HAGGLE :**
   (A) alleviate
   (B) reject
   (C) expel
   (D) occupy
   (E) wrangle

5. **INFALLIBLE :**
   (A) haughty
   (B) timorous
   (C) haunted
   (D) unerring
   (E) well-bred

6. **LIBERAL :**
   (A) giving
   (B) indestructible
   (C) shrewd
   (D) haggard
   (E) pretentious

7. **NEMESIS :**
   (A) catastrophe
   (B) extremity
   (C) adversary
   (D) posture
   (E) model

8. **PROFUSE :**
   (A) suitable
   (B) copious
   (C) transient
   (D) graphic
   (E) moving

9. **RECOIL :**
   (A) gleam
   (B) flinch
   (C) magnify
   (D) forsake
   (E) thrive

10. **TANGIBLE :**
    (A) murky
    (B) indecent
    (C) secured
    (D) real
    (E) religious

"I've learned that people will forget what you said,
people will forget what you did,
but people will never forget how you made them feel."

— Maya Angelou —
American writer

사람들은 당신이 한 말을 잊을 것이고, 당신이 한 일도 잊을 것이지만,
당신이 어떻게 느끼도록 했는지 결코 잊지 않을 것을 안다.

Greek and Latin Roots & Prefixes 59

★ FER = to carry

con (together)	confer	상의하다, 수여하다
dis (apart)	conference	회의, 회담
circum (around)	circumference	원주, 둘레
de (down)	defer	미루다, 연기하다
re (back)	refer	조회하다, 참조하게 하다
in (into)	infer	추론하다, 암시하다
inter (between)	interfere	간섭하다, 훼방을 놓다
pre (before)	prefer	선호하다, 좋아하다
trans (across)	transfer	옮기다, 이동하다
voco (call)	vociferous	소리 높여 말하는

DAY

59

WORDS TO LEARN

- [ ] agenda
- [ ] archaic
- [ ] benevolent
- [ ] cajole
- [ ] congenital
- [ ] contradict
- [ ] defect
- [ ] devious
- [ ] eavesdrop

- [ ] eddy
- [ ] embargo
- [ ] facile
- [ ] fluctuate
- [ ] genesis
- [ ] hale
- [ ] harass
- [ ] impromptu
- [ ] infamy

- [ ] intermittent
- [ ] juxtapose
- [ ] liberate
- [ ] maniac
- [ ] miserly
- [ ] neophyte
- [ ] oracle
- [ ] penchant
- [ ] precocious

- [ ] replica
- [ ] rotund
- [ ] servile
- [ ] snarl
- [ ] subjugate
- [ ] sweltering
- [ ] trickle
- [ ] vacate
- [ ] woe

01

agenda
[*uh*-jen-duh]

n. a list, plan, outline of things to be done
회의 일정, 논의할 의제
The committee placed the issue of safety at the top of the **agenda**.[1]

> *syn.* schedule, plan, program

02

archaic
[ahr-key-ik]

adj. marked by the characteristics of an earlier period
고대의, 오래된
Her advertisement idea seemed like an **archaic** notion and was not approved by her boss.[2]

> *syn.* antiquated, obsolete

03

benevolent
[b*uh*-nev-*uh*-lu*h*nt]

adj. expressing goodwill or kind feelings
자비로운, 인자한, 인정 많은
Students were happy with gifts from several **benevolent** alumni.[3]

> *syn.* good, kind, generous, charitable

예문 해석

01 그 위원회는 안전 문제를 첫 안건으로 올렸다.　**02** 그녀의 광고 아이디어는 낡은 생각처럼 보였고 상사의 승인을 받지 못했다.
03 학생들은 몇몇 인자한 동문으로부터의 선물에 기뻐했다.

04

cajole
[k*uh*-johl]

v. to persuade by flattery or promises
감언이설로 속이다
He has bribed and **cajoled**.[4]

syn. wheedle, coax

05

congenital
[k*uh*n-jen-i-tl]

adj. present at birth but not necessarily hereditary
선천적인, 타고난
The baby was born with a **congenital** disease, so the parents looked into proper accommodations.[5]

syn. innate, inborn, inherent

06

contradict
[kon-tr*uh*-dikt]

v. to assert the opposite of
부인하다, 반박하다
I hate to **contradict** you, but I don't agree.[6]

syn. negate, deny, belie

07

defect
[dee-fekt]

n. a failing or deficiency
결점, 결함
There was a **defect** in the machine.[7]

syn. flaw, fault, failing

08

devious
[dee-vee-*uhs*]

adj. not straightforward
정도를 벗어난, 구불구불한, 사악한
He was **devious**, prepared to say one thing in public and another in private.[8]

syn. deceitful, tricky, shifty

예문 해석

04 그는 뇌물을 주고 감언이설로 속였다. **05** 아기가 선천성 질환을 갖고 태어났기 때문에 부모는 적절한 숙소를 알아봤다. **06** 반박하고 싶진 않지만, 나는 그렇게 생각하지 않는다. **07** 기계에 결함이 있었다. **08** 그는 안에서 하는 말과 밖에서 하는 말이 다른 믿지 못할 사람이었다.

09

eavesdrop
[eevz-drop]

v. to listen secretly to a private conversation

엿듣다, 도청하다

The boy **eavesdropped** on his parents in an attempt to find out what he might get for his birthday.[9]

syn. overhear, tap, wire

10

eddy
[ed-ee]

n. a miniature whirlpool or whirlwind

회오리, 소용돌이

He stared at an **eddy** as a kid when the water was draining out of the bathtub.[10]

syn. whirlpool, whirlwind, swirl

11

embargo
[em-bahr-goh]

n. a prohibition of the movement of merchant ships into or out of a country's ports

금수조치, 경제 교류를 중단하는 조치

Because of the protest, there was an **embargo**.[11]

syn. boycott, ban, prohibition

12

facile
[fas-il]

adj. too easily achieved

힘들지 않는, 쉽사리 얻을 수 있는

The team winning did not mean much because of their **facile** victory.[12]

syn. simplistic, effortless

13

fluctuate
[fluck-chu-ate]

v. to change a lot in an irregular way

오르락내리락하다, 변동하다

The **fluctuating** price of oil seems to consistently take people by surprise.[13]

syn. vacillate, oscillate, waver

 예문 해석

09 그 소년은 생일에 무엇을 받을지 알아보기 위해 부모님의 말을 엿들었다. **10** 그는 아이처럼 욕조에서 물이 빠지고 있을 때 작은 소용돌이를 응시했다. **11** 시위 때문에 금수 조치가 내려졌다. **12** 수월한 승리 때문에 팀의 승리는 큰 의미가 없었다. **13** 기름값의 등락은 끊임없이 사람들을 놀라게 하는 것 같다.

14

genesis
[jen-*uh*-sis]

n. an origin, creation, or beginning
기원, 발생, 창조
This book is about the **genesis** of the fashion design.[14]

syn. creation, origin, beginning

15

hale
[heyl]

adj. free from disease or infirmity
(특히 노인이) 건강한, 정정한
Even in his 80s, he was **hale**, hearty, and could lift a piano easily.[15]

syn. robust, vigorous, healthy

16

harass
[h*uh*-ras]

v. to pester and torment aggressively and repeatedly
(압력을 가하거나 불쾌한 말이나 행동으로) 괴롭히다, 희롱하다
The bully at school **harasses** some poor kids verbally and physically.[16]

syn. badger, pester, vex

17

impromptu
[im-promp-too]

adj. made or done without previous preparation
즉흥적인
I had to give an **impromptu** speech at the gala.[17]

syn. extemporized, improvised

18

infamy
[in-*fuh*-mee]

n. extremely bad reputation
불명예, 악명
The **infamy** of the villain was well known throughout the village.[18]

syn. notoriety, disgrace, disrepute

19

intermittent
[in-ter-mit-nt]

adj. alternately ceasing and beginning again
간헐적인
A diet that is popular these days to lose weight is known as **intermittent** fasting.[19]

syn. sporadic, occasional, periodic

예문 해석

14 이 책은 패션 디자인의 기원에 대한 책이다.   **15** 그는 80대인데도 정정했고 피아노도 쉽게 들 수 있었다.   **16** 학교에서 다른 사람들을 괴롭히는 사람은 몇몇 불쌍한 아이들을 언어적, 육체적으로 괴롭힌다.   **17** 나는 축제에서 즉석 연설을 해야 했다.   **18** 그 악당의 악명은 마을 전체에 널리 알려져 있었다.   **19** 요즘 체중 감량을 위해 유행하는 다이어트는 간헐적 단식이라고 알려져 있다.

20

juxtapose
[ju*h*k-st*uh*-pohz]

v. to place close together or side by side
나란히 늘어놓다, 병렬로 정렬하다
In the exhibit, his father's paintings are **juxtaposed** with those of other famous painters.[20]

syn. place side by side, connect, appose

21

liberate
[lib-er-eyt]

v to free from confinement
풀어주다, 자유롭게 해주다, 노예를 해방하다
Meditation helps to **liberate** the mind and soul.[21]

syn. release, unfetter, emancipate

22

maniac
[mey-nee-ak]

n. a raving or violently insane person
열광자, 마니아
Because of her behavior, others viewed her like a **maniac**.[22]

syn. lunatic, fanatic, zealot

23

miserly
[mai-zer-lee]

adj. of a person hating to spend money
인색한, 욕심 많은
He is **miserly** with both his time and his money.[23]

syn. stingy, greedy, parsimonious

24

neophyte
[nee-*uh*-fait]

n. someone who's brand new at something
초심자, 신참자, 초보자
Neophyte teachers barely out of college instruct students who are sometimes older than they are.[24]

syn. tyro, novice, recruit

25

oracle
[awr-*uh*-k*uh*l]

n. the advice that the gods gave
신탁, 신탁을 전하는 사제
The king consulted the **oracle** before going to battle.[25]

syn. prophecy, augury, divination

 예문 해석

20 전시회에는 그의 아버지의 그림들이 다른 유명 화가의 작품들과 나란히 걸려 있었다. **21** 명상은 마음과 영혼을 해방시키는 데 도움이 된다. **22** 그녀의 행동 때문에 다른 사람들은 그녀를 미치광이처럼 보았다. **23** 그는 시간과 돈에 매우 인색하다. **24** 대학을 갓 졸업한 새내기 선생님들은 때로는 자기보다 나이가 많은 학생들을 가르친다. **25** 왕은 전투에 나가기 전에 신탁을 받는 사제와 상의했다.

26

penchant
[pen-ch*uh*nt]

n. a strong and continued inclination
강하게 좋아하는 경향, 성향
She has a **penchant** for sitting by the window.[26]

syn. predilection, proclivity, propensity

27

precocious
[pri-koh-sh*uh*s]

adj. ahead of normal development
조숙한, 발달이 빠른
She was a **precocious** child for her age.[27]

syn. advanced, early

28

replica
[rep-li-k*uh*]

n. an exact copy
복제본
I have yet to see a life-sized **replica** of the Statue of Liberty.[28]

syn. copy, facsimile, duplicate

29

rotund
[roh-t*uh*nd]

adj. round or rounded in form
(살이 쪄서) 통통한, 둥실둥실한
He has a **rotund** face.[29]

syn. stout, plump, round

30

servile
[sur-vil]

adj. slavishly respectful or obedient
노예근성의, 비굴한
He is subservient and **servile** like a slave.[30]

syn. abject, cringing, subservient

31

snarl
[snahrl]

v. to utter in an angry, sharp, or abrupt tone
(화가 나서) 으르렁거리다
A dog's snarl says, "Back off!"[31]

syn. growl, bark, mutter

예문 해석

26 그녀는 창가에 앉는 것을 매우 좋아하는 경향이 있다. **27** 그녀는 나이에 비해 조숙한 아이였다. **28** 나는 아직 자유의 여신상의 실물 크기 복제품을 보지 못했다. **29** 그는 둥글둥글한 얼굴을 하고 있다. **30** 그는 복종적이고 노예처럼 비굴하다. **31** 개의 으르렁거림은 "물러서"라고 말하는 것이다.

32

subjugate
[su*h*b-*juh*-geyt]

v. to force to submit or subdue

지배하에 두다, 예속시키다

The powers try to **subjugate** the weak countries.[32]

> *syn.* overpower, defeat, conquer

33

sweltering
[swel-ter-ing]

adj. excessively hot and humid

무더운, 매우 덥고 습한

Walking a long way home on a **sweltering** day left him exhausted.[33]

> *syn.* torrid, scorching, sizzling

34

trickle
[trik-*uhl*]

v. to flow or make something flow in a thin slow stream or drops

액체가 뚝뚝 떨어지다, 졸졸 흐르다

A tear **trickled** down the girl's cheek.[34]

> *syn.* drip, dribble, drop

35

vacate
[vey-keyt]

v. to leave behind empty

비우다, 떠나다

The landlady asked him to **vacate** the room, so he packed up his things and went out.[35]

> *syn.* empty out, evacuate, abandon

36

woe
[woh]

n. misery resulting from affliction

슬픔

She listened to his whole tale of **woe**.[36]

> *syn.* misery, anguish, grief

 예문 해석

32 강대국들은 약소국들을 정복하려고 한다.   **33** 푹푹 찌는 날 집까지 먼 길을 걸었더니 그는 녹초가 되었다.   **34** 소녀의 뺨을 타고 눈물이 뚝뚝 떨어졌다.   **35** 집주인이 방을 비워달라고 해서 그는 짐을 싸서 나갔다.   **36** 그녀는 그의 슬픈 이야기를 다 들어 주었다.

Directions   Each of the following questions consists of one word followed by five words or phrases. You are to select the one word or phrase whose meaning is closest to the word in capital letters.

1. AGENDA :
- (A) reverence
- (B) argument
- (C) predicament
- (D) schedule
- (E) tribute

2. ARCHAIC :
- (A) nimble
- (B) antiquated
- (C) sluggish
- (D) conversational
- (E) fictional

3. CAJOLE :
- (A) scorn
- (B) mortify
- (C) wheedle
- (D) compensate
- (E) wander

4. DEFECT :
- (A) improper
- (B) flaw
- (C) din
- (D) cleft
- (E) stutter

5. EAVESDROP :
- (A) overhear
- (B) retaliation
- (C) abscond
- (D) request
- (E) disquiet

6. FACILE :
- (A) illustrative
- (B) simplistic
- (C) unflagging
- (D) ingenious
- (E) frantic

7. INTERMITTENT :
- (A) ingenuous
- (B) provisional
- (C) nautical
- (D) sporadic
- (E) inconsequential

8. LIBERATE :
- (A) expend
- (B) pester
- (C) intimidate
- (D) release
- (E) weaken

9. ORACLE :
- (A) prophecy
- (B) ruse
- (C) charlatan
- (D) velocity
- (E) tumult

10. REPLICA :
- (A) parole
- (B) frivolity
- (C) insanity
- (D) quandary
- (E) copy

"Great minds discuss ideas; Average minds discuss events;
Small minds discuss people."

— Eleanor Roosevelt —
U.S. diplomat & reformer

위대한 사람은 아이디어를 논한다. 보통의 사람은 사건을 논한다.
소인배들은 사람들에 대해 논한다.

Greek and Latin Roots & Prefixes 60

★ VOCO = call

-al (adj.)	vocal	목소리의
-tion (n.)	vocation	천직, 소명
ab (away from)	avocation	취미, 여가 활동
in (into)	invoke	들먹이다, 부르다
pro (before)	provoke	화나게 하다, 도발하다
re (back)	revoke	취소하다, 폐지하다
sub (down)	subvocal	목소리를 거의 내지 않는
ad (toward)	advocate	지지하다, 지지자

DAY

60

WORDS TO LEARN

☐ aggravate	☐ embellish	☐ interpose	☐ repose
☐ archipelago	☐ emancipate	☐ keen	☐ rue
☐ bequeath	☐ facilitate	☐ manifest	☐ sever
☐ colloquial	☐ flutter	☐ misery	☐ spat
☐ compile	☐ genial	☐ nestle	☐ spite
☐ coterie	☐ hallow	☐ orator	☐ tantalize
☐ defer	☐ hurl	☐ penitent	☐ trifling
☐ devise	☐ improvise	☐ plod	☐ vehement
☐ distaste	☐ infatuated	☐ prowl	☐ versatile

01

aggravate
[ag-*ruh*-veyt]

v. to make something even worse
악화시키다
Military intervention **aggravated** the conflict even further.[1]

syn. intensify, worsen, exacerbate

02

archipelago
[ahr-*kuh*-pel-*uh*-goh]

n. a large group or chain of islands
군도(무리를 이룬 섬), 열도
The family had a goal to go see the Japanese **archipelago**.[2]

syn. islands, enclave, islet

03

bequeath
[bih-kweeth]

v. to hand down
물려주다, 유증하다
She **bequeathed** half of her assets to her daughter.[3]

syn. endow, transmit, pass on

예문 해석

01 군사적 개입은 갈등을 더욱 악화시켰다.　**02** 그 가족은 일본 열도를 보러 가는 것이 목표였다.　**03** 그녀는 자산의 반을 딸에게 물려주었다.

04

colloquial
[k*uh*-loh-kwee-*uh*l]

adj. used in or characteristic of familiar and informal conversation

구어체의, 일상 회화식 표현의

Do not use **colloquial** expressions in a formal essay.[4]

syn. conversational, informal, nonformal

05

compile
[k*uh*m-pahyl]

v. to get or gather together

(여러 출처에서 자료를 가져와) 엮다, 편집하다

He **complied** his favorite songs and made his playlist for his love.[5]

syn. assemble, collect, accumulate

06

coterie
[koh-t*uh*-ree]

n. an exclusive circle of people with a common purpose

소규모 집단

Directly below the queen was a **coterie** of intellectuals possessing a mind of the highest intellect.[6]

syn. clique, circle, set

07

defer
[dih-fur]

v. to put off to a future time

뒤로 미루다, 연기하다

The decision has been **deferred** until next week.[7]

syn. put off, delay, postpone

08

devise
[di-vaiz]

v. to come up with an idea, theory, or principle after a mental effort

고안하다, 발명하다

We **devised** an innovative way to help him.[8]

syn. contrive, invent, formulate

예문 해석

04 공식적인 에세이에 구어적 표현은 사용하지 마세요. **05** 그는 자신이 좋아하는 노래를 엮어 사랑하는 사람을 위한 플레이리스트를 만들었다. **06** 여왕 바로 아래에는 최고의 지성을 가진 지식인들이 모여 있었다. **07** 결정은 다음 주로 연기되었다. **08** 우리는 그를 도와 줄 혁신적인 방법을 고안했다.

distaste
[dis-teyst]

n. a felling of intense dislike

불쾌함, 혐오함

His mother had a **distaste** for the sport of boxing, while his boxing-loving dad's distaste was for ballet.[9]

syn. disgust, antipathy, aversion

emancipate
[ih-man-*suh*-peyt]

v. to free from slavery or servitude

해방시키다

At the end of the Civil War, slaves were **emancipated**.[10]

syn. set free, liberate, loosen

embellish
[em-bel-ish]

v. to decorate

장식하다, 꾸미다

She **embellished** her home with flowers.[11]

syn. decorate, adorn, bedeck

facilitate
[*fuh*-sil-i-teyt]

v. to make something easier

일을 쉽게 하다, 용이하게 하다

The new airport **facilitated** the development of tourism.[12]

syn. aid, help, ease

flutter
[fl*uh*t-er]

v. to flap the wings rapidly

펄럭거리다, 퍼덕이다

School banners **fluttered** in the breeze.[13]

syn. flap, flop, drift

genial
[jeen-y*uh*l]

adj. diffusing warmth and freindliness

친절한, 상냥한

The teachers were always **genial**.[14]

syn. congenial, amiable, agreeable

예문 해석

09 그의 어머니는 권투 스포츠를 싫어했고, 그의 복싱을 사랑하는 아버지는 발레를 싫어했다.   **10** 남북전쟁이 끝나자 노예들은 해방되었다.   **11** 그녀는 자신의 집을 꽃으로 장식했다.   **12** 새 공항은 관광산업 발전을 더 용이하게 했다.   **13** 학교 깃발들이 미풍에 펄럭거렸다.   **14** 선생님들은 늘 친절했다.

15

hallow
[hal-oh]

v. to make holy
신성한 것으로 숭배하다
Our Father which art in heaven, **hallowed** be thy name.[15]

> *syn.* sanctify, consecrate

16

hurl
[hurl]

v. to throw violently
세게 내던지다
The angry crowd **hurled** stones at the police.[16]

> *syn.* fling, throw, fling

17

improvise
[im-pr*uh*-vaiz]

v. to compose and perform or deliver without previous preparation
(연주나 말을) 즉흥적으로 하다
When asked for the names of famous scientists, he **improvised**.[17]

> *syn.* make up, ad-lib, extemporize

18

infatuated
[in-fach-oo-eytid]

adj. having strong feelings of love or passion which make it hard to think sensibly
심취한, 매혹된, 열중한
He was utterly **infatuated** with her.[18]

> *syn.* obsessed, enamored, bewitched

19

interpose
[in-ter-pohz]

v. to put something between or in the way of
사이에 끼워넣다, 개입하다, 중재하다
She **interposed** herself between her mother and father.[19]

> *syn.* interrupt, arbitrate, mediate

20

keen
[keen]

adj. intense, sharp or focused
날카로운, 예리한
He has a **keen** eye for detail.[20]

> *syn.* intense, acute, sharp

예문 해석

15 하늘에 계신 우리 아버지여, 이름이 거룩히 여김을 받으시오며. (성경 Matthew 마태복음에 나오는 '주기도문'의 첫 구절)   **16** 화난 군중들이 경찰에게 돌을 던졌다.   **17** 유명한 과학자 이름을 대보라는 말에 그는 그 자리에서 지어내었다.   **18** 그는 완전히 그녀에게 푹 빠져 있었다.   **19** 그녀는 엄마 아빠 사이에 끼어들었다.   **20** 그는 세세한 것을 잘 보는 눈이 있다.

21

manifest
[man-*uh*-fest]

adj. easily seen or perceived
명백한, 분명한
It's **manifest** at a glance.[21]

syn. apparent, obvious, patent

22

misery
[miz-*uh*-ree]

n. suffering caused by need or poverty
비참함, 곤궁, 불행
A country's **misery** index is a barometer of people's economic conditions.[22]

syn. distress, anguish, suffering

23

nestle
[nes-*uhl*]

v. to sit or lie down in a warm or soft place
편안하게 자리 잡다
She **nestled** her first child in her arms.[23]

syn. snuggle, cozy up, huddle

24

orator
[awr-*uh*-ter]

n. someone who is skilled at making formal speeches
웅변가, 연설자
Lenin was the great **orator** of the Russian Revolution.[24]

syn. speaker, lecturer, rhetorician

25

penitent
[pen-i-*tuh*nt]

adj. feeling or expressing regretful pain or sorrow for sins or offenses
뉘우치는, 참회하는, 회개하는
She strongly lambasted him for not being **penitent** for his past wrongdoings.[25]

syn. contrite, repentant, atoning

 예문 해석

21 한 눈에 보기에도 확실하다.　**22** 한 나라의 불행 지수란 그 나라 사람들의 경제 상황의 지표이다.　**23** 그녀는 자기 첫 아이를 품에 편안하게 안았다.　**24** 레닌은 러시아 혁명의 위대한 웅변가였다.　**25** 그녀는 그가 지난 잘못을 뉘우치지 않는 것에 대해 심하게 비난했다.

plod
[plod]

v. to walk slowly, heavily, and deliberately

터벅터벅 걷다

He **plodded** home at the end of a long day.[26]

syn. trudge, tramp, lumber

prowl
[proul]

v. to rove or go about stealthily, as in search of prey

(먹이를 찾아 살금살금) 돌아다니다, 배회하다

The jaguar **prowled** around to search for prey.[27]

syn. roam, loiter, scavenge

repose
[ree-pohz]

n. the state of reposing or being at rest

휴식, 수면, 고요한 상태

She had a still, almost blank face in **repose**.[28]

syn. restfulness, calmness, relaxation

rue
[roo]

v. to feel regret or remorse for something

후회하다

Shakespeare's famous phrase "**rue** the day" means bitterly regretting a moment.[29]

syn. regret, grieve, mourn

sever
[sev-er]

v. to cut completely

자르다, 잘라내다

He **severed** connection with his company.[30]

syn. cut apart, split, separate

spat
[spat]

n. a trivial or petty fight or quarrel

말다툼, 싸움

She had a **spat** with a janitor in her apartment.[31]

syn. dispute, quarrel, altercation

예문 해석

26 그는 긴 하루를 마치고 집으로 터벅터벅 걸어갔다. **27** 그 재규어는 먹이를 찾기 위해 돌아다녔다. **28** 그녀는 거의 아무 생각도 없는 듯한 무표정한 얼굴을 하고 있었다. **29** 셰익스피어의 유명한 구절 "Rue the day"는 한 순간을 뼈저리게 후회한다는 뜻이다. **30** 그는 동료와 연락을 끊었다. **31** 그녀는 아파트 수위와 말다툼을 했다.

spite
[spait]

n. a malicious desire to harm another person

앙심, 악의

He said sarcastic remarks out of **spite** in a cruel way.[32]

syn. malice, ill will, malevolence

tantalize
[tan-tl-aiz]

v. to tease someone by keeping something they want just out of reach

애타게 하다, 감질나게 하다

The dream of being a famous singer has **tantalized** her.[33]

syn. taunt, tempt, tease

trifling
[trai-fling]

adj. unimportant or trivial

하찮은, 시시한

These difficulties may seem fairly **trifling**.[34]

syn. trivial, insignificant, worthless

vehement
[vee-*uh*-muhnt]

adj. expressed with strong feeling or firm conviction

열렬한, 열정적인

She suddenly became a **vehement** fan, jumping around and shouting.[35]

syn. zealous, passionate, fervent

versatile
[vur-*suh*-tl]

adj. capable in many areas and able to turn with ease from one thing to another

다재다능한

She is a **versatile** writer who crosses many genres.[36]

syn. adjustable, adaptable, resourceful

 예문 해석

32 그는 앙심을 품고 비꼬는 말을 잔인하게 했다.　**33** 가수가 되고자 하는 꿈이 그녀를 안달나게 했다.　**34** 이런 어려움은 별것도 아닌 것처럼 보일 수 있다.　**35** 그녀는 갑자기 열정적인 팬이 되어 뛰고 소리를 질렀다.　**36** 그녀는 여러 장르를 넘나드는 다재다능한 작가이다.

Directions   Each of the following questions consists of one word followed by five words or phrases. You are to select the one word or phrase whose meaning is closest to the word in capital letters.

1. **AGGRAVATE :**
   (A) curtail
   (B) surround
   (C) abridge
   (D) intensify
   (E) clinch

2. **COMPILE :**
   (A) arbitrate
   (B) jeer
   (C) assemble
   (D) deplore
   (E) overlook

3. **COTERIE :**
   (A) recreation
   (B) clique
   (C) frontier
   (D) deficiency
   (E) surfeit

4. **EMBELLISH :**
   (A) decorate
   (B) loiter
   (C) condole
   (D) weaken
   (E) ignite

5. **HURL :**
   (A) disguise
   (B) pulverize
   (C) fling
   (D) incense
   (E) evacuate

6. **MANIFEST :**
   (A) robust
   (B) apparent
   (C) dormant
   (D) conflicting
   (E) alternative

7. **PENITENT :**
   (A) myriad
   (B) pedestrian
   (C) contrite
   (D) meddlesome
   (E) visionary

8. **PROWL :**
   (A) magnify
   (B) roam
   (C) decrease
   (D) occupy
   (E) split

9. **TRIFLING :**
   (A) trivial
   (B) stationary
   (C) timorous
   (D) dogged
   (E) mocking

10. **VERSATILE :**
   (A) mellow
   (B) adjustable
   (C) wispy
   (D) haughty
   (E) dazzling

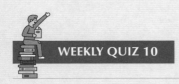
Directions   Each of the following questions consists of one word followed by five words or phrases. You are to select the one word or phrase whose meaning is closest to the word in capital letters.

1. DEVASTATE :
   (A) daydream
   (B) forgo
   (C) settle
   (D) demolish
   (E) withdraw

2. FLIPPANT :
   (A) frightful
   (B) supercilious
   (C) instructive
   (D) frivolous
   (E) obsolete

3. HACKNEYED :
   (A) trite
   (B) complicated
   (C) authentic
   (D) initial
   (E) belated

4. HUE :
   (A) color
   (B) drapery
   (C) brood
   (D) posture
   (E) courage

5. VALIANT :
   (A) unnecessary
   (B) callow
   (C) intrepid
   (D) tentative
   (E) unflagging

6. INDIGENT :
   (A) destitute
   (B) congenial
   (C) puzzling
   (D) genetic
   (E) disorganized

7. SERENE :
   (A) ferocious
   (B) nautical
   (C) obedient
   (D) irritated
   (E) placid

8. HAIL :
   (A) lean on
   (B) keep away
   (C) call to
   (D) put up
   (E) depend on

9. HUMILIATE :
   (A) hoist
   (B) mortify
   (C) attack
   (D) moan
   (E) chant

10. IMPOVERISHED :
    (A) genetic
    (B) murky
    (C) skillful
    (D) penurious
    (E) venturesome

11. TAINT :
    (A) wield
    (B) sully
    (C) reject
    (D) approve
    (E) embody

12. WILY :
    (A) postmortem
    (B) callow
    (C) artful
    (D) supple
    (E) derisive

13. COLLABORATE :
    (A) halt
    (B) pine
    (C) table
    (D) displace
    (E) cooperate

14. MANEUVER :
    (A) frugality
    (B) judge
    (C) stratagem
    (D) debacle
    (E) prudence

15. OPULENT :
    (A) fickle
    (B) odd
    (C) luxurious
    (D) steadfast
    (E) charming

16. DEVIOUS :
    (A) aloof
    (B) straitlaced
    (C) submissive
    (D) deceitful
    (E) petty

17. PRECOCIOUS :
    (A) advanced
    (B) placid
    (C) fervent
    (D) articulate
    (E) disillusioned

18. ROTUND :
    (A) stout
    (B) wintry
    (C) preposterous
    (D) wretched
    (E) brazen

19. SERVILE :
    (A) harmonious
    (B) abject
    (C) logical
    (D) permanent
    (E) frosty

20. PLOD :
    (A) covet
    (B) trudge
    (C) ignore
    (D) chuckle
    (E) hesitate

DAILY & WEEKLY

—

QUIZ
ANSWERS

DAILY QUIZ ANSWERS

DAILY QUIZ 01~06

day 1	1.D	2.E	3.E	4.B	5.D	6.A	7.A	8.B	9.B	10.D
day 2	1.E	2.A	3.A	4.C	5.E	6.A	7.D	8.E	9.A	10.D
day 3	1.D	2.E	3.A	4.C	5.A	6.A	7.D	8.B	9.B	10.B
day 4	1.B	2.C	3.A	4.C	5.A	6.D	7.B	8.A	9.E	10.C
day 5	1.D	2.E	3.A	4.B	5.B	6.A	7.A	8.D	9.B	10.B
day 6	1.A	2.D	3.B	4.B	5.A	6.E	7.B	8.A	9.A	10.C

DAILY QUIZ 07~12

day 7	1.C	2.B	3.D	4.B	5.A	6.A	7.B	8.B	9.C	10.E
day 8	1.A	2.C	3.B	4.E	5.C	6.B	7.C	8.E	9.C	10.C
day 9	1.E	2.C	3.E	4.B	5.A	6.A	7.D	8.E	9.E	10.D
day 10	1.D	2.E	3.A	4.A	5.A	6.D	7.B	8.A	9.C	10.D
day 11	1.A	2.A	3.A	4.B	5.B	6.D	7.E	8.D	9.B	10.B
day 12	1.E	2.B	3.D	4.A	5.C	6.C	7.D	8.C	9.D	10.E

DAILY QUIZ 13~18

day 13	1.D	2.E	3.A	4.A	5.E	6.C	7.C	8.D	9.B	10.D
day 14	1.E	2.E	3.A	4.C	5.A	6.A	7.A	8.E	9.B	10.A
day 15	1.C	2.C	3.B	4.E	5.C	6.A	7.C	8.D	9.C	10.B
day 16	1.A	2.D	3.C	4.A	5.D	6.E	7.D	8.E	9.B	10.C
day 17	1.C	2.D	3.A	4.B	5.E	6.B	7.E	8.C	9.A	10.E
day 18	1.B	2.A	3.A	4.D	5.B	6.C	7.A	8.D	9.D	10.C

DAILY QUIZ 19~24

day 19	1.E	2.B	3.E	4.C	5.D	6.D	7.C	8.A	9.A	10.A
day 20	1.D	2.A	3.E	4.D	5.E	6.D	7.A	8.C	9.C	10.E
day 21	1.D	2.B	3.D	4.B	5.E	6.A	7.A	8.E	9.A	10.B
day 22	1.E	2.A	3.B	4.B	5.A	6.C	7.D	8.A	9.B	10.A
day 23	1.A	2.E	3.C	4.B	5.C	6.D	7.B	8.B	9.C	10.C
day 24	1.D	2.A	3.E	4.E	5.C	6.B	7.A	8.C	9.A	10.E

DAILY QUIZ 25~30

day 25	1.E	2.D	3.C	4.C	5.A	6.C	7.E	8.C	9.A	10.A
day 26	1.E	2.A	3.C	4.E	5.D	6.E	7.A	8.D	9.A	10.E
day 27	1.E	2.C	3.E	4.C	5.A	6.A	7.D	8.D	9.C	10.D
day 28	1.A	2.E	3.A	4.B	5.A	6.B	7.A	8.B	9.E	10.E
day 29	1.B	2.C	3.A	4.B	5.A	6.E	7.C	8.A	9.B	10.A
day 30	1.A	2.E	3.A	4.A	5.E	6.A	7.C	8.E	9.A	10.B

DAILY QUIZ 31~36

day 31	1.B	2.B	3.E	4.B	5.E	6.D	7.C	8.A	9.B	10.A
day 32	1.A	2.C	3.B	4.A	5.B	6.A	7.B	8.D	9.E	10.A
day 33	1.E	2.D	3.E	4.C	5.A	6.B	7.D	8.D	9.D	10.E
day 34	1.E	2.B	3.D	4.B	5.A	6.C	7.E	8.C	9.B	10.B
day 35	1.A	2.C	3.E	4.D	5.E	6.B	7.E	8.C	9.C	10.D
day 36	1.D	2.B	3.D	4.C	5.E	6.D	7.C	8.A	9.C	10.E

DAILY QUIZ 37~42

day 37	1.D	2.C	3.B	4.D	5.C	6.B	7.C	8.A	9.C	10.E
day 38	1.C	2.C	3.E	4.D	5.A	6.D	7.D	8.C	9.E	10.E
day 39	1.E	2.B	3.D	4.A	5.E	6.A	7.B	8.D	9.D	10.E
day 40	1.D	2.B	3.B	4.A	5.D	6.C	7.C	8.D	9.B	10.D
day 41	1.A	2.A	3.C	4.D	5.A	6.C	7.D	8.E	9.D	10.E
day 42	1.D	2.B	3.E	4.A	5.A	6.A	7.C	8.D	9.C	10.E

DAILY QUIZ 43~48

day 43	1.A	2.E	3.C	4.B	5.D	6.D	7.A	8.B	9.E	10.D
day 44	1.A	2.E	3.C	4.D	5.B	6.C	7.C	8.D	9.C	10.A
day 45	1.E	2.C	3.C	4.A	5.D	6.A	7.B	8.C	9.B	10.D
day 46	1.E	2.D	3.A	4.C	5.D	6.D	7.C	8.B	9.B	10.E
day 47	1.B	2.A	3.E	4.D	5.D	6.B	7.A	8.B	9.C	10.E
day 48	1.D	2.C	3.B	4.A	5.B	6.C	7.D	8.E	9.B	10.A

DAILY QUIZ 49~54

day 49	1.C	2.B	3.E	4.D	5.C	6.B	7.B	8.D	9.D	10.D
day 50	1.C	2.D	3.D	4.C	5.B	6.B	7.B	8.C	9.B	10.B
day 51	1.B	2.E	3.B	4.E	5.E	6.C	7.C	8.E	9.A	10.D
day 52	1.D	2.A	3.C	4.E	5.B	6.B	7.B	8.B	9.A	10.C
day 53	1.B	2.D	3.D	4.B	5.B	6.B	7.A	8.A	9.C	10.C
day 54	1.D	2.C	3.D	4.C	5.C	6.A	7.B	8.A	9.C	10.D

DAILY QUIZ 55~60

day 55	1.E	2.E	3.C	4.C	5.A	6.A	7.B	8.B	9.B	10.A
day 56	1.D	2.D	3.B	4.A	5.B	6.E	7.B	8.C	9.B	10.E
day 57	1.C	2.C	3.D	4.E	5.C	6.E	7.A	8.D	9.A	10.E
day 58	1.A	2.B	3.D	4.E	5.D	6.A	7.C	8.B	9.B	10.D
day 59	1.D	2.B	3.C	4.B	5.A	6.B	7.D	8.D	9.A	10.E
day 60	1.D	2.C	3.B	4.A	5.C	6.B	7.C	8.B	9.A	10.B

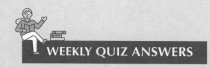

WEEKLY QUIZ ANSWERS

| WEEKLY QUIZ 01 | 1.A | 2.A | 3.D | 4.C | 5.C | 6.E | 7.C | 8.B | 9.A | 10.E |
| | 11.E | 12.D | 13.A | 14.C | 15.A | 16.C | 17.C | 18.D | 19.B | 20.A |

| WEEKLY QUIZ 02 | 1.B | 2.D | 3.D | 4.D | 5.B | 6.B | 7.E | 8.C | 9.A | 10.D |
| | 11.B | 12.D | 13.A | 14.A | 15.D | 16.D | 17.D | 18.B | 19.C | 20.C |

| WEEKLY QUIZ 03 | 1.B | 2.C | 3.B | 4.B | 5.E | 6.B | 7.D | 8.A | 9.C | 10.B |
| | 11.A | 12.D | 13.D | 14.E | 15.C | 16.B | 17.C | 18.C | 19.A | 20.E |

| WEEKLY QUIZ 04 | 1.D | 2.C | 3.D | 4.A | 5.C | 6.A | 7.B | 8.A | 9.B | 10.E |
| | 11.A | 12.E | 13.E | 14.C | 15.C | 16.E | 17.B | 18.E | 19.D | 20.B |

| WEEKLY QUIZ 05 | 1.A | 2.A | 3.A | 4.A | 5.B | 6.B | 7.E | 8.C | 9.C | 10.D |
| | 11.C | 12.B | 13.A | 14.A | 15.E | 16.A | 17.A | 18.D | 19.E | 20.C |

| WEEKLY QUIZ 06 | 1.E | 2.E | 3.D | 4.A | 5.D | 6.E | 7.E | 8.D | 9.D | 10.B |
| | 11.D | 12.C | 13.C | 14.B | 15.B | 16.A | 17.C | 18.B | 19.A | 20.E |

| WEEKLY QUIZ 07 | 1.D | 2.A | 3.E | 4.C | 5.A | 6.A | 7.B | 8.D | 9.B | 10.E |
| | 11.A | 12.B | 13.A | 14.B | 15.C | 16.E | 17.E | 18.A | 19.B | 20.C |

| WEEKLY QUIZ 08 | 1.D | 2.D | 3.E | 4.C | 5.B | 6.E | 7.A | 8.D | 9.D | 10.C |
| | 11.E | 12.E | 13.E | 14.E | 15.B | 16.C | 17.B | 18.B | 19.A | 20.D |

| WEEKLY QUIZ 09 | 1.A | 2.A | 3.A | 4.D | 5.A | 6.D | 7.D | 8.A | 9.B | 10.C |
| | 11.D | 12.C | 13.B | 14.B | 15.D | 16.D | 17.C | 18.E | 19.B | 20.B |

| WEEKLY QUIZ 10 | 1.D | 2.D | 3.A | 4.A | 5.C | 6.A | 7.E | 8.C | 9.B | 10.D |
| | 11.B | 12.C | 13.E | 14.C | 15.C | 16.D | 17.A | 18.A | 19.B | 20.B |

AMERICAN COLLEGE VOCABULARY 101
미국 대입 필수 영단어

초판 1쇄 발행 2021년 5월 31일

지은이 한세희
발행처 헤르몬하우스
발행인 최영민
감수 Veronica L. Wilson
디자이너 김정아, 이연수
Contributors 필립림, 이지은, 양수아
주소 경기도 파주시 신촌로 16
전화 031-8071-0088
팩스 031-942-8688
전자우편 hermonh@naver.com
출판등록 2015년 3월 27일
등록번호 제406-2015-31호

ISBN 979-11-91188-91-2 53740

MEMO

MEMO